AQUARIAN AGE JUVENILE ORION™

オリオンの少年

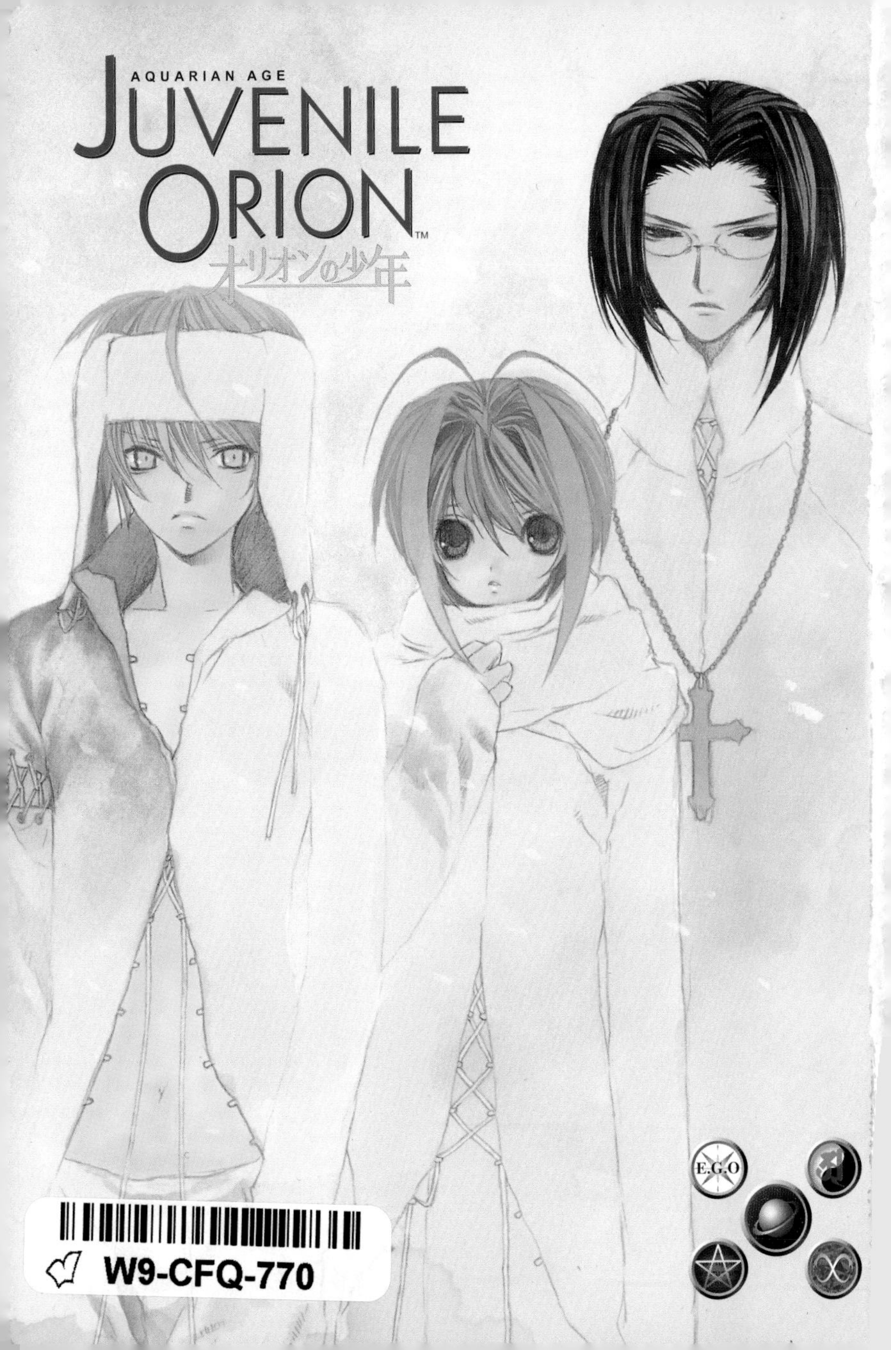
E.G.O

Other titles available from Broccoli Books

Galaxy Angel
The Angel Troupe has one mission; they must protect Prince Shiva, the sole survivor of the royal family decimated by a coup d'état. Milfeulle, Ranpha, Mint, Forte, and Vanilla each possess special gifts, making them ideal for the job at hand. Takuto finds himself leading the mission, getting caught between the five unique Angels and...space whales!?
Story & Art by Kanan
Suggested Retail Price: $9.99

Until the Full Moon
Marlo is half vampire, half werewolf with a problem. On nights when the full moon shines, Marlo undergoes a mysterious transformation... he turns into a girl.
Story & Art by Sanami Matoh
Suggested Retail Price: $9.99

Di Gi Charat Theater – Dejiko's Summer Vacation & Piyoko is Number One!
Join Dejiko and the gang as they hit the beach, switch bodies, blow up the Black Gema Gema Gang, and discover the secret of Hokke Mirin and her cat corp! And watch out Dejiko! Piyoko and her gang attempt to steal the show with their very own book!
Story & Art by Koge-Donbo and others
Suggested Retail Price: $9.99 each

Di Gi Charat Theater – Leave it to Piyoko! (December 2004)
Follow the daily adventures of the Black Gema Gema Gang, as they continue their road to evil.
Story & Art by Hina.
Suggested Retail Price: $9.99
Volumes 1-2 Coming Soon!

Di Gi Charat Theater – Dejiko's Adventure
Dejiko has destroyed the Gamers retail store! Now it's up to her and the rest of the gang as they search for the secret treasure that will save Gamers.
Story & Art by Yuki Kiriga
Suggested Retail Price: $9.99
Volumes 2-3 Coming Soon!

For more information about Broccoli Books titles,
check out **bro-usa.com!**

AQUARIAN AGE

JUVENILE ORION ③

オリオンの少年

by Sakurako Gokurakuin
Original Concept by BROCCOLI • Marekatsu Nakai

brought to you by
BROCCOLI BOOKS
A DIVISION OF BROCCOLI INTERNATIONAL USA

Aquarian Age™ – Juvenile Orion Volume 3

English Adaptation Staff
Translation: Rie Hagihara
English Adaptation: Elizabeth Hanel
Clean-Up, Touch-Up & Lettering: Fawn "tails" Lau
Cover & Layout: Chris McDougall

Editor: Satsuki Yamashita
Sales Manager: Ardith D. Santiago
Managing Editor: Shizuki Yamashita
Publisher: Hideki Uchino

Email: editor@broccolibooks.com
Website: www.bro-usa.com

A  BROCCOLI BOOKS Manga
Broccoli Books is a division of Broccoli International USA, Inc.
12211 W. Washington Blvd, Suite 110, Los Angeles CA 90066

© 2002, 2004 BROCCOLI
© 2002, 2004 Sakurako Gokurakuin. All Rights Reserved.
First published in Japan in 2002 by SQUARE ENIX CO., LTD., Tokyo. English translation
rights arranged with SQUARE ENIX CO., LTD. through BROCCOLI Co., Ltd.

Aquarian Age is a trademark of BROCCOLI Co., Ltd
Juvenile Orion logo is a trademark of Broccoli International USA, Inc.
All rights reserved.
No portion of this book may be reproduced or transmitted in any form without written
permission from the copyright holders.
The stories, characters, and incidents mentioned in this book are entirely fictional.

ISBN: 1-932480-11-0

Published by Broccoli International USA, Inc.
Second printing, October 2004
First printing, May 2004

All illustrations by Sakurako Gokurakuin.

www.bro-usa.com

10 9 8 7 6 5 4 3 2
Printed in the United States

AQUARIAN AGE
JUVENILE ORION
3

CONTENTS

JUVENILE ORION
CHARACTERS

MANA KIRIHARA
Mind Breaker
16 years old

Mana has just transferred to Seika High. Because of her strong need to protect her loved ones, she agrees to participate in the Aquarian Age. She is kind and hardworking, but can be clutzy at times. She cares deeply for Kaname.

Her parents passed away, and she currently lives with her aunt, who is a writer.

 ### KANAME KUSAKABE
DARKLORE
16 years old

Kaname considers himself a typical high school student. He is a little stubborn but straightforward. He lost his parents in an accident when he was younger, and lives with his older sister.

He is in the basketball team at school.

 ### NAOYA ITSUKI
E.G.O.
17 years old

Naoya is the only male kin of the Itsuki family, an influential power in the E.G.O. He has telepathic abilities, and has the potential to become a strong Mind Breaker. He is outgoing and friendly.

He does many odd jobs to support his family, and therefore spends most of his time at school napping.

ISSHIN SHIBA
ARAYASHIKI

18 years old

Isshin is the heir to a Chinese conglomerate, and an expert in Chinese martial arts. His hobbies include motorcycles and basketball, and is in the same basketball team as Kaname. He is very proper and strait-laced.

TSUKASA AMOU
ERASER

16 years old

Tsukasa was suffering from amnesia, wandering the streets until Tomonori found him and took him into his home. He is kind and gentle, but gets depressed easily because of his memory loss.

TOMONORI NAKAURA
WIZ-DOM

24 years old

Tomonori grew up in a WIZ-DOM orphanage, and used to live alone until he found Tsukasa. He is a math teacher at Seika High. He is a little strict, but is well-liked by his students. He is a great cook, but has a low tolerance to alcohol.

HARUNA ITSUKI
E.G.O.

17 years old

Naoya's twin sister, she is currently bedridden and connected to a machine that controls her strong powers.

JUVENILE ORION
CHARACTERS

KAORU
Mind Breaker

Kaoru is a strong Mind Breaker who is interested in Mana for reasons unknown.

 ## LAFAYEL
ERASER

Lafayel is a mysterious boy who attacks Mana and Tsukasa. He seems to know Tsukasa from before. Lafayel has a strong hatred towards Tsukasa and is determined to kill him.

 ## MIZUNAGI
E.G.O.

Mizunagi is a cool and calm guy. He is one of the psychic hunters.

AMA-INU

DARKLORE

Ama-Inu is a hot-blooded psychic who takes enjoyment in killing people.

KUGA

WIZ-DOM

Kuga is a handsome psychic who is the closest to Kaoru.

KASEI

ARAYASHIKI

Kasei is a mysterious psychic who doesn't talk much. He carries a long sword on his back.

JUVENILE ORION
CHARACTERS

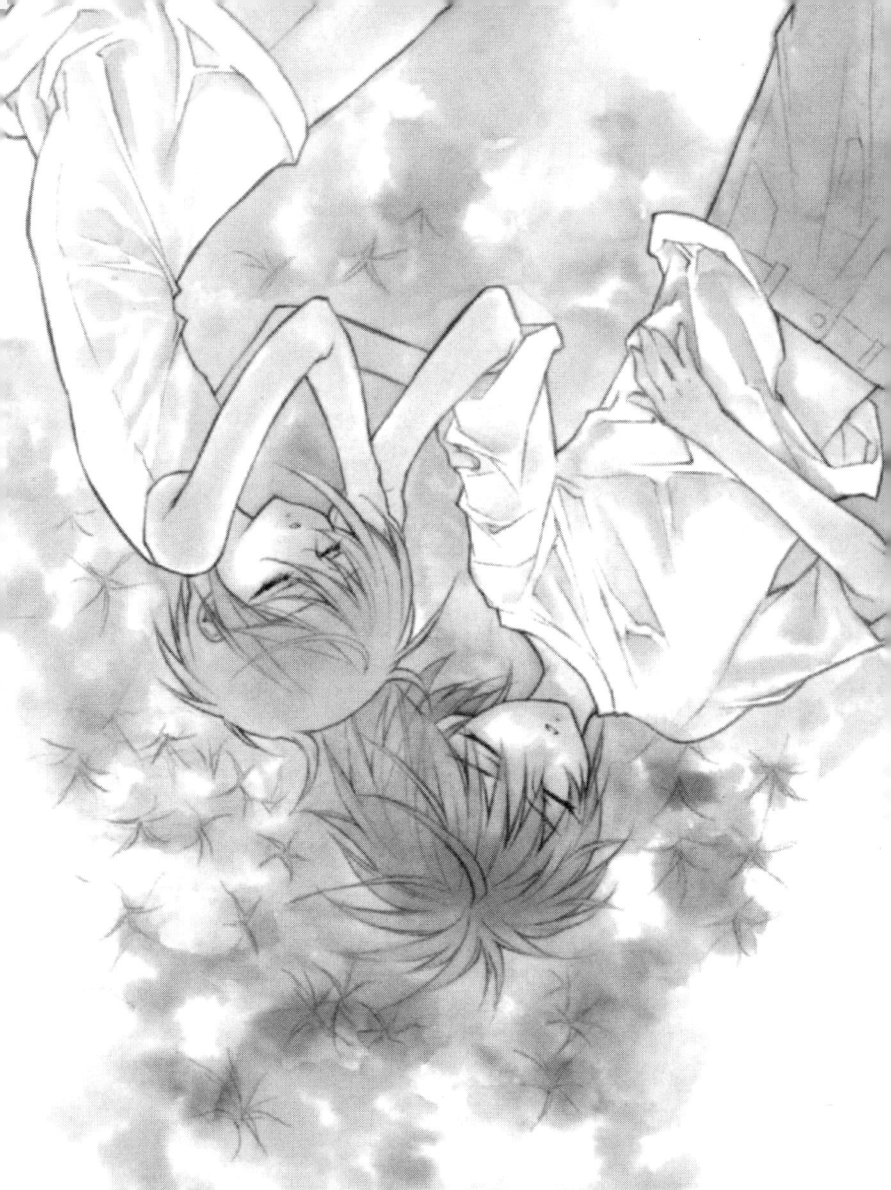

turn.11

Mana and Haruna

I love drawing girls.
Drawing girls make the picture cheerful.

Haruna-- "Master, you're bigger than me!! Not fair!!"
Mana-- "Where are you looking???"

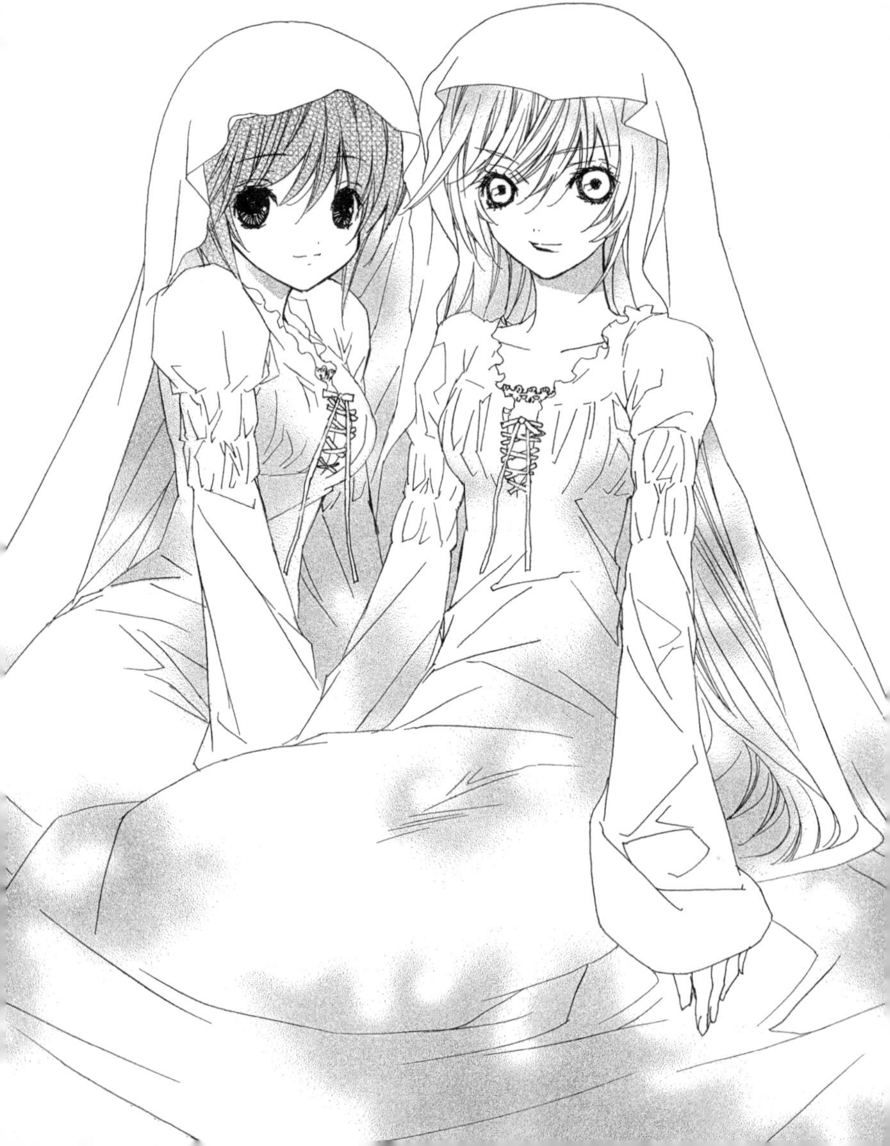

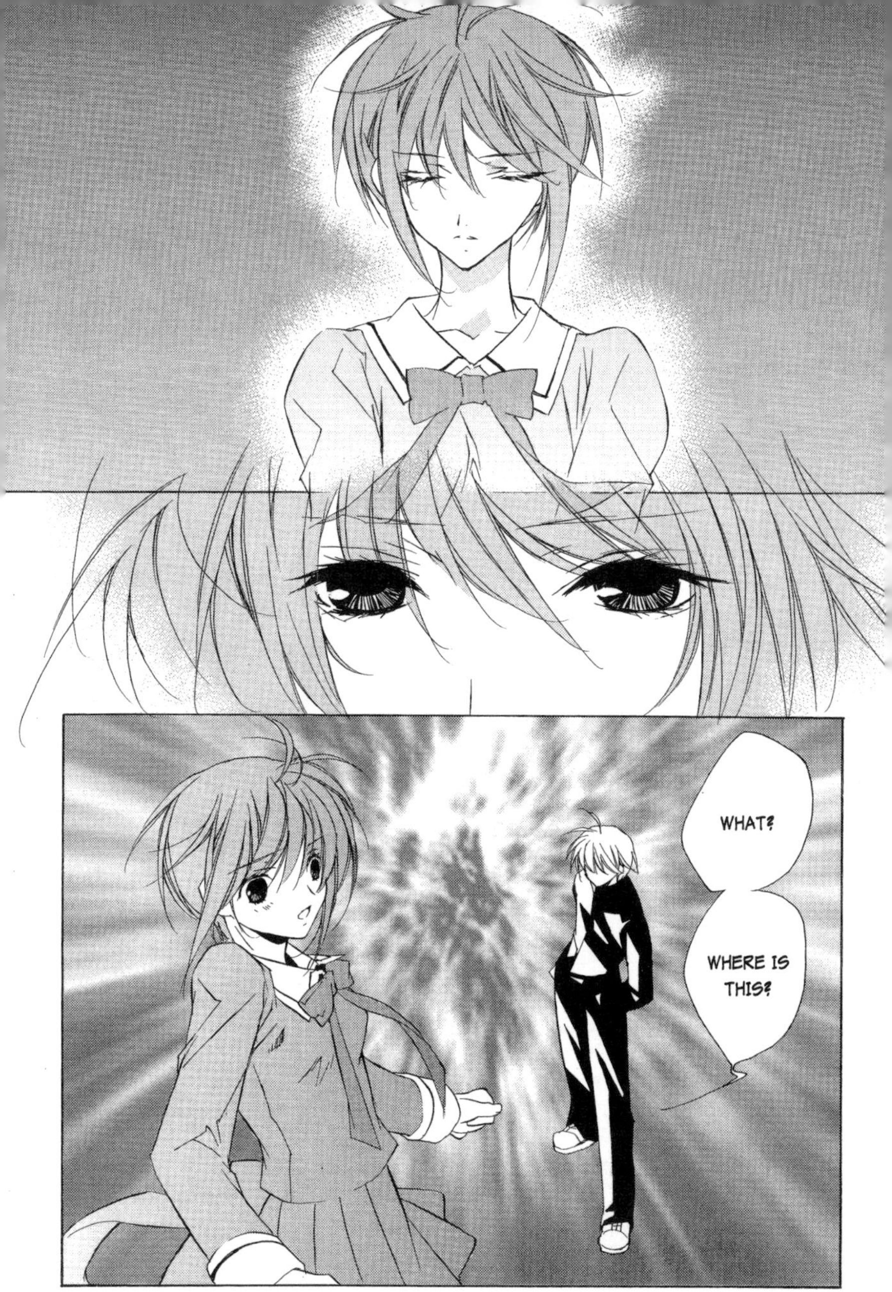
WHAT?
WHERE IS THIS?

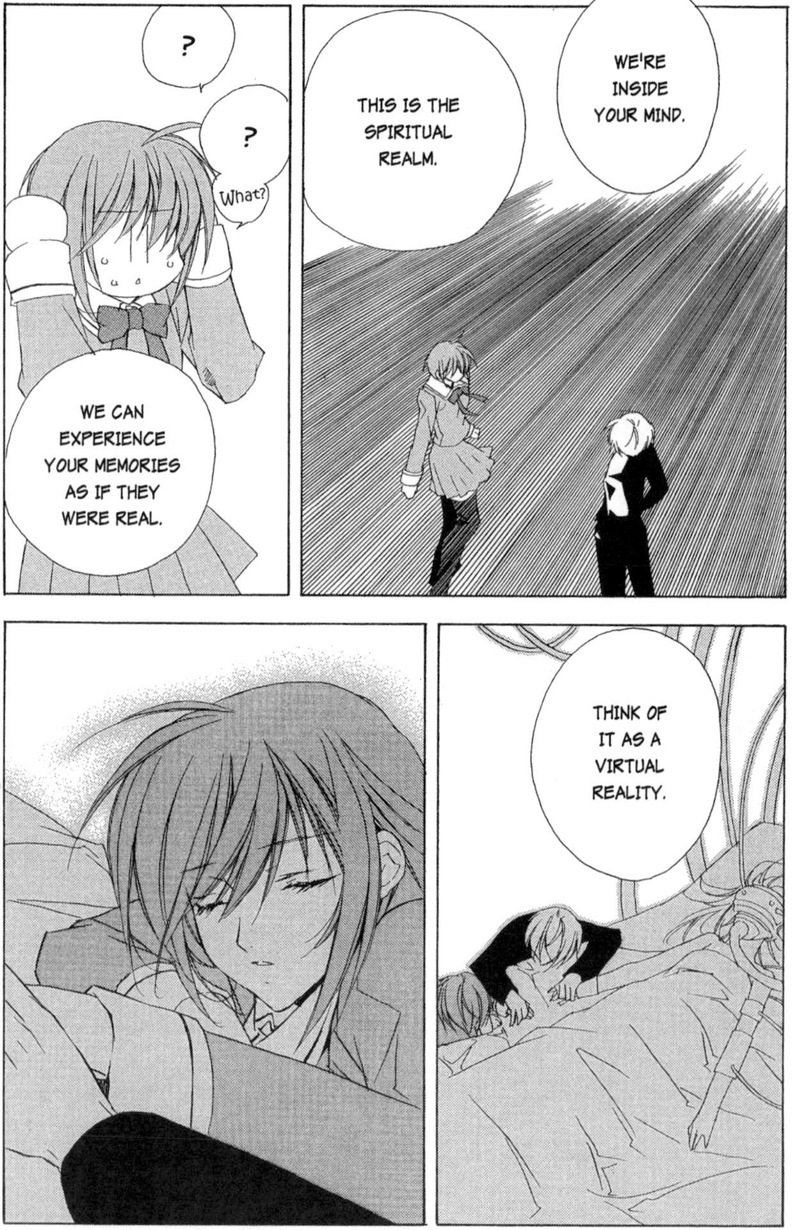
WE'RE INSIDE YOUR MIND.
THIS IS THE SPIRITUAL REALM.
?
?
What?
WE CAN EXPERIENCE YOUR MEMORIES AS IF THEY WERE REAL.
THINK OF IT AS A VIRTUAL REALITY.

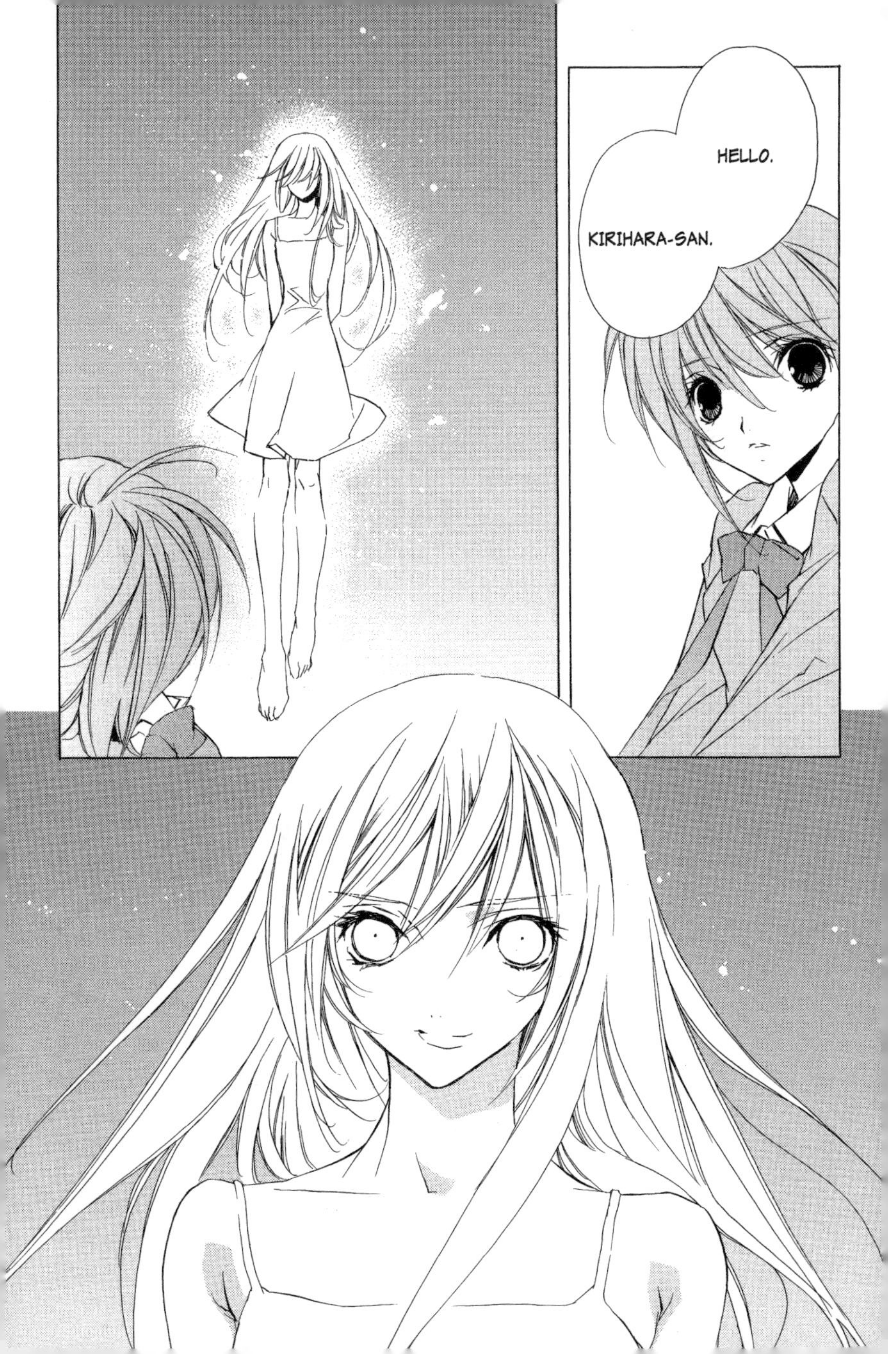
HELLO.
KIRIHARA-SAN.

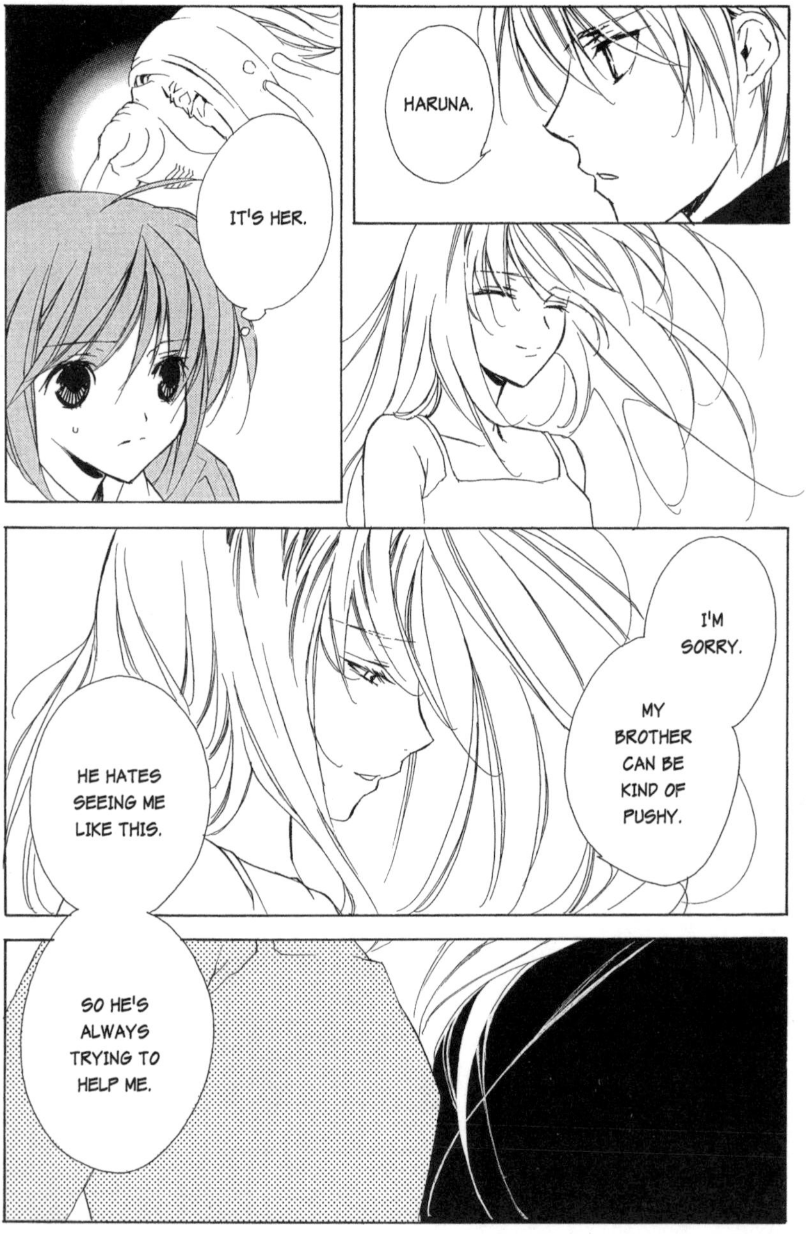
HARUNA.
IT'S HER.
I'M SORRY.
MY BROTHER CAN BE KIND OF PUSHY.
HE HATES SEEING ME LIKE THIS.
SO HE'S ALWAYS TRYING TO HELP ME.

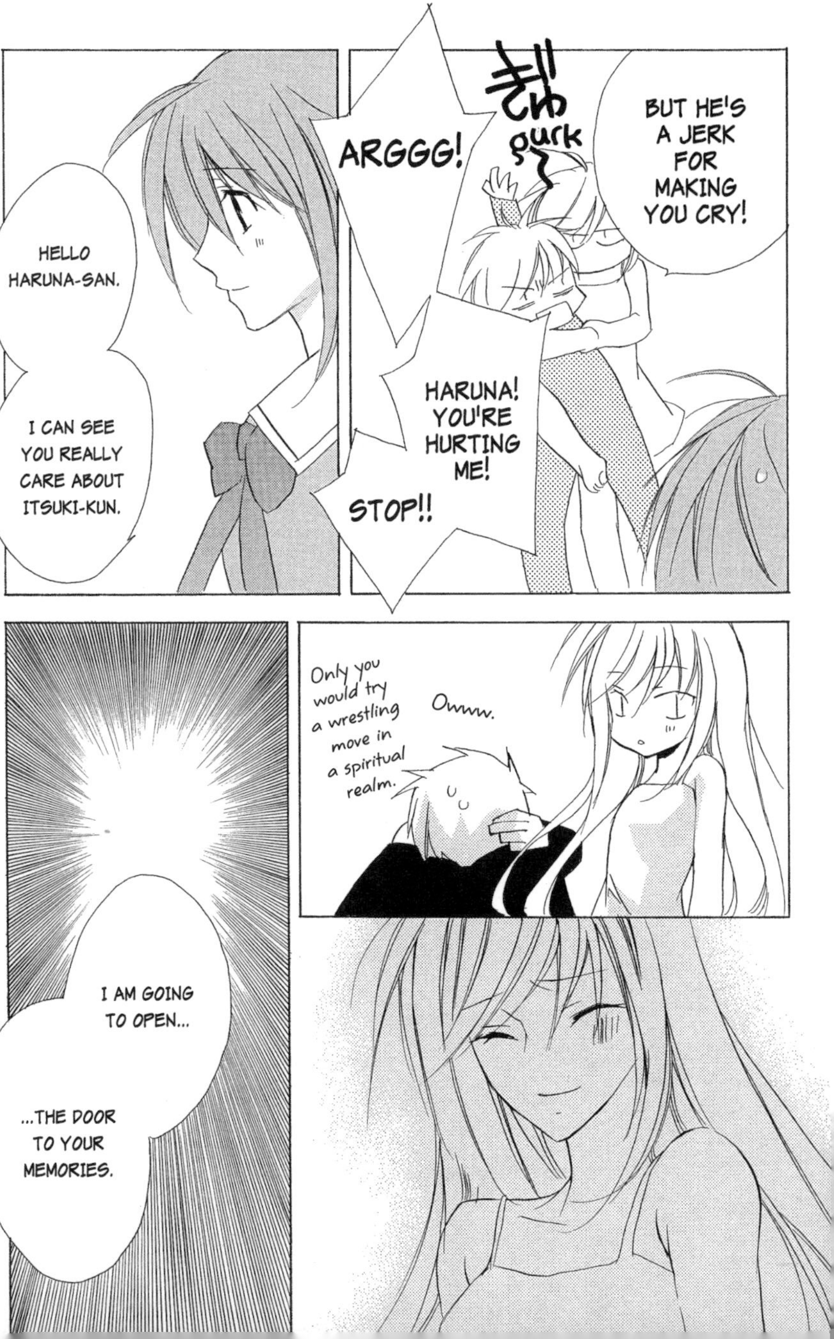
BUT HE'S A JERK FOR MAKING YOU CRY!
gurk
ARGGG!
HARUNA! YOU'RE HURTING ME!
STOP!!
HELLO HARUNA-SAN.
I CAN SEE YOU REALLY CARE ABOUT ITSUKI-KUN.
Owww.
Only you would try a wrestling move in a spiritual realm.
I AM GOING TO OPEN...
...THE DOOR TO YOUR MEMORIES.

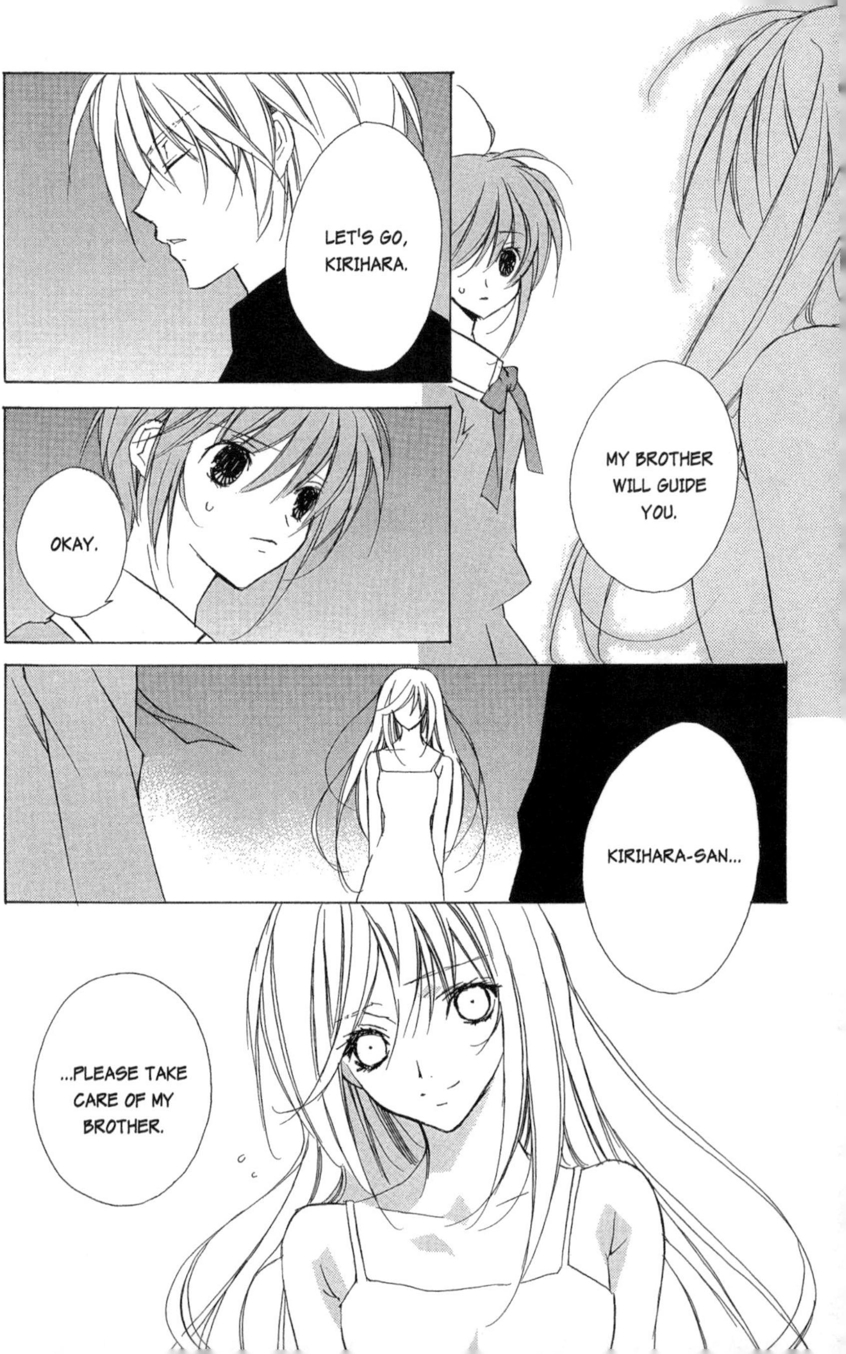
MY BROTHER WILL GUIDE YOU.
LET'S GO, KIRIHARA.
OKAY.
KIRIHARA-SAN...
...PLEASE TAKE CARE OF MY BROTHER.

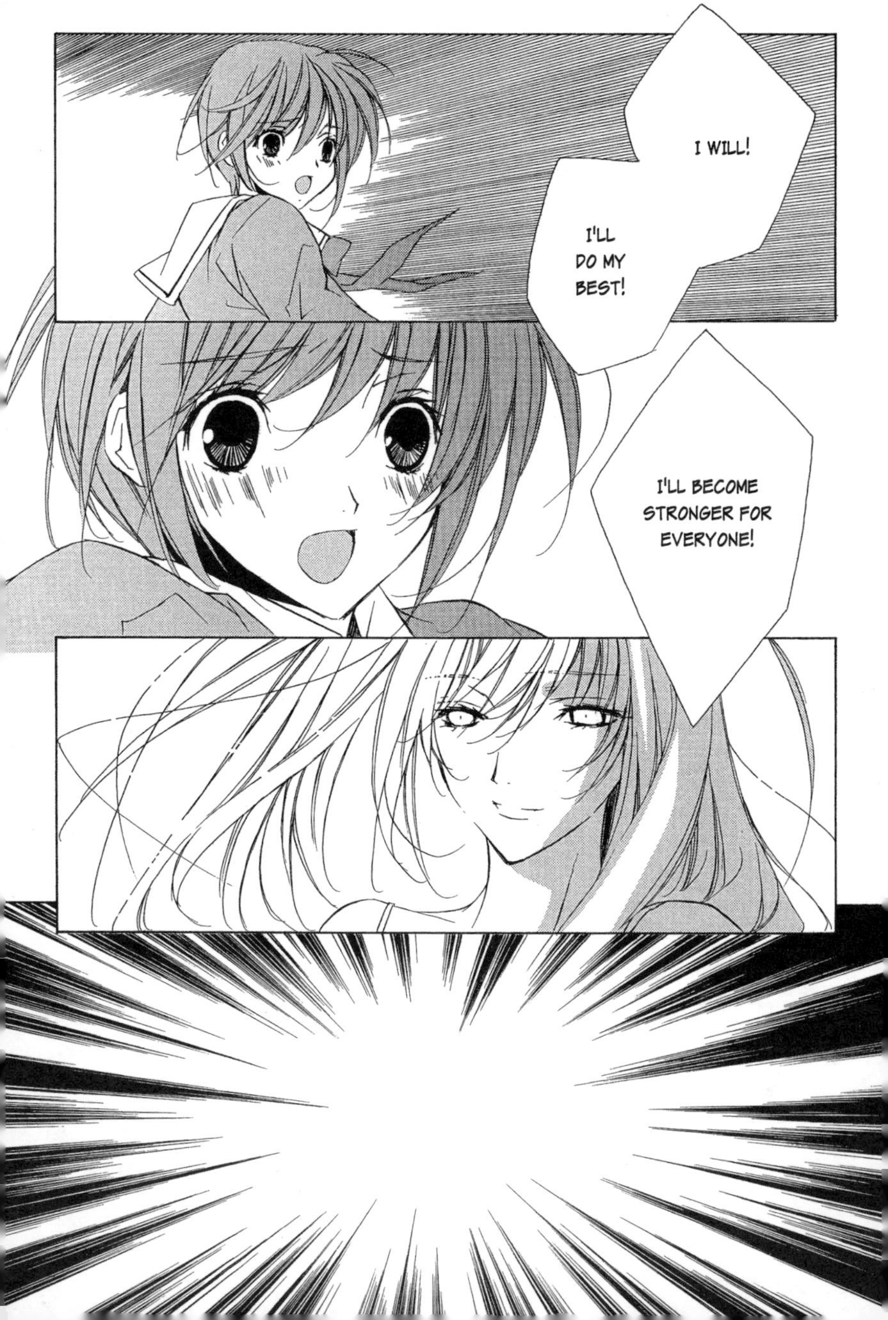
I WILL!
I'LL DO MY BEST!
I'LL BECOME STRONGER FOR EVERYONE!

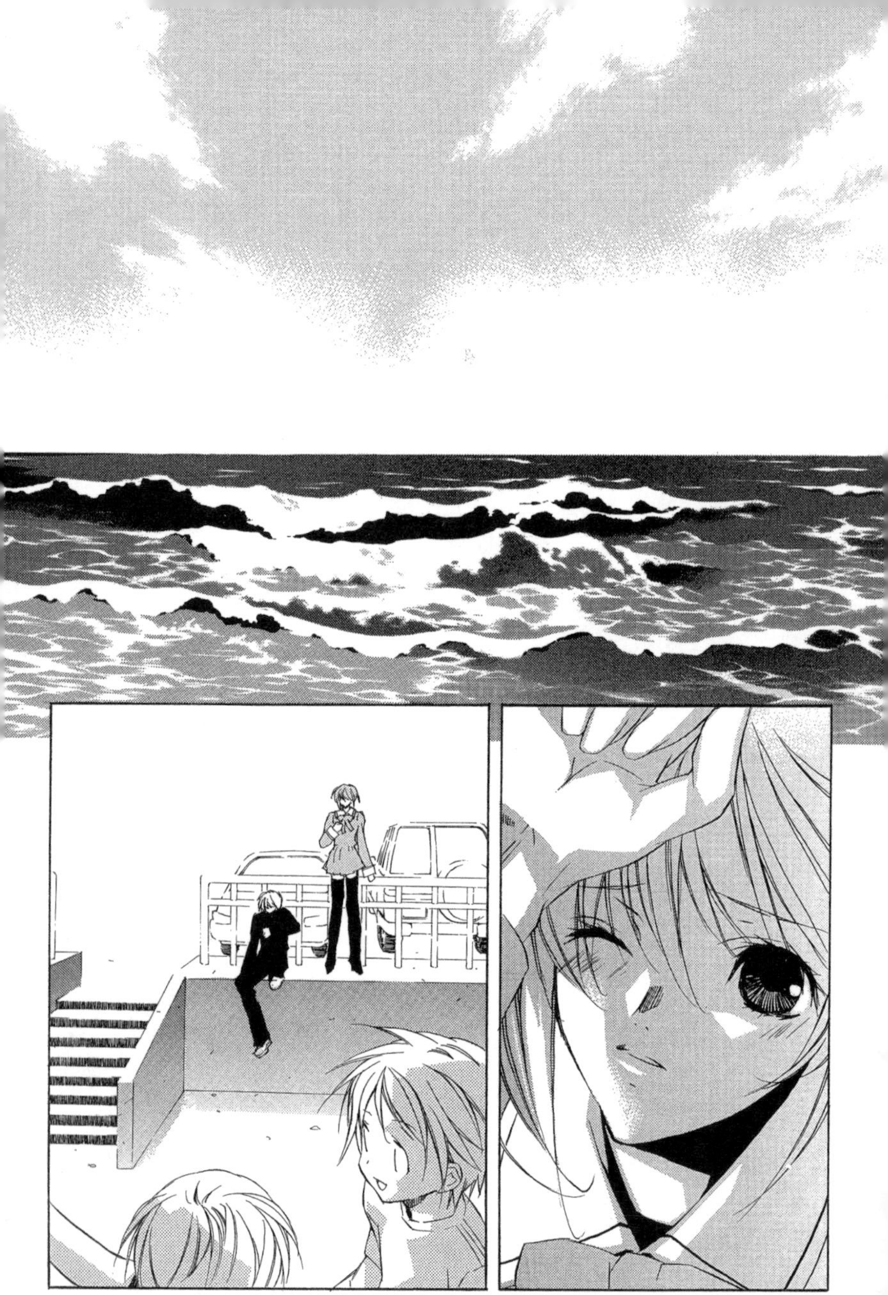

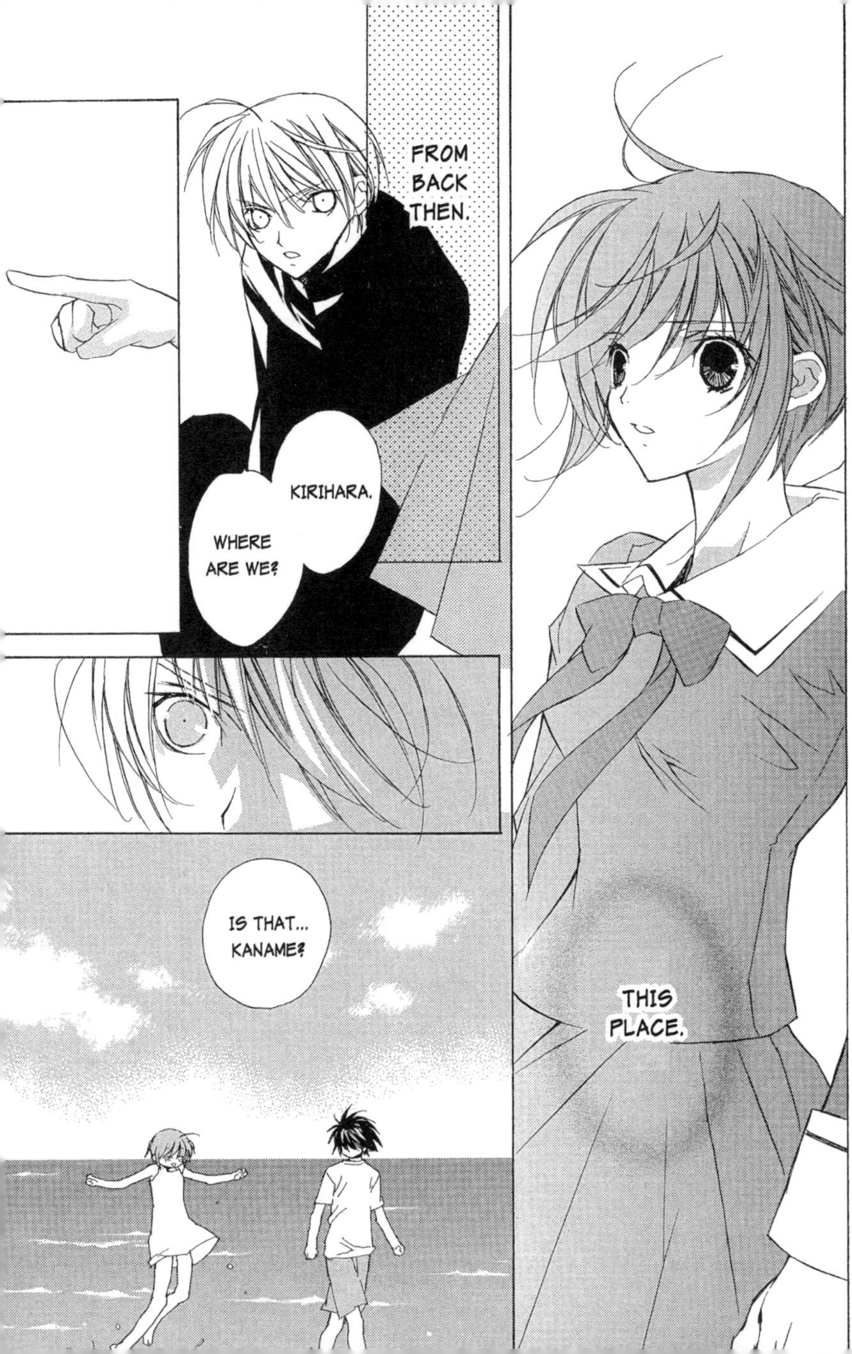
THIS PLACE.
FROM BACK THEN.
KIRIHARA.
WHERE ARE WE?
IS THAT... KANAME?

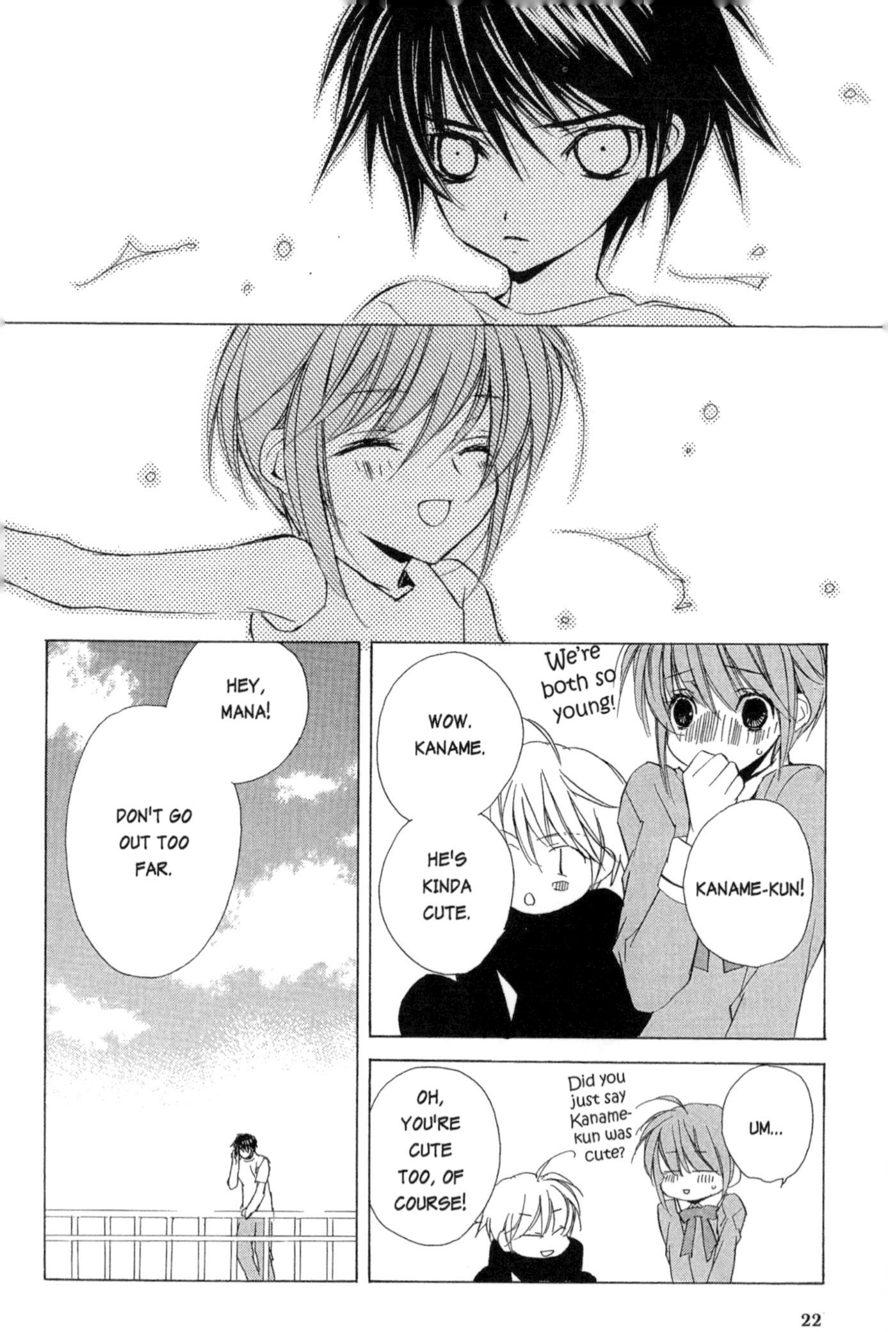
KANAME-KUN!
We're both so young!
WOW. KANAME.
HE'S KINDA CUTE.
UM...
Did you just say Kaname-kun was cute?
OH, YOU'RE CUTE TOO, OF COURSE!
HEY, MANA!
DON'T GO OUT TOO FAR.

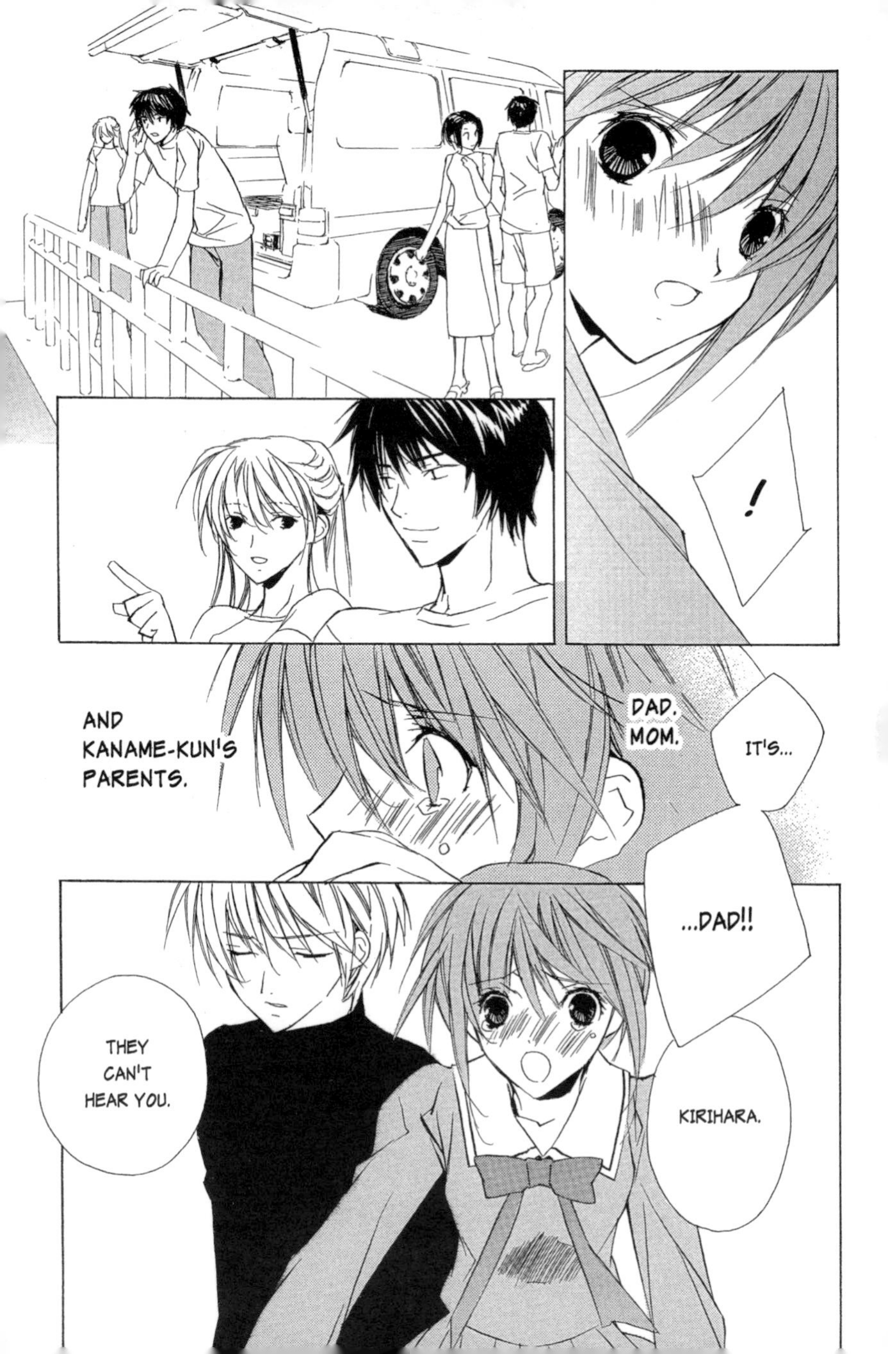
!
IT'S...
DAD. MOM.
AND KANAME-KUN'S PARENTS.
...DAD!!
KIRIHARA.
THEY CAN'T HEAR YOU.

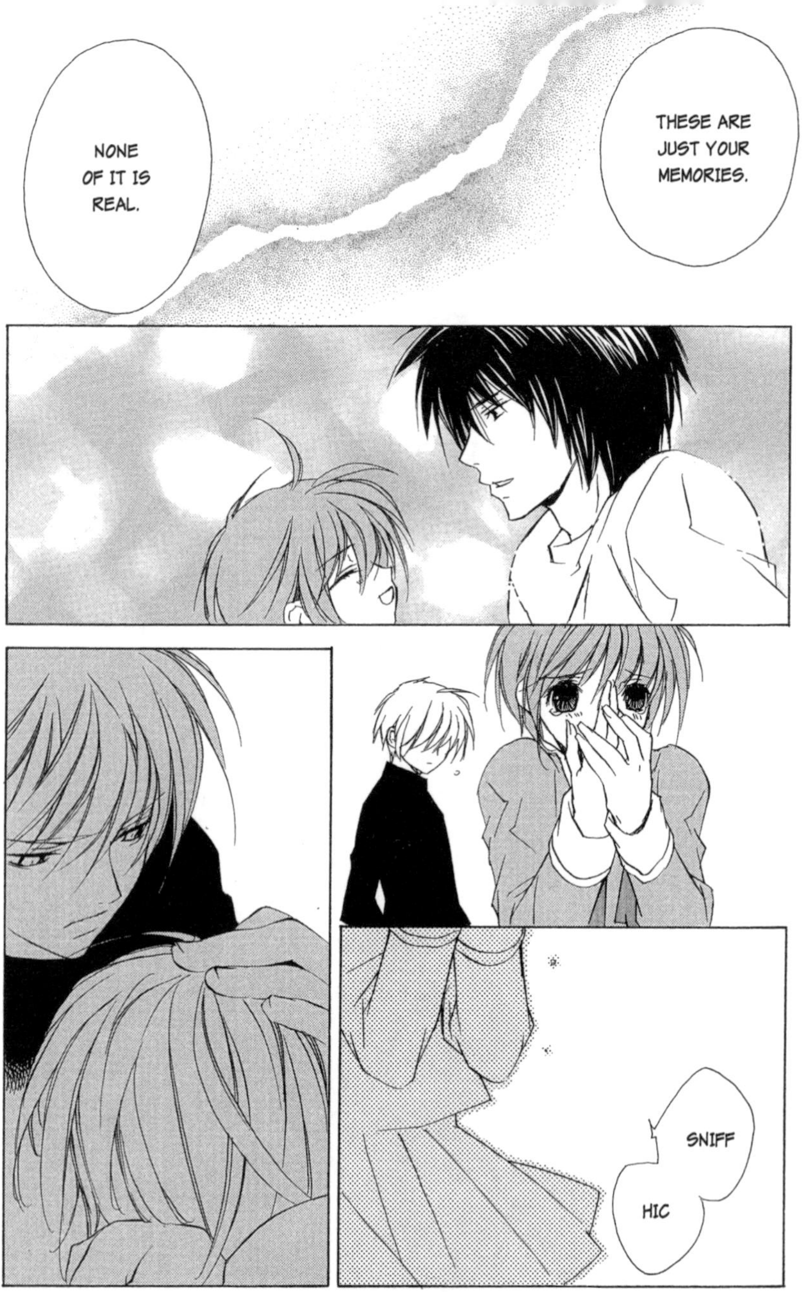
THESE ARE JUST YOUR MEMORIES.
NONE OF IT IS REAL.
SNIFF
HIC

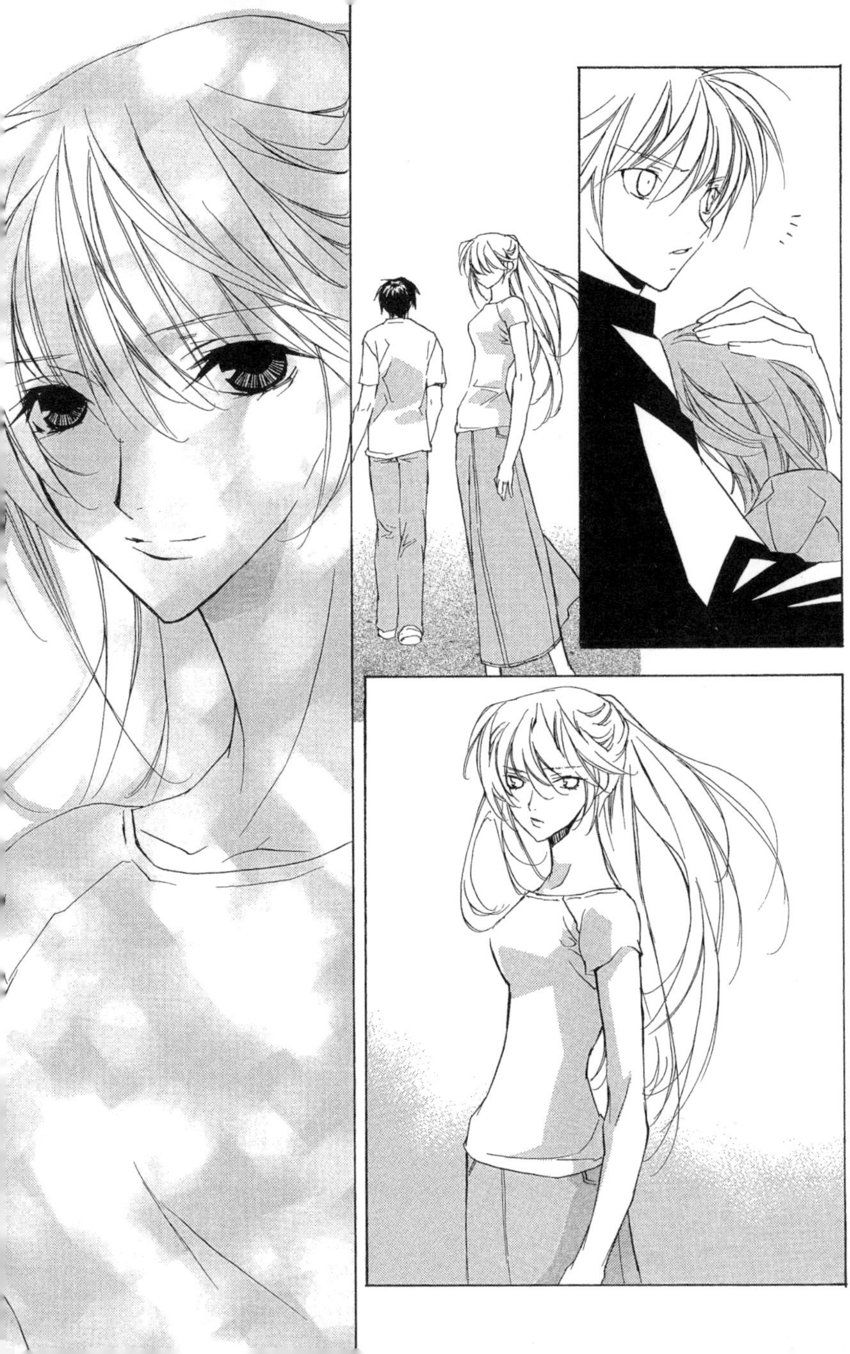

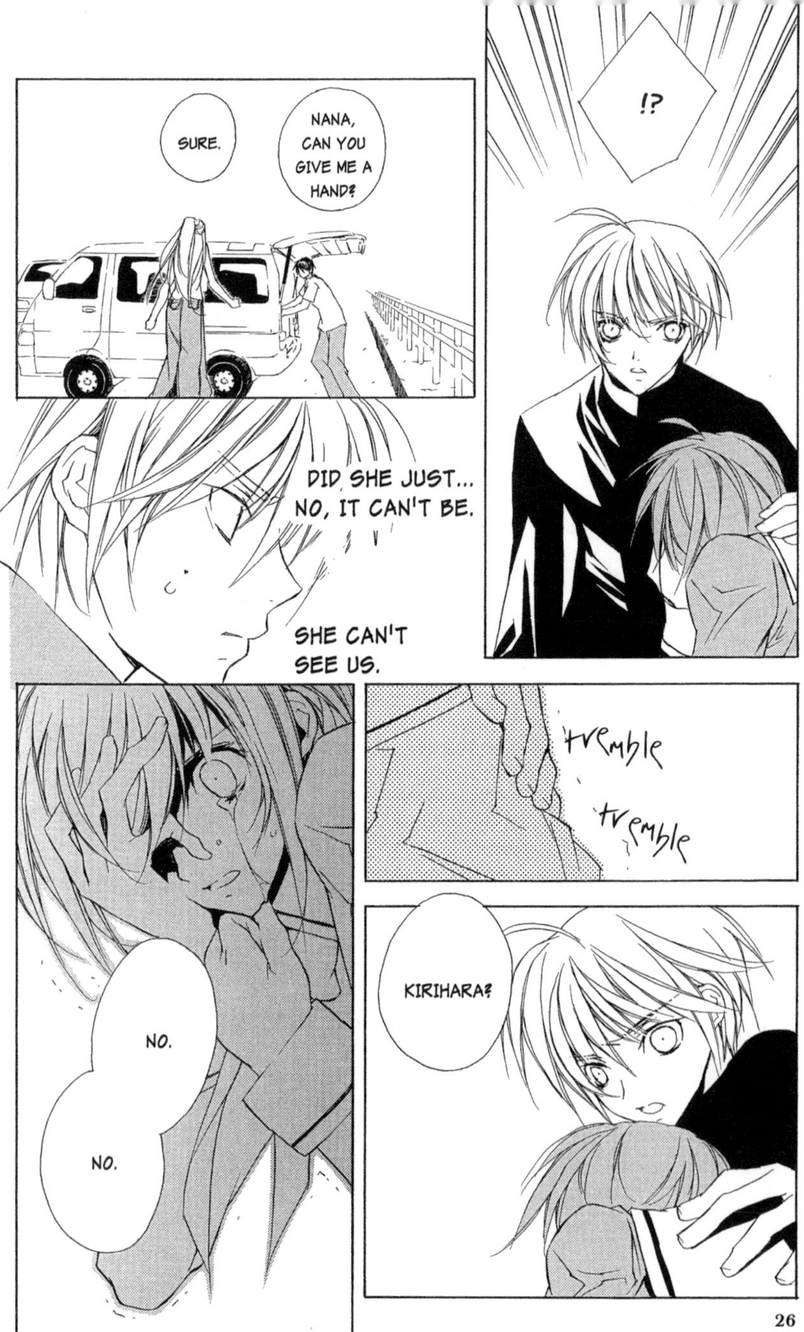
!?
NANA, CAN YOU GIVE ME A HAND?
SURE.
DID SHE JUST... NO, IT CAN'T BE.
SHE CAN'T SEE US.
tremble
tremble
KIRIHARA?
NO.
NO.

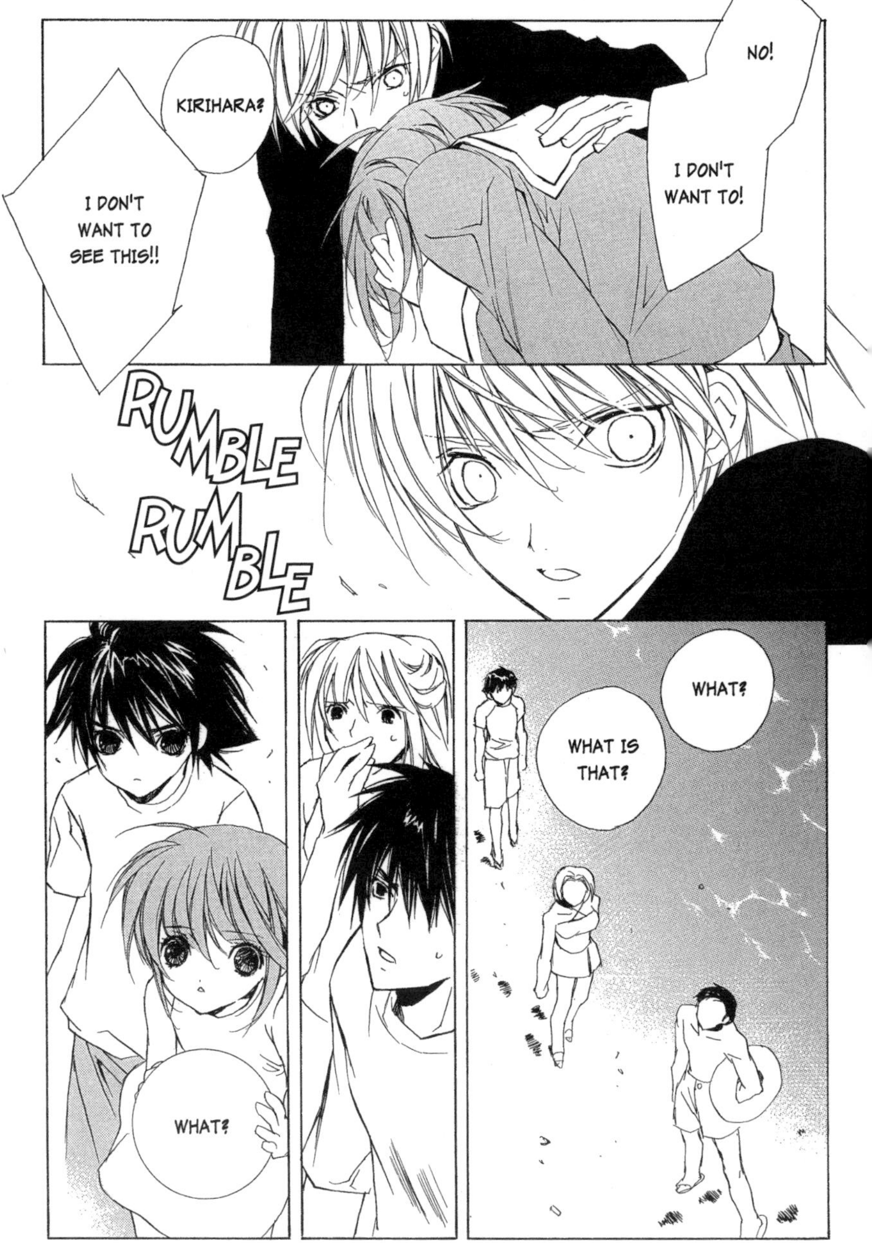
NO!
I DON'T WANT TO!
KIRIHARA?
I DON'T WANT TO SEE THIS!!
RUMBLE RUMBLE
WHAT?
WHAT IS THAT?
WHAT?

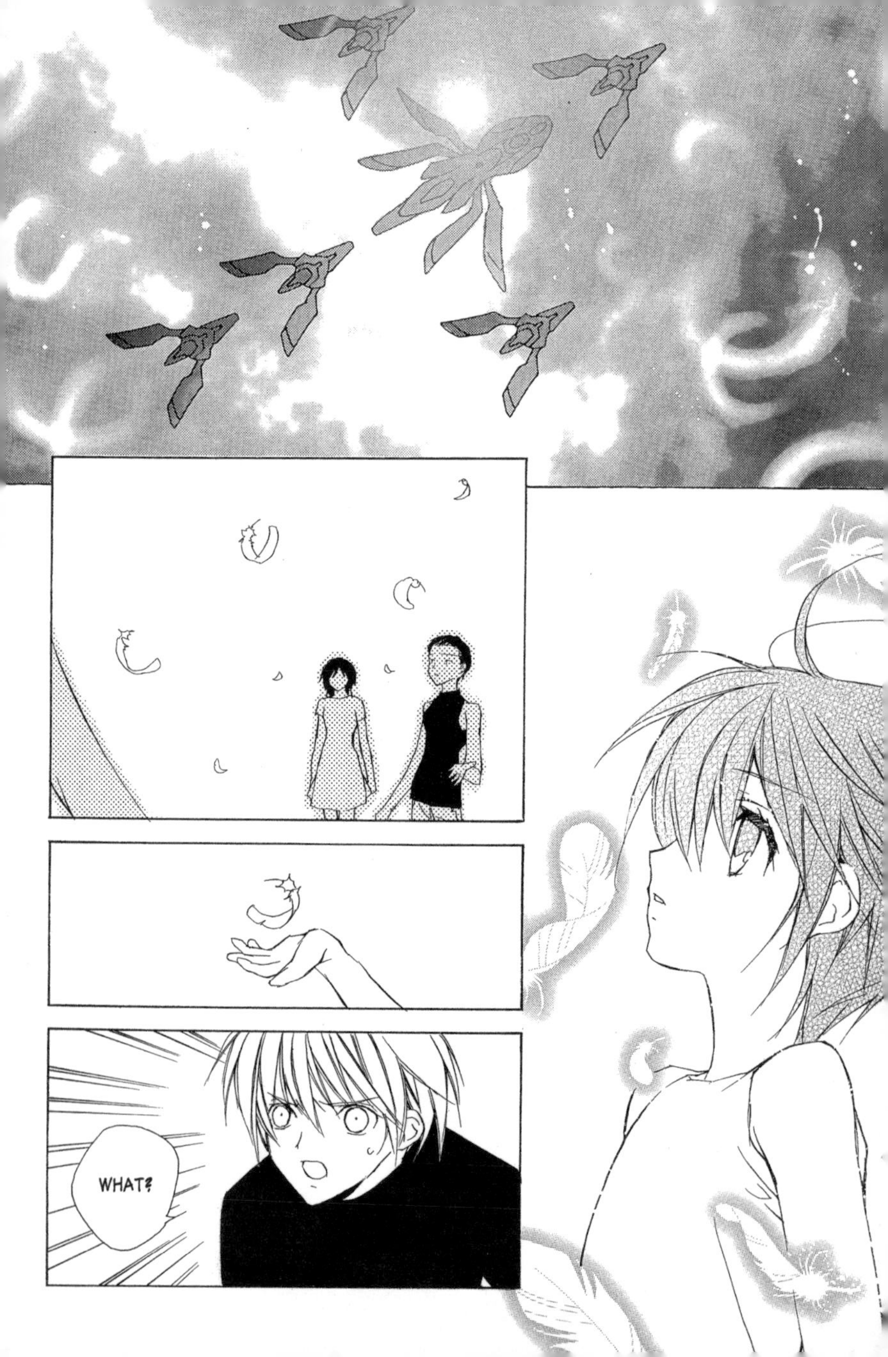
WHAT?

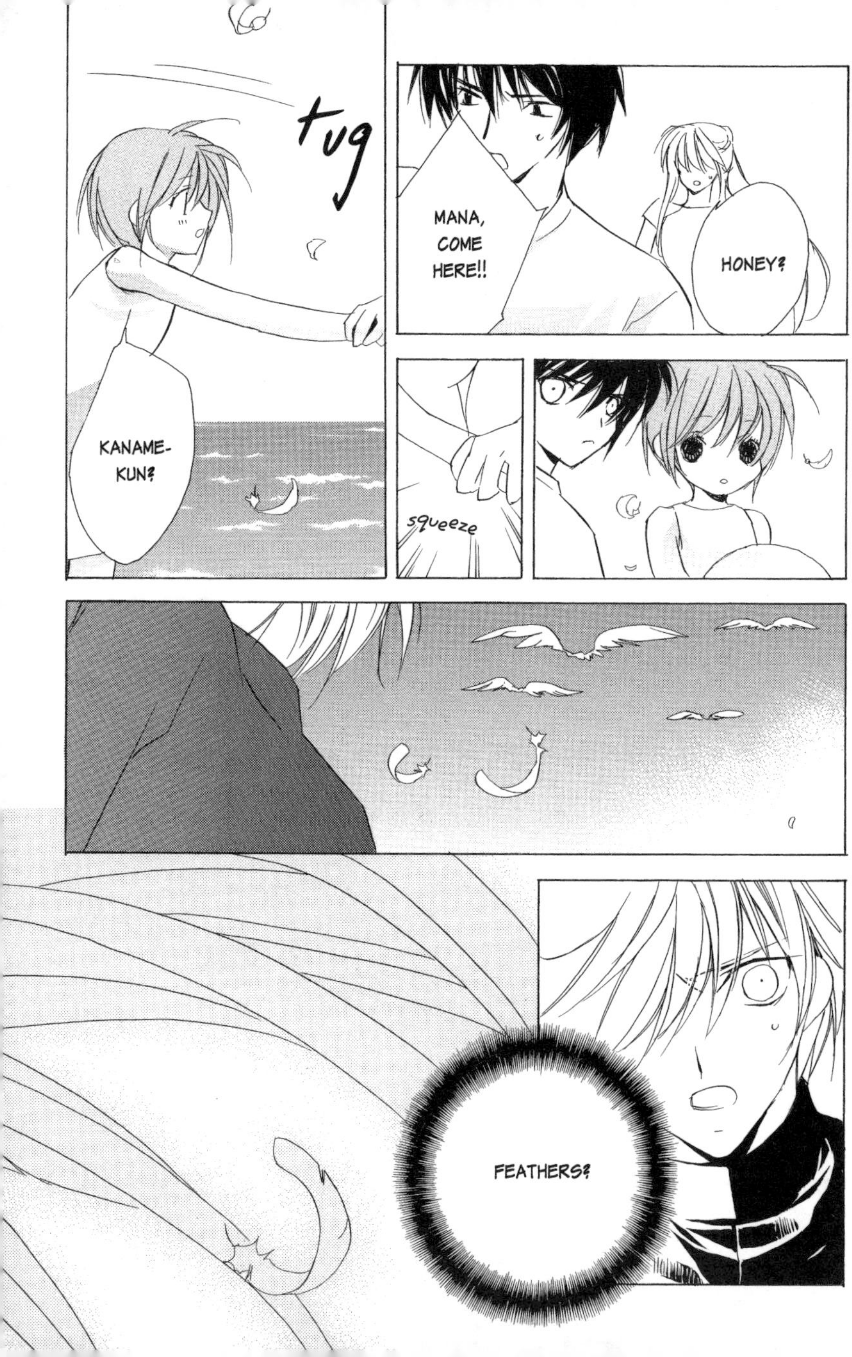
HONEY?
MANA, COME HERE!!
squeeze
tug
KANAME-KUN?
FEATHERS?

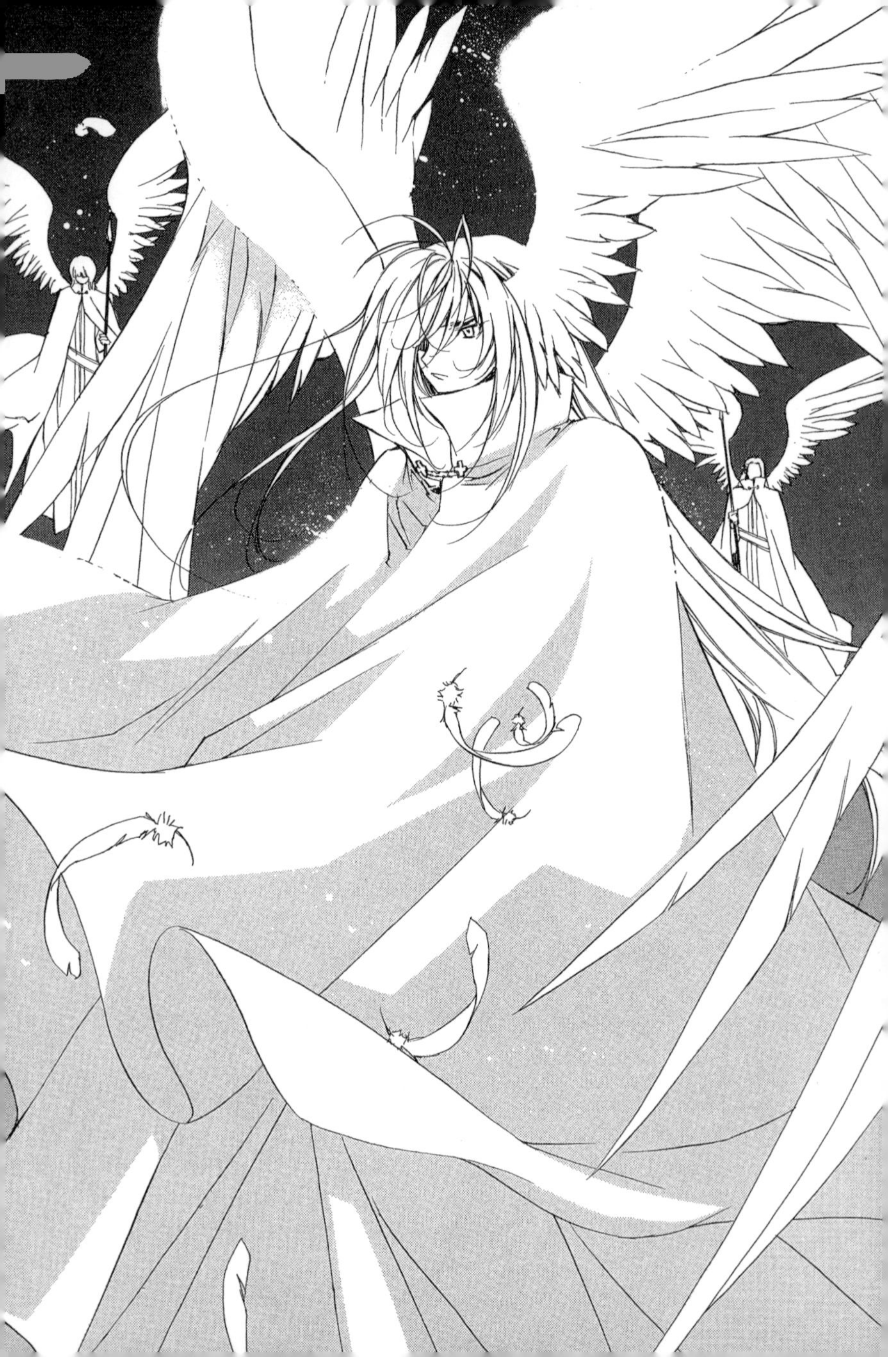

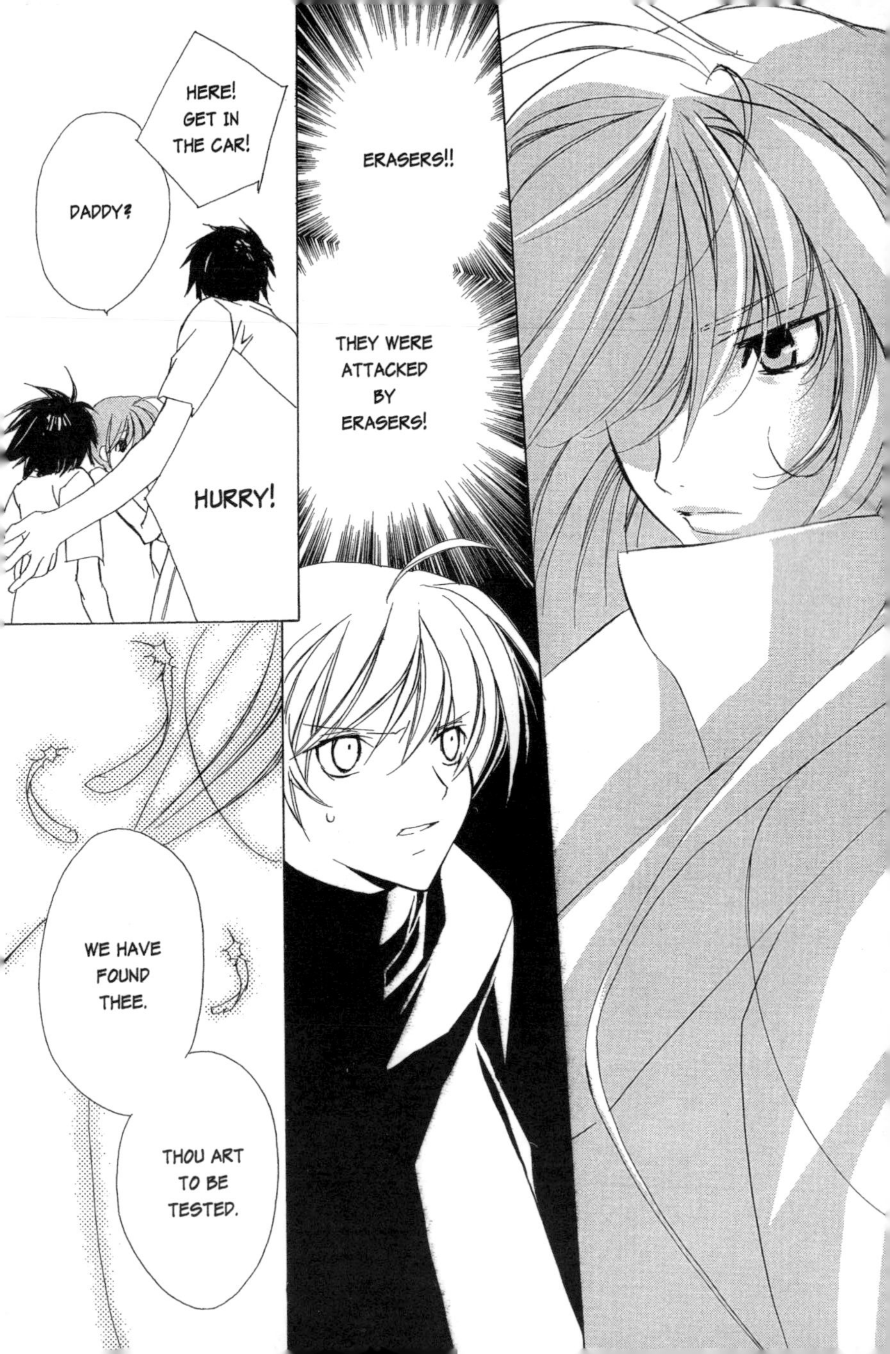

ERASERS!!
THEY WERE ATTACKED BY ERASERS!
HERE! GET IN THE CAR!
DADDY?
HURRY!
WE HAVE FOUND THEE.
THOU ART TO BE TESTED.

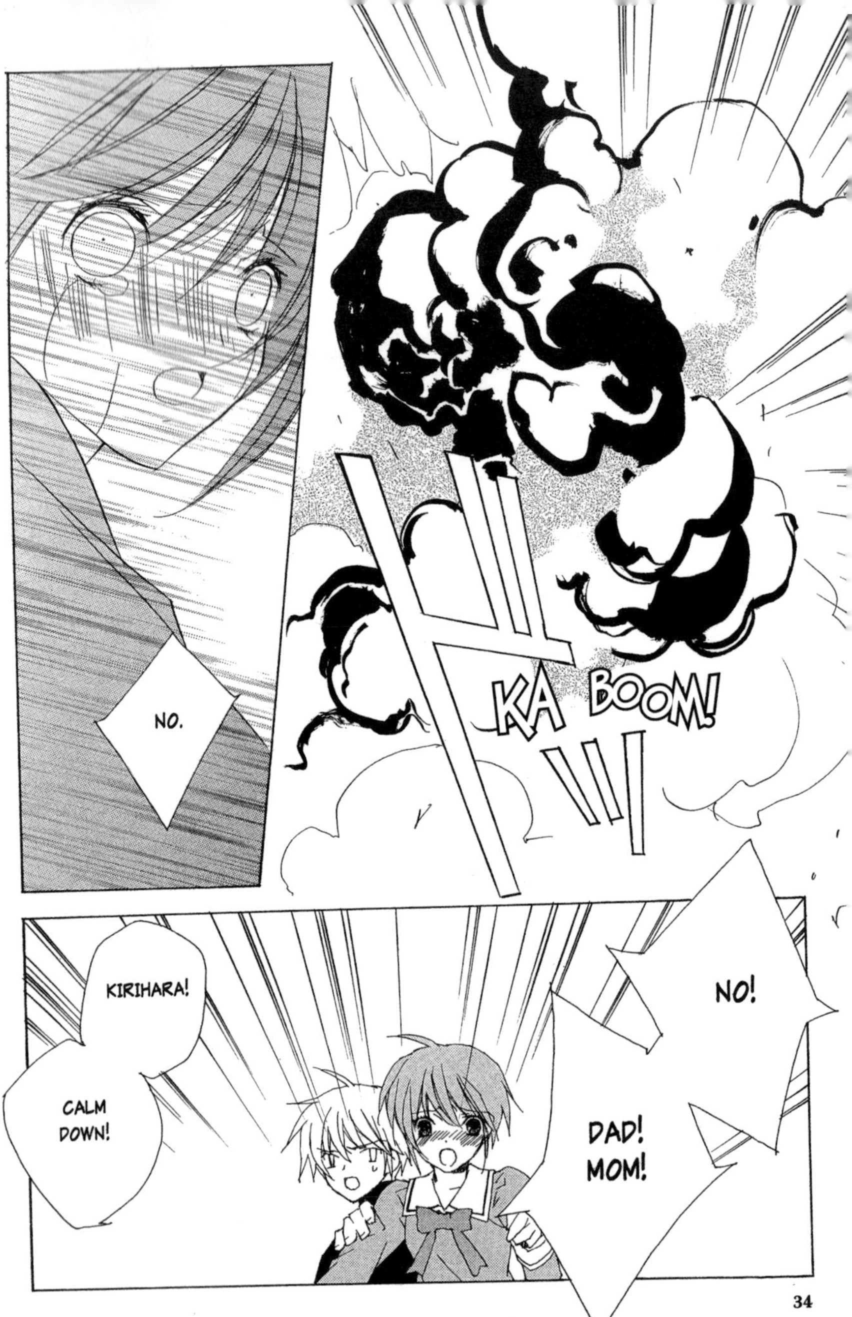
KA BOOM!
NO.
NO!
DAD! MOM!
KIRIHARA!
CALM DOWN!

TO MAKE YOU GO THROUGH THIS AGAIN.

...

NO.

I'M SORRY.

I'M SO SORRY.

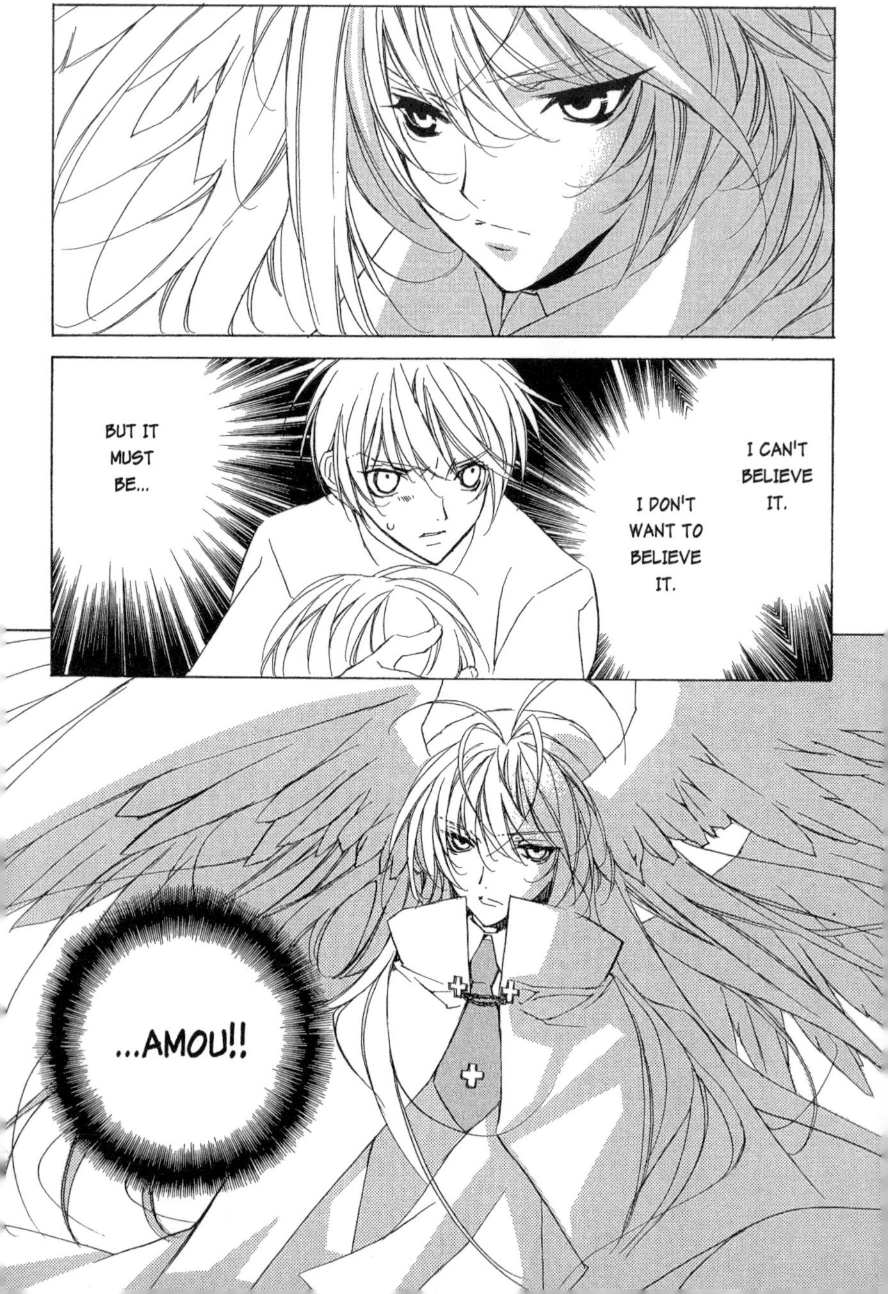
I CAN'T BELIEVE IT.
I DON'T WANT TO BELIEVE IT.
BUT IT MUST BE...
...AMOU!!

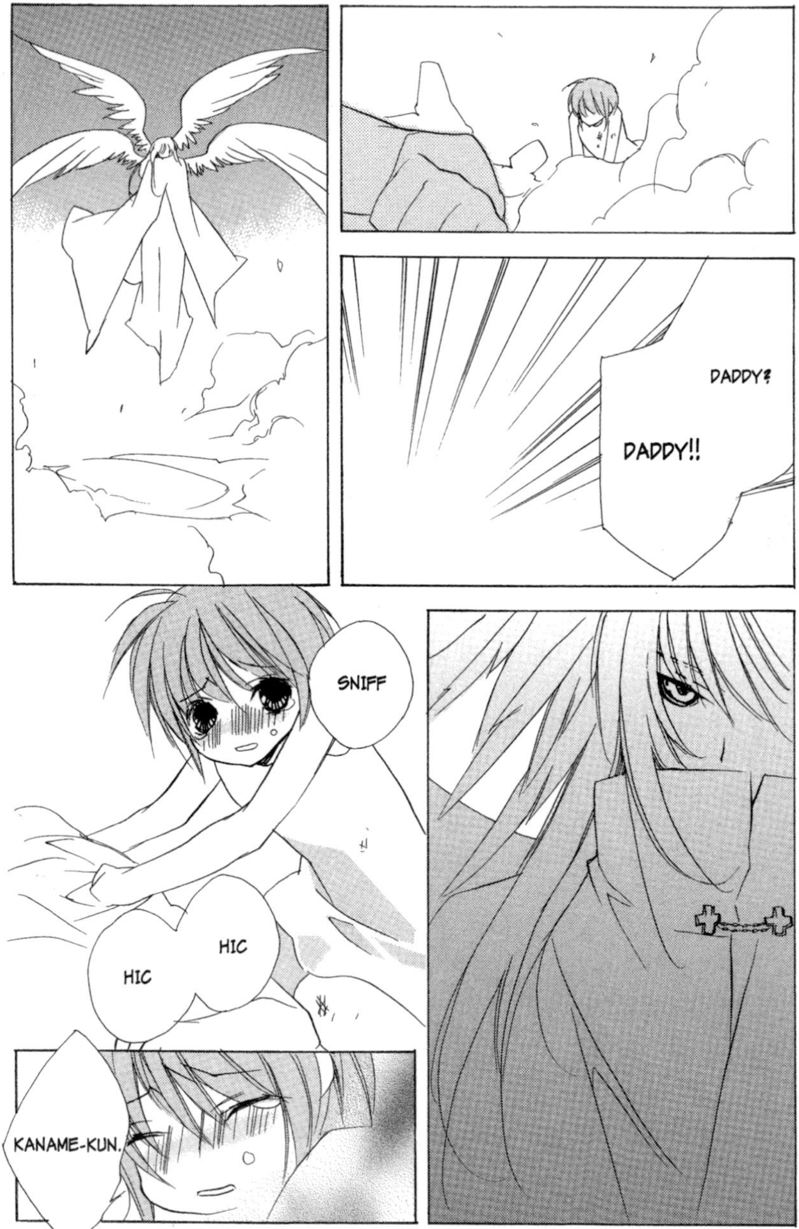
DADDY?
DADDY!!
SNIFF
HIC
HIC
KANAME-KUN.

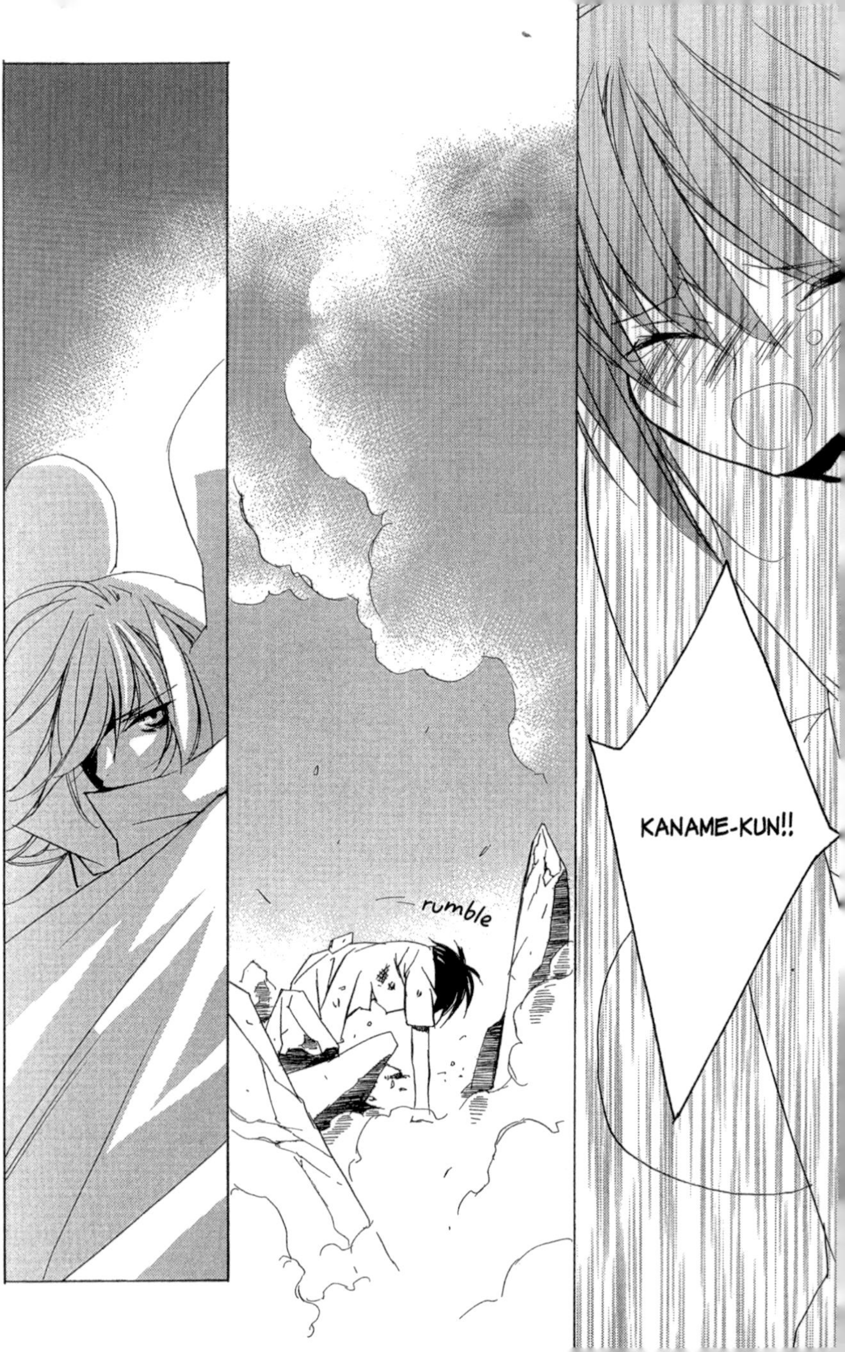
KANAME-KUN!!
rumble

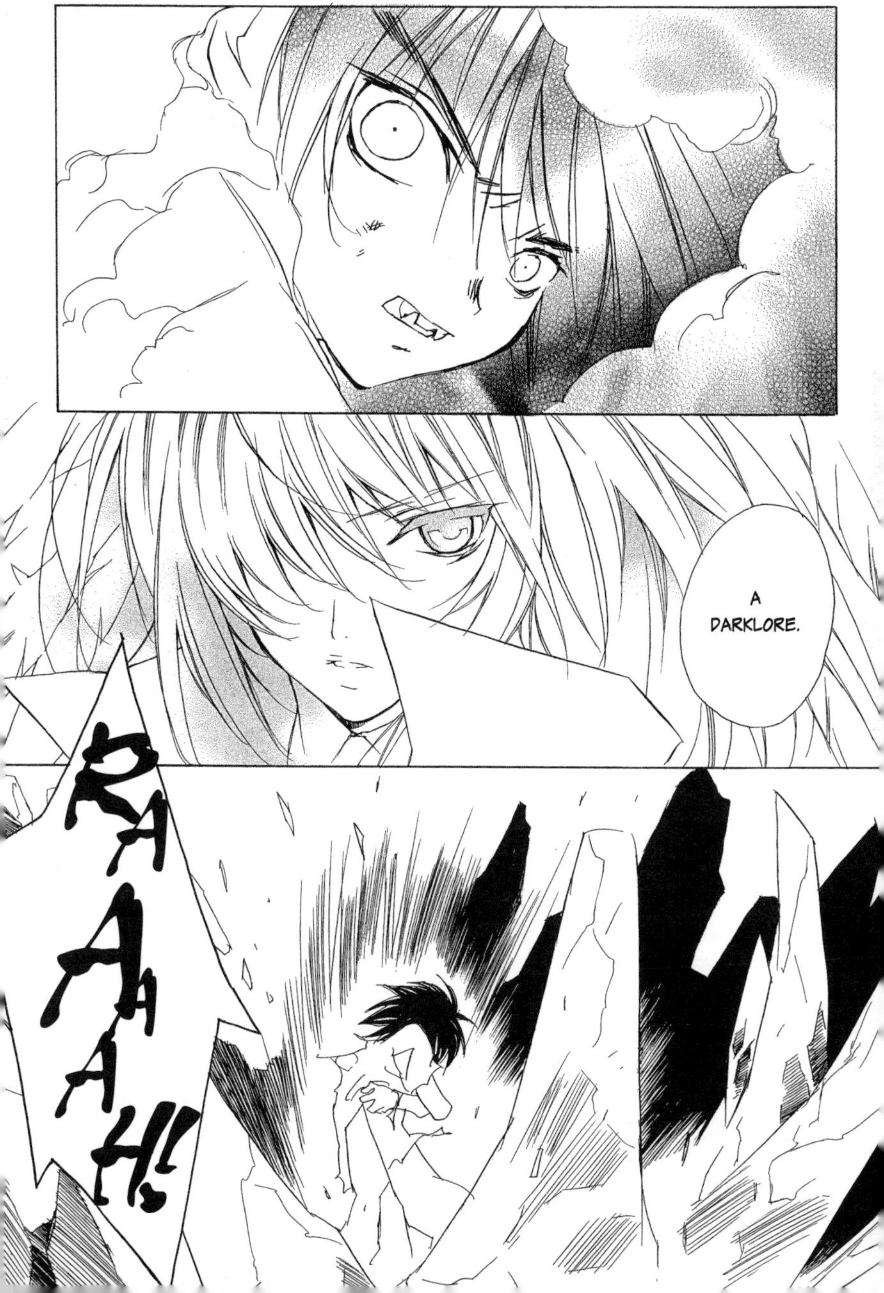

A DARKLORE.
RAAAAAH!!

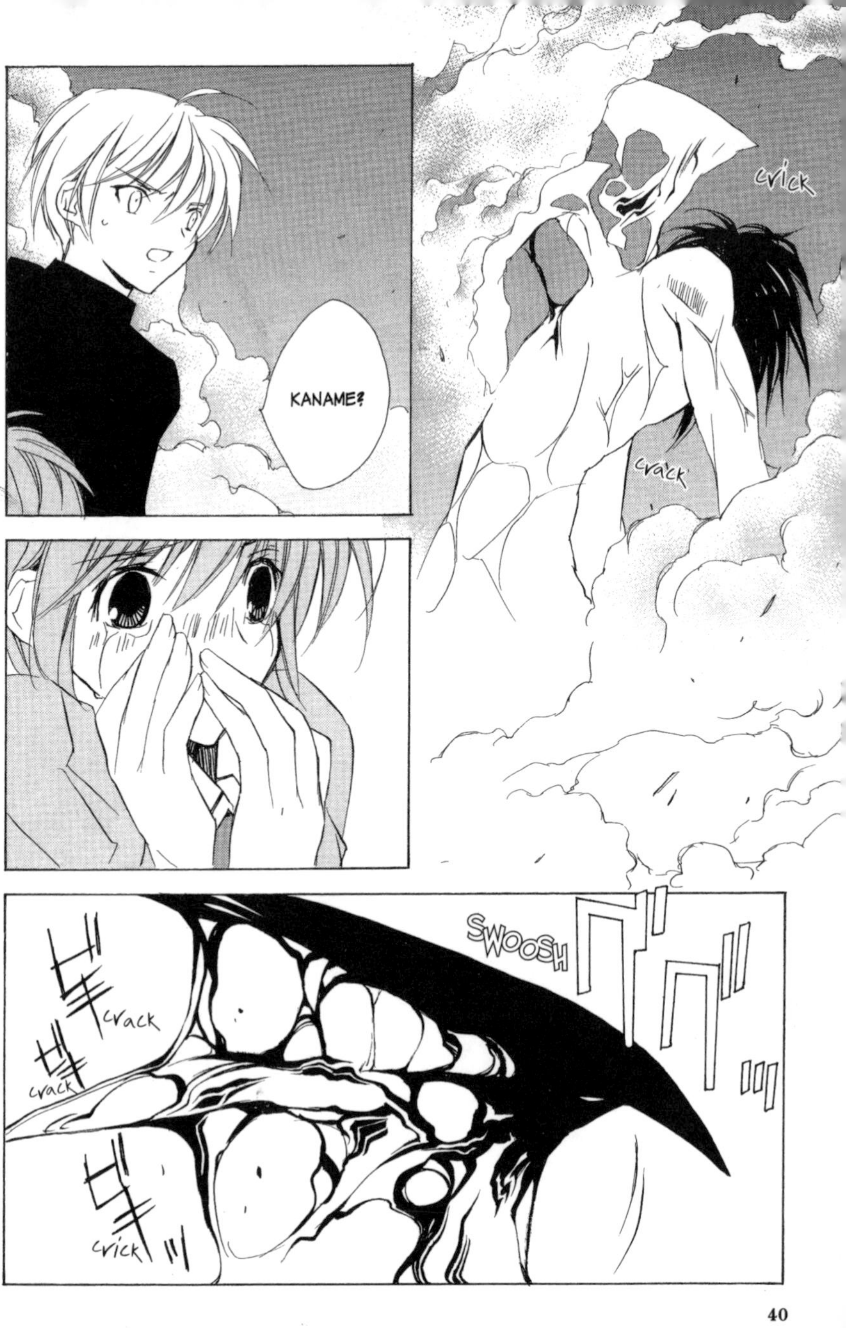
crick
crack
KANAME?
SWOOSH
crack
crack
crick

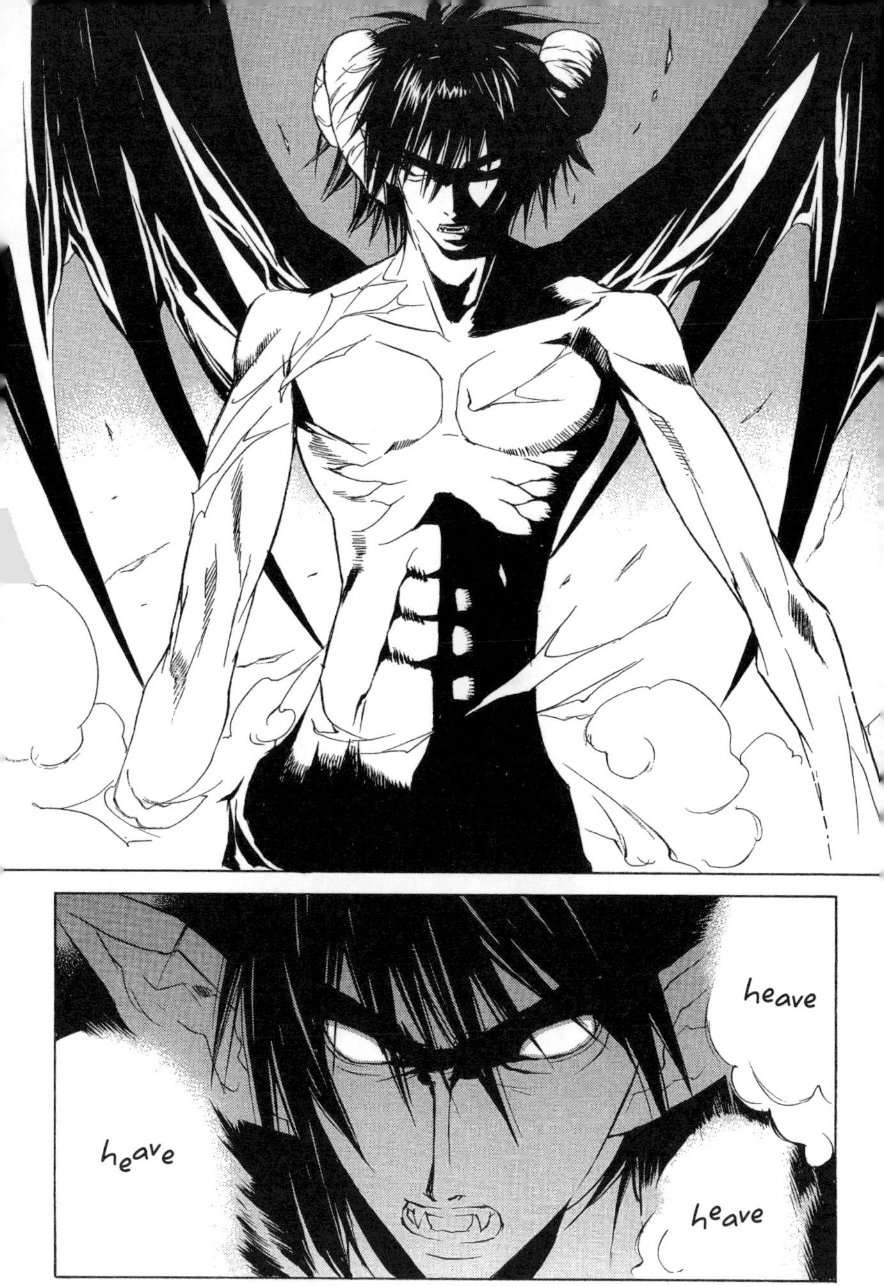
heave
heave
heave

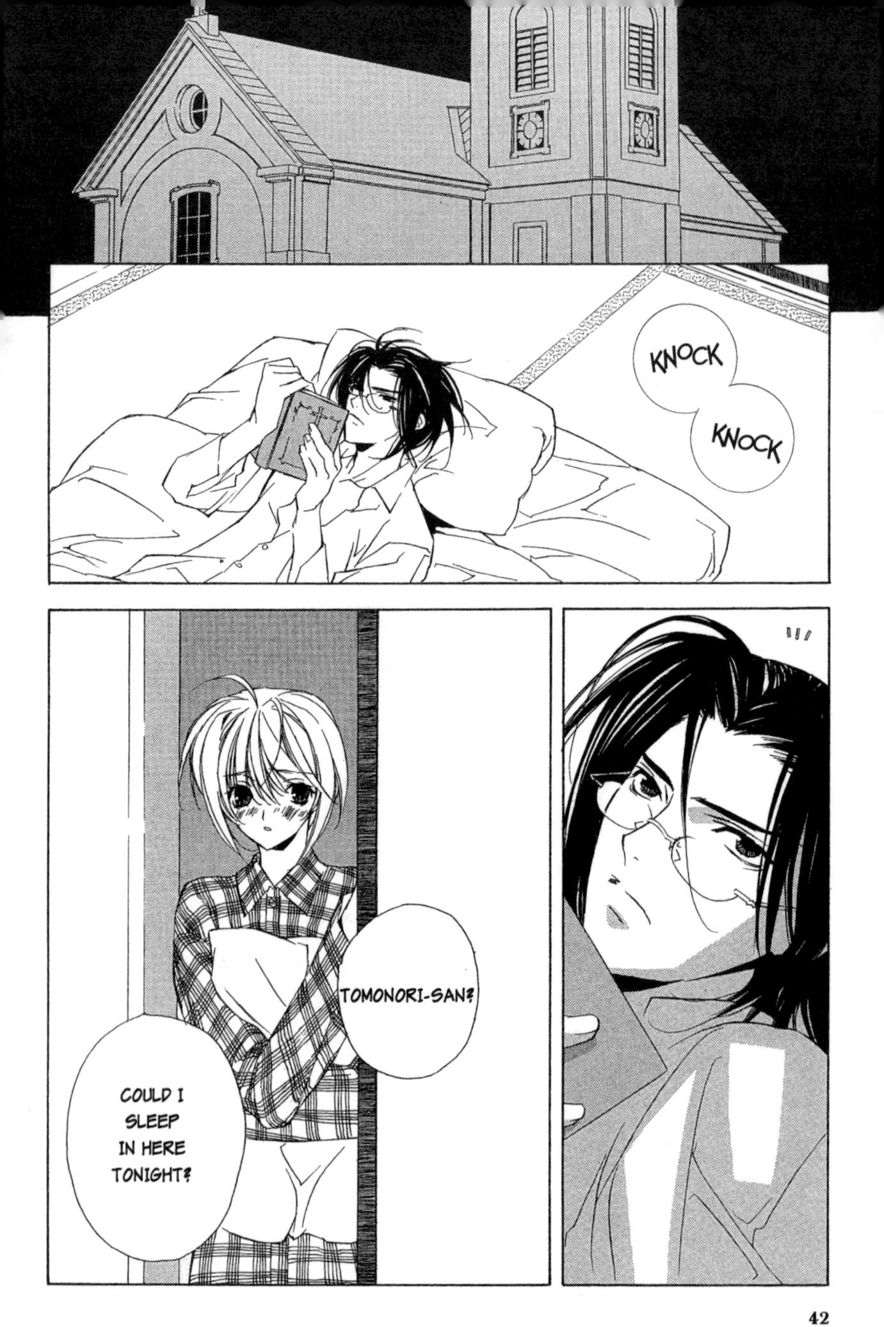
KNOCK
KNOCK
TOMONORI-SAN?
COULD I SLEEP IN HERE TONIGHT?

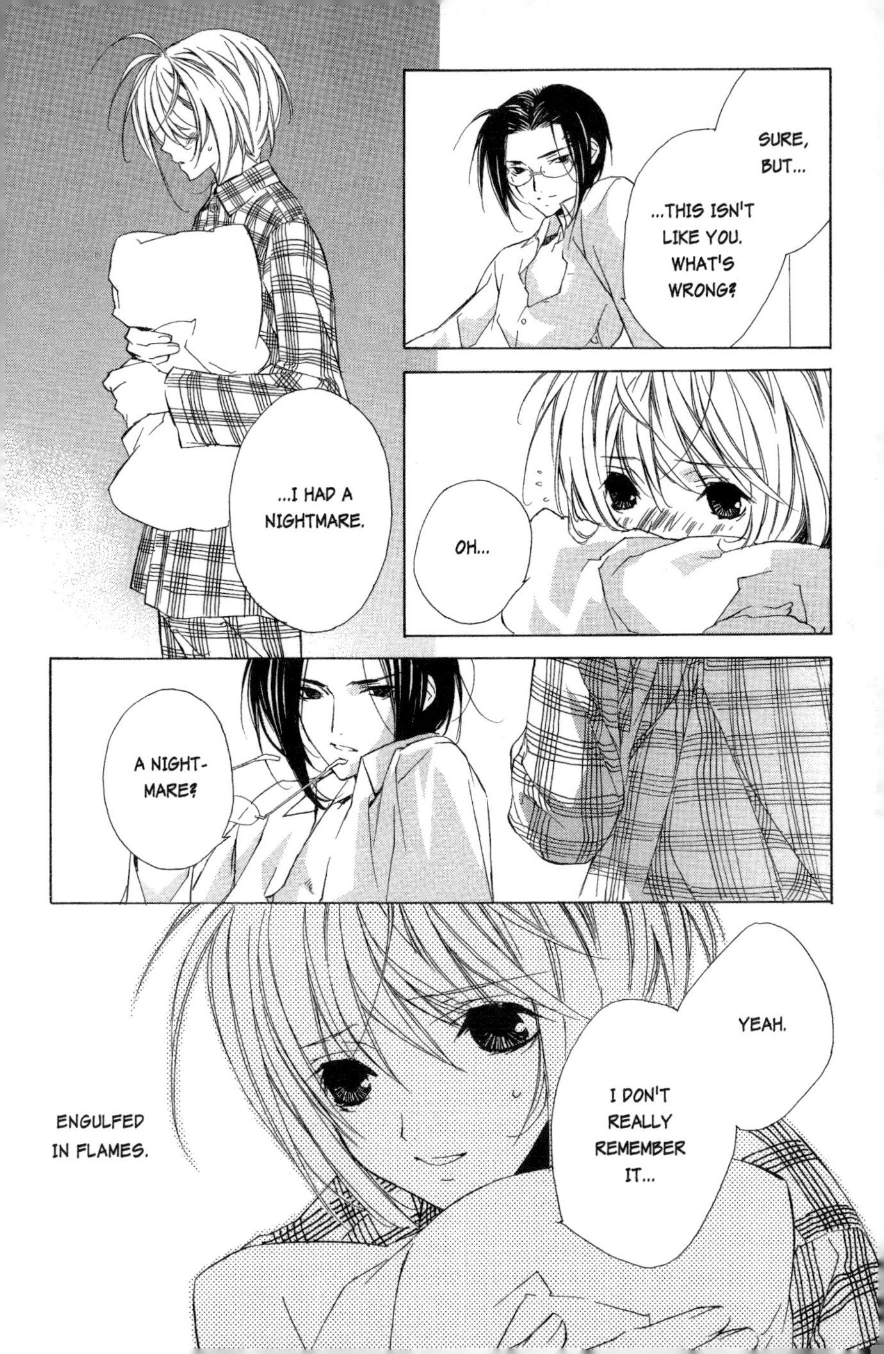
SURE, BUT...
...THIS ISN'T LIKE YOU. WHAT'S WRONG?
OH...
...I HAD A NIGHTMARE.
A NIGHT-MARE?
YEAH.
I DON'T REALLY REMEMBER IT...
ENGULFED IN FLAMES.

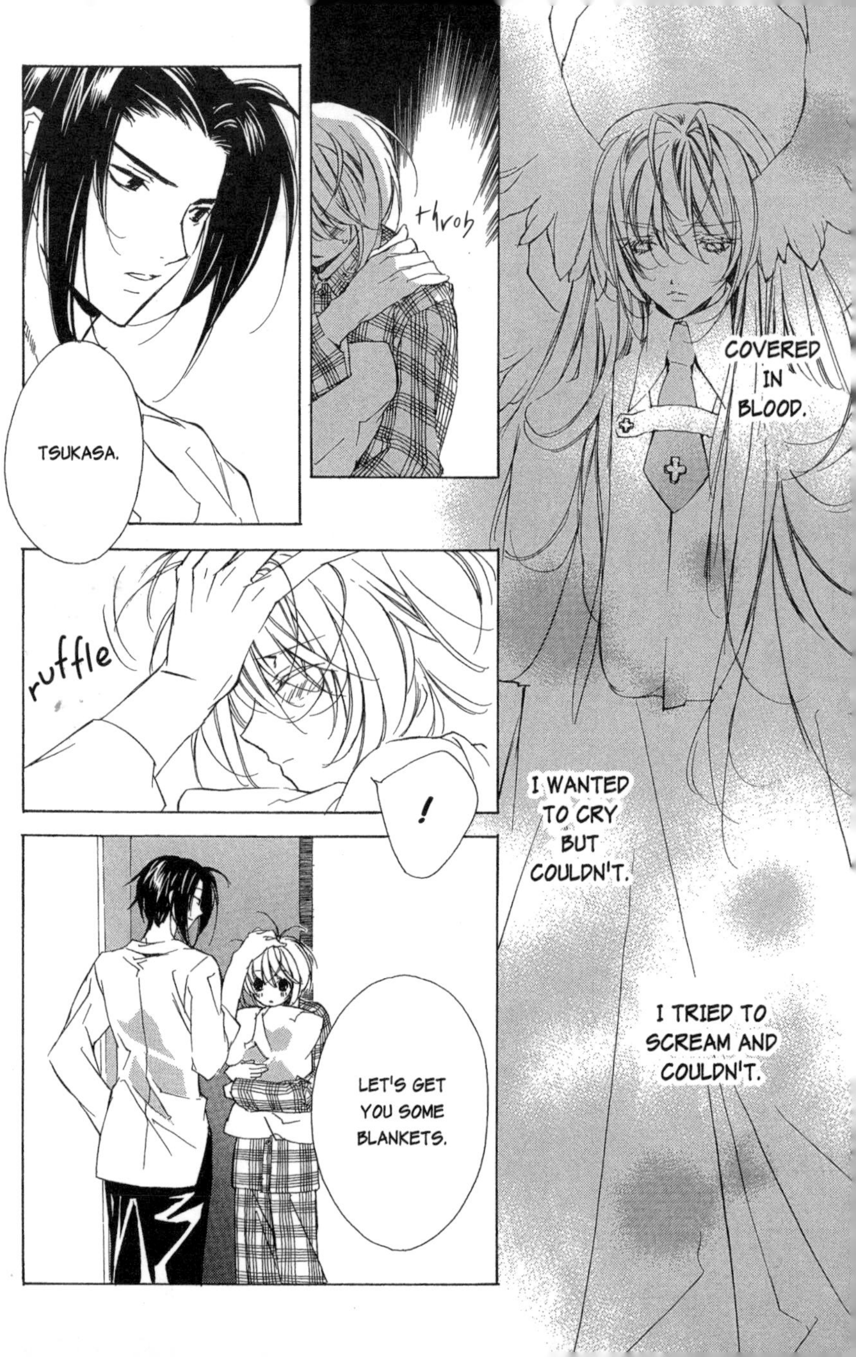
COVERED IN BLOOD.
I WANTED TO CRY BUT COULDN'T.
I TRIED TO SCREAM AND COULDN'T.
throb
TSUKASA.
ruffle
!
LET'S GET YOU SOME BLANKETS.

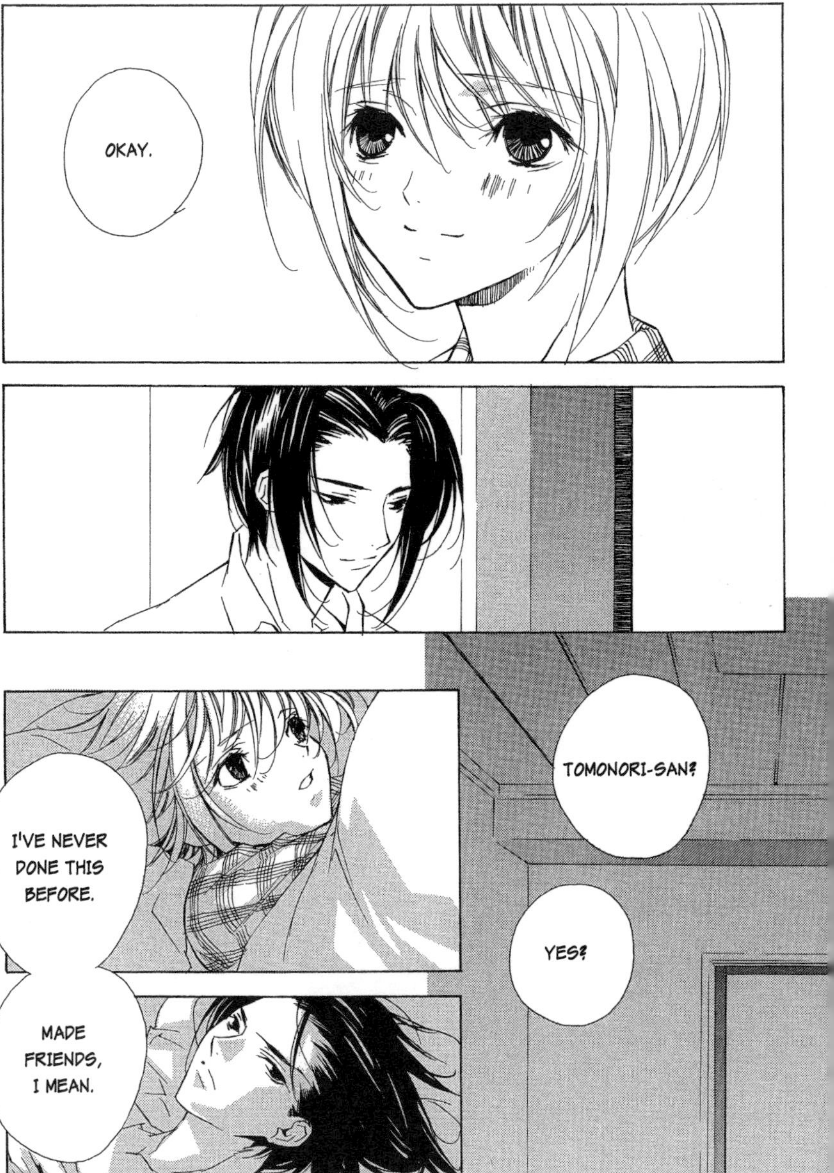
OKAY.
TOMONORI-SAN?
YES?
I'VE NEVER DONE THIS BEFORE.
MADE FRIENDS, I MEAN.

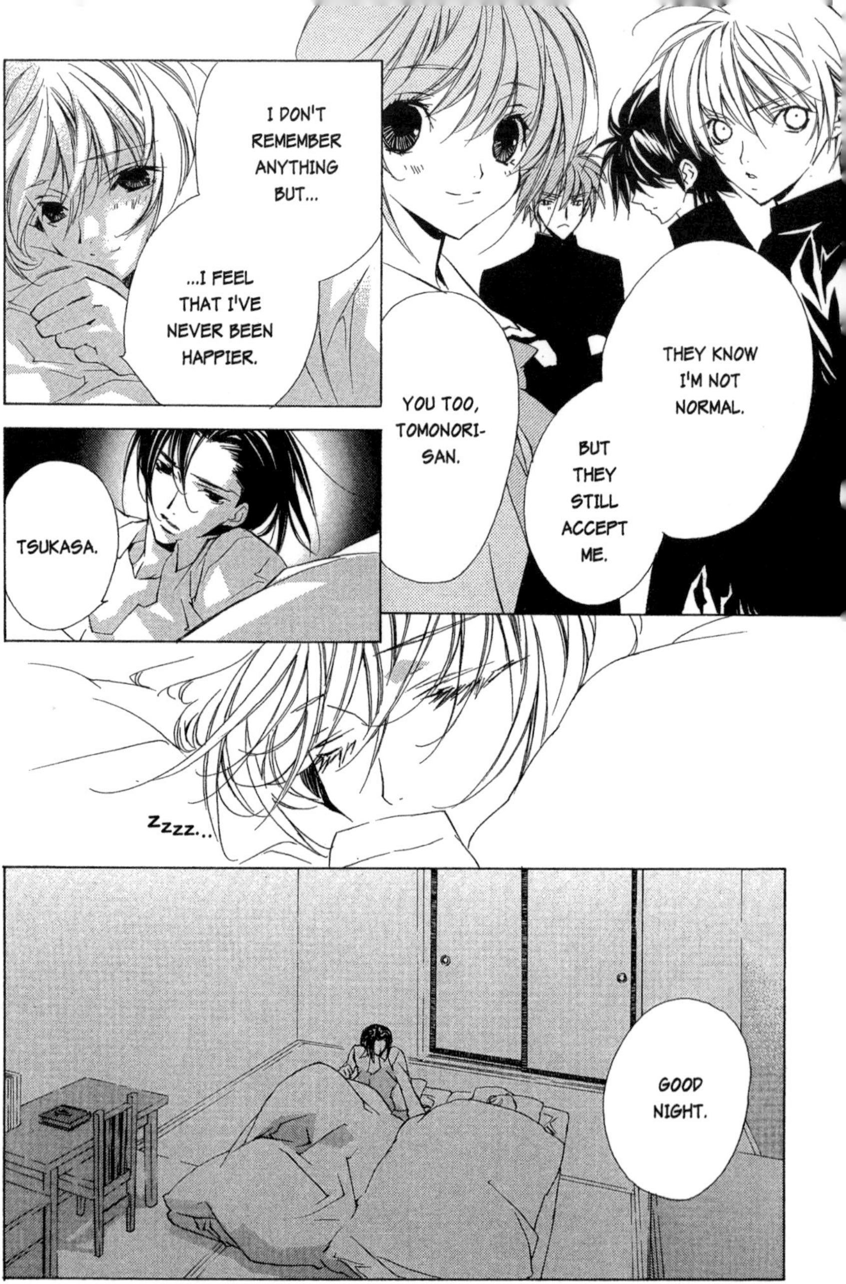

THEY KNOW I'M NOT NORMAL.
BUT THEY STILL ACCEPT ME.
YOU TOO, TOMONORI-SAN.
I DON'T REMEMBER ANYTHING BUT...
...I FEEL THAT I'VE NEVER BEEN HAPPIER.
TSUKASA.
Zzzz...
GOOD NIGHT.

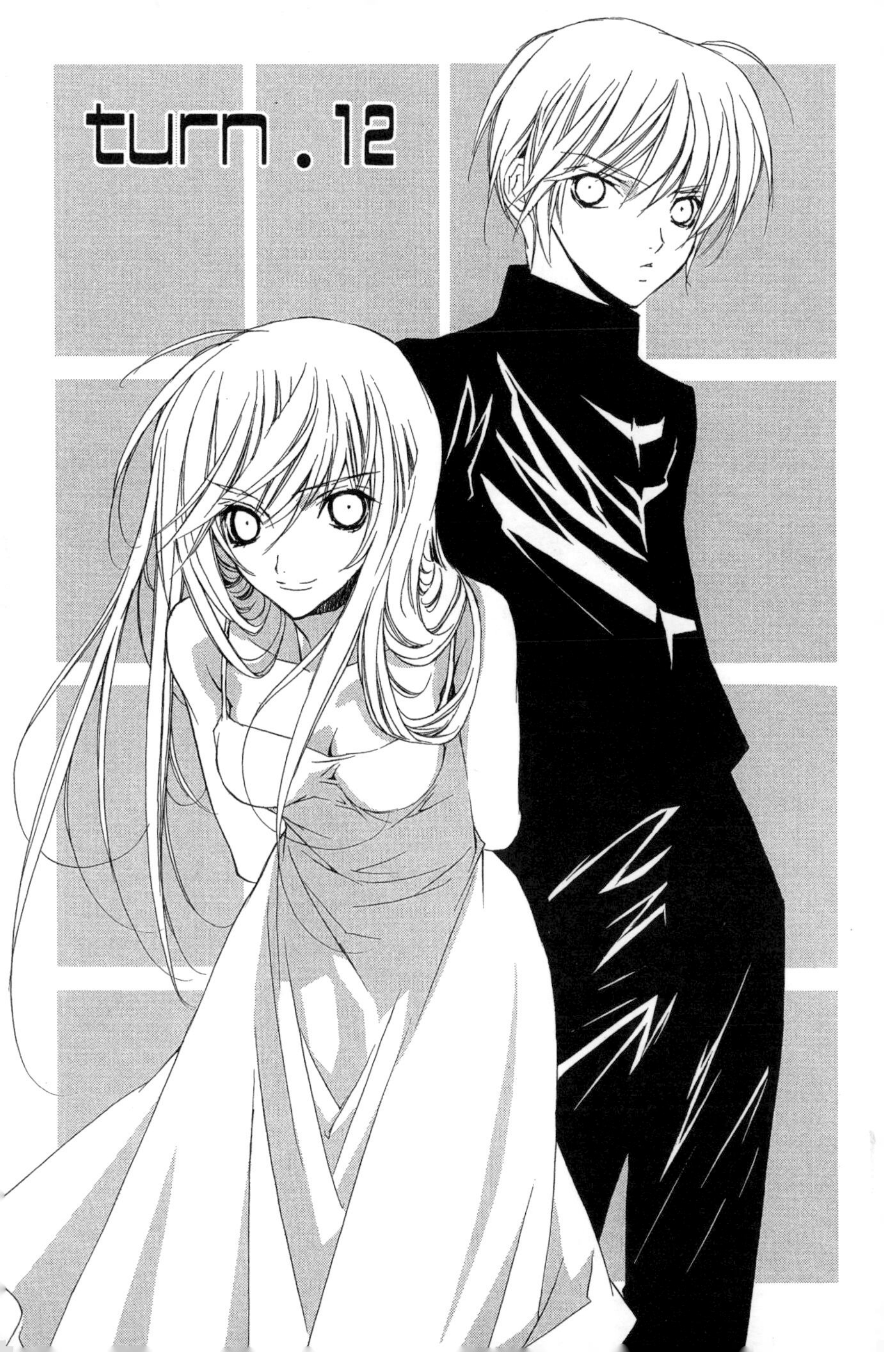
turn . 12

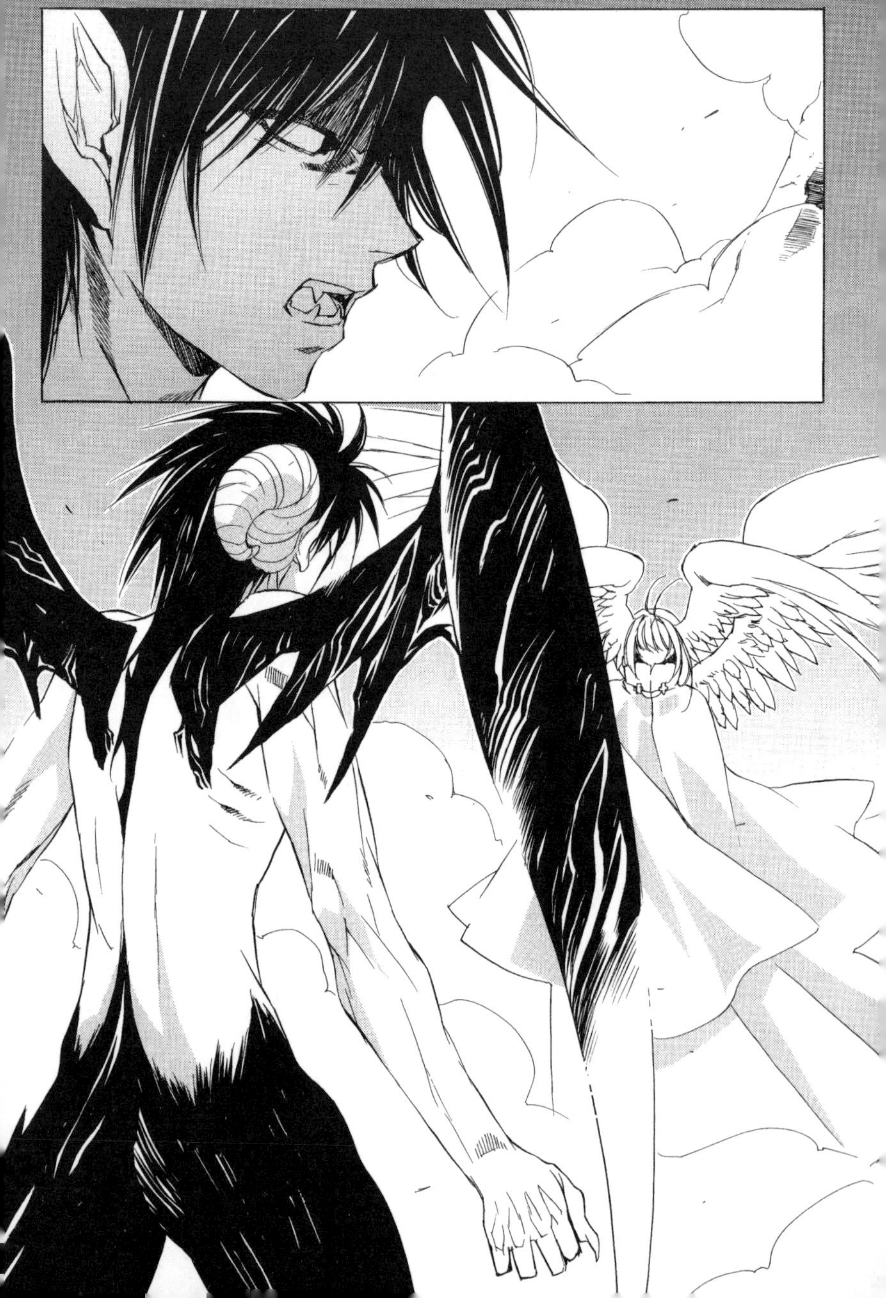

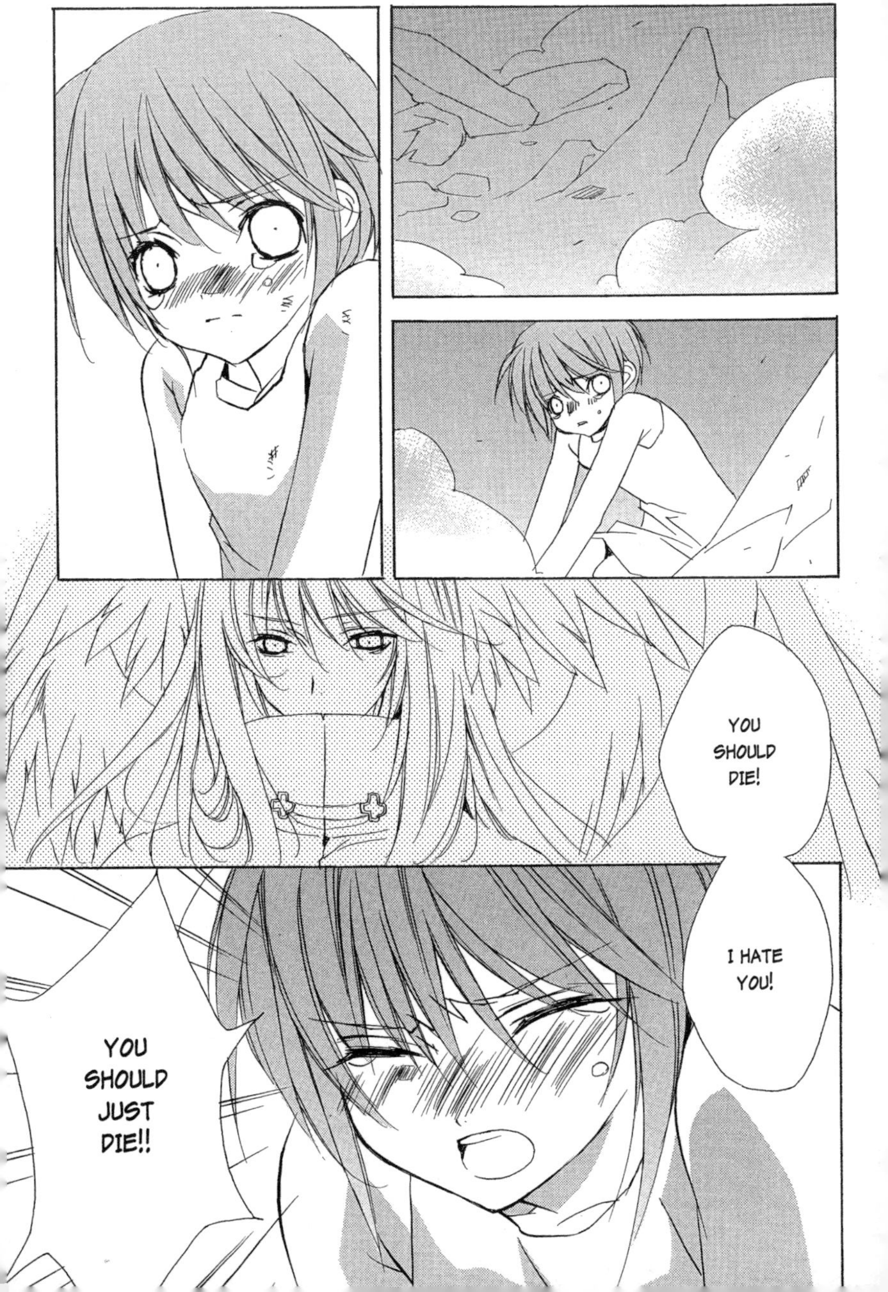
YOU SHOULD DIE!
I HATE YOU!
YOU SHOULD JUST DIE!!

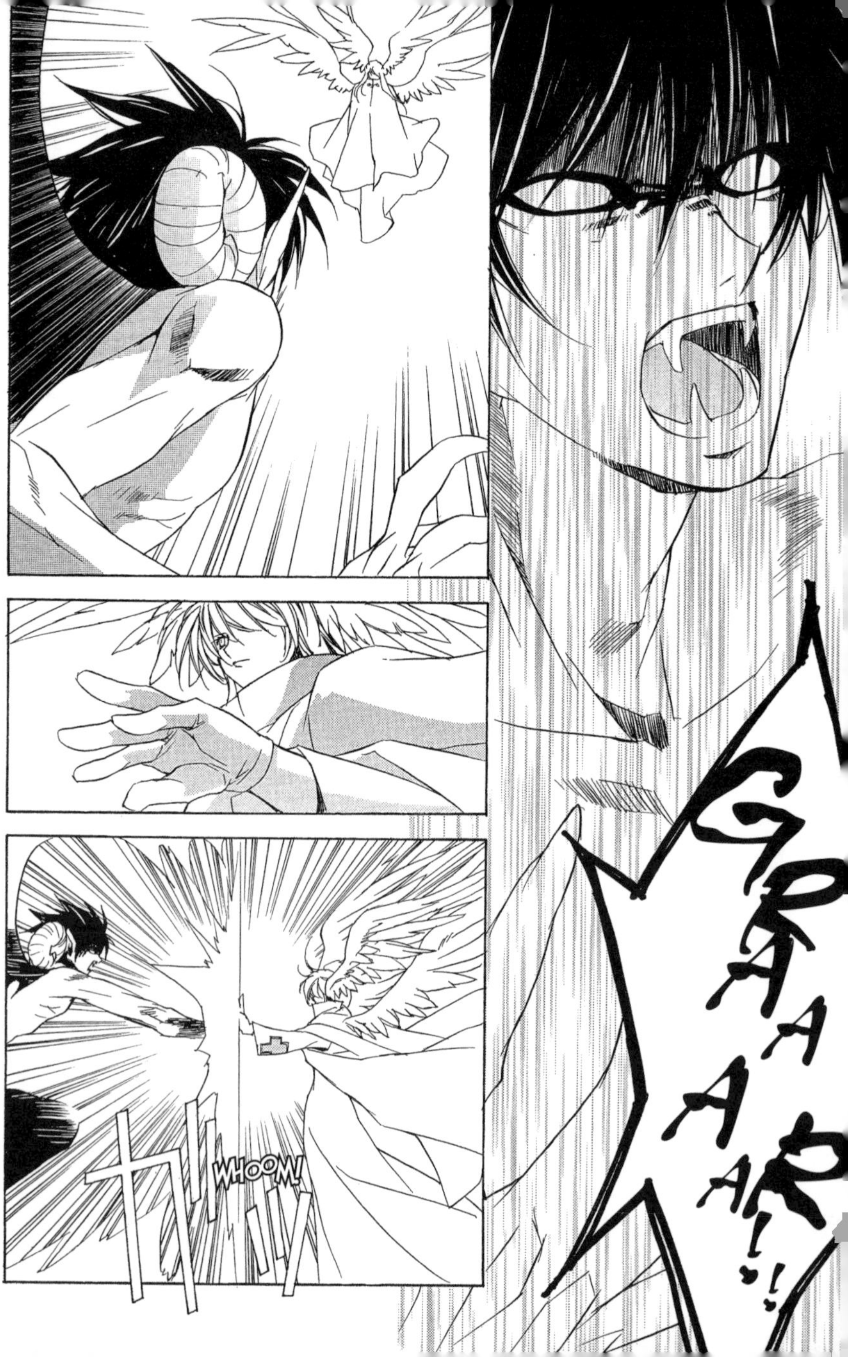
GRAAAAR!!!
WHOOM!

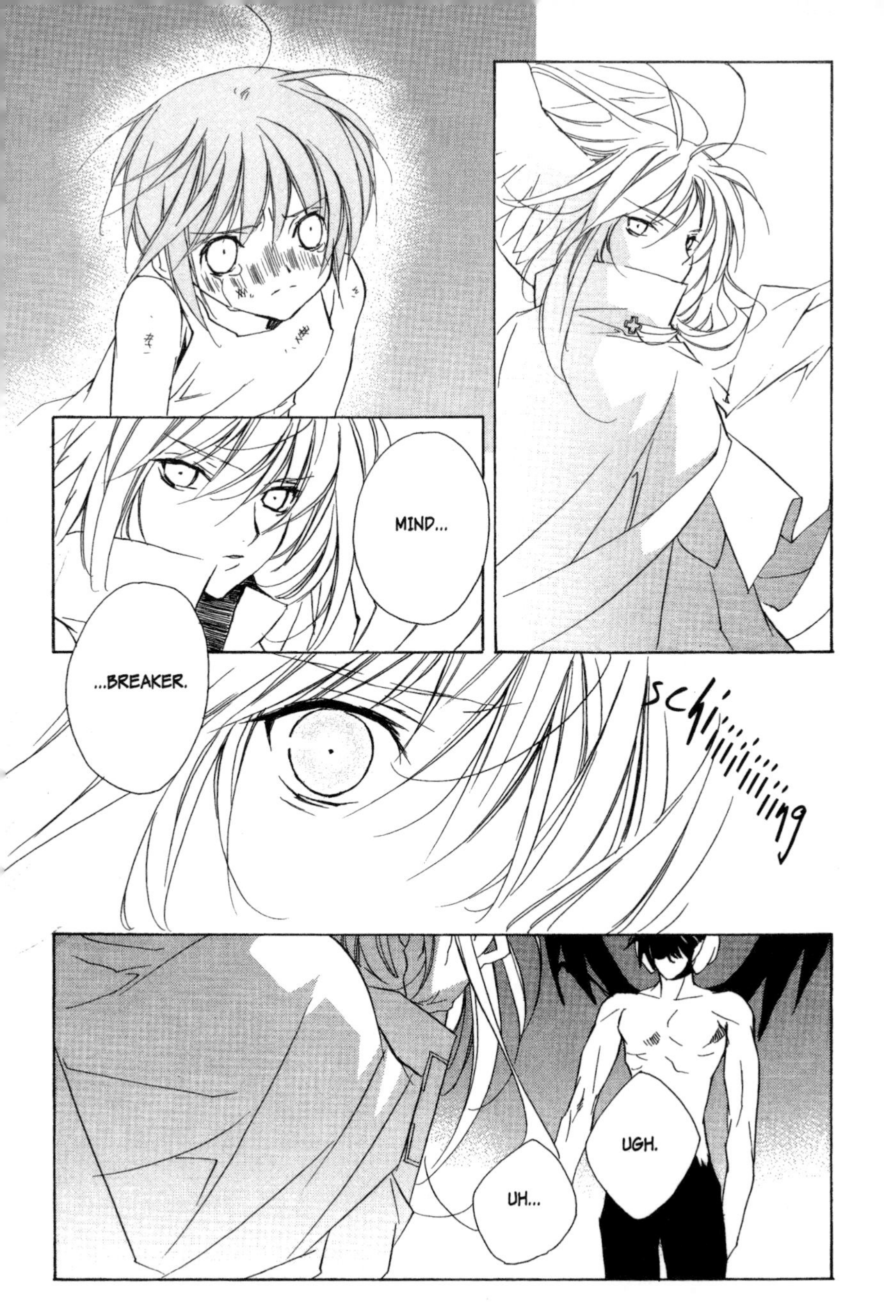
MIND...
...BREAKER.
schiiiiiiiiiing
UGH.
UH...

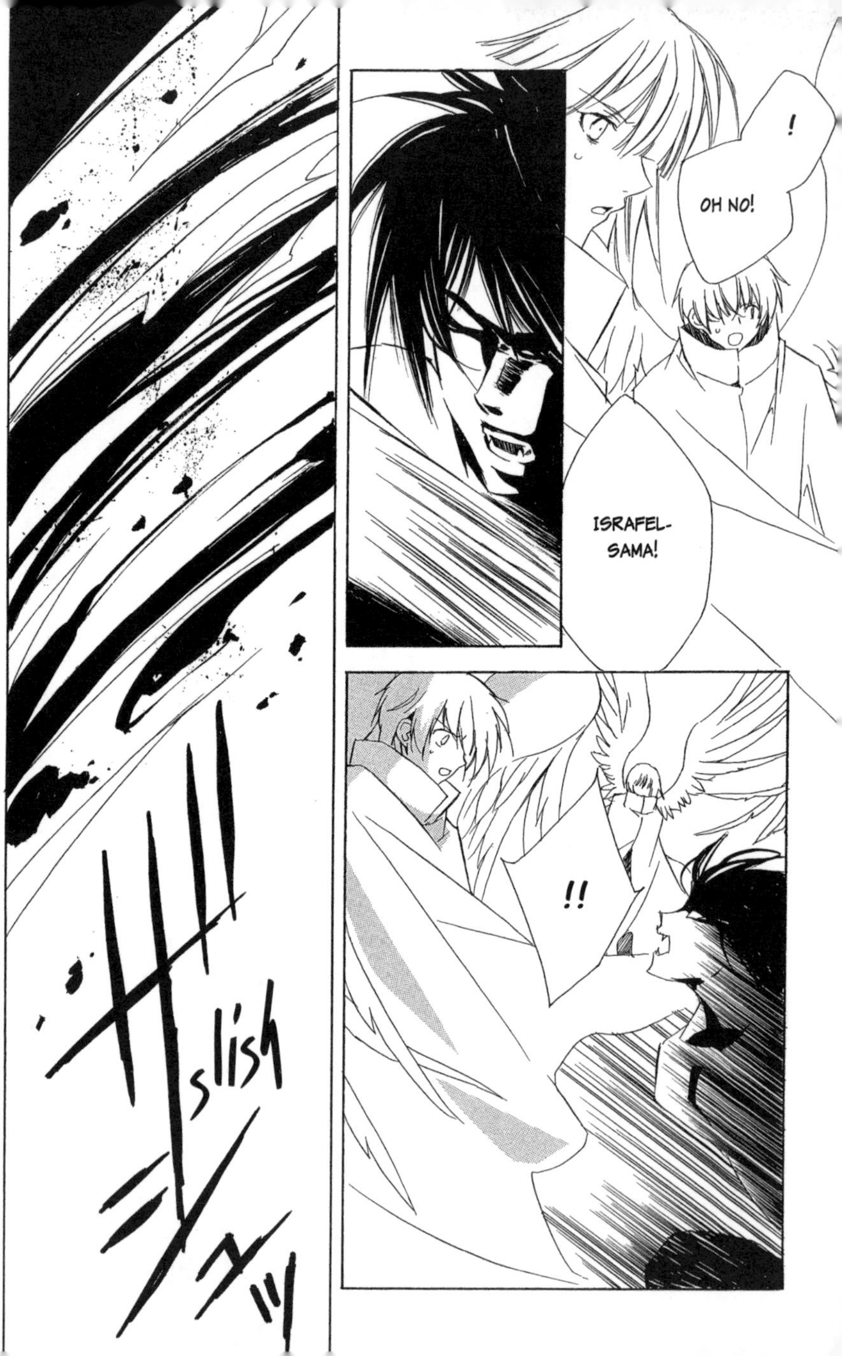

!
OH NO!
ISRAFEL-SAMA!
!!
slish

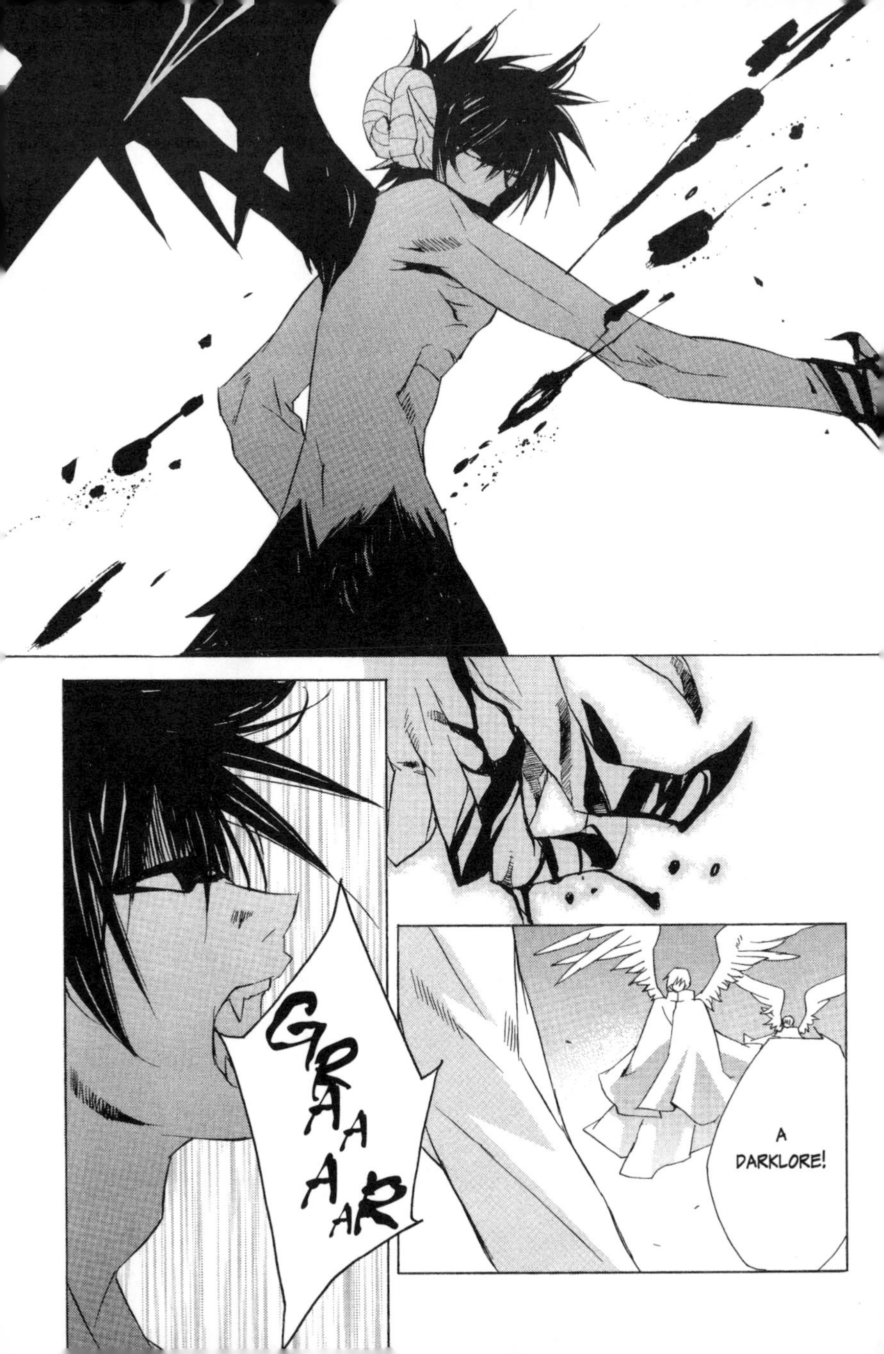
A DARKLORE!
GRAAAAAR

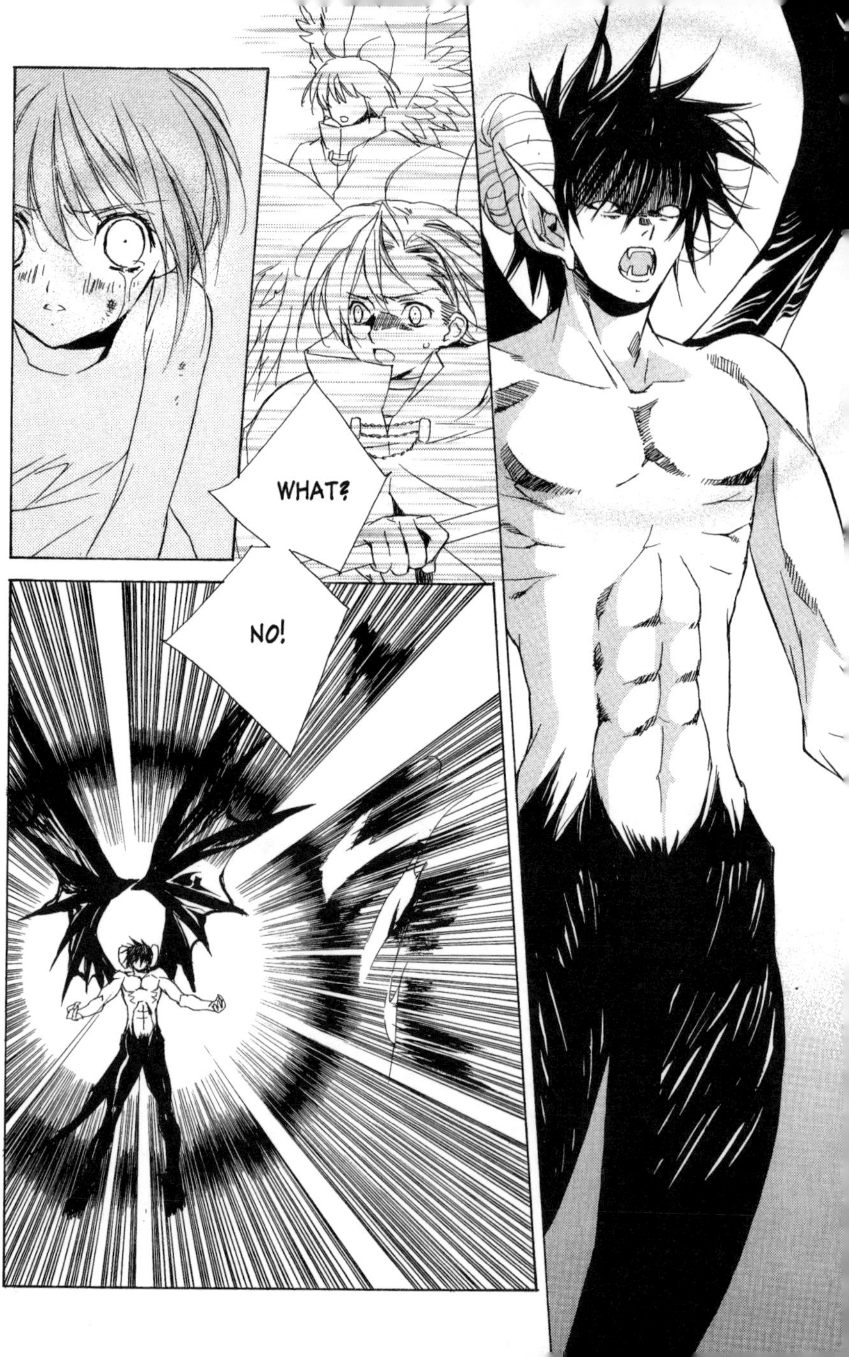
WHAT?
NO!

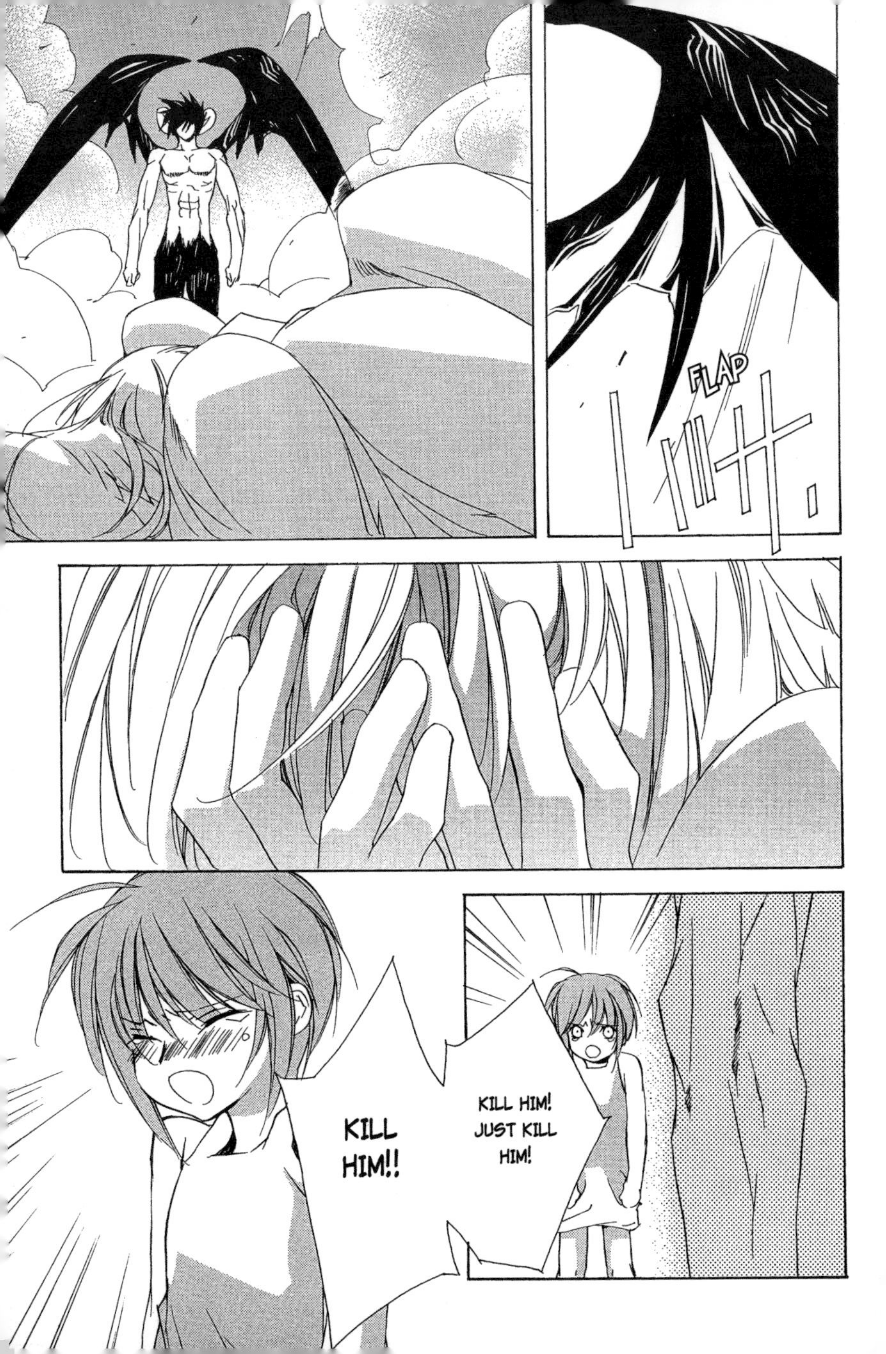
FLAP
KILL HIM! JUST KILL HIM!
KILL HIM!!

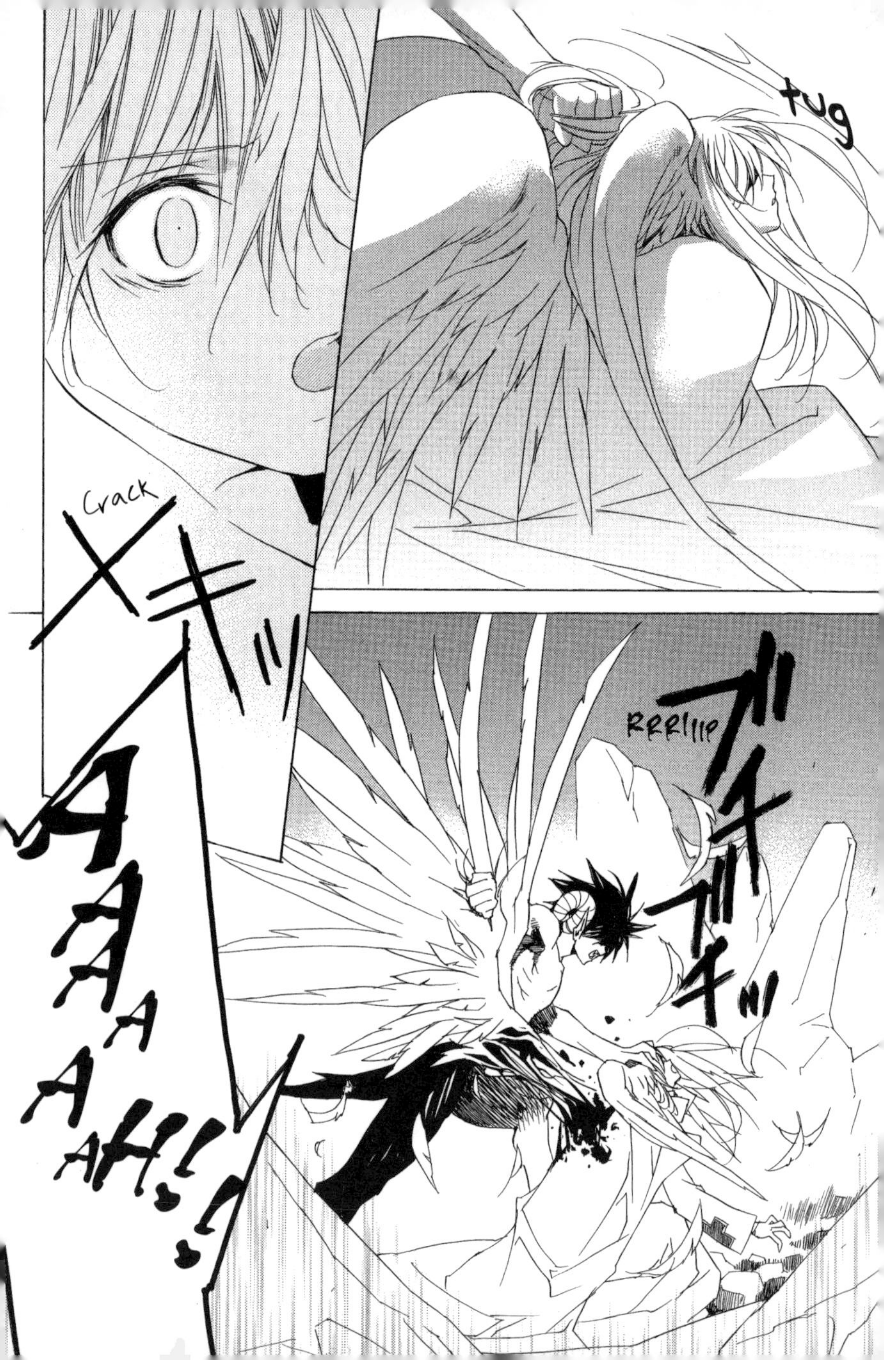
tug
Crack
メキッ
RRRIIIP
ブチブチッ
AAAAAAAH!!

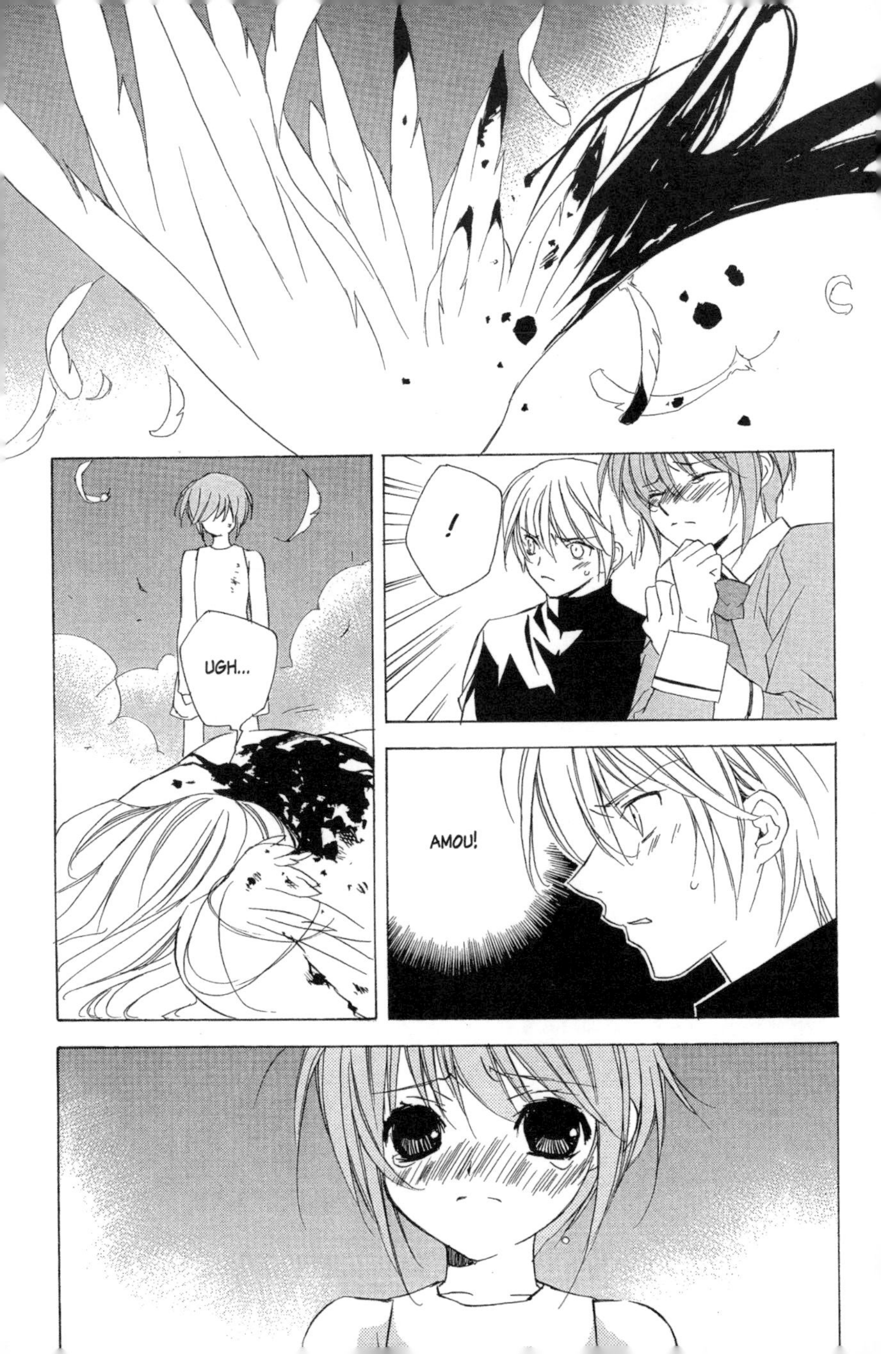
!
AMOU!
UGH...

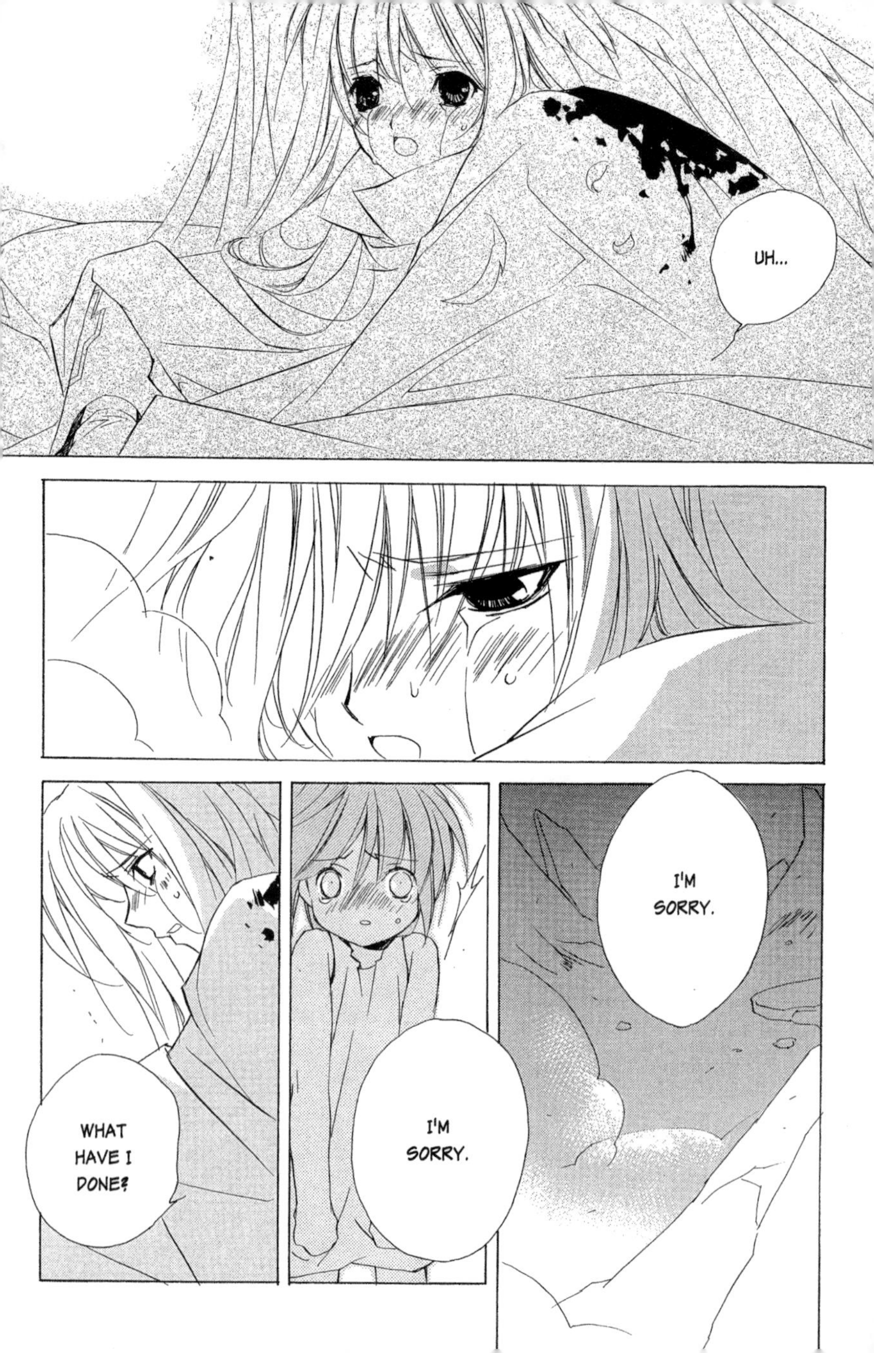
UH...
I'M SORRY.
I'M SORRY.
WHAT HAVE I DONE?

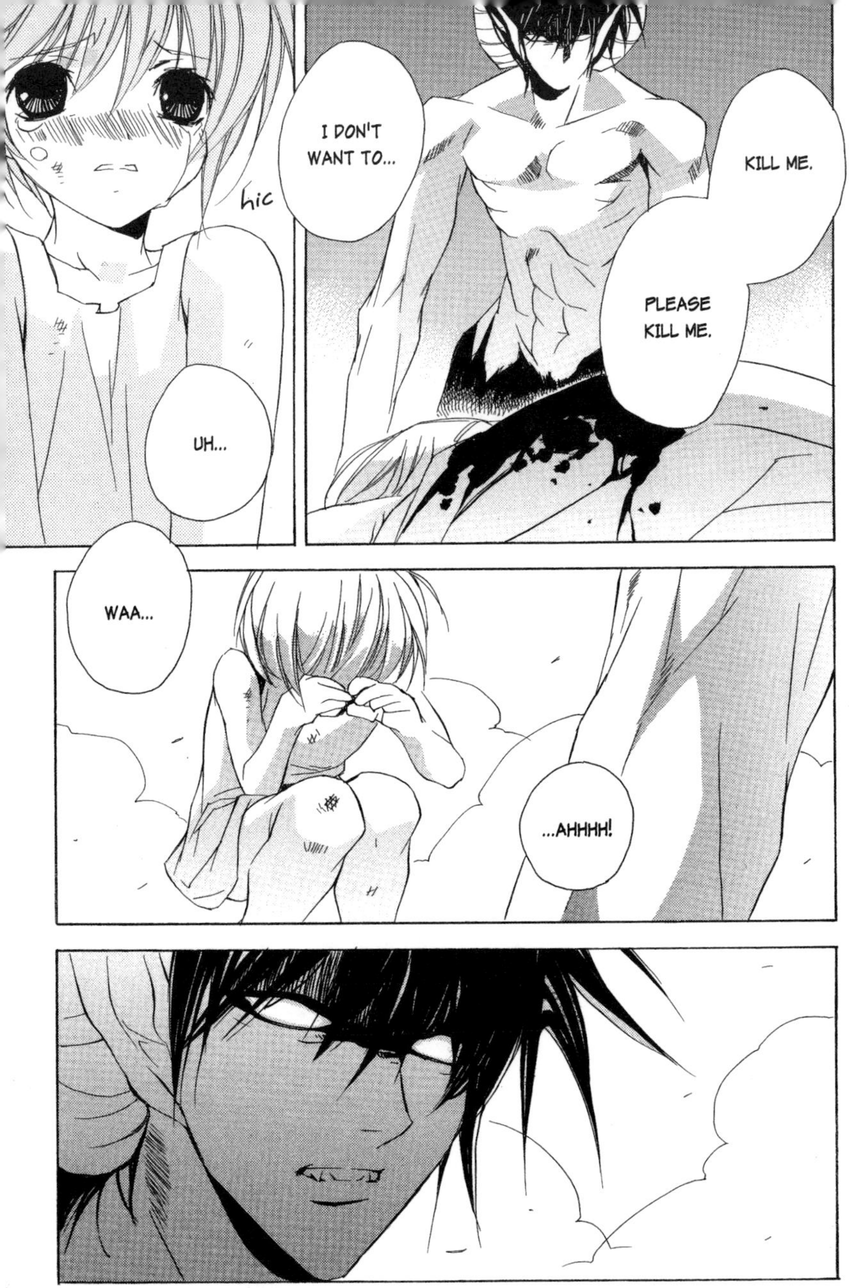
KILL ME.
I DON'T WANT TO...
PLEASE KILL ME.
hic
UH...
WAA...
...AHHHH!

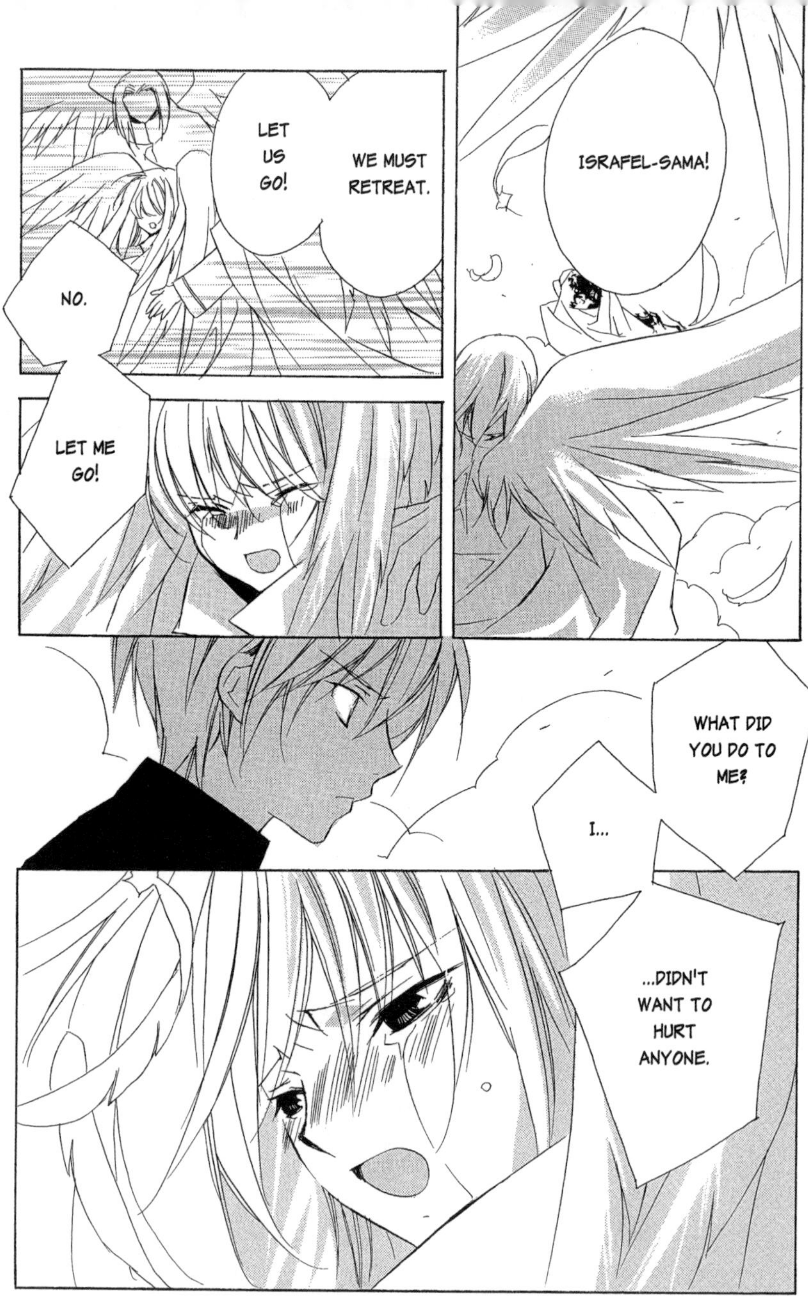
ISRAFEL-SAMA!
WE MUST RETREAT.
LET US GO!
NO.
LET ME GO!
WHAT DID YOU DO TO ME?
I...
...DIDN'T WANT TO HURT ANYONE.

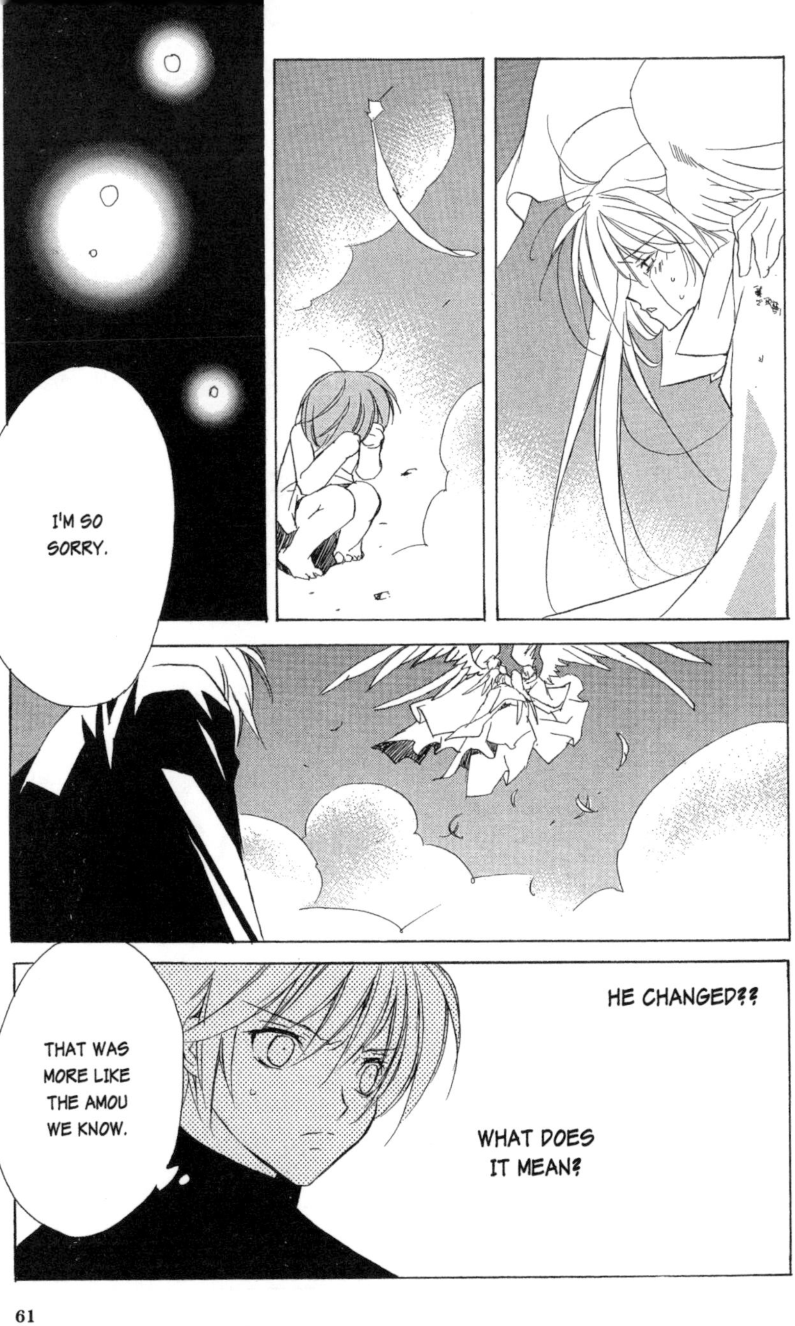
I'M SO SORRY.
HE CHANGED??
WHAT DOES IT MEAN?
THAT WAS MORE LIKE THE AMOU WE KNOW.

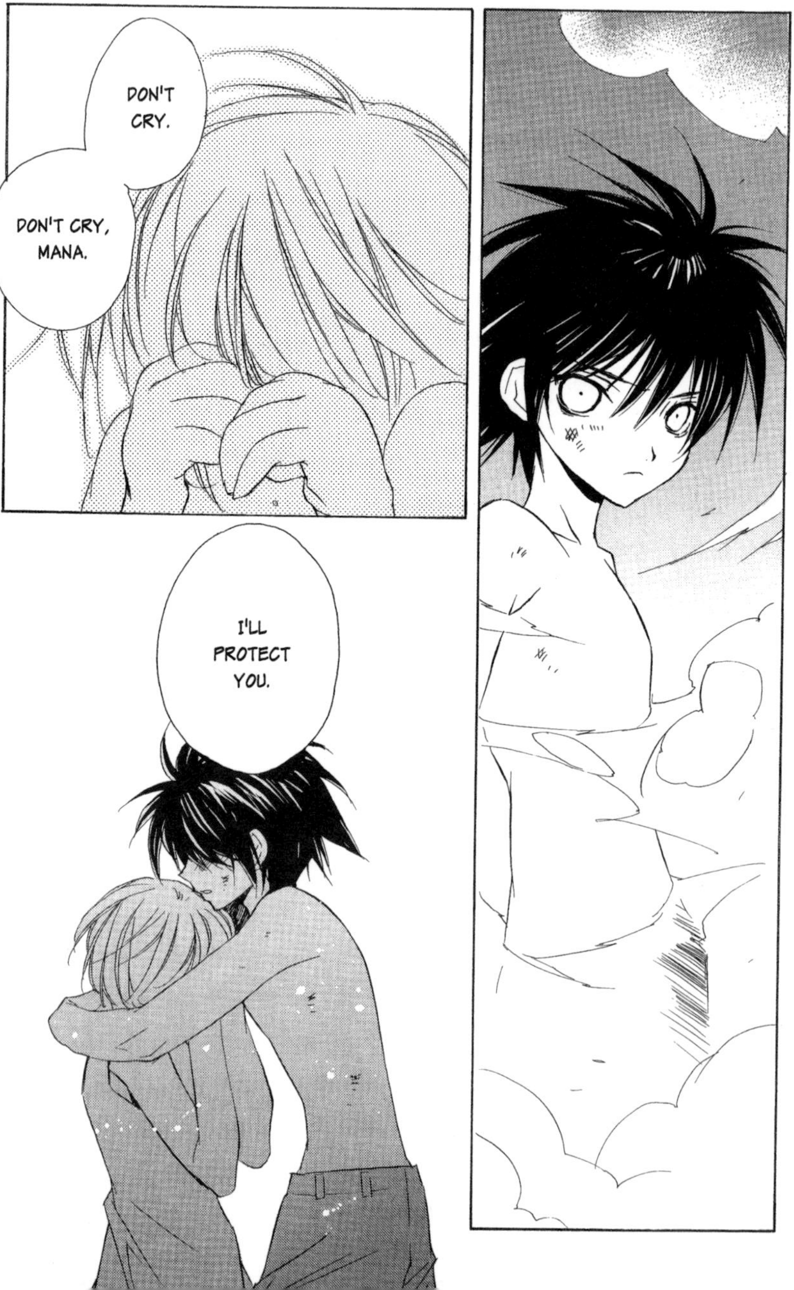
DON'T CRY.
DON'T CRY, MANA.
I'LL PROTECT YOU.

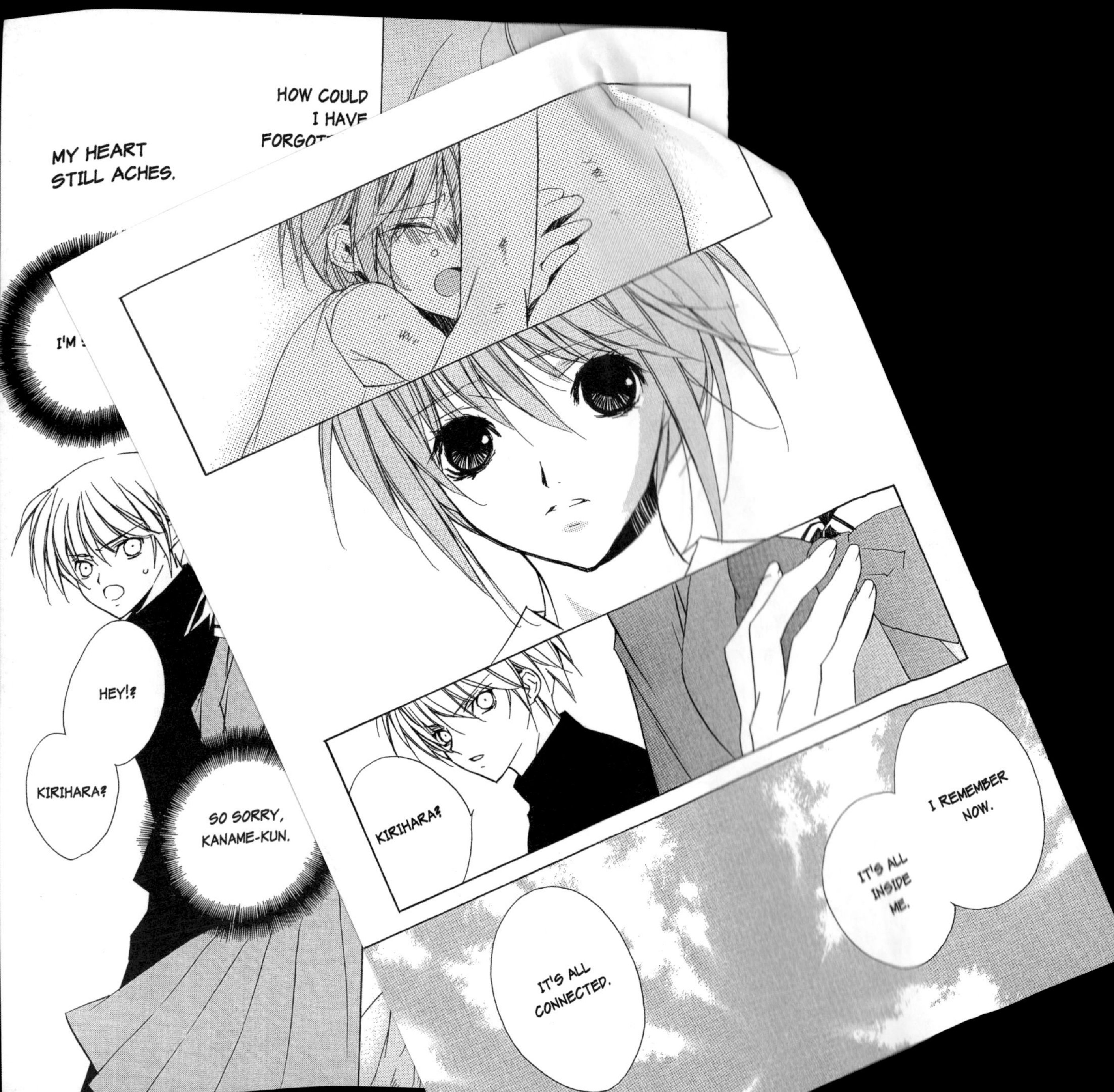

KIRIHARA?
I REMEMBER NOW.
IT'S ALL INSIDE ME.
IT'S ALL CONNECTED.
HOW COULD I HAVE FORGOT
MY HEART STILL ACHES.
I'M
SO SORRY, KANAME-KUN.
HEY!?
KIRIHARA?

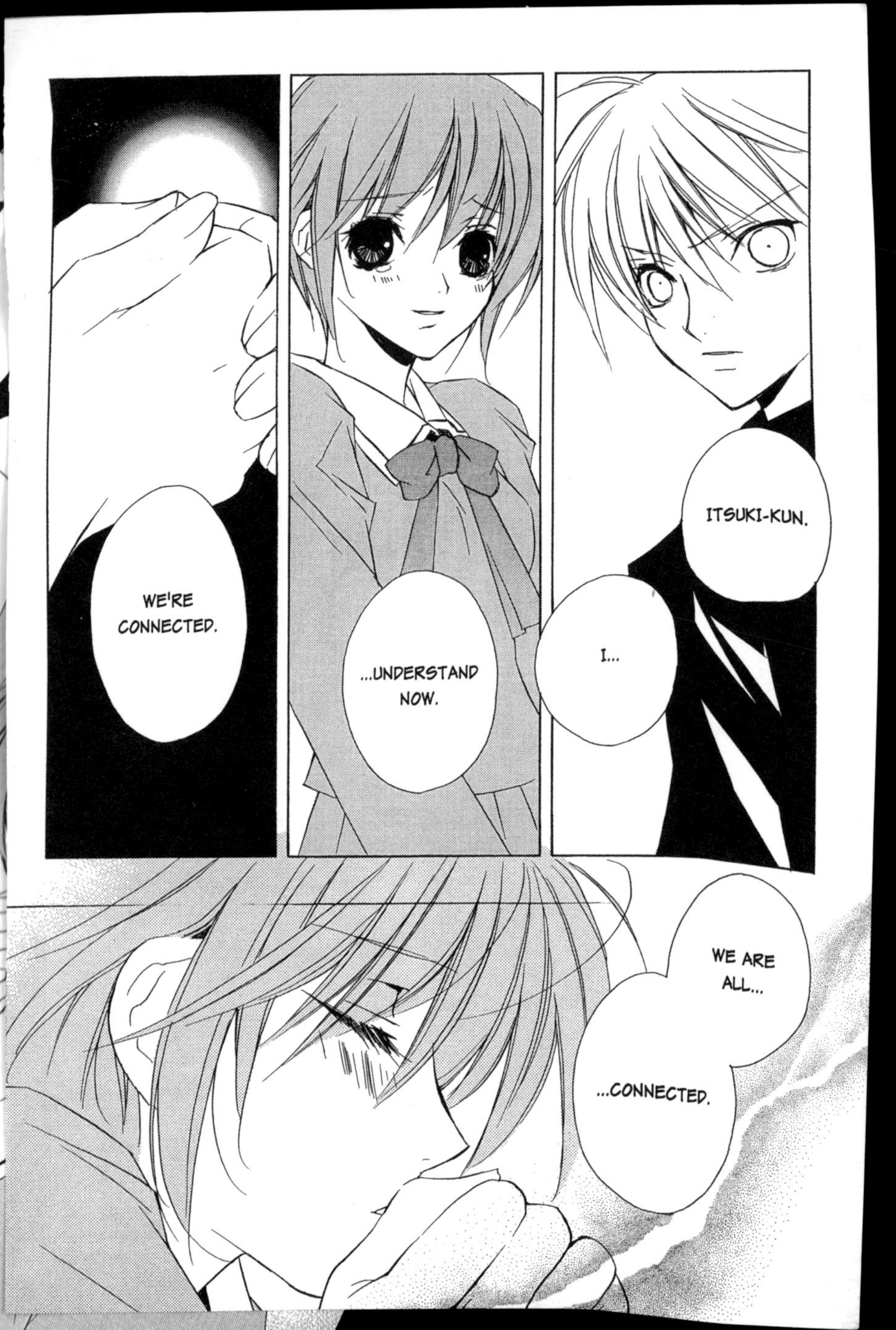
ITSUKI-KUN.
I...
...UNDERSTAND NOW.
WE'RE CONNECTED.
WE ARE ALL...
...CONNECTED.
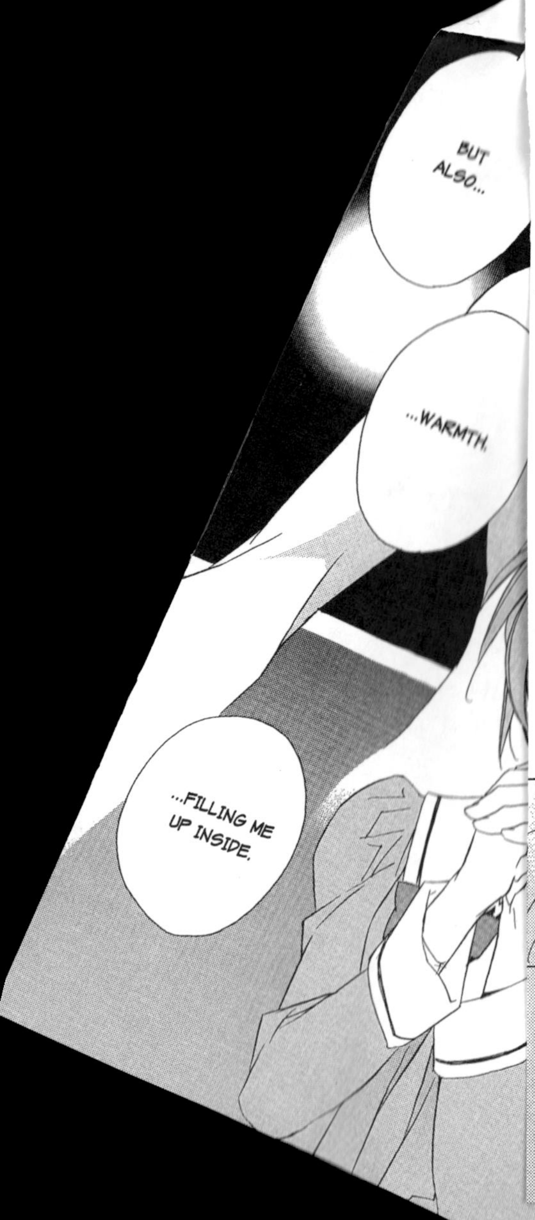
BUT ALSO...
...WARMTH.
...FILLING ME UP INSIDE.

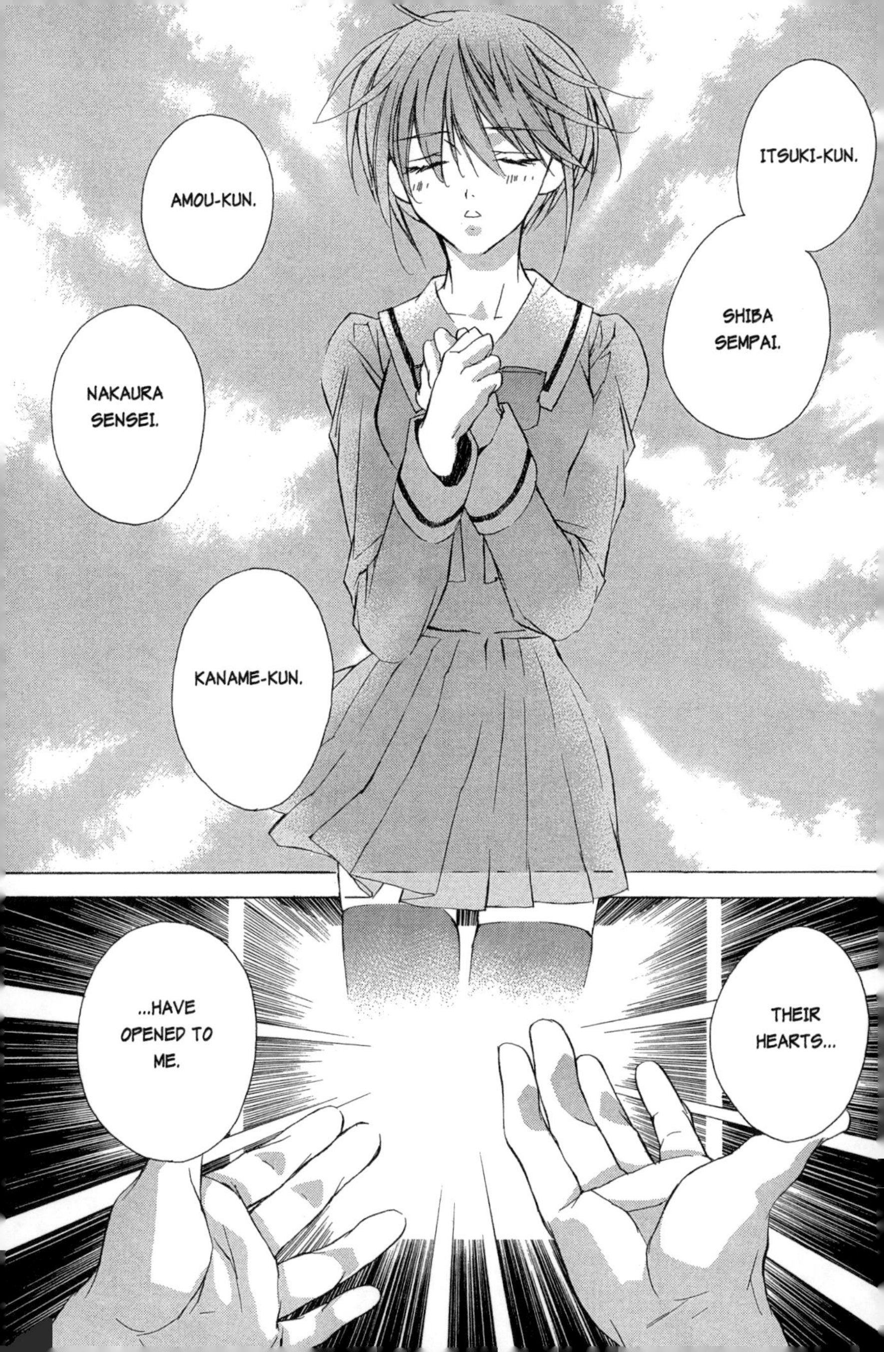
ITSUKI-KUN.
AMOU-KUN.
SHIBA SEMPAI.
NAKAURA SENSEI.
KANAME-KUN.
THEIR HEARTS...
...HAVE OPENED TO ME.

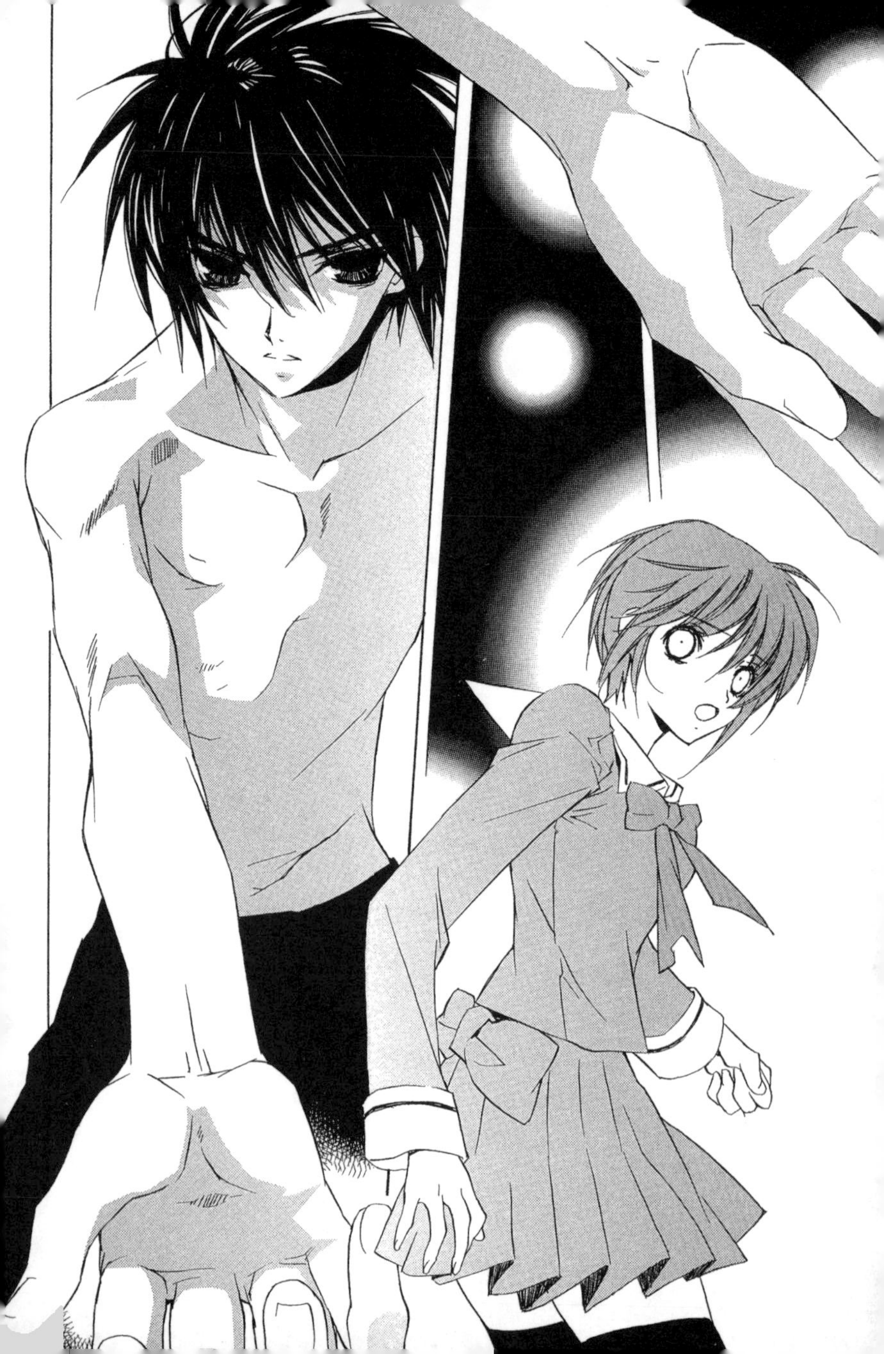

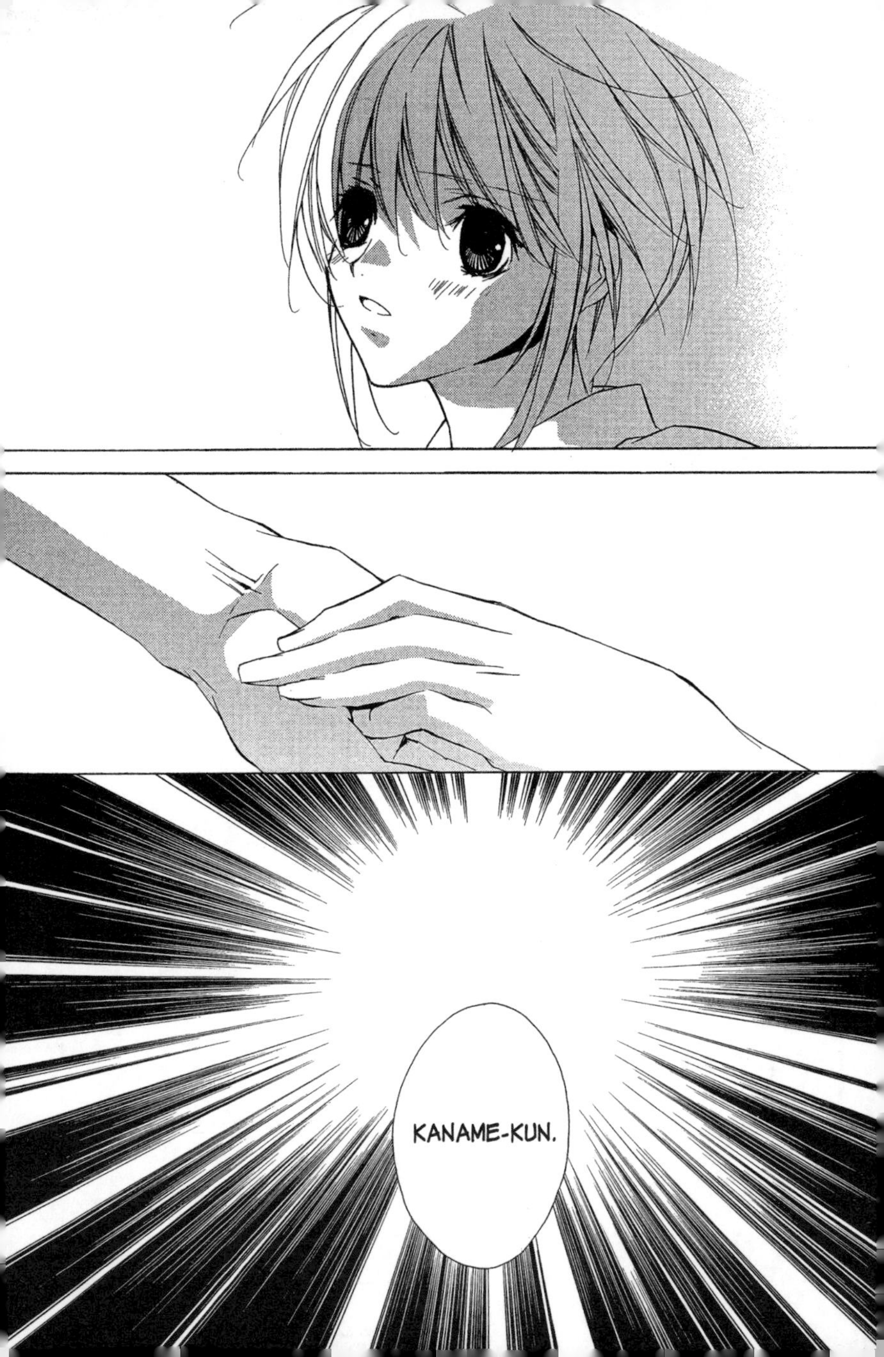
KANAME-KUN.

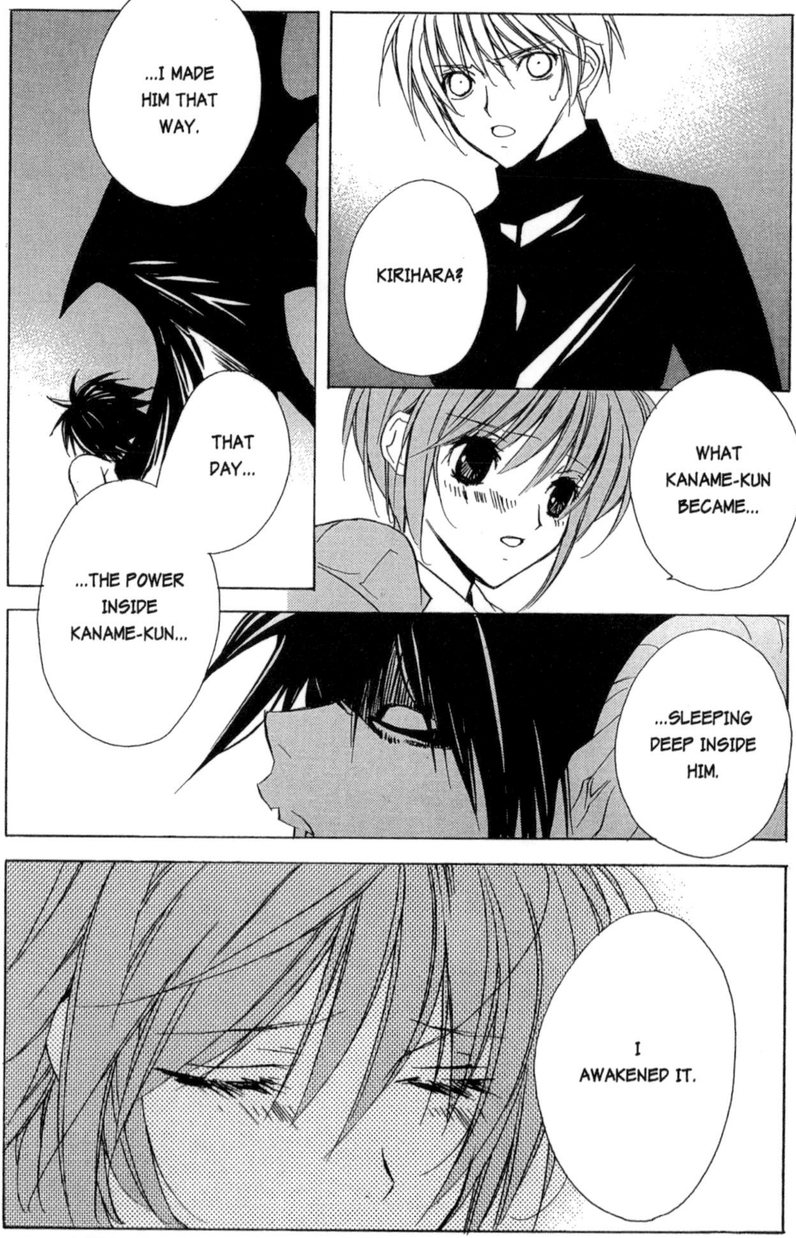
KIRIHARA?
WHAT KANAME-KUN BECAME...
...I MADE HIM THAT WAY.
THAT DAY...
...THE POWER INSIDE KANAME-KUN...
...SLEEPING DEEP INSIDE HIM.
I AWAKENED IT.

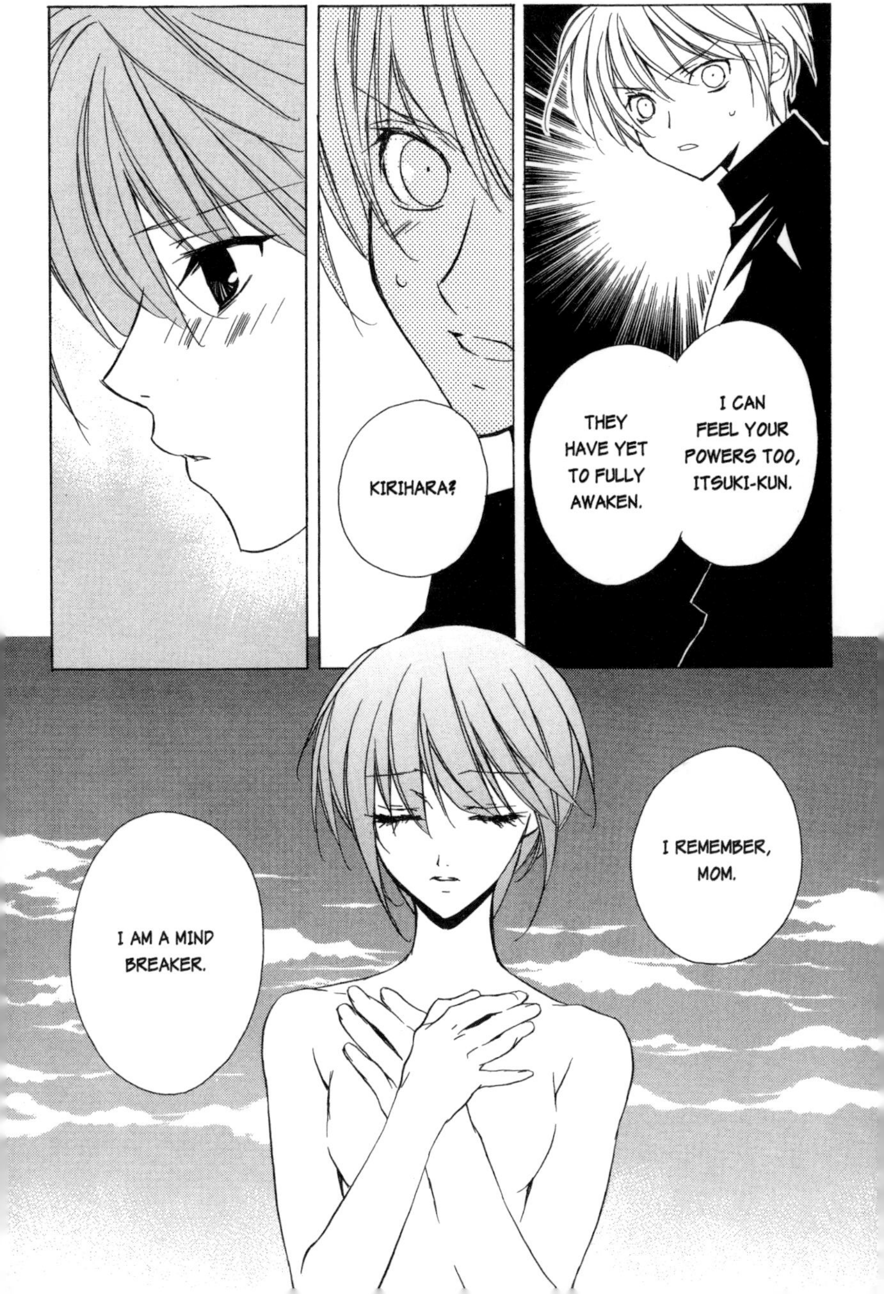
I CAN FEEL YOUR POWERS TOO, ITSUKI-KUN.
THEY HAVE YET TO FULLY AWAKEN.
KIRIHARA?
I REMEMBER, MOM.
I AM A MIND BREAKER.

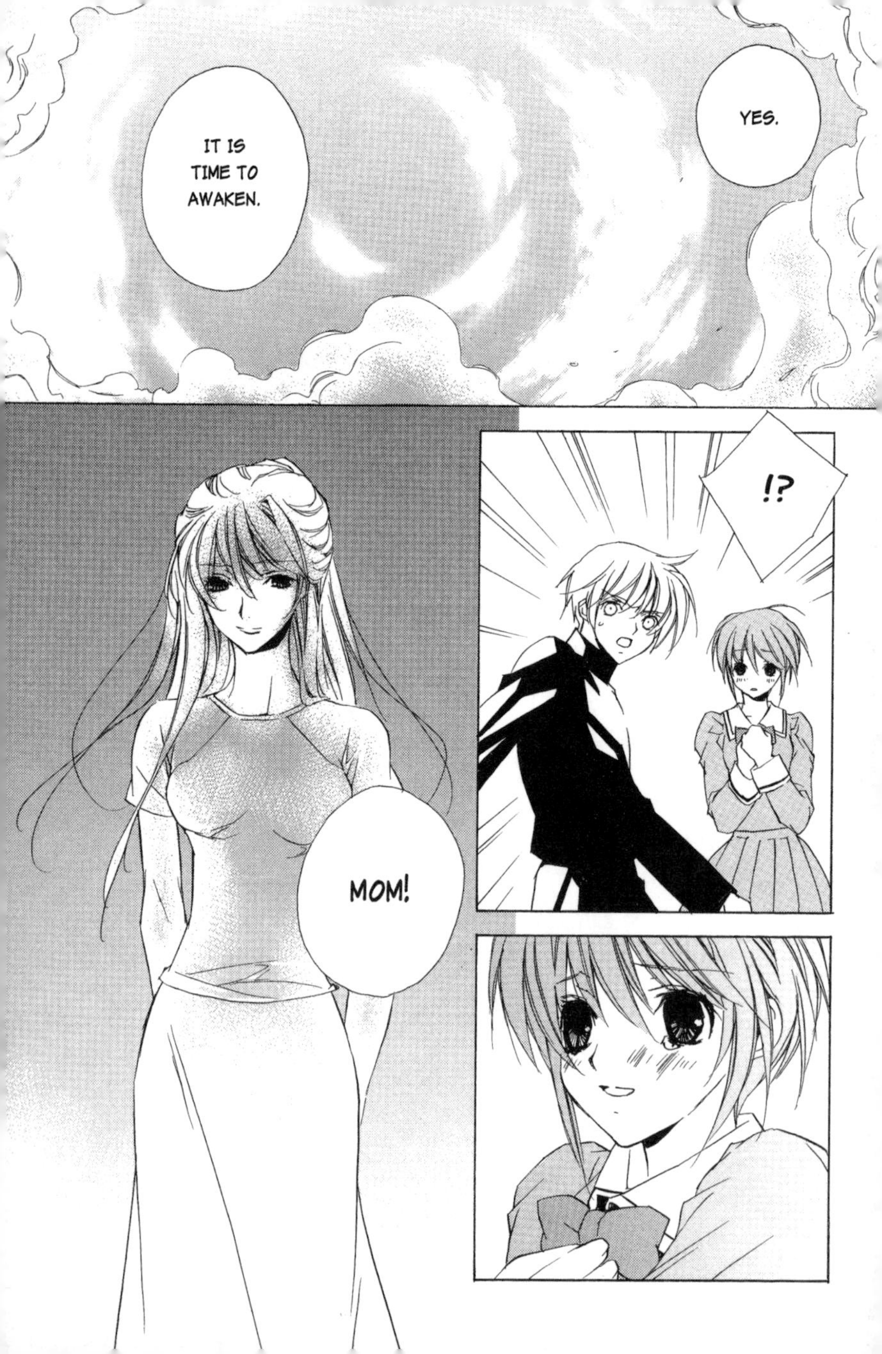
YES.
IT IS TIME TO AWAKEN.
!?
MOM!

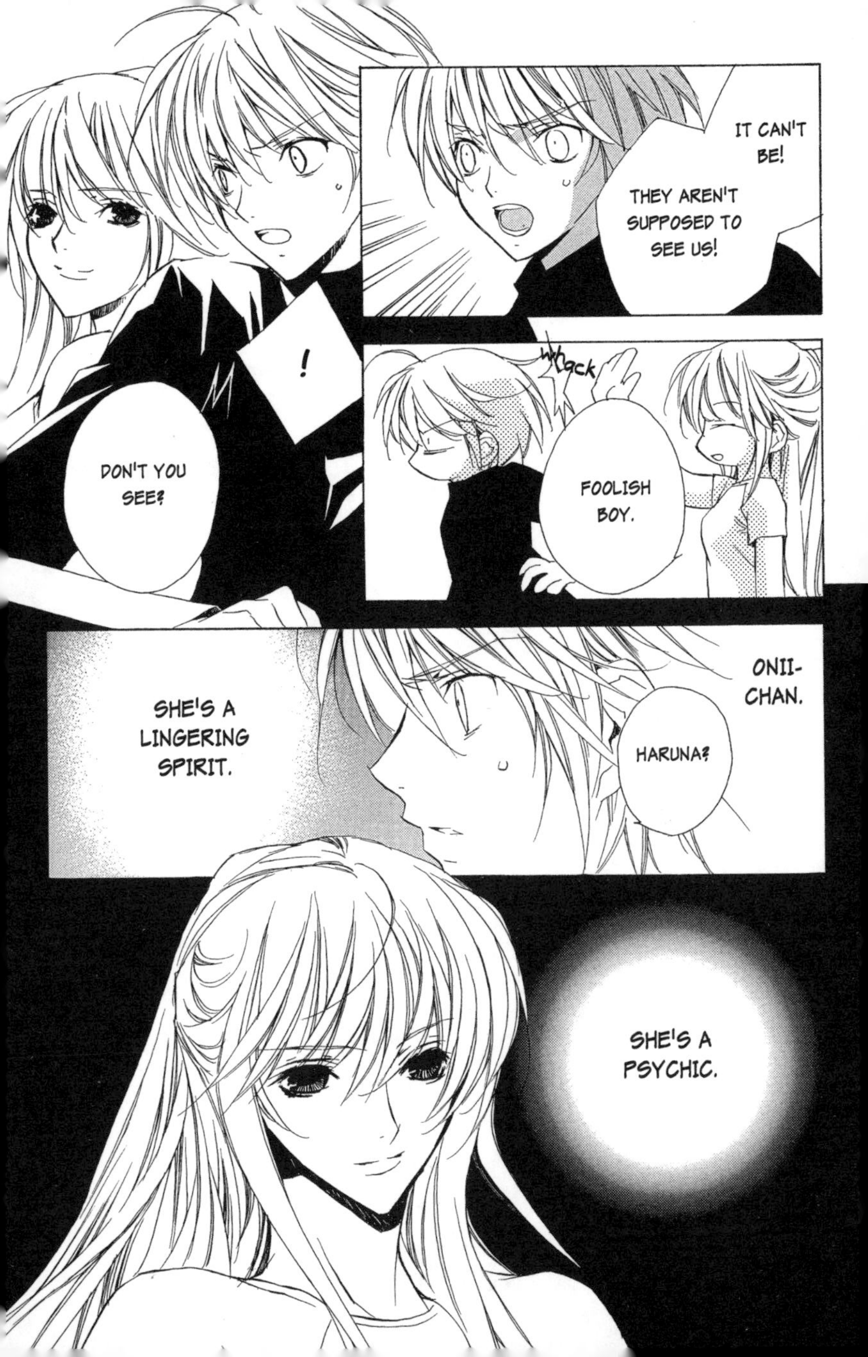
IT CAN'T BE!
THEY AREN'T SUPPOSED TO SEE US!
whack
FOOLISH BOY.
!
DON'T YOU SEE?
ONII-CHAN.
HARUNA?
SHE'S A LINGERING SPIRIT.
SHE'S A PSYCHIC.

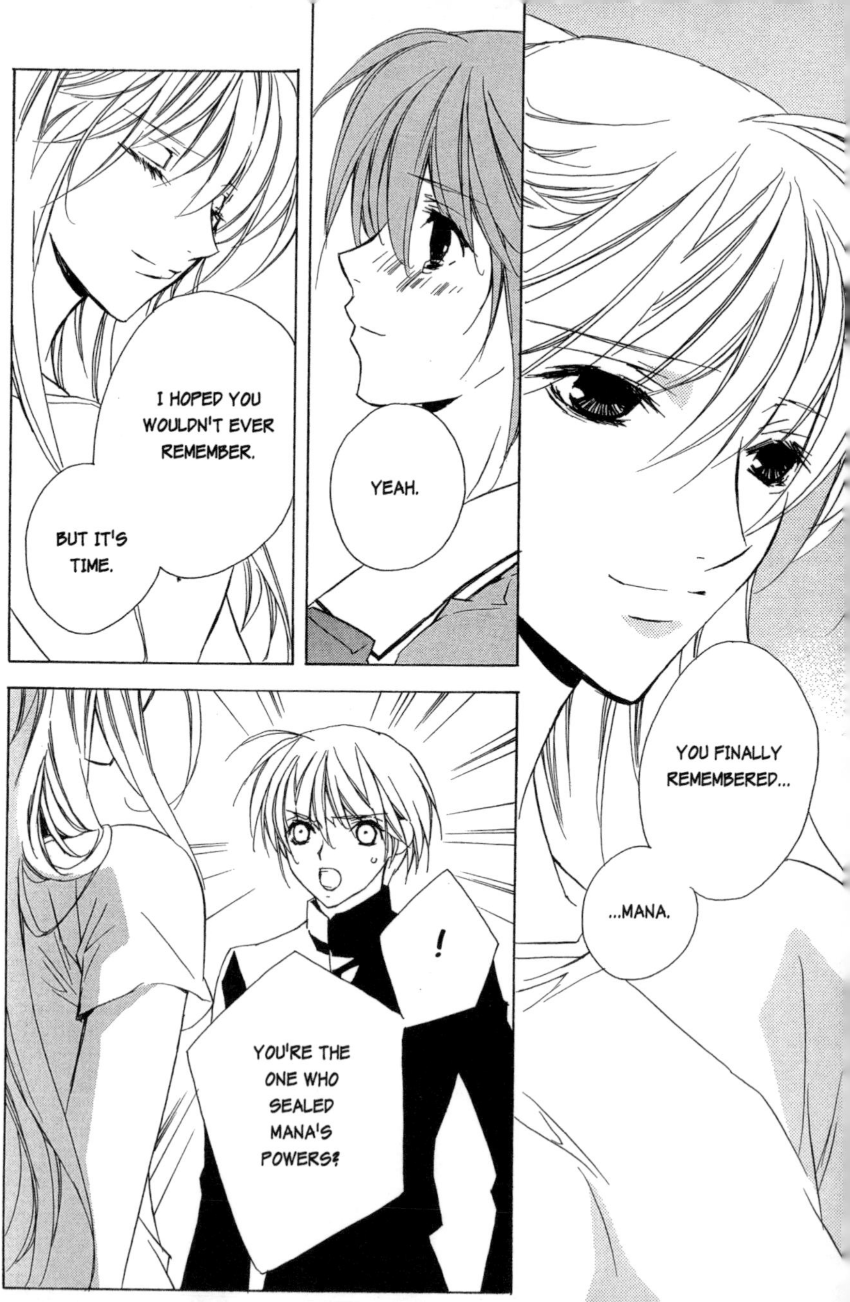
YOU FINALLY REMEMBERED...
...MANA.
YEAH.
I HOPED YOU WOULDN'T EVER REMEMBER.
BUT IT'S TIME.
!
YOU'RE THE ONE WHO SEALED MANA'S POWERS?

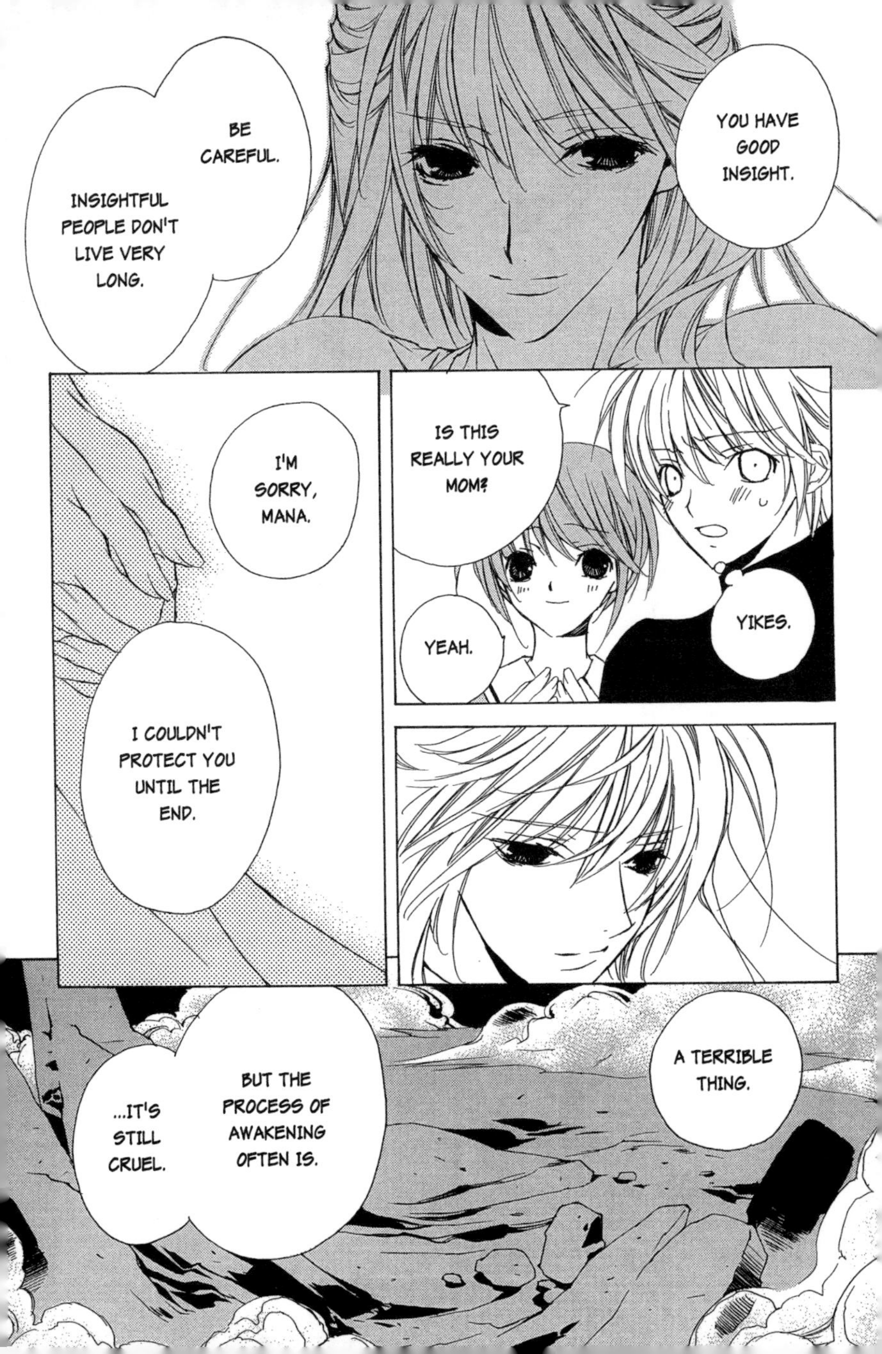
YOU HAVE GOOD INSIGHT.
BE CAREFUL.
INSIGHTFUL PEOPLE DON'T LIVE VERY LONG.
IS THIS REALLY YOUR MOM?
YIKES.
YEAH.
I'M SORRY, MANA.
I COULDN'T PROTECT YOU UNTIL THE END.
A TERRIBLE THING.
BUT THE PROCESS OF AWAKENING OFTEN IS.
...IT'S STILL CRUEL.

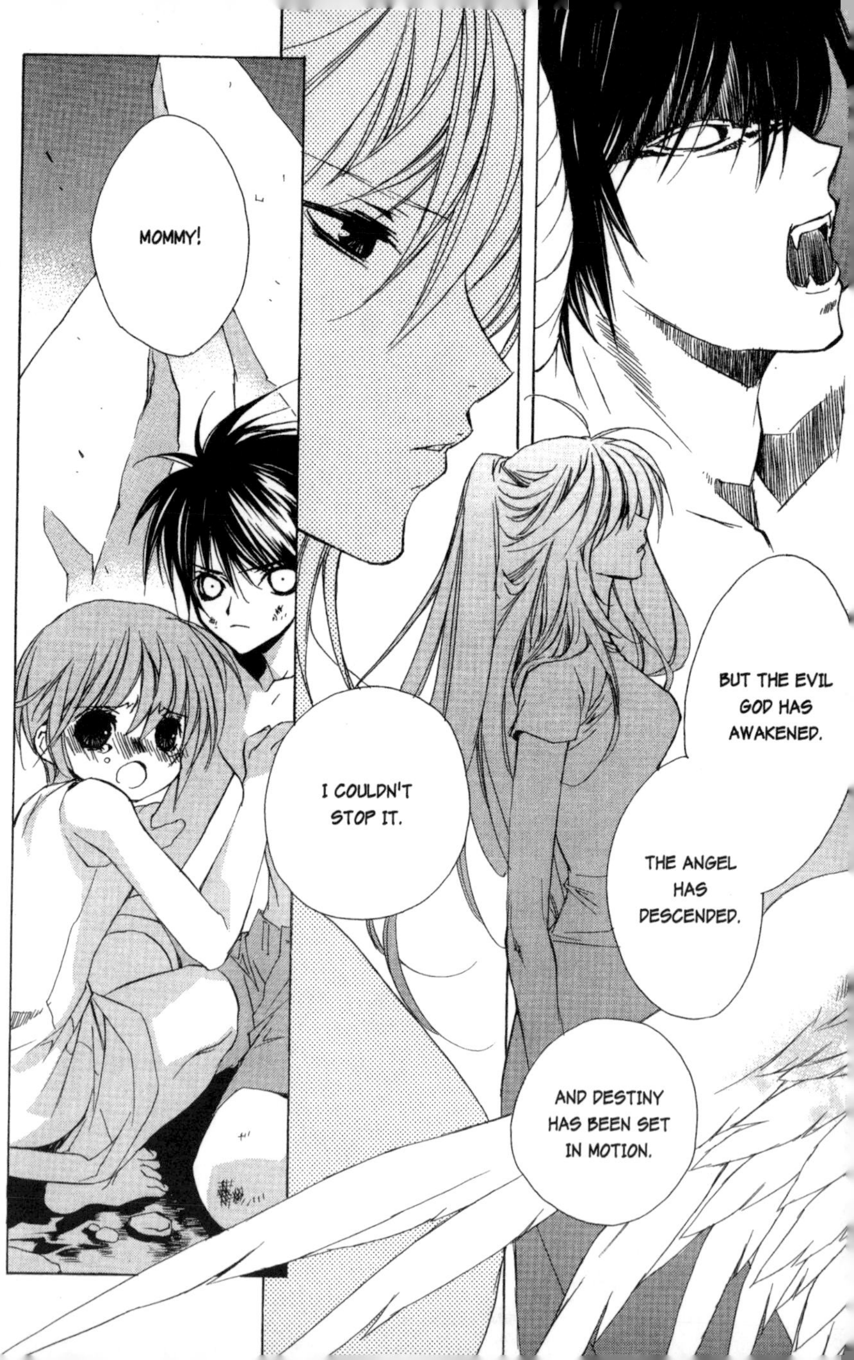
BUT THE EVIL GOD HAS AWAKENED.
THE ANGEL HAS DESCENDED.
AND DESTINY HAS BEEN SET IN MOTION.
I COULDN'T STOP IT.
MOMMY!

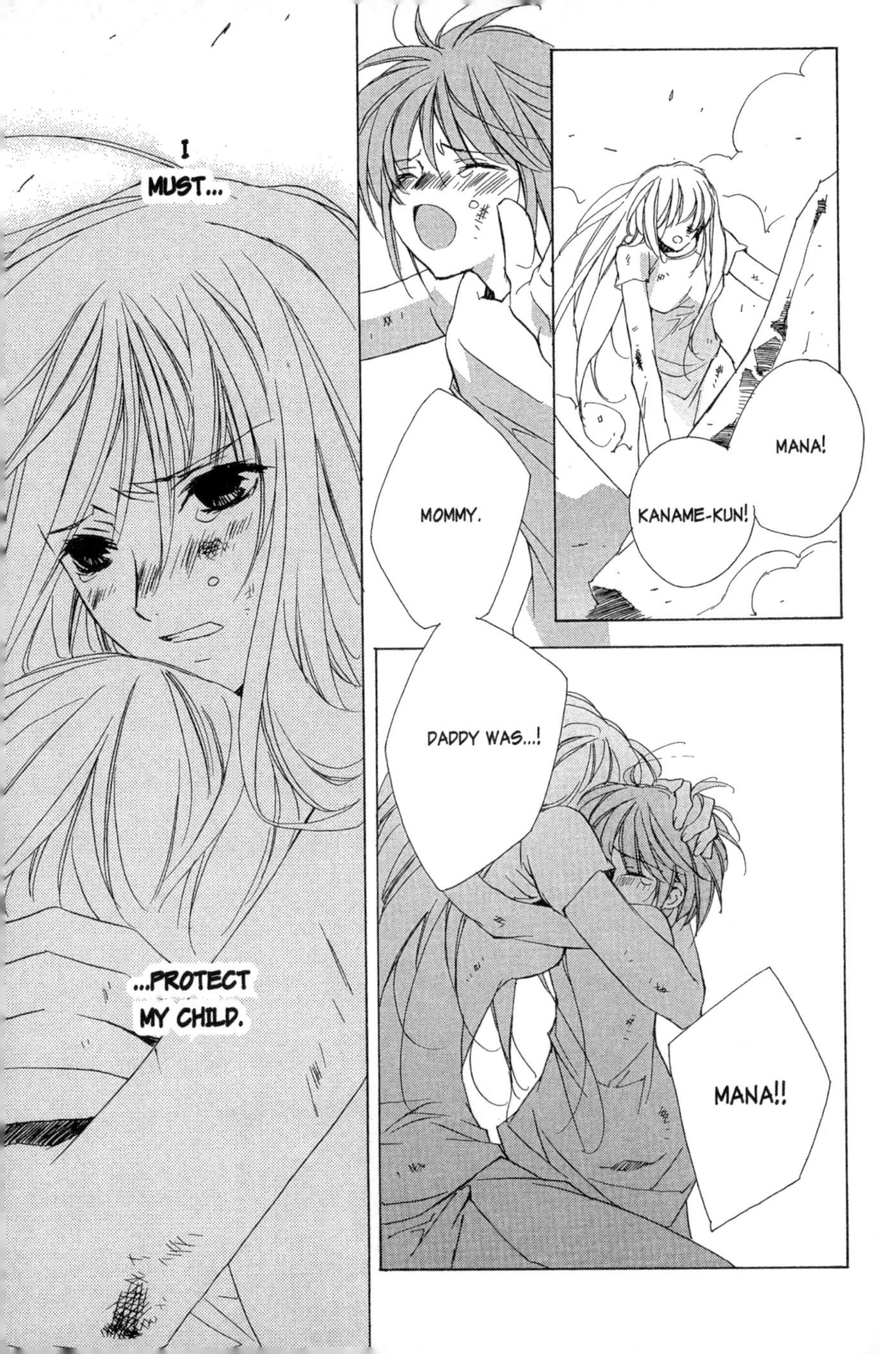
MANA!
KANAME-KUN!
MOMMY.
DADDY WAS...!
MANA!!
I MUST...
...PROTECT MY CHILD.

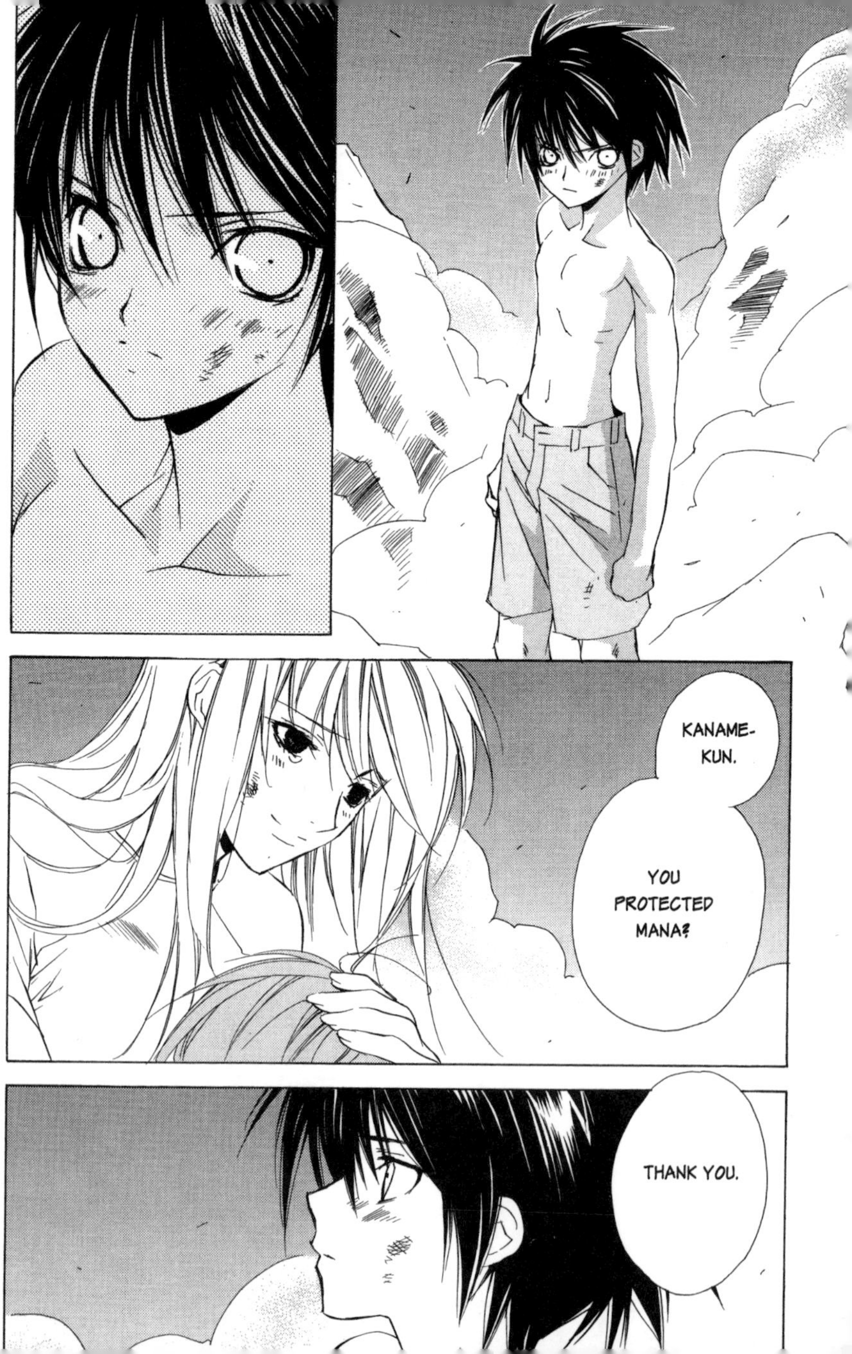
KANAME-
KUN.
YOU
PROTECTED
MANA?
THANK YOU.

THANK YOU...

FLASH

I'M SORRY.

thud

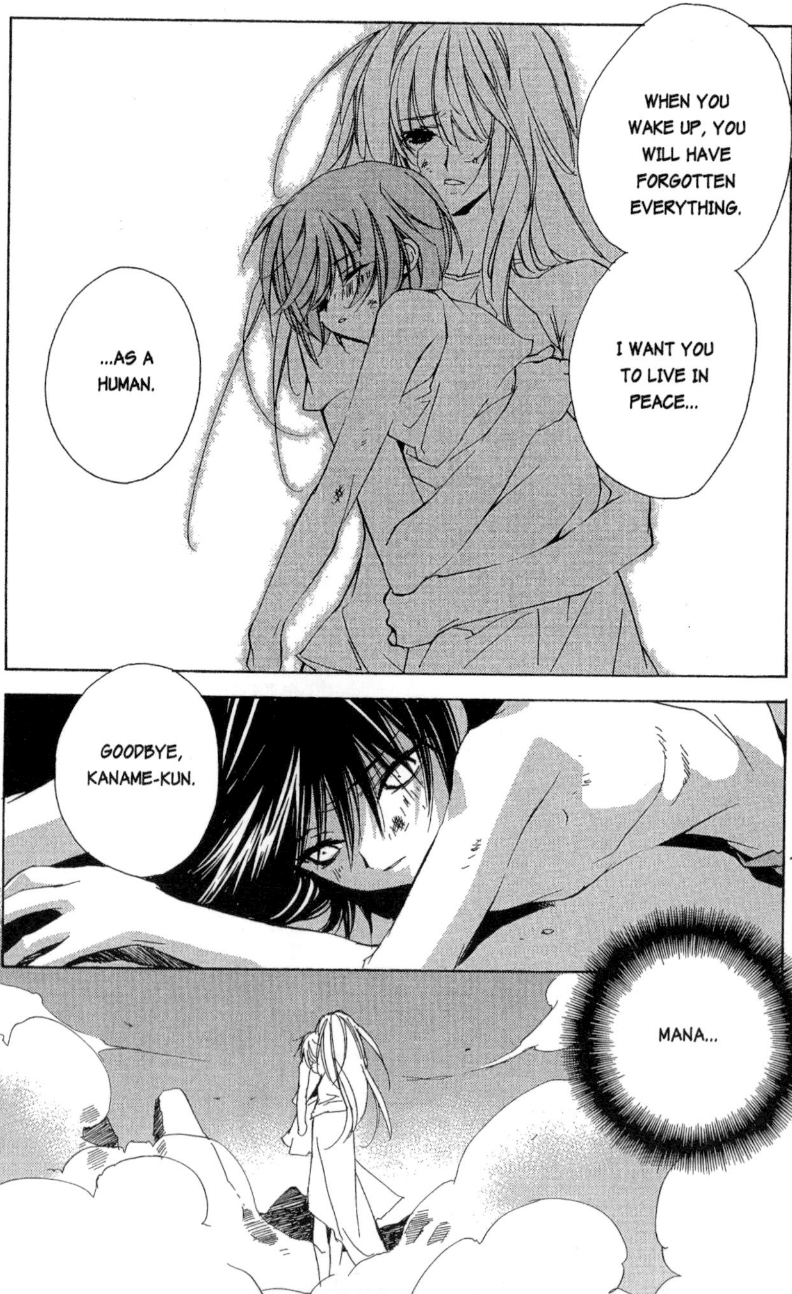
WHEN YOU WAKE UP, YOU WILL HAVE FORGOTTEN EVERYTHING.
I WANT YOU TO LIVE IN PEACE...
...AS A HUMAN.
GOODBYE, KANAME-KUN.
MANA...

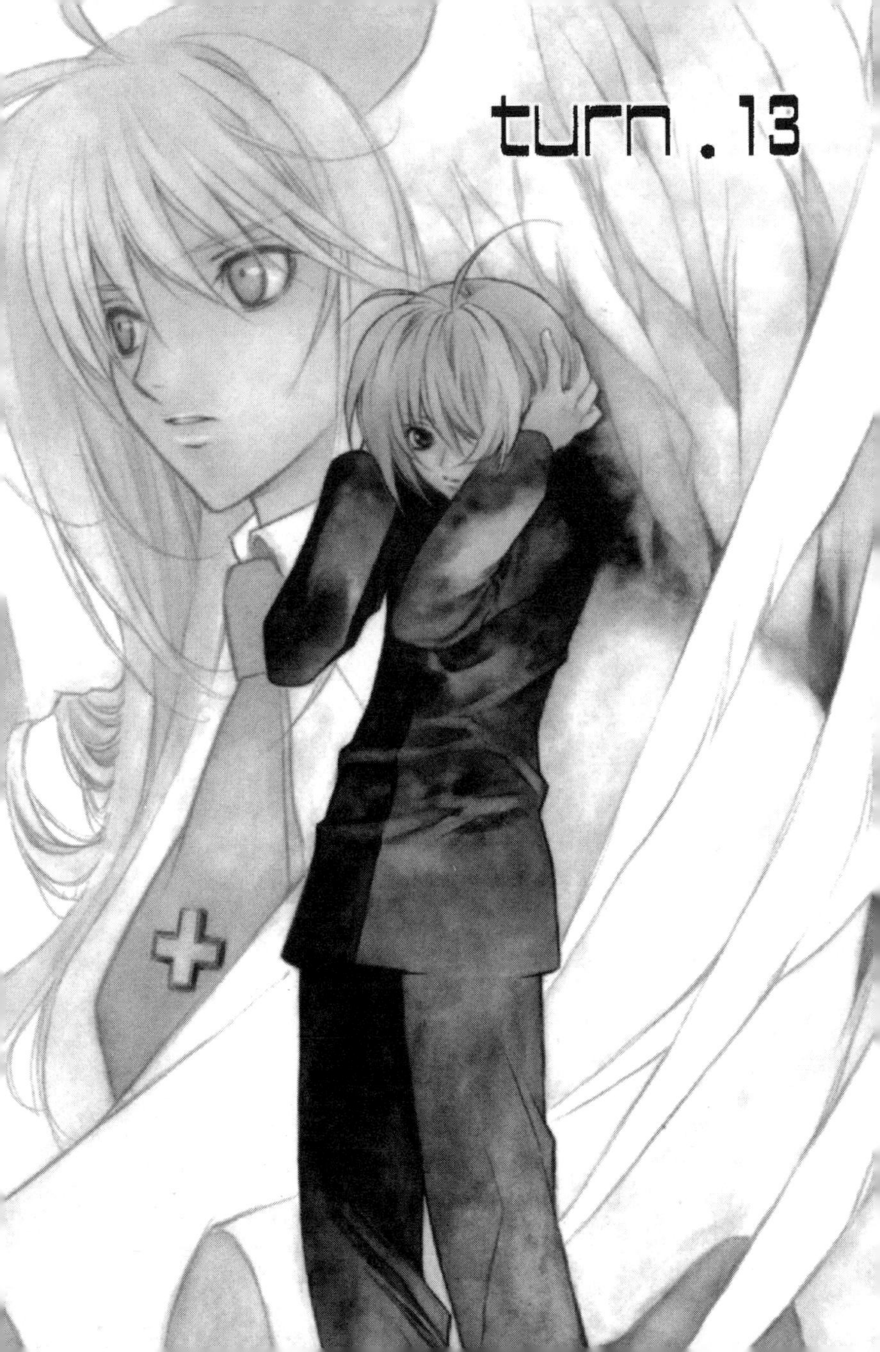
turn . 13

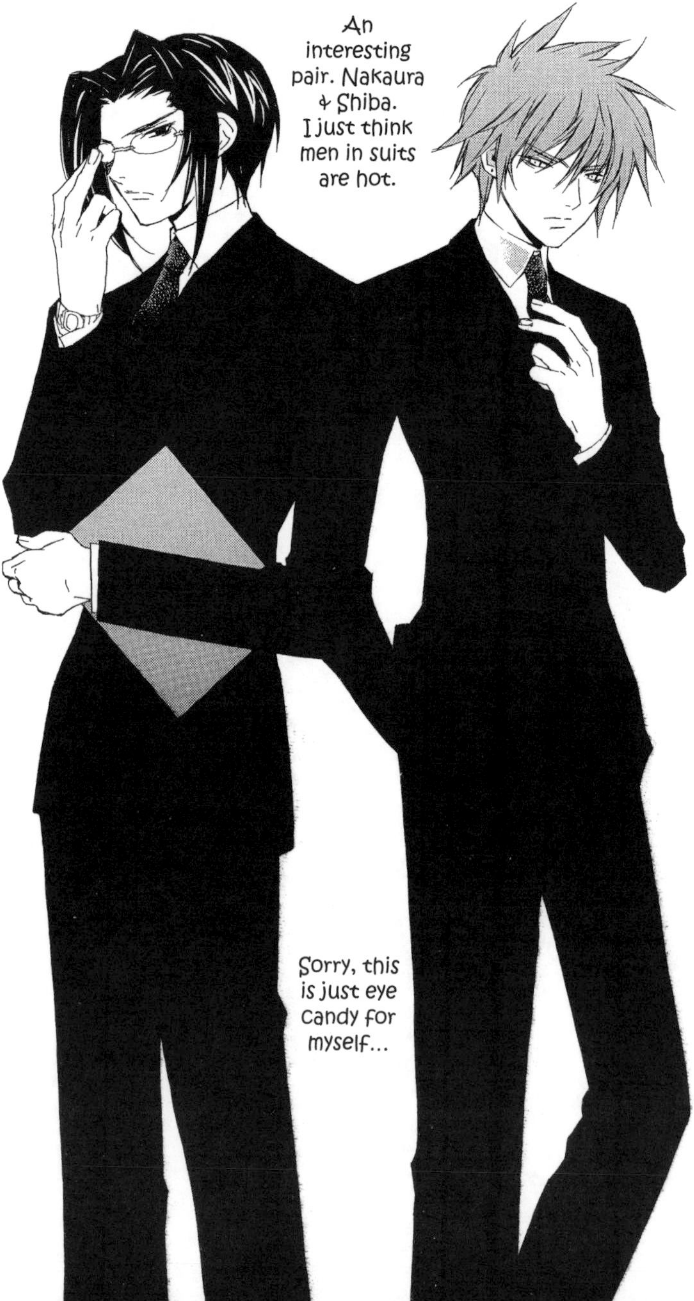
An interesting pair. Nakaura & Shiba. I just think men in suits are hot.
Sorry, this is just eye candy for myself...

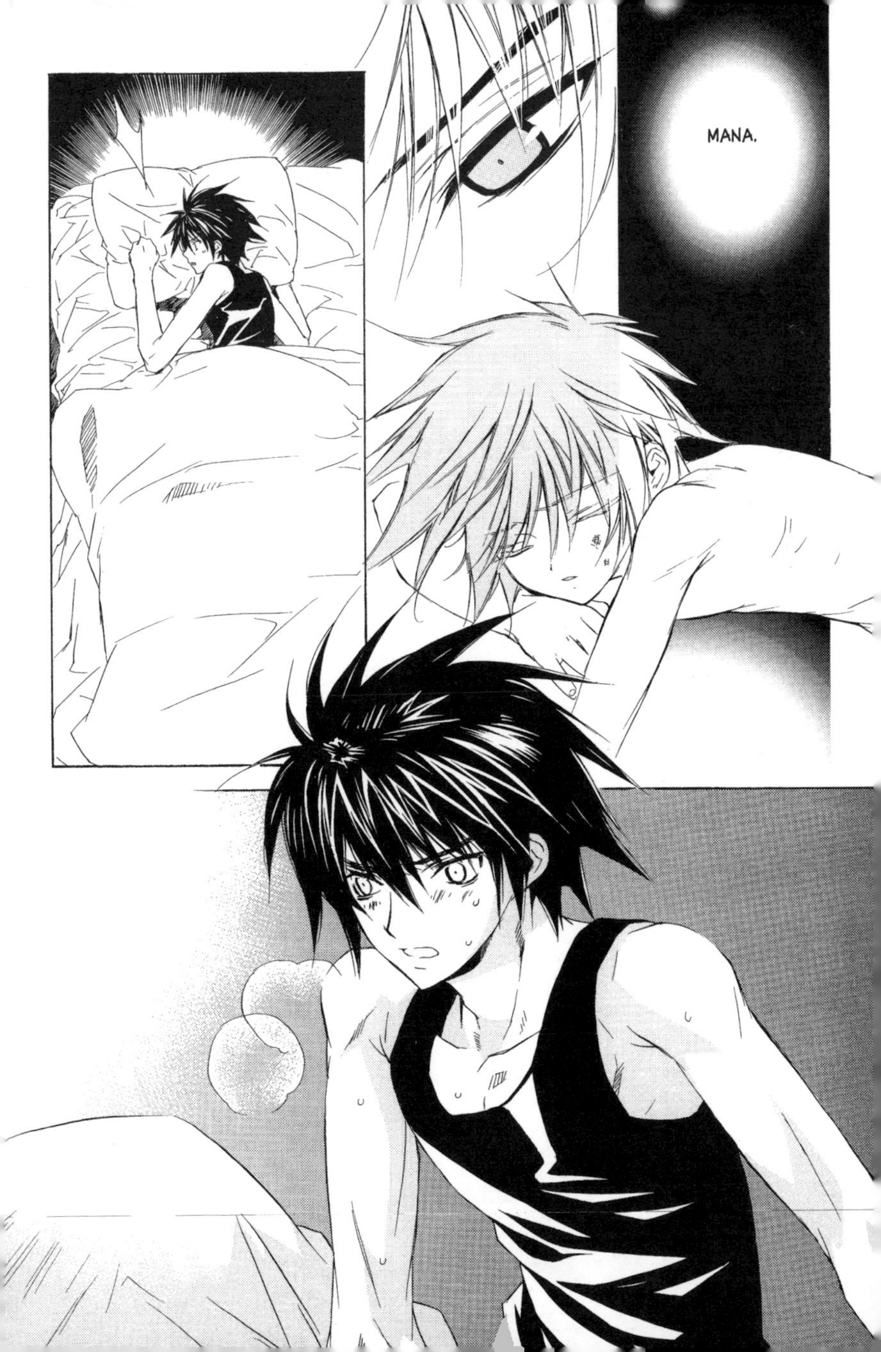
MANA.

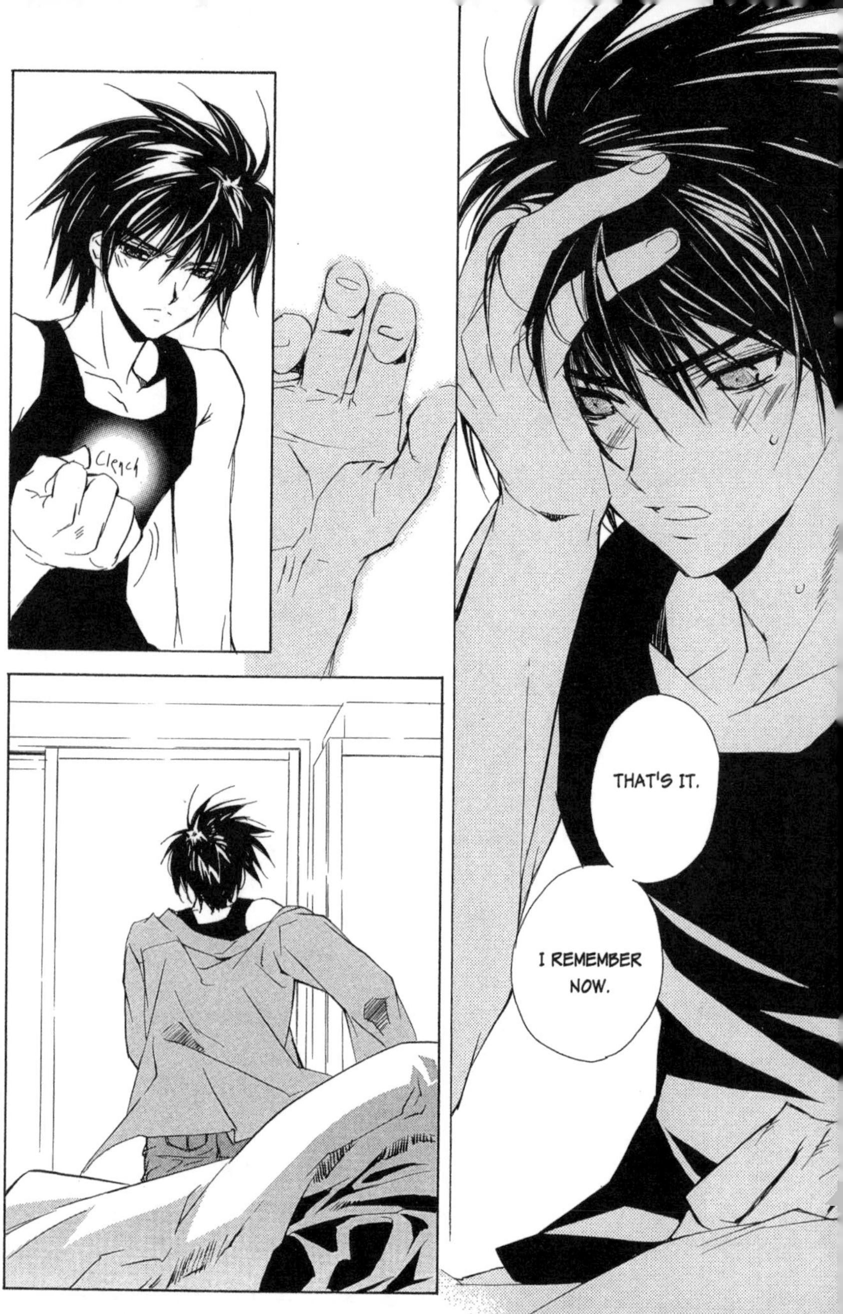
THAT'S IT.
I REMEMBER NOW.
Clench

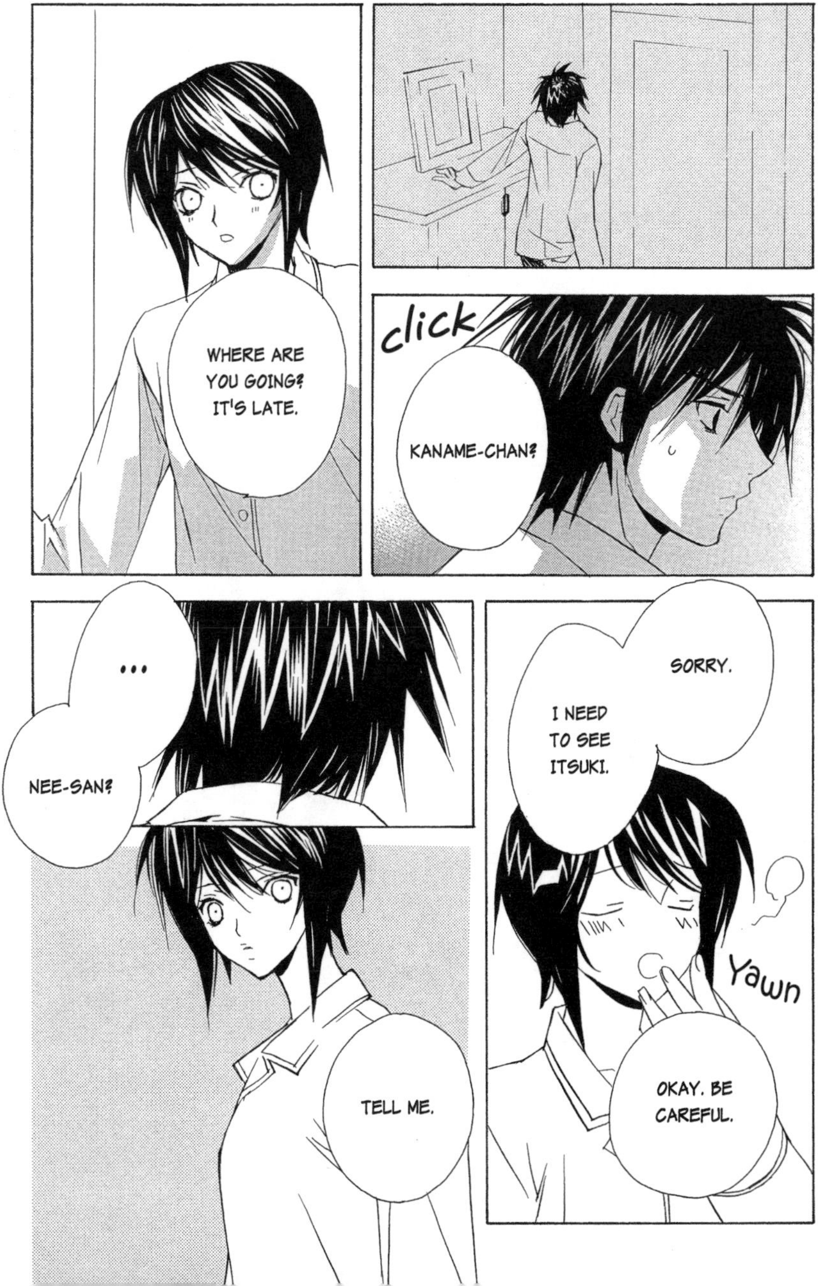
click
KANAME-CHAN?
WHERE ARE YOU GOING? IT'S LATE.
SORRY.
I NEED TO SEE ITSUKI.
Yawn
OKAY. BE CAREFUL.
...
NEE-SAN?
TELL ME.

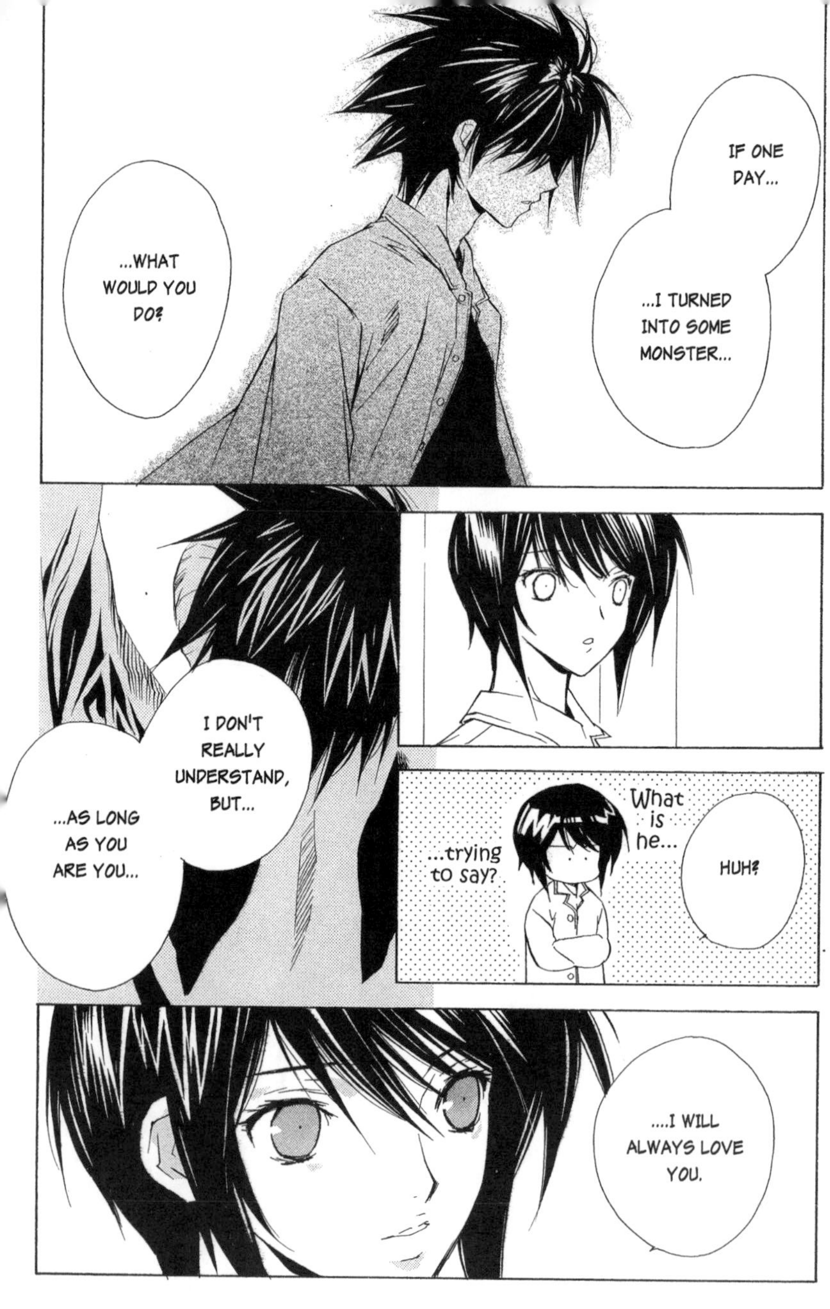
IF ONE DAY... ...I TURNED INTO SOME MONSTER...
...WHAT WOULD YOU DO?
HUH?
What is he... ...trying to say?
I DON'T REALLY UNDERSTAND, BUT...
...AS LONG AS YOU ARE YOU...
....I WILL ALWAYS LOVE YOU.

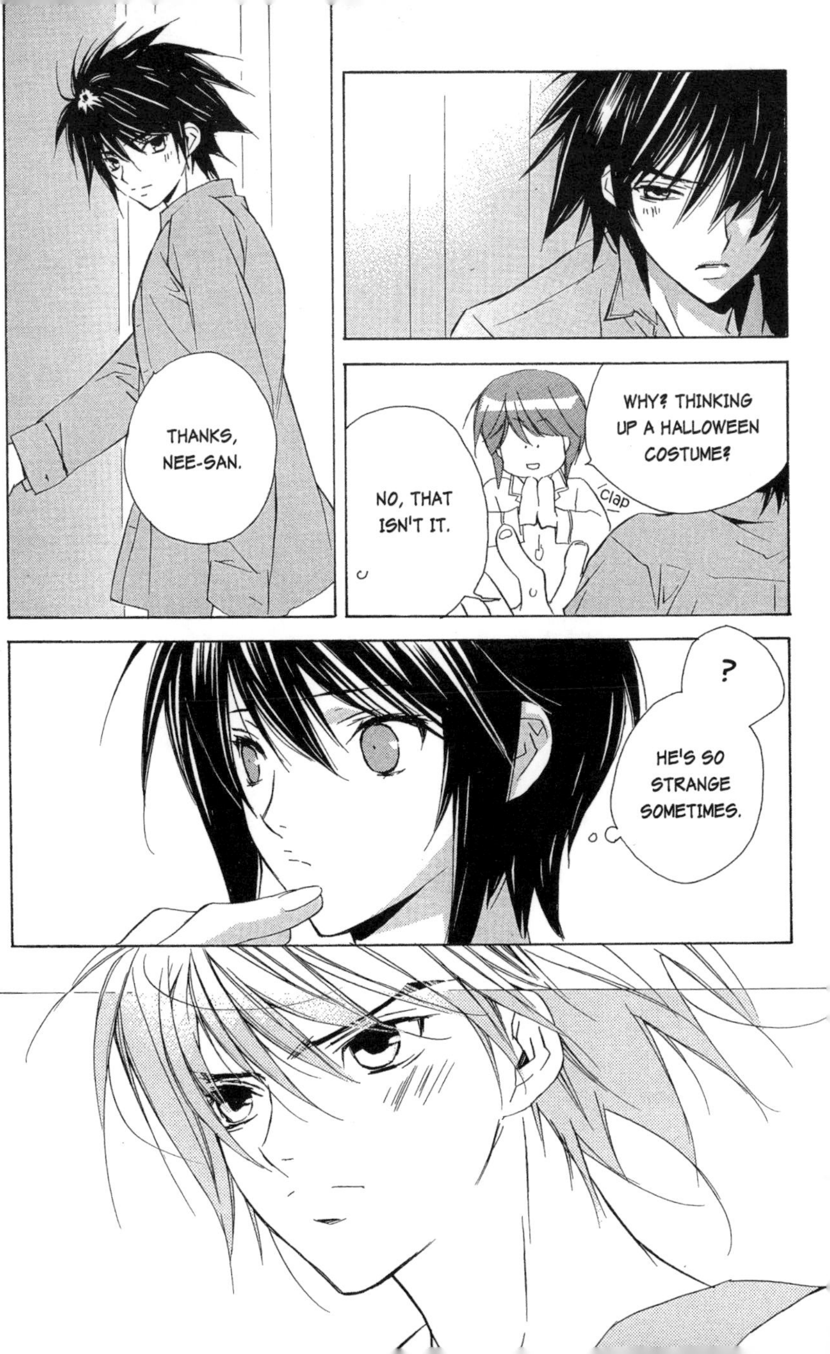
WHY? THINKING UP A HALLOWEEN COSTUME?
clap
NO, THAT ISN'T IT.
THANKS, NEE-SAN.
?
HE'S SO STRANGE SOMETIMES.

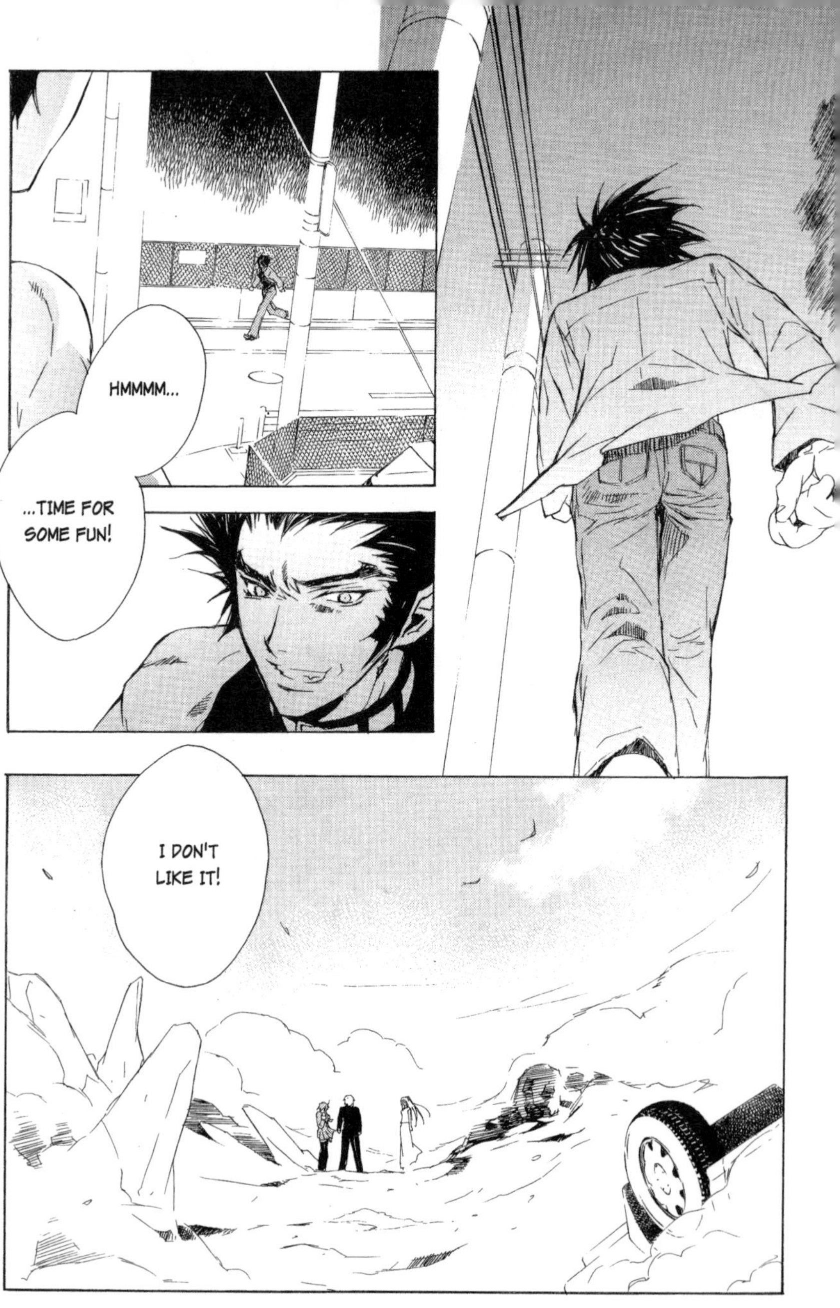
HMMMM...
...TIME FOR SOME FUN!
I DON'T LIKE IT!

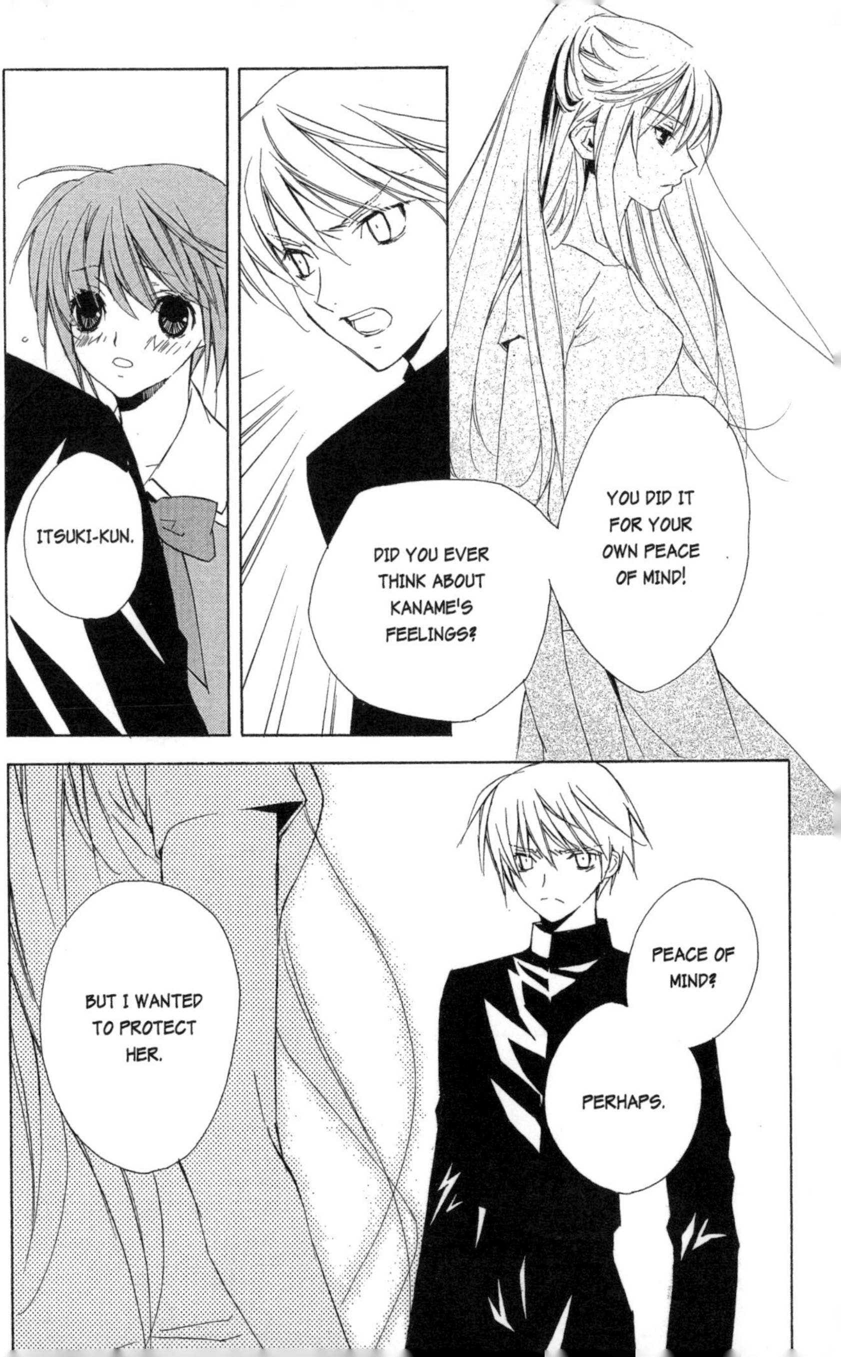
YOU DID IT FOR YOUR OWN PEACE OF MIND!
DID YOU EVER THINK ABOUT KANAME'S FEELINGS?
ITSUKI-KUN.
PEACE OF MIND?
PERHAPS.
BUT I WANTED TO PROTECT HER.

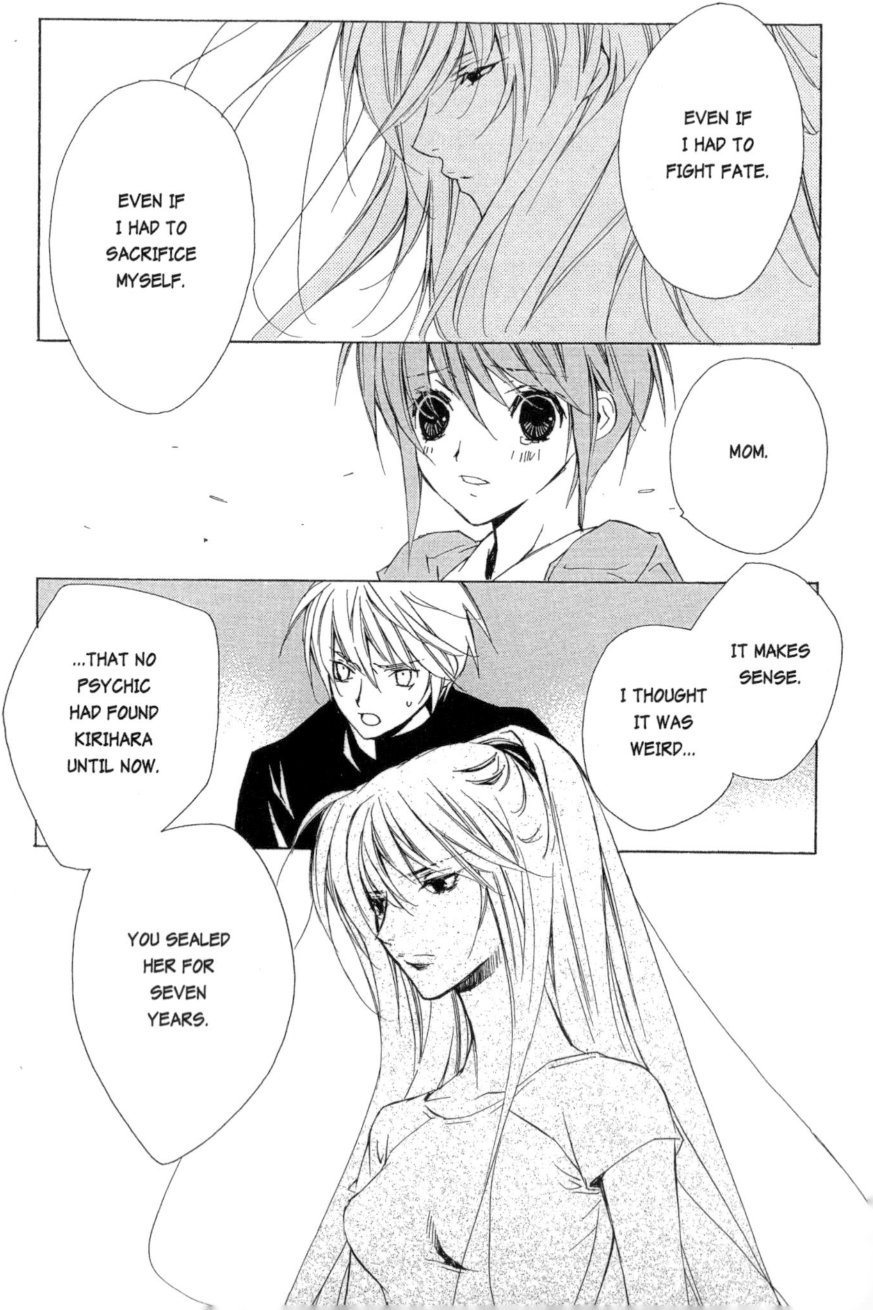
EVEN IF I HAD TO FIGHT FATE.
EVEN IF I HAD TO SACRIFICE MYSELF.
MOM.
IT MAKES SENSE.
I THOUGHT IT WAS WEIRD...
...THAT NO PSYCHIC HAD FOUND KIRIHARA UNTIL NOW.
YOU SEALED HER FOR SEVEN YEARS.

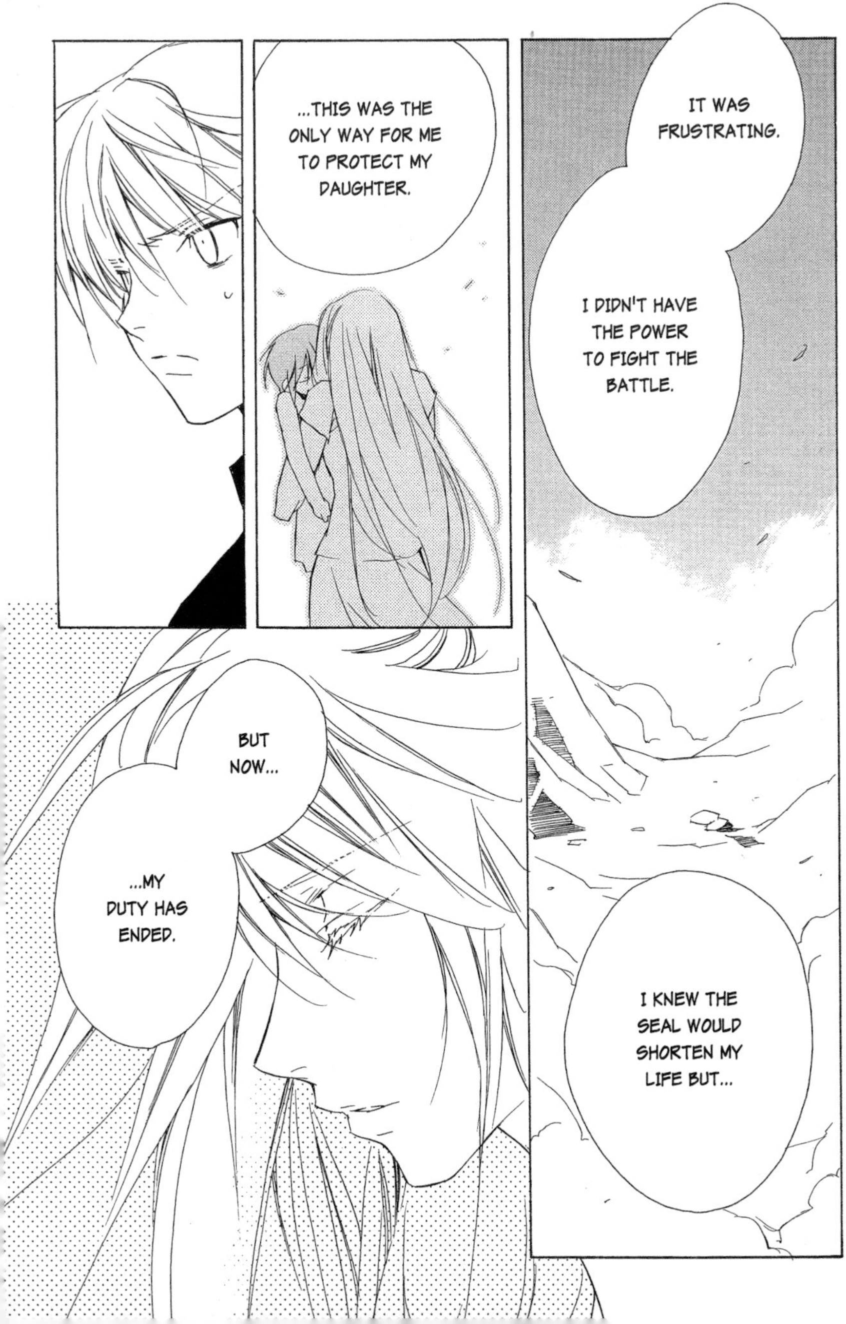
IT WAS FRUSTRATING.
I DIDN'T HAVE THE POWER TO FIGHT THE BATTLE.
I KNEW THE SEAL WOULD SHORTEN MY LIFE BUT...
...THIS WAS THE ONLY WAY FOR ME TO PROTECT MY DAUGHTER.
BUT NOW...
...MY DUTY HAS ENDED.

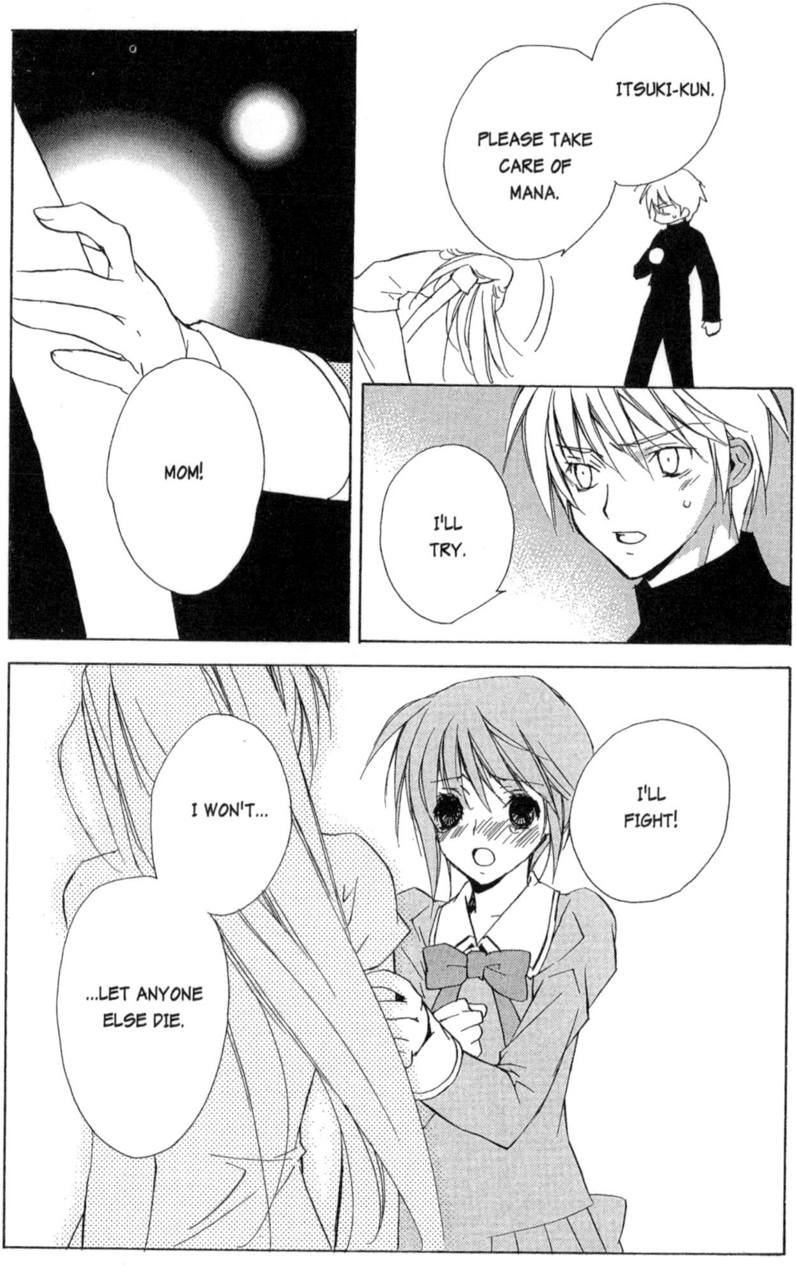
ITSUKI-KUN.
PLEASE TAKE CARE OF MANA.
I'LL TRY.
MOM!
I'LL FIGHT!
I WON'T...
...LET ANYONE ELSE DIE.

I'LL WATCH OVER YOU.

ALWAYS, MANA.

TELL KANAME-KUN...

...THAT I'M SORRY.

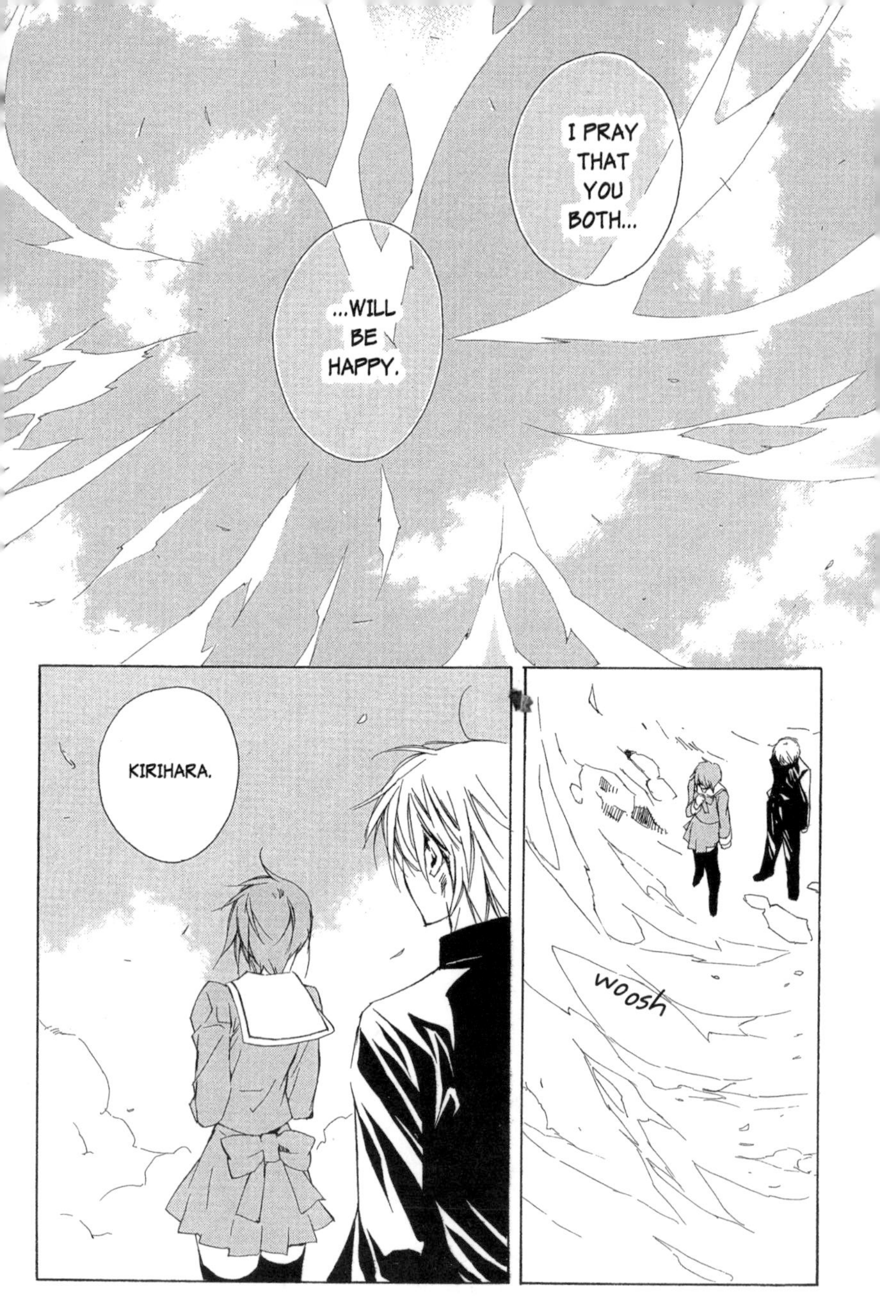
I PRAY THAT YOU BOTH...
...WILL BE HAPPY.
woosh
KIRIHARA.

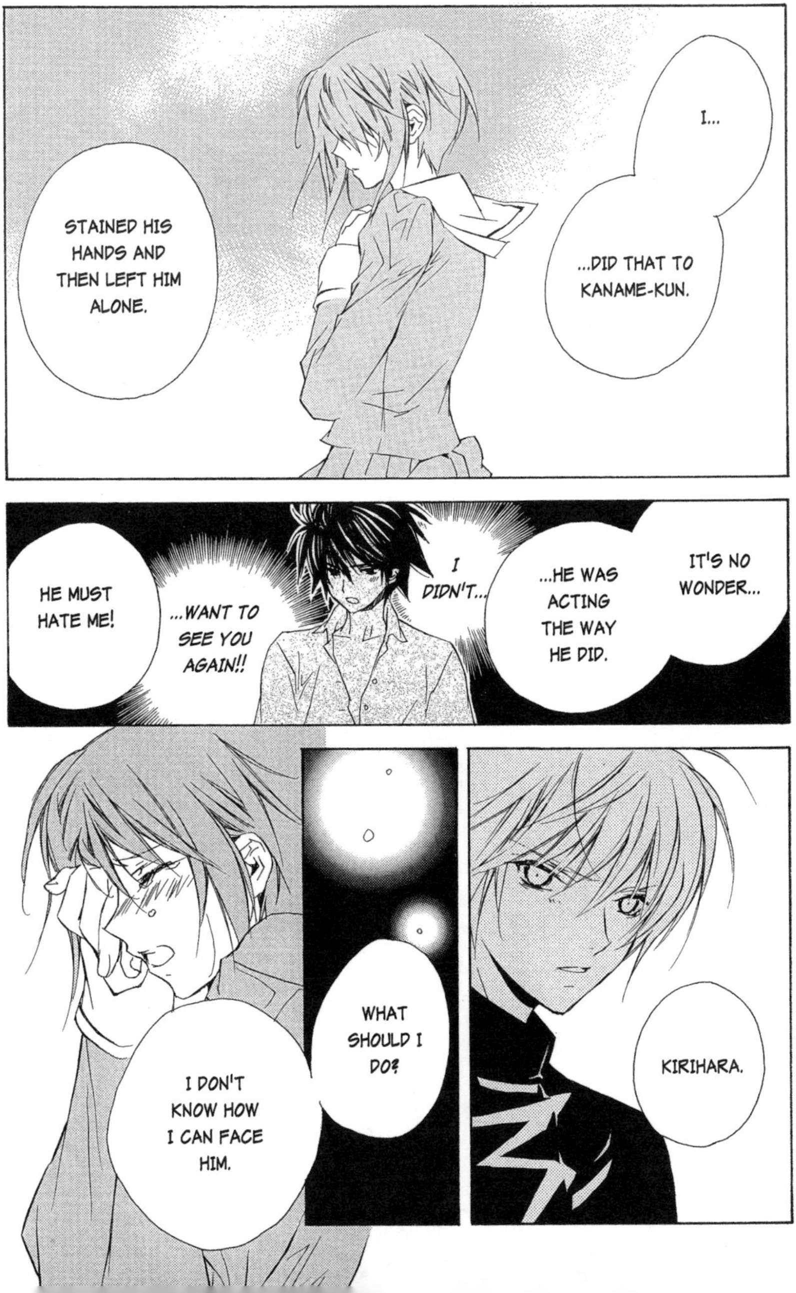
I...
...DID THAT TO KANAME-KUN.
STAINED HIS HANDS AND THEN LEFT HIM ALONE.
IT'S NO WONDER...
...HE WAS ACTING THE WAY HE DID.
I DIDN'T...
...WANT TO SEE YOU AGAIN!!
HE MUST HATE ME!
KIRIHARA.
WHAT SHOULD I DO?
I DON'T KNOW HOW I CAN FACE HIM.

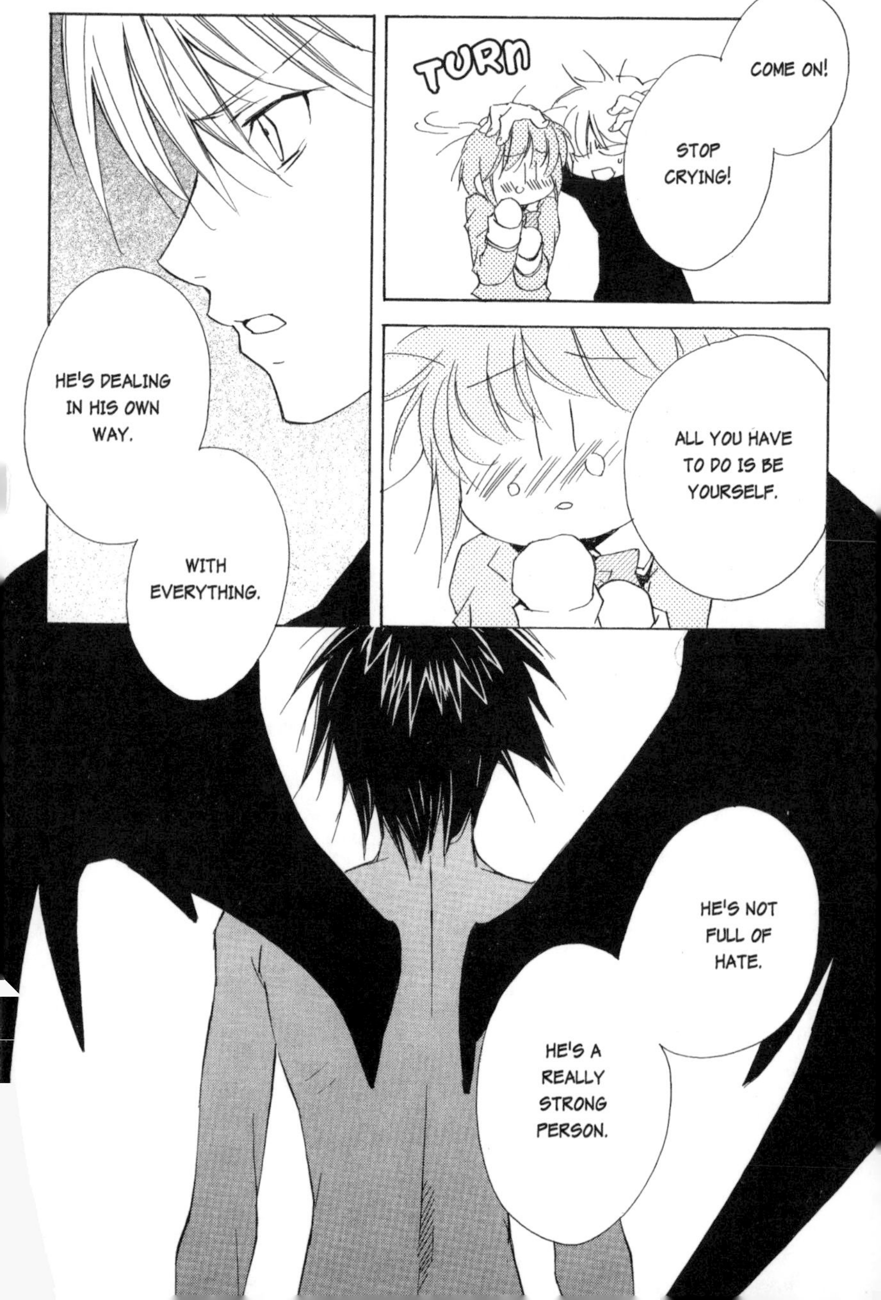
COME ON!
STOP CRYING!
TURN
ALL YOU HAVE TO DO IS BE YOURSELF.
HE'S DEALING IN HIS OWN WAY.
WITH EVERYTHING.
HE'S NOT FULL OF HATE.
HE'S A REALLY STRONG PERSON.

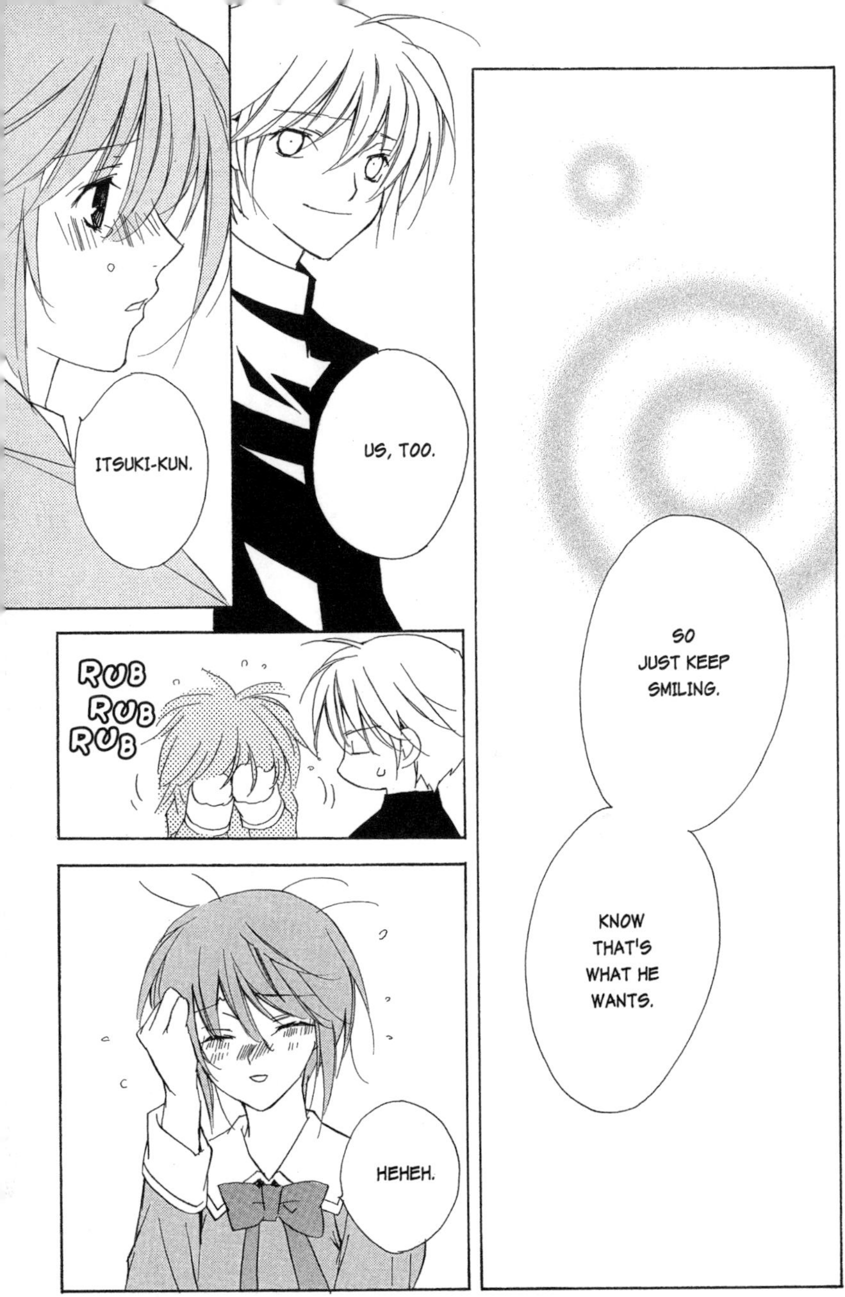
SO JUST KEEP SMILING.
KNOW THAT'S WHAT HE WANTS.
US, TOO.
ITSUKI-KUN.
RUB RUB RUB
HEHEH.

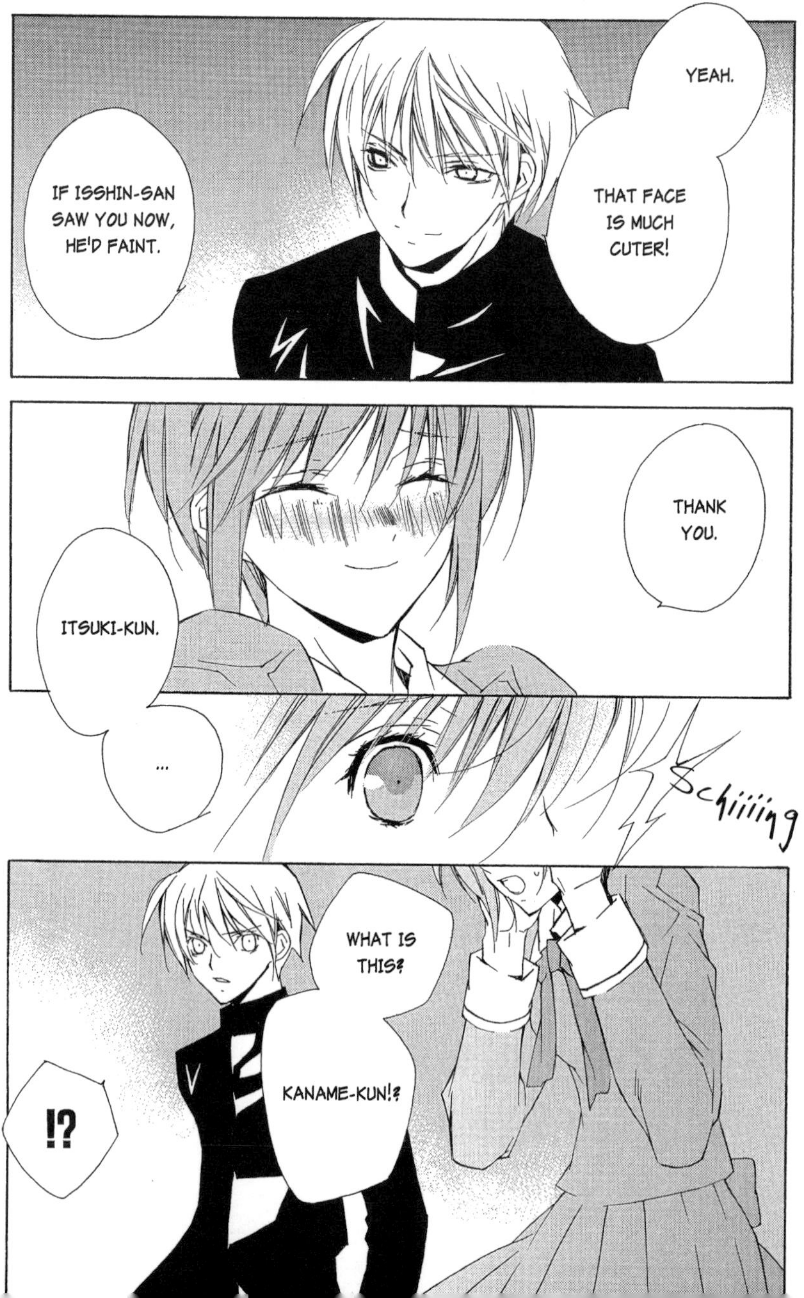
YEAH.
THAT FACE IS MUCH CUTER!
IF ISSHIN-SAN SAW YOU NOW, HE'D FAINT.
THANK YOU.
ITSUKI-KUN.
Schiiiing
...
WHAT IS THIS?
KANAME-KUN!?
!?

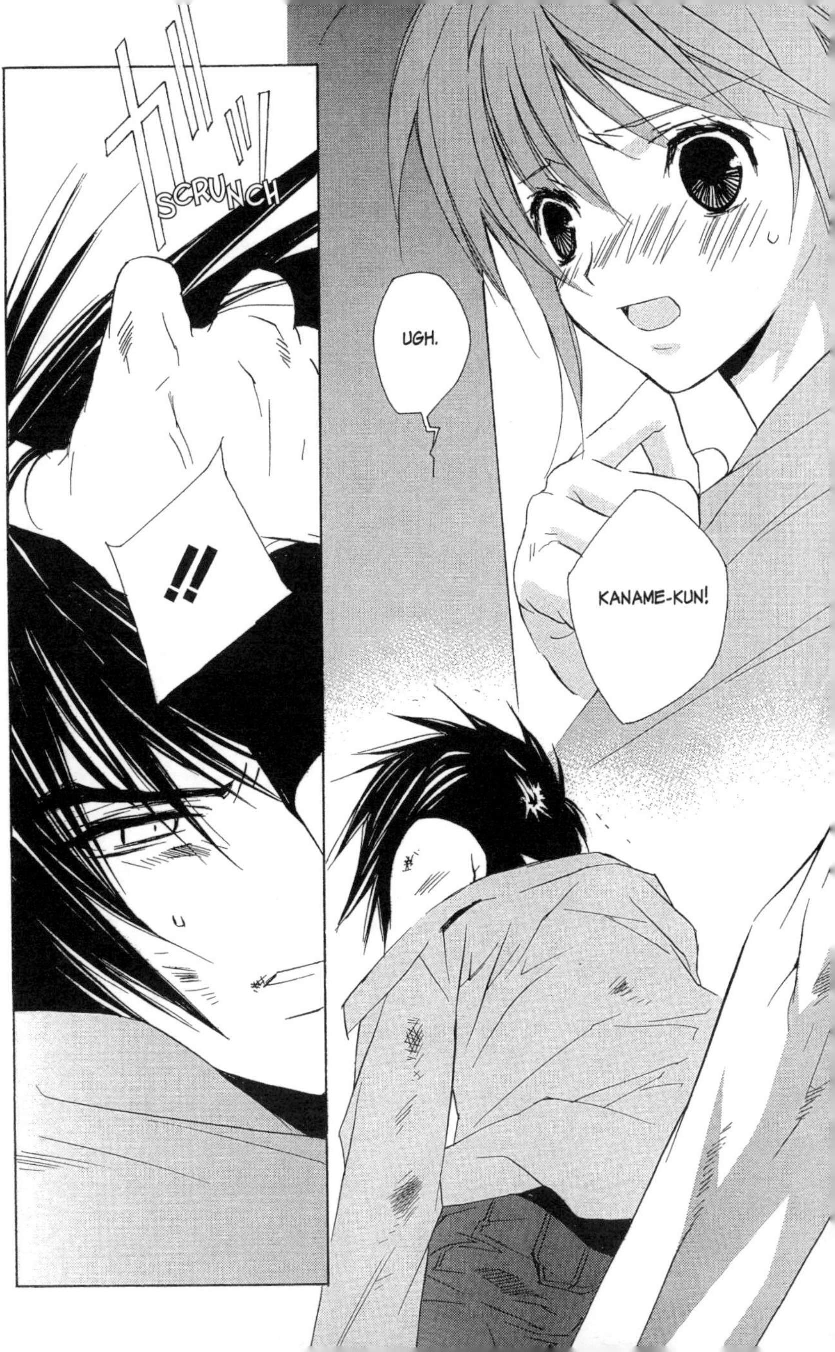
KANAME-KUN!
UGH.
カッ
SCRUNCH
!!

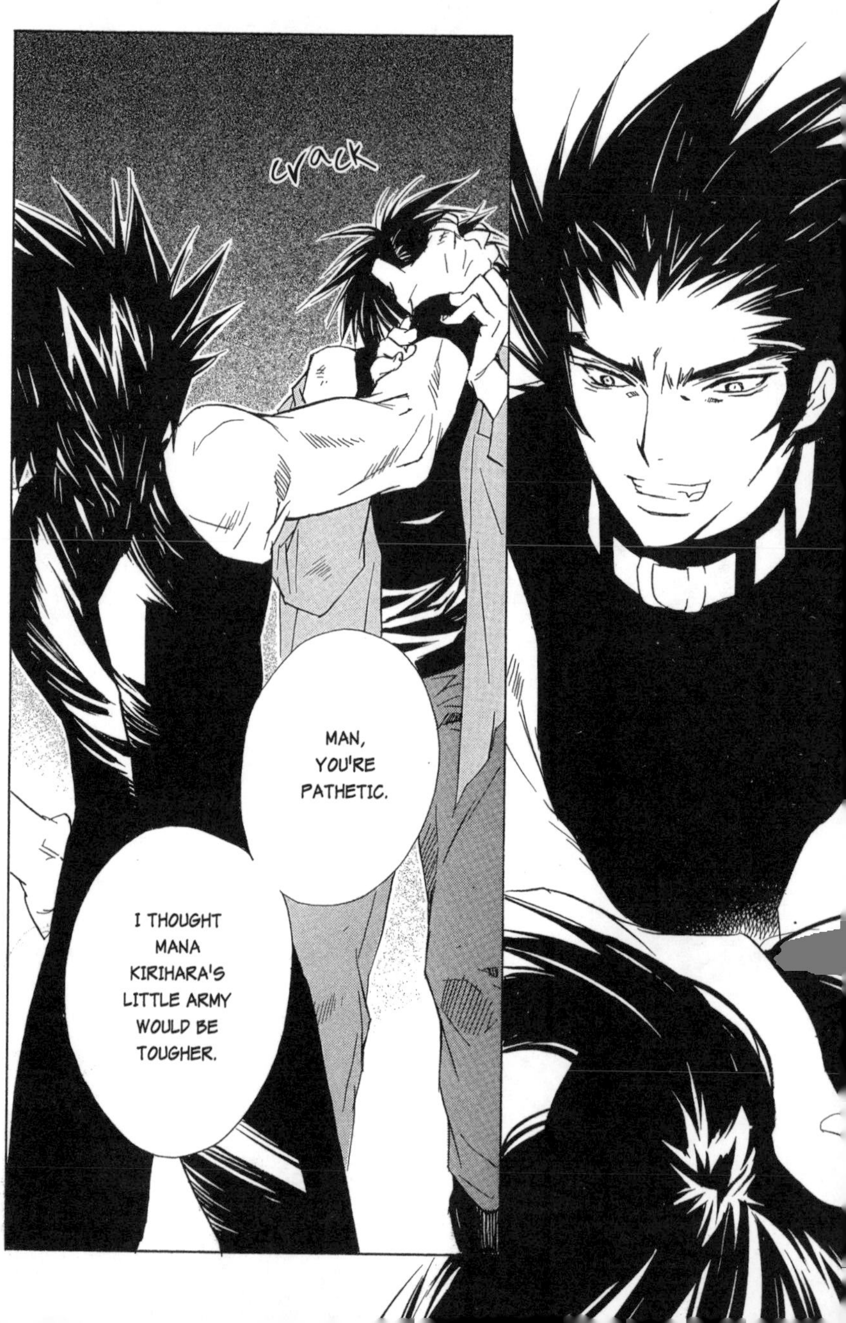
crack
MAN, YOU'RE PATHETIC.
I THOUGHT MANA KIRIHARA'S LITTLE ARMY WOULD BE TOUGHER.

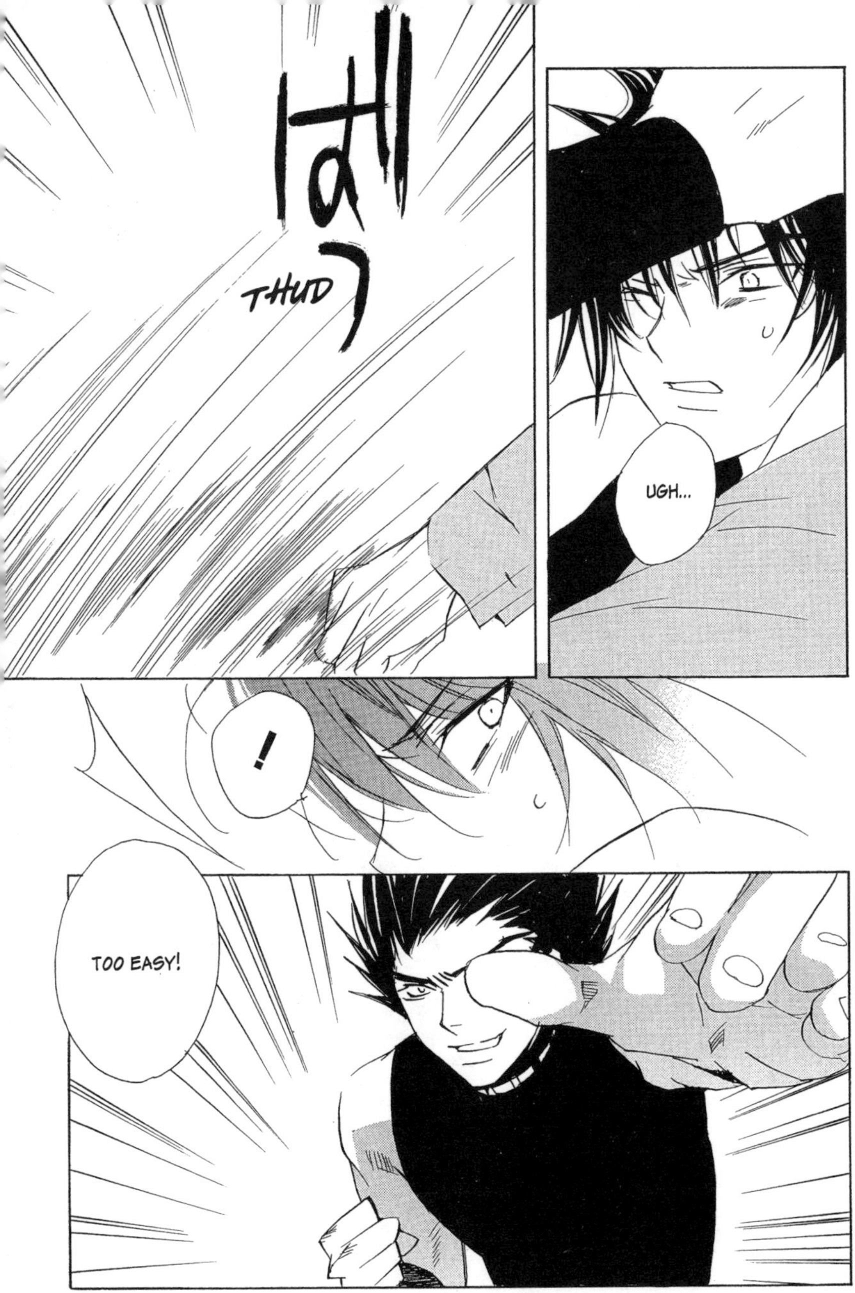
UGH...
THUD
!
TOO EASY!

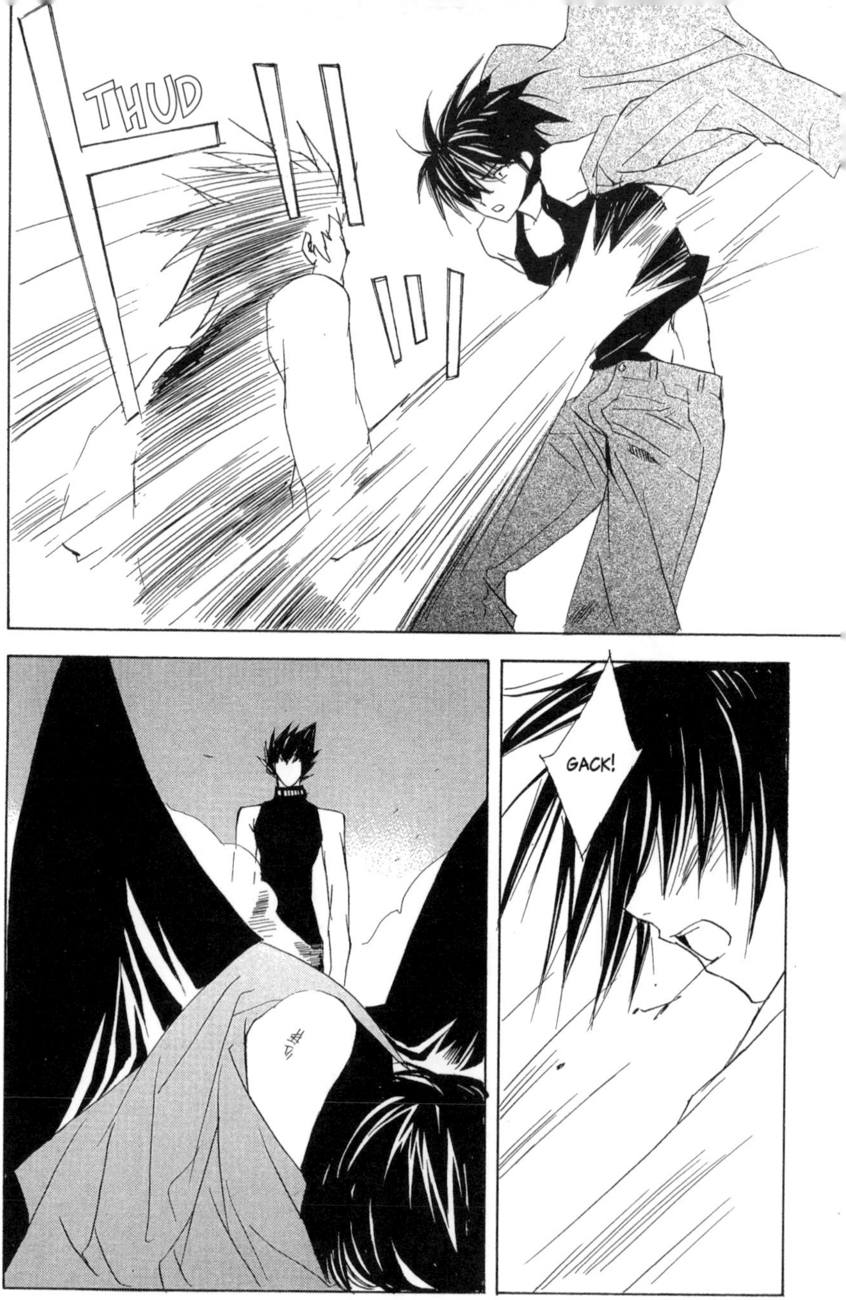
THUD
GACK!

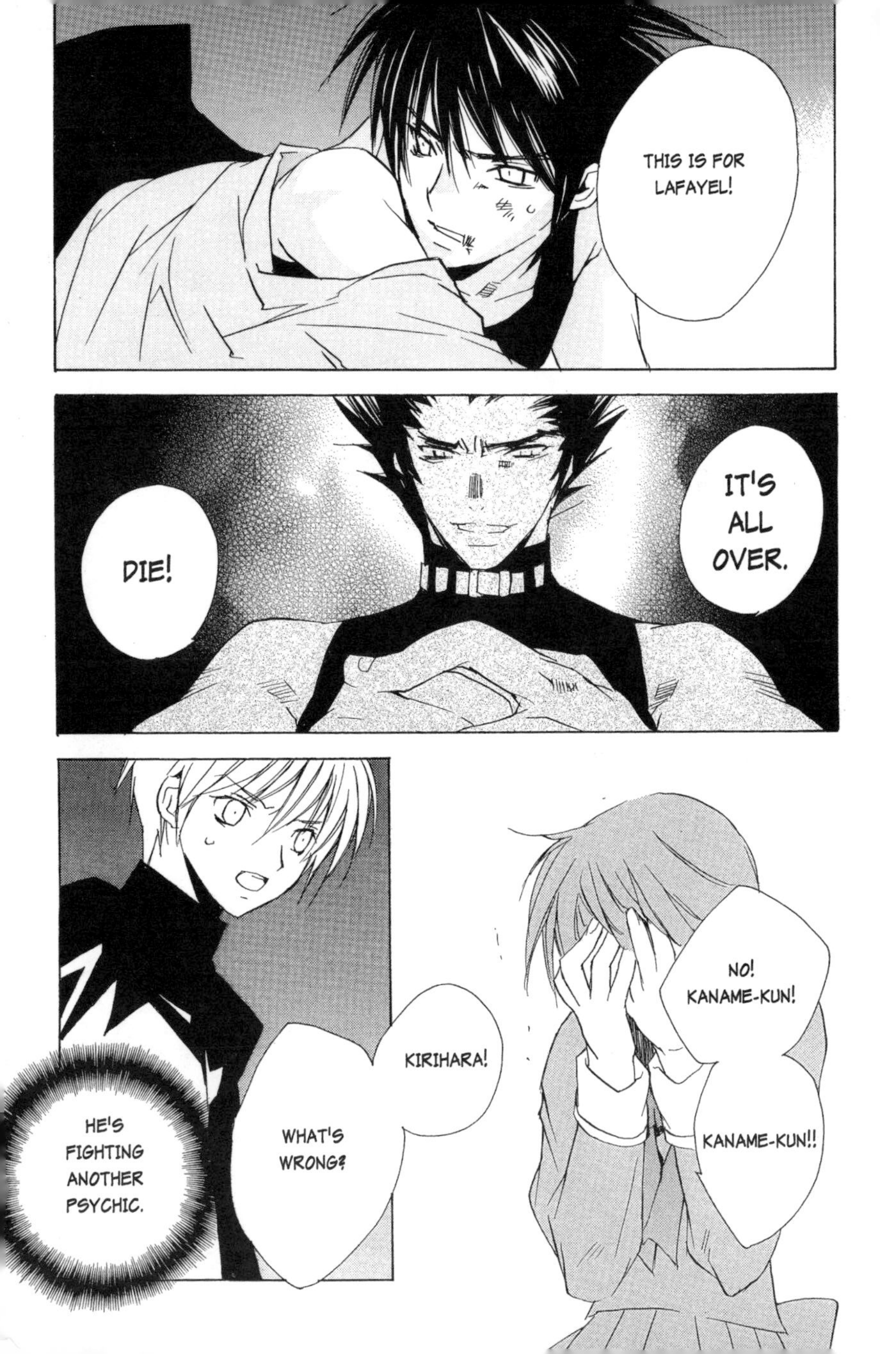
THIS IS FOR LAFAYEL!
IT'S ALL OVER.
DIE!
NO! KANAME-KUN!
KANAME-KUN!!
KIRIHARA!
WHAT'S WRONG?
HE'S FIGHTING ANOTHER PSYCHIC.

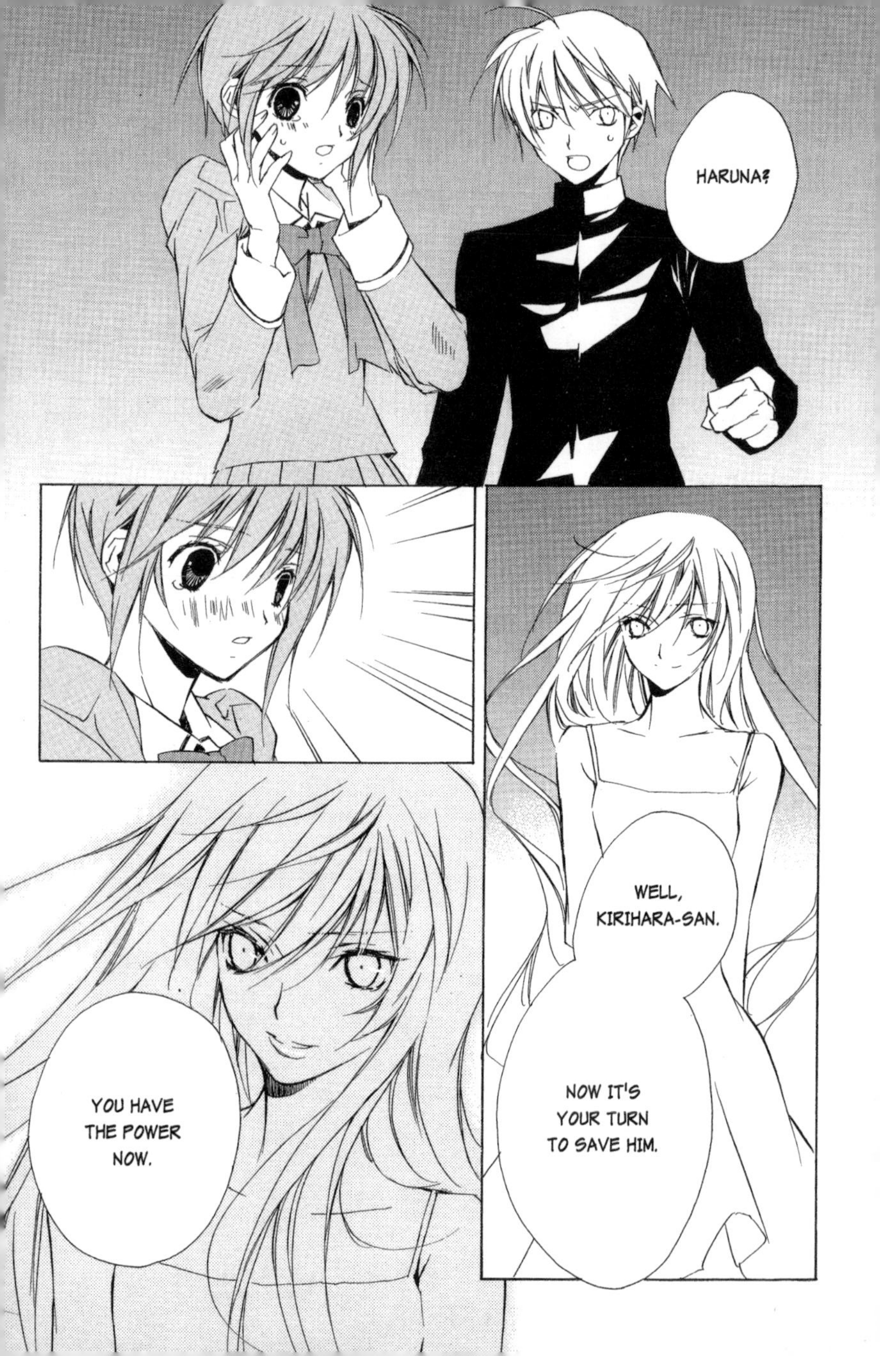
HARUNA?
WELL, KIRIHARA-SAN.
NOW IT'S YOUR TURN TO SAVE HIM.
YOU HAVE THE POWER NOW.

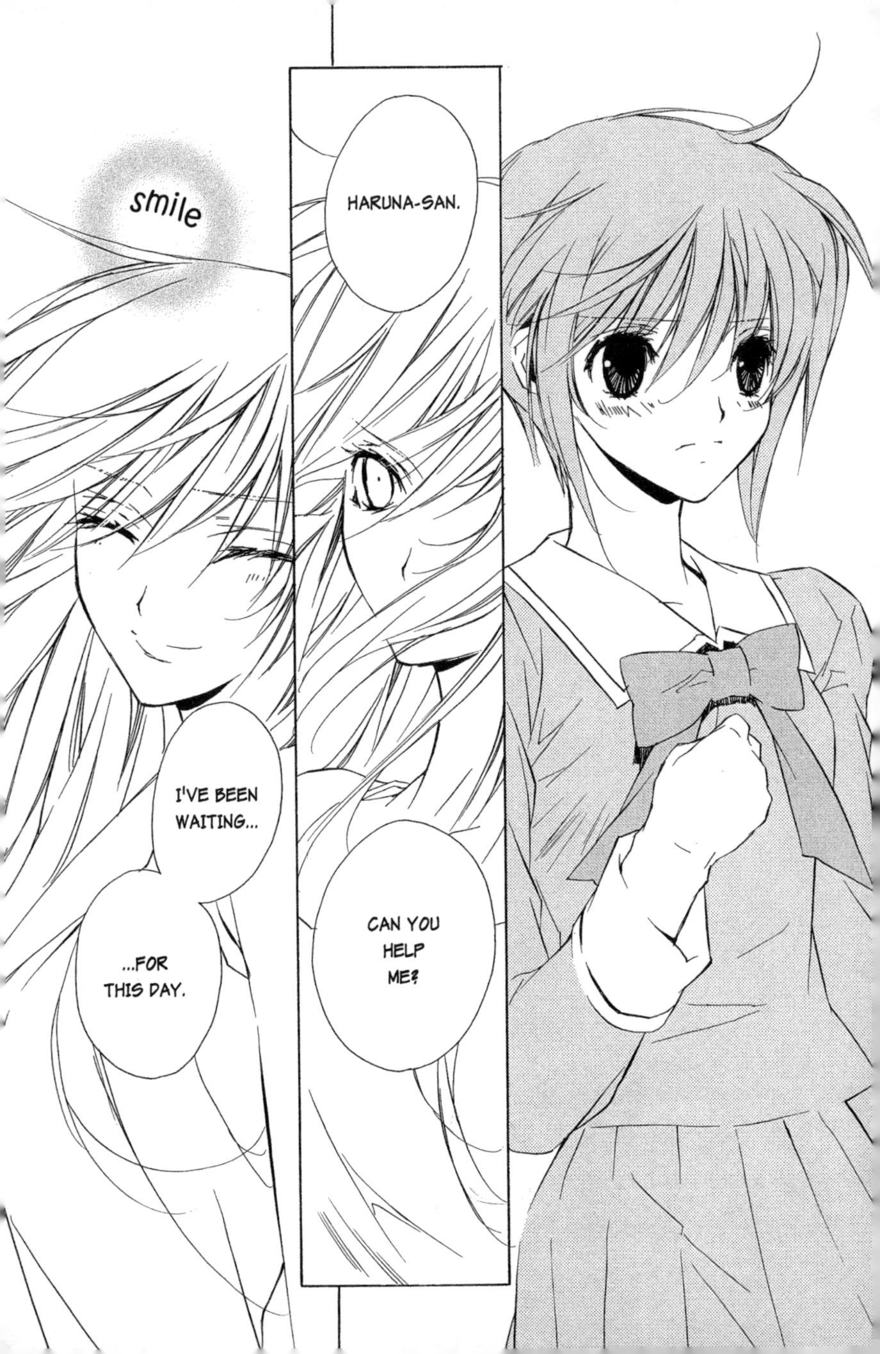
HARUNA-SAN.
CAN YOU HELP ME?
smile
I'VE BEEN WAITING...
...FOR THIS DAY.

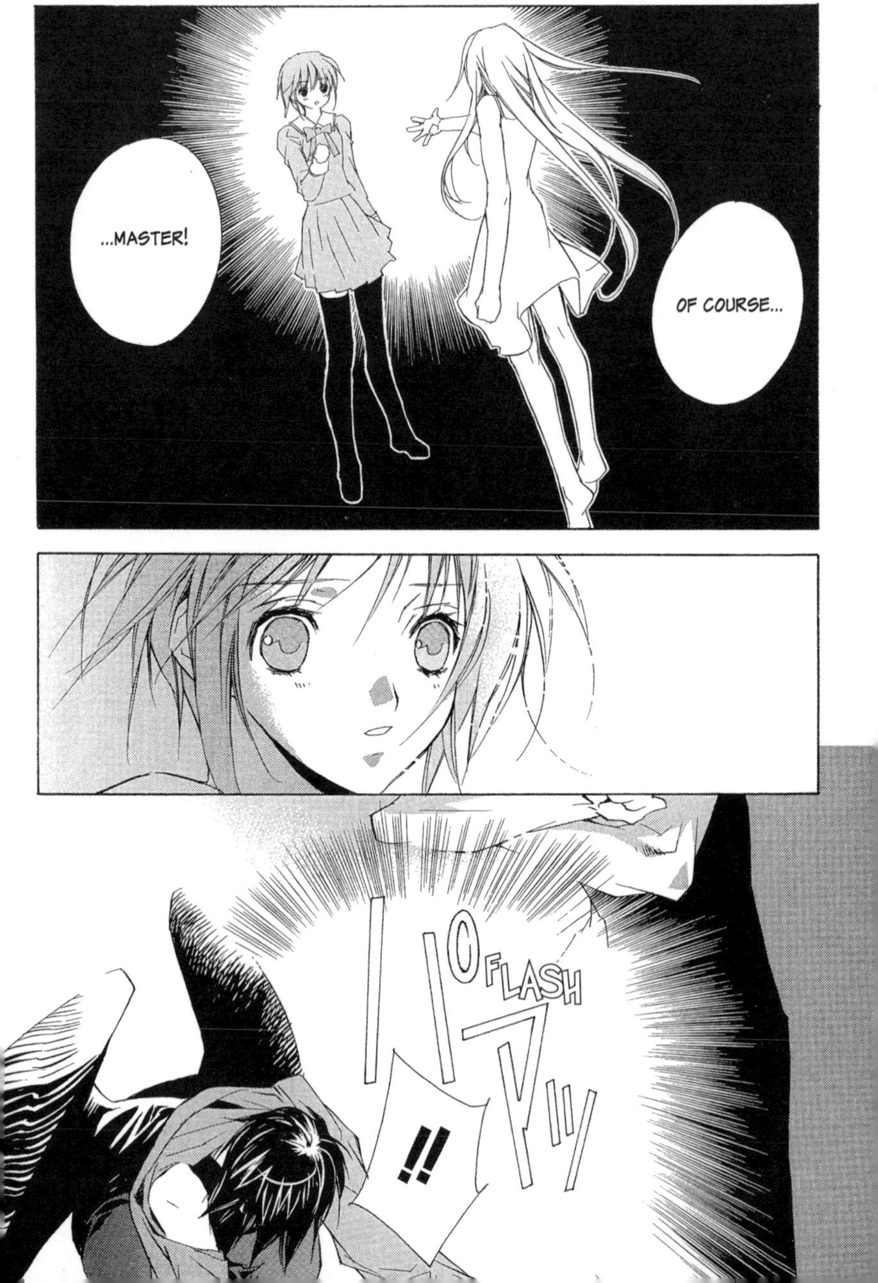
OF COURSE...
...MASTER!
FLASH
!!

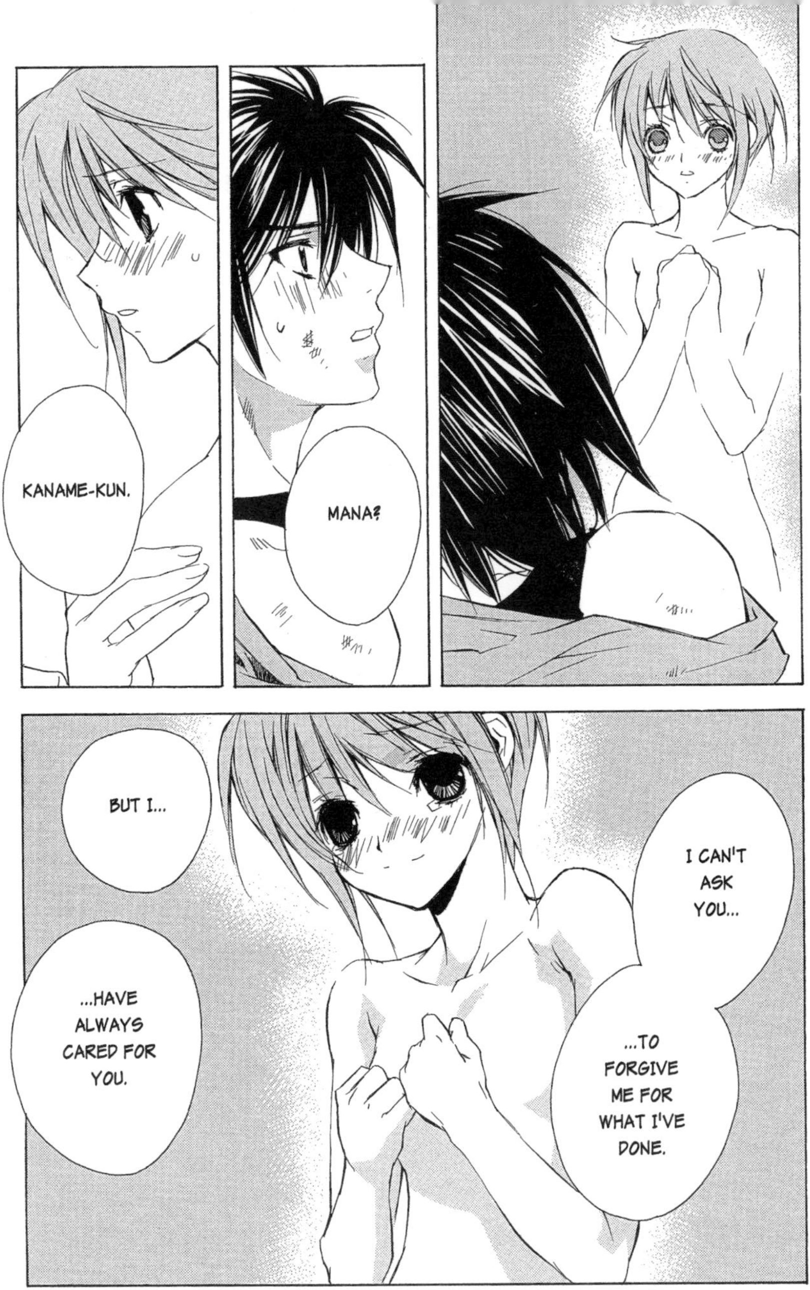
MANA?
KANAME-KUN.
I CAN'T ASK YOU...
...TO FORGIVE ME FOR WHAT I'VE DONE.
BUT I...
...HAVE ALWAYS CARED FOR YOU.

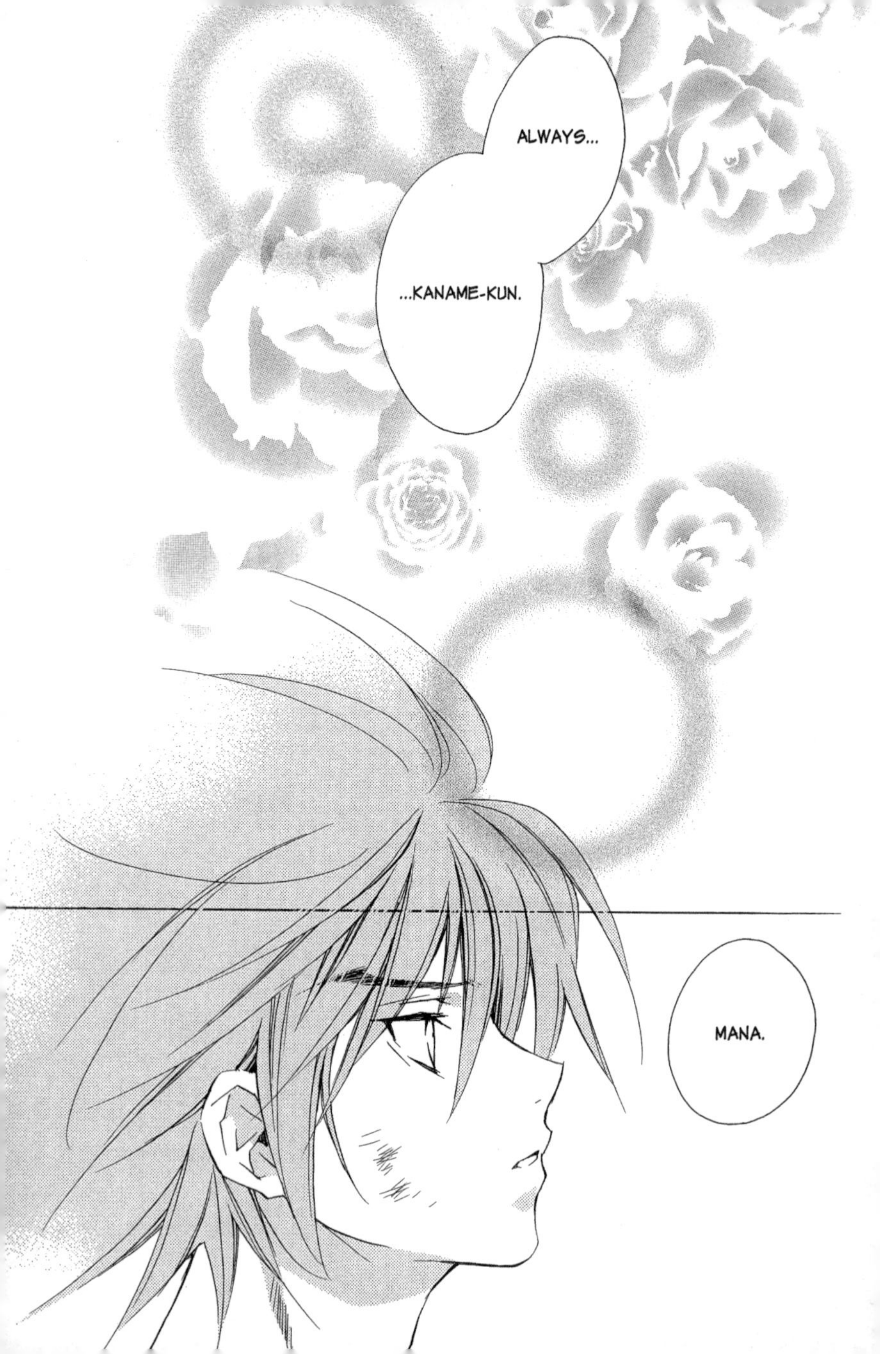
ALWAYS...
...KANAME-KUN.
MANA.

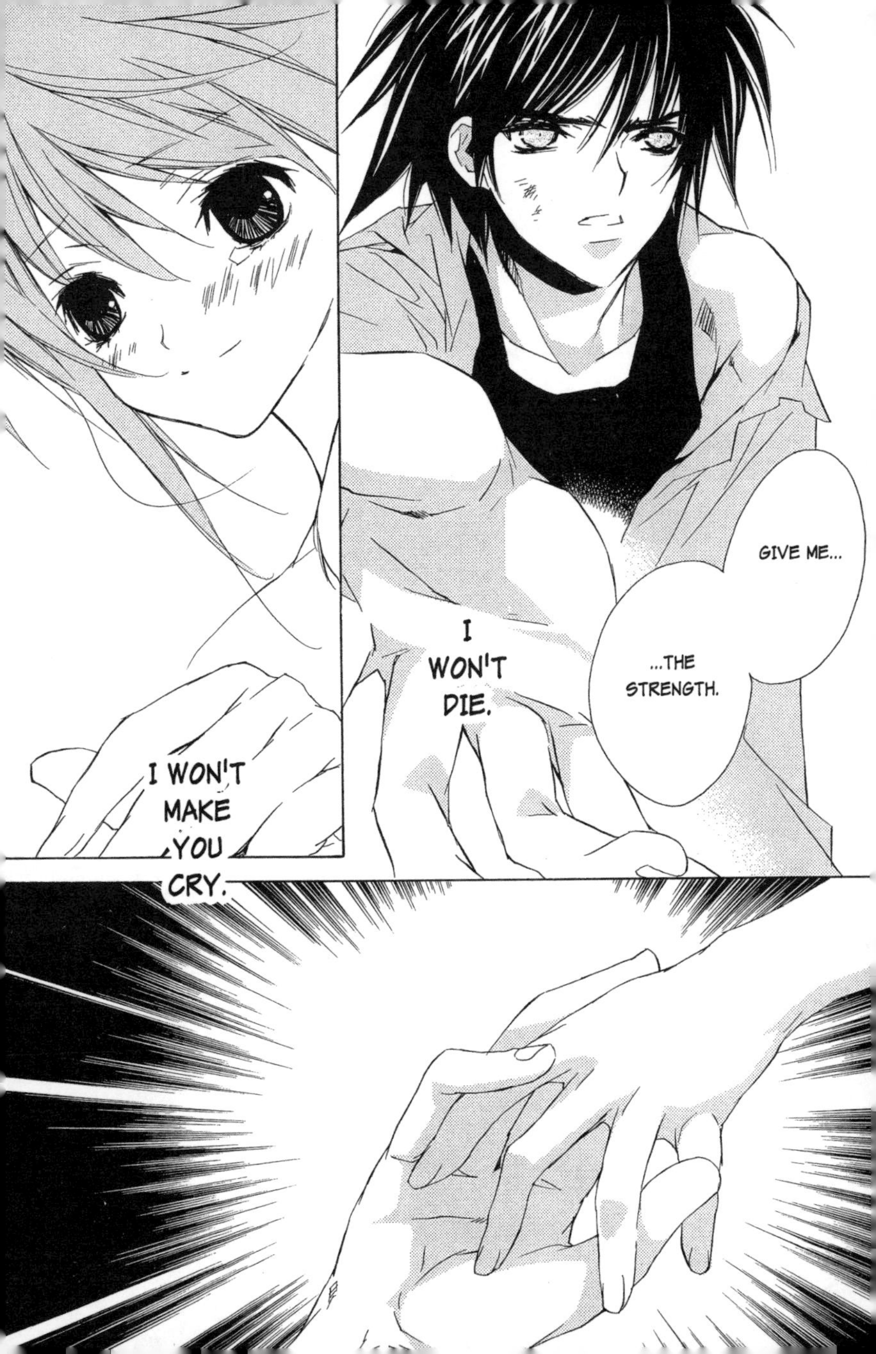
GIVE ME...
...THE STRENGTH.
I WON'T DIE.
I WON'T MAKE YOU CRY.

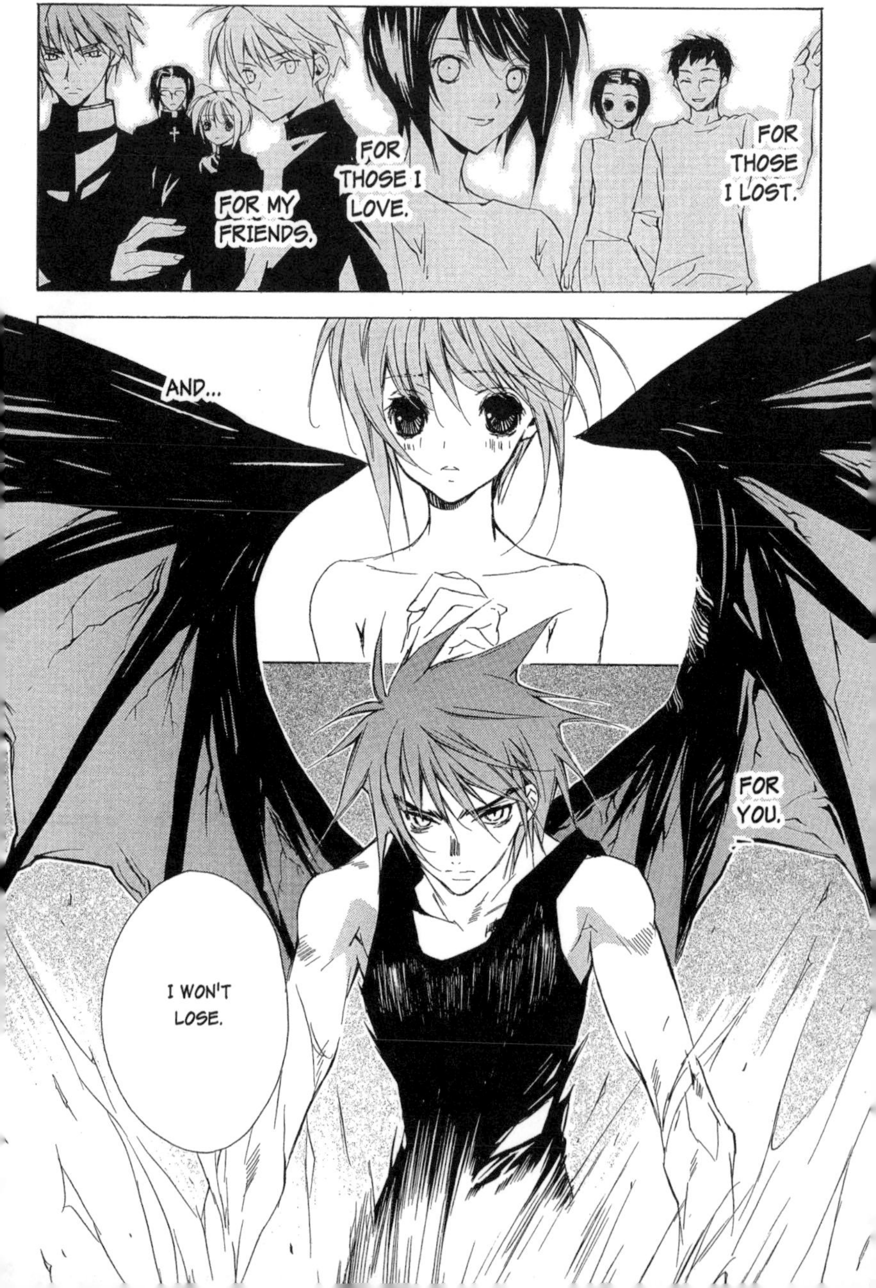
FOR THOSE I LOST.
FOR THOSE I LOVE.
FOR MY FRIENDS.
AND...
FOR YOU.
I WON'T LOSE.

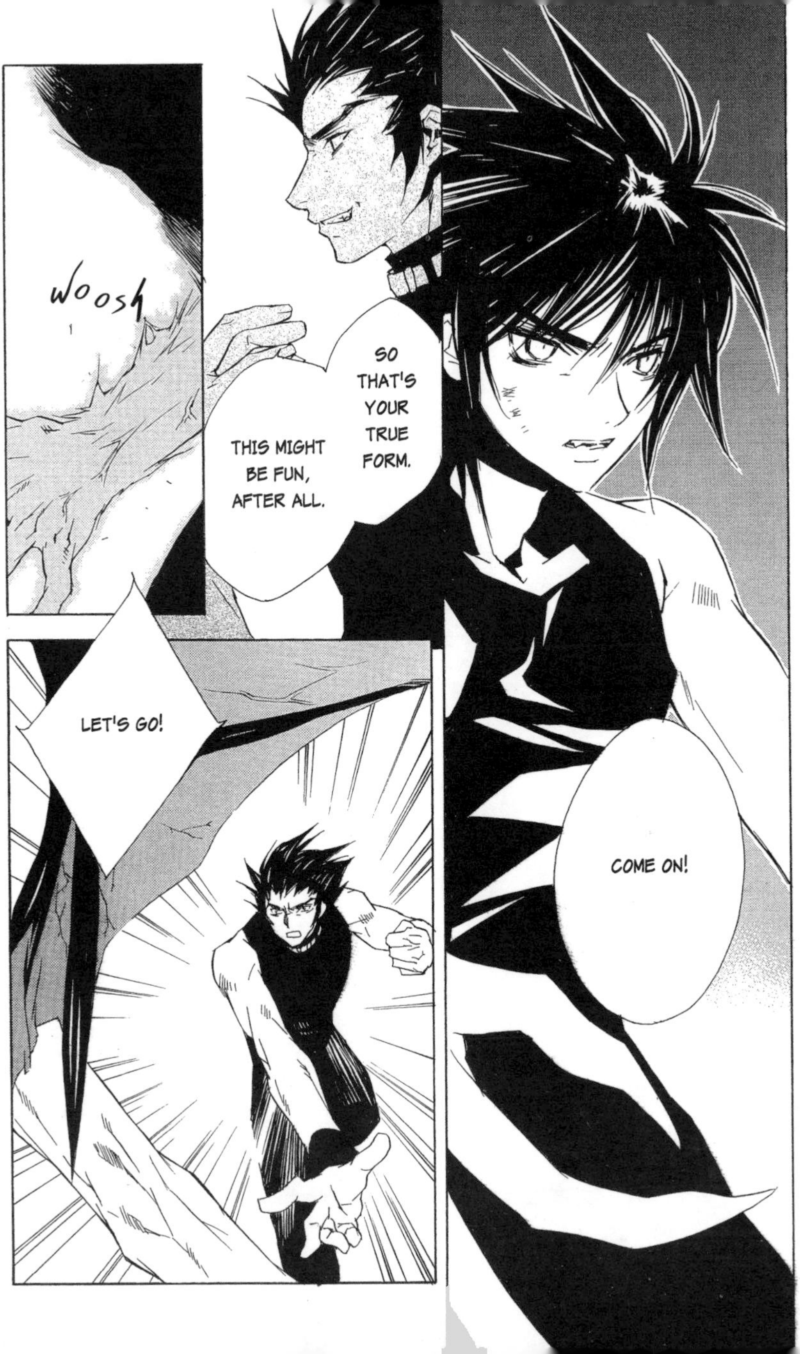
SO THAT'S YOUR TRUE FORM.
THIS MIGHT BE FUN, AFTER ALL.
woosh
COME ON!
LET'S GO!

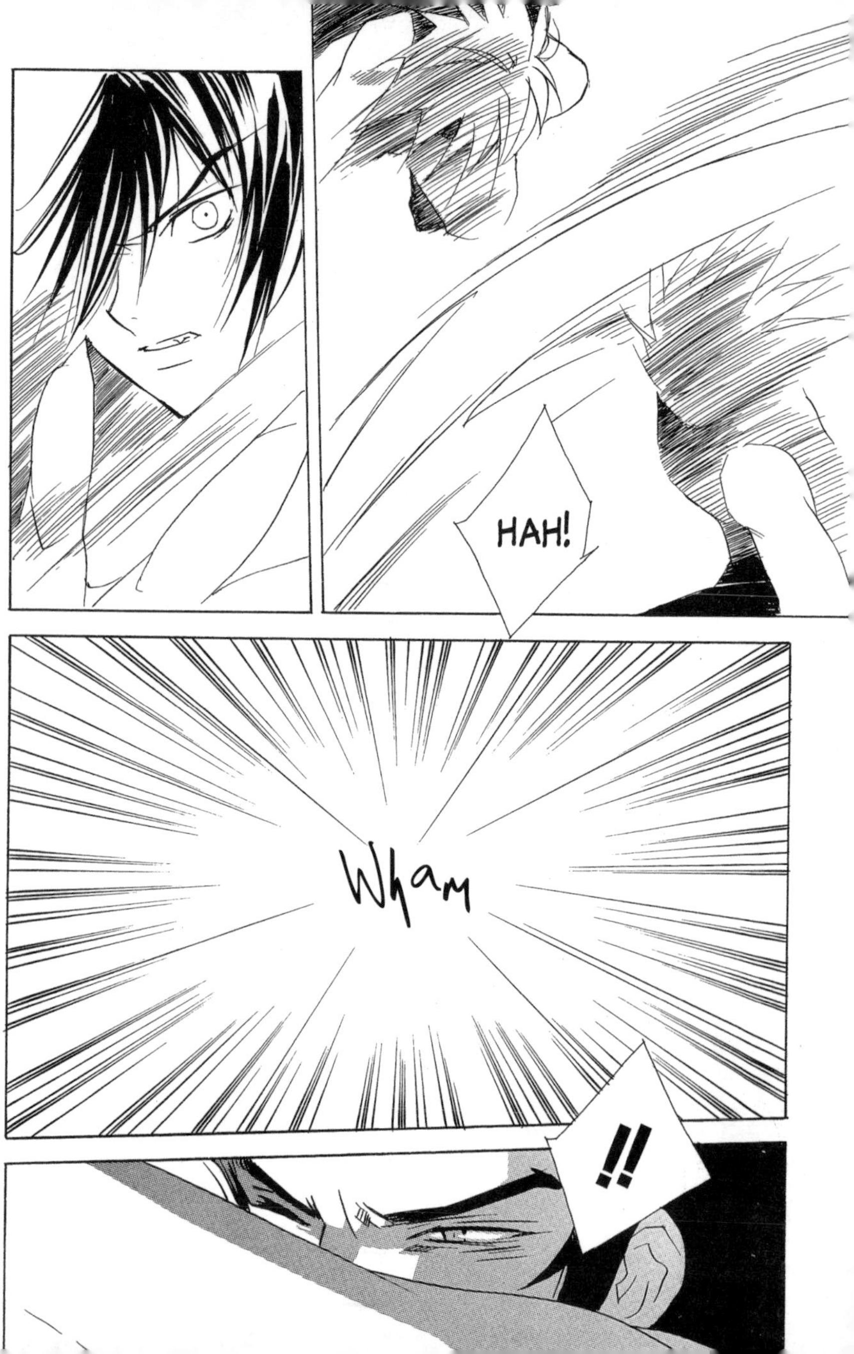
HAH!
Wham
!!

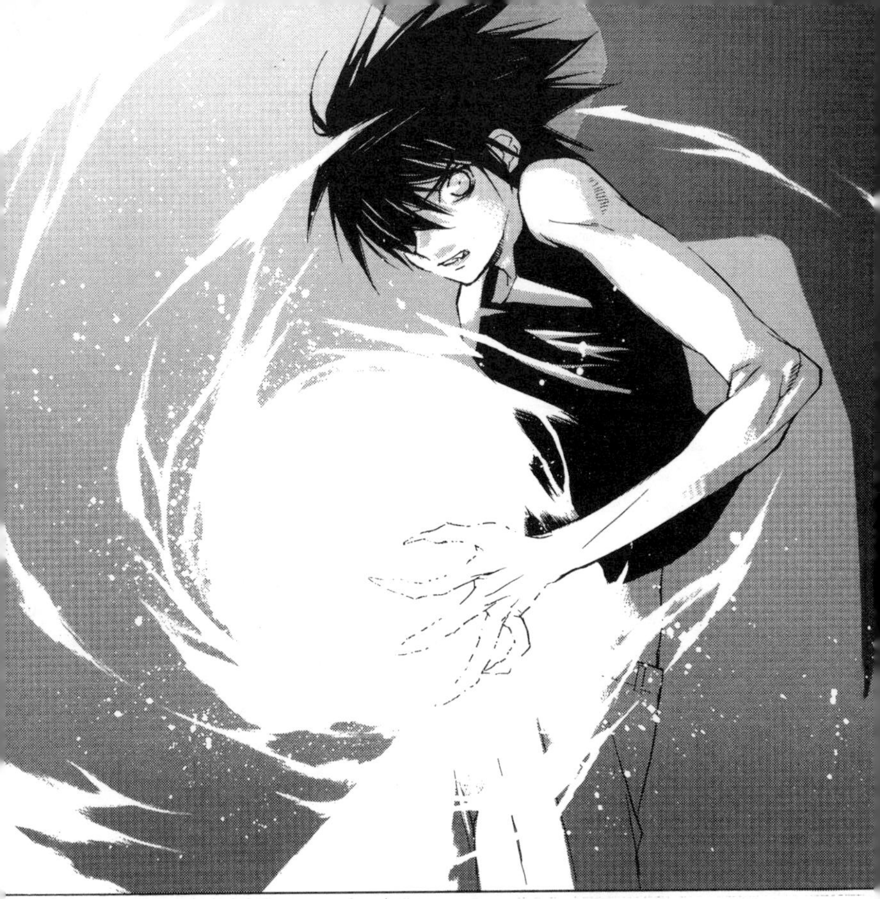

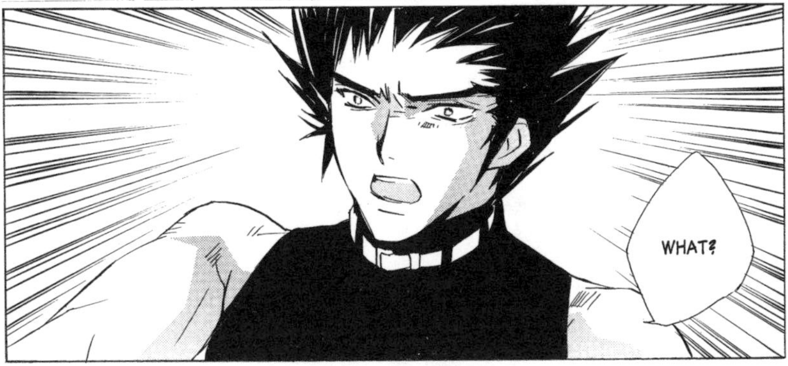
WHAT?

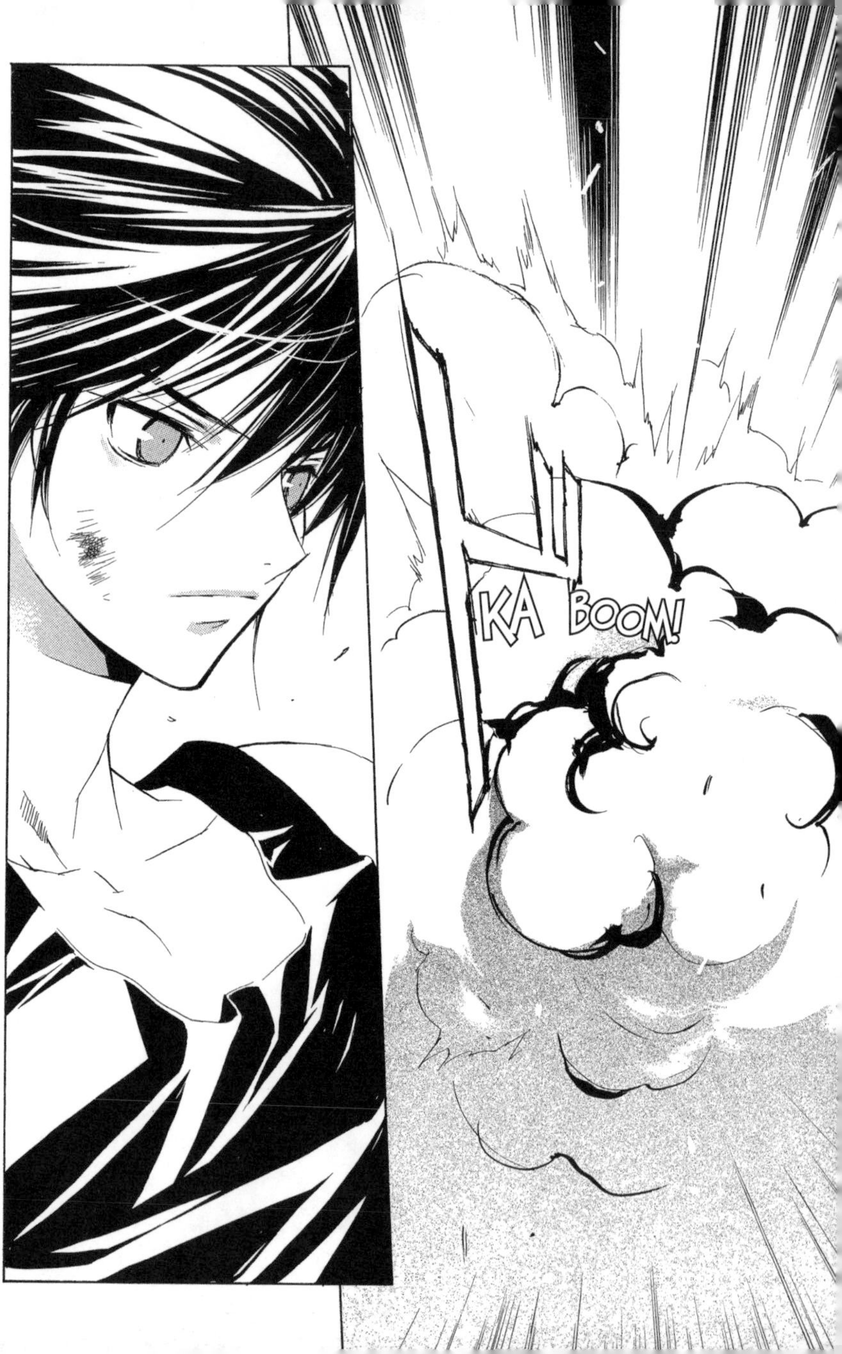
KA BOOM!

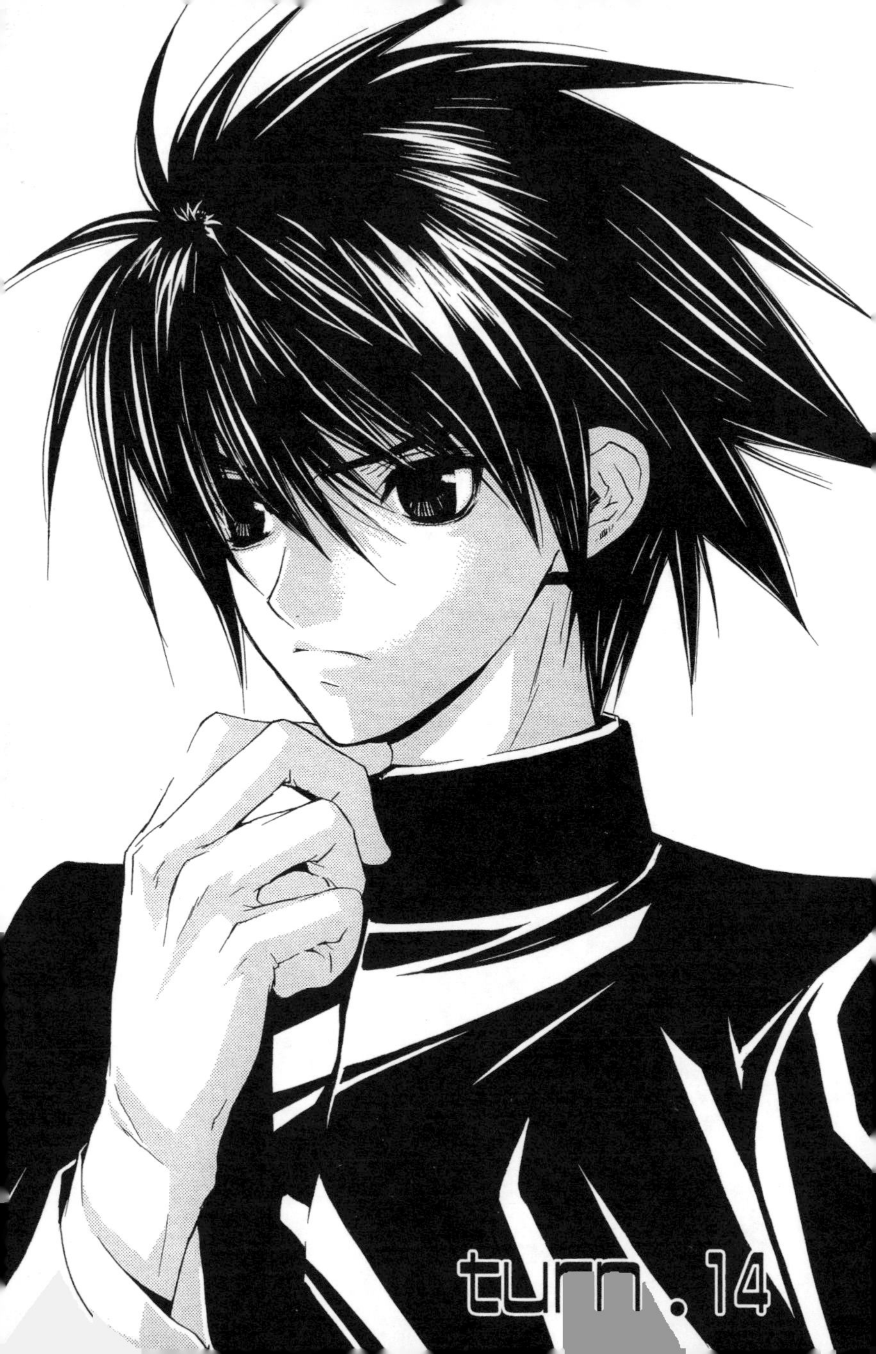
turn . 14

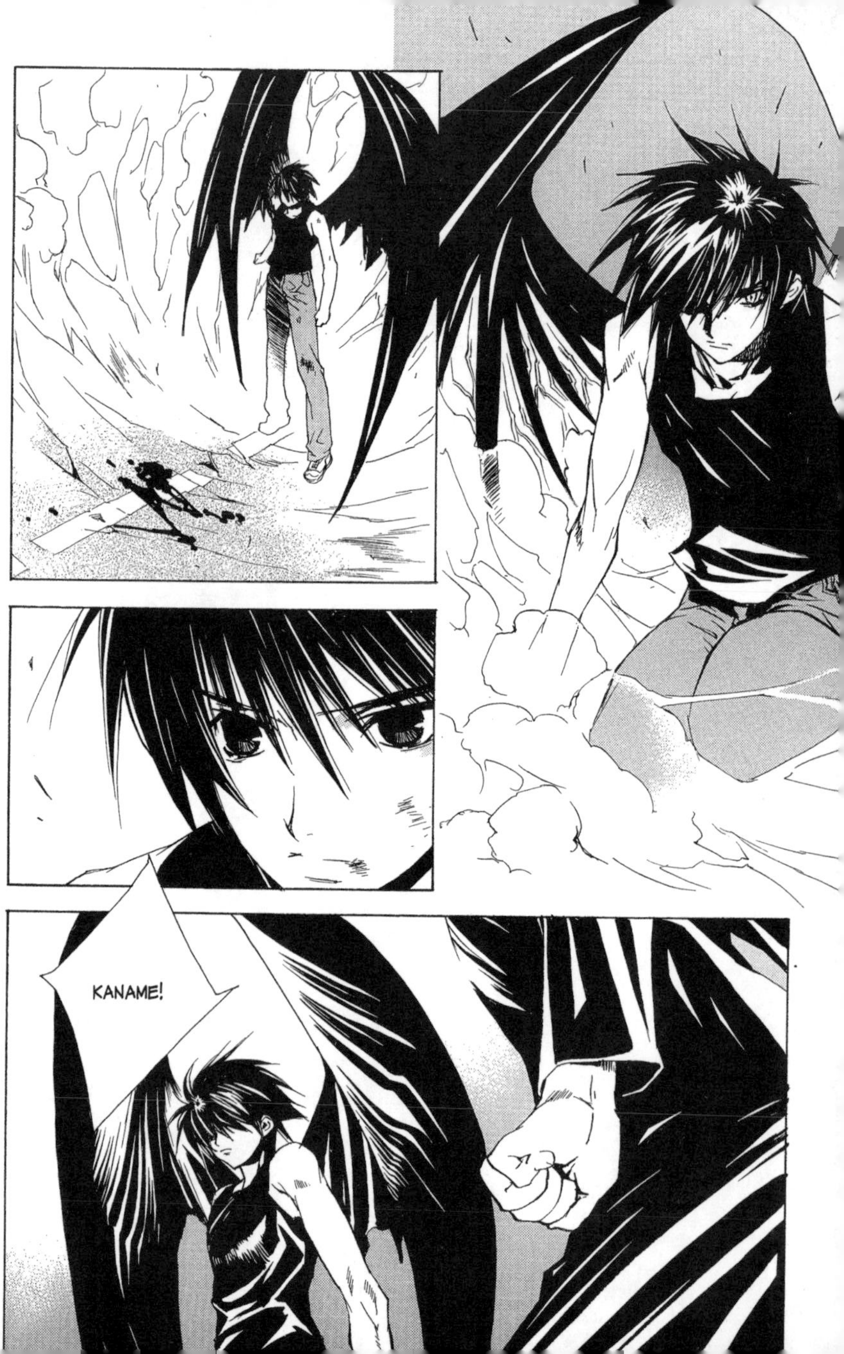
KANAME!

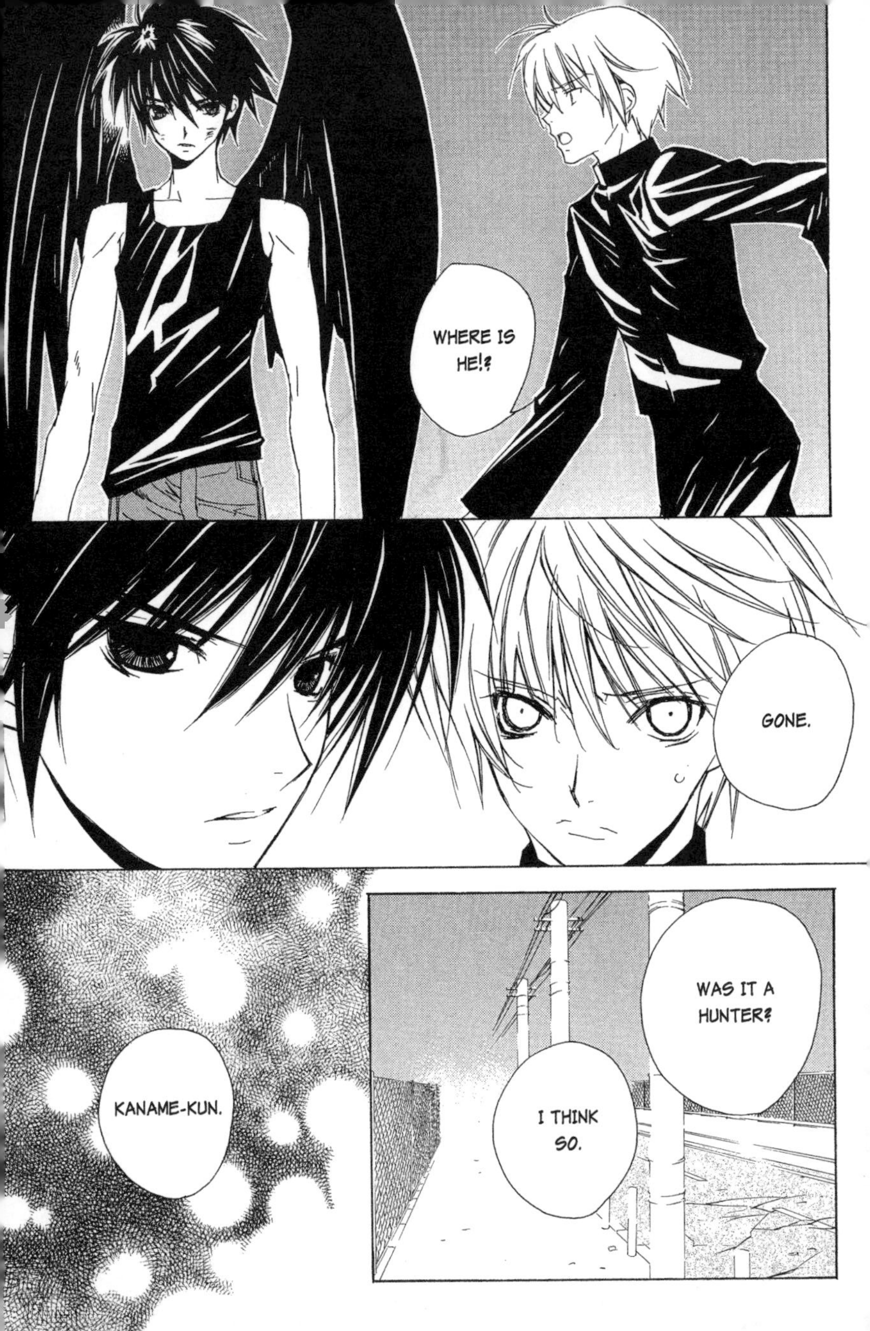
WHERE IS HE!?
GONE.
WAS IT A HUNTER?
I THINK SO.
KANAME-KUN.

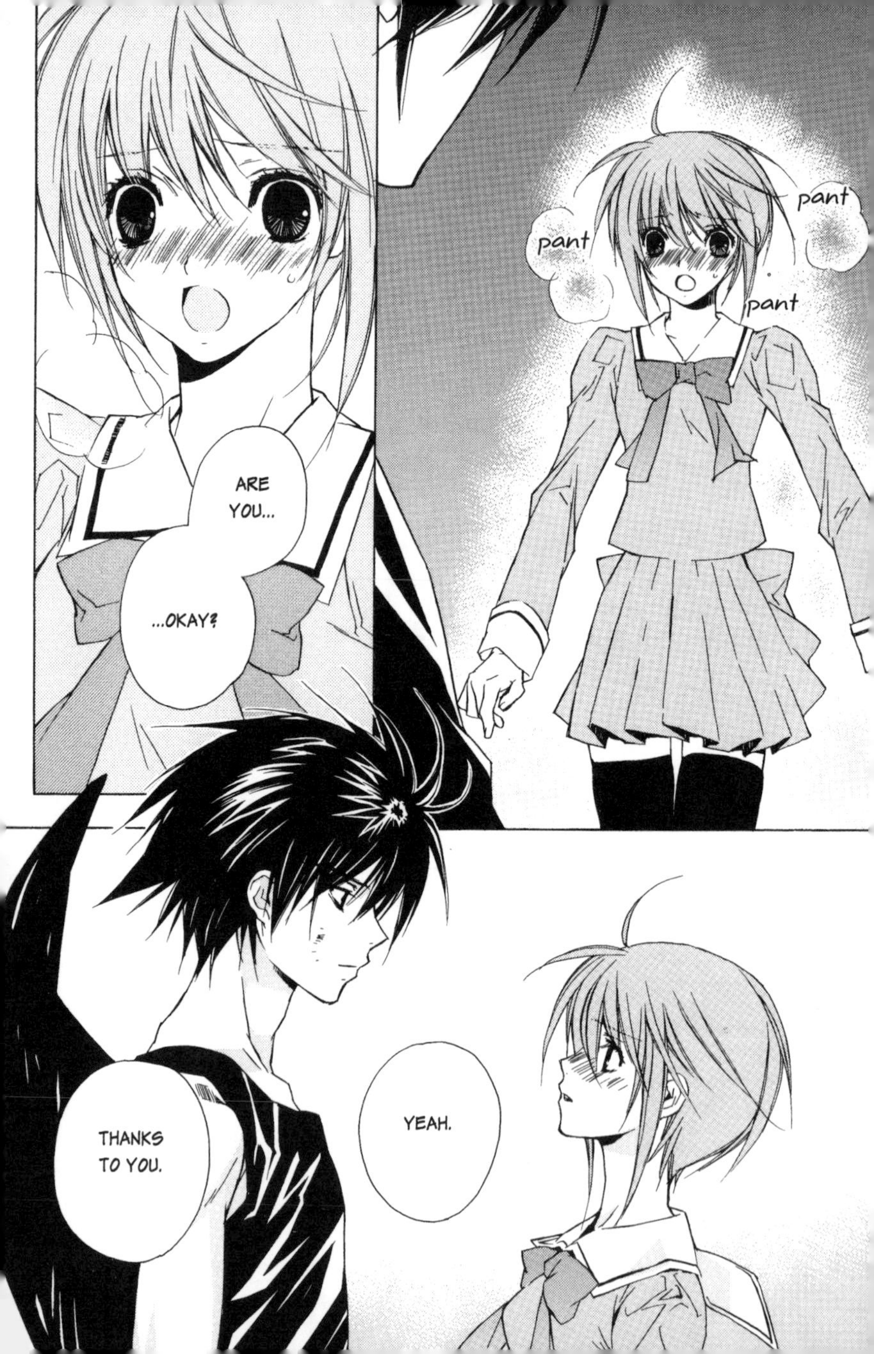
pant
pant
pant
ARE YOU...
...OKAY?
YEAH.
THANKS TO YOU.

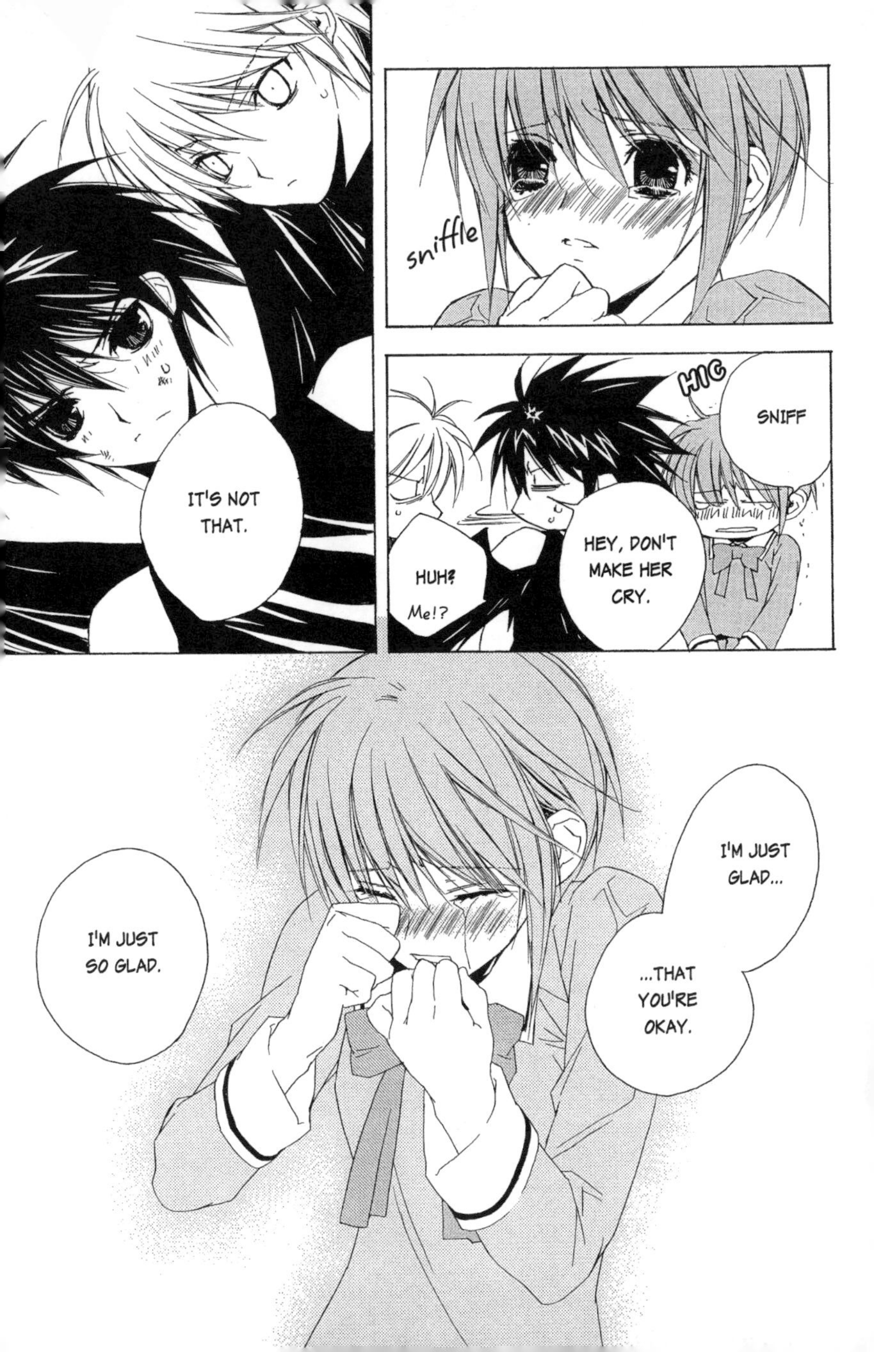
sniffle
HIC
SNIFF
HEY, DON'T MAKE HER CRY.
HUH? Me!?
IT'S NOT THAT.
I'M JUST GLAD...
...THAT YOU'RE OKAY.
I'M JUST SO GLAD.

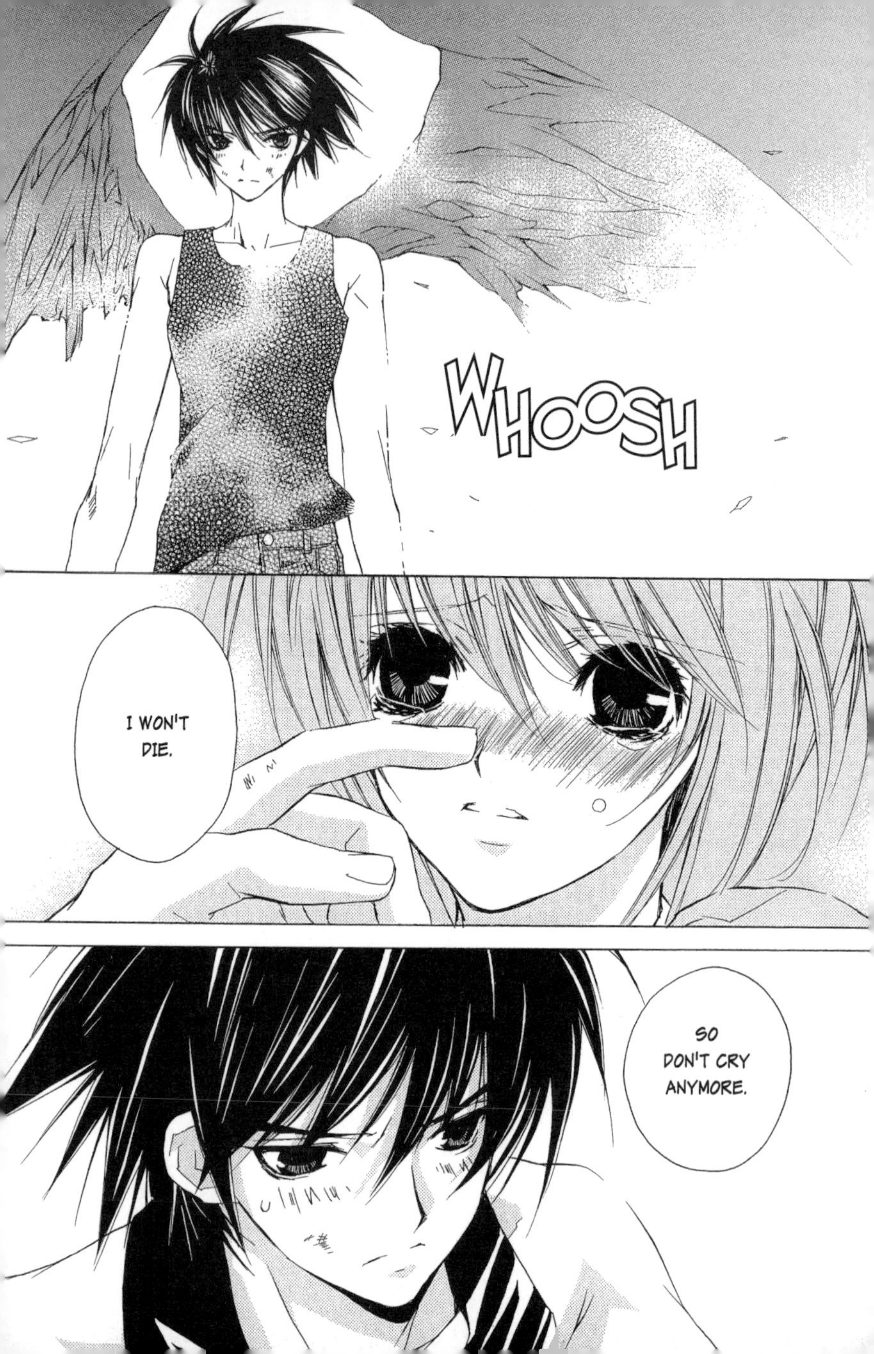
WHOOSH
I WON'T DIE.
SO DON'T CRY ANYMORE.

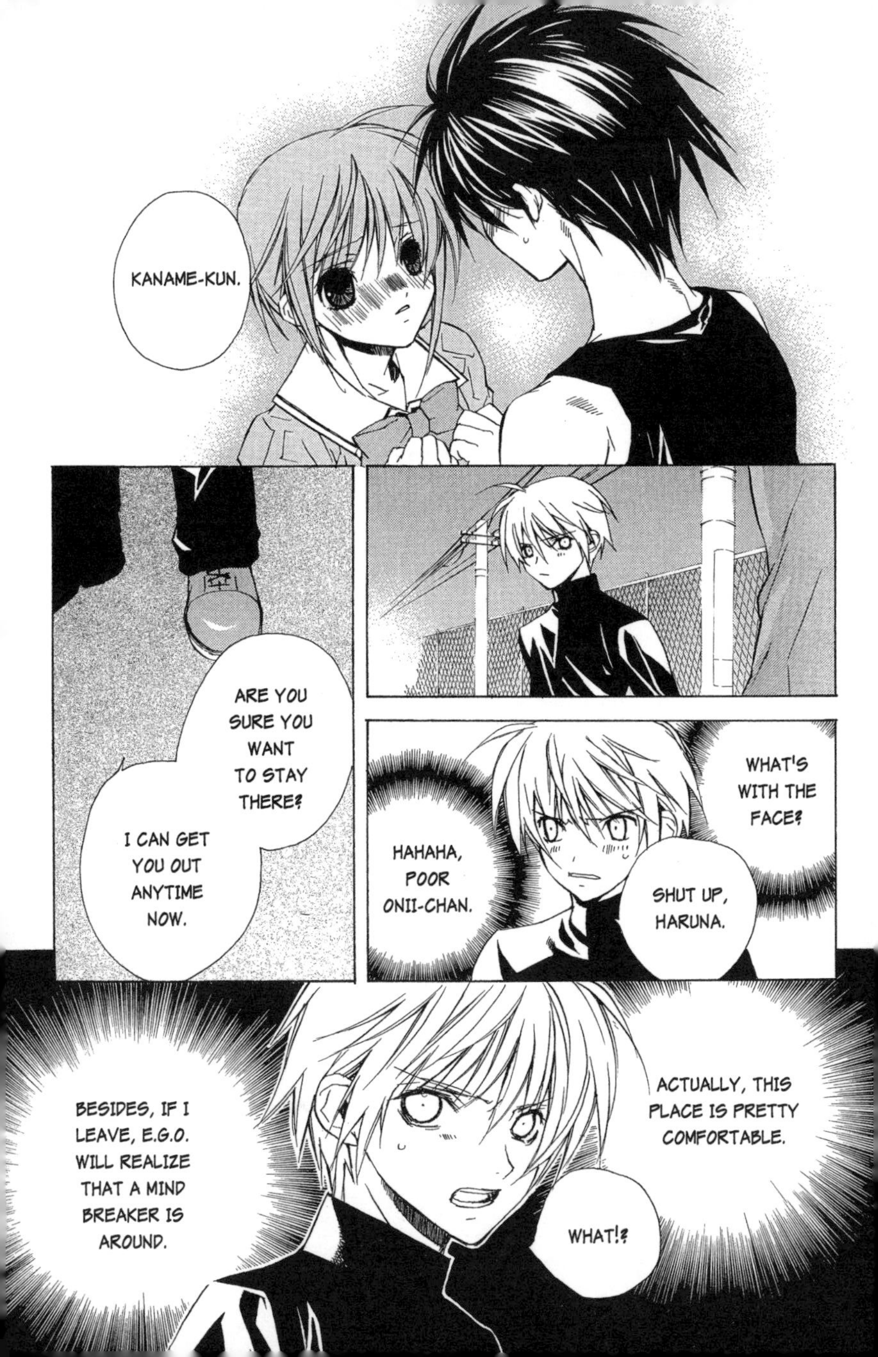
KANAME-KUN.
WHAT'S WITH THE FACE?
HAHAHA, POOR ONII-CHAN.
SHUT UP, HARUNA.
ARE YOU SURE YOU WANT TO STAY THERE?
I CAN GET YOU OUT ANYTIME NOW.
ACTUALLY, THIS PLACE IS PRETTY COMFORTABLE.
WHAT!?
BESIDES, IF I LEAVE, E.G.O. WILL REALIZE THAT A MIND BREAKER IS AROUND.

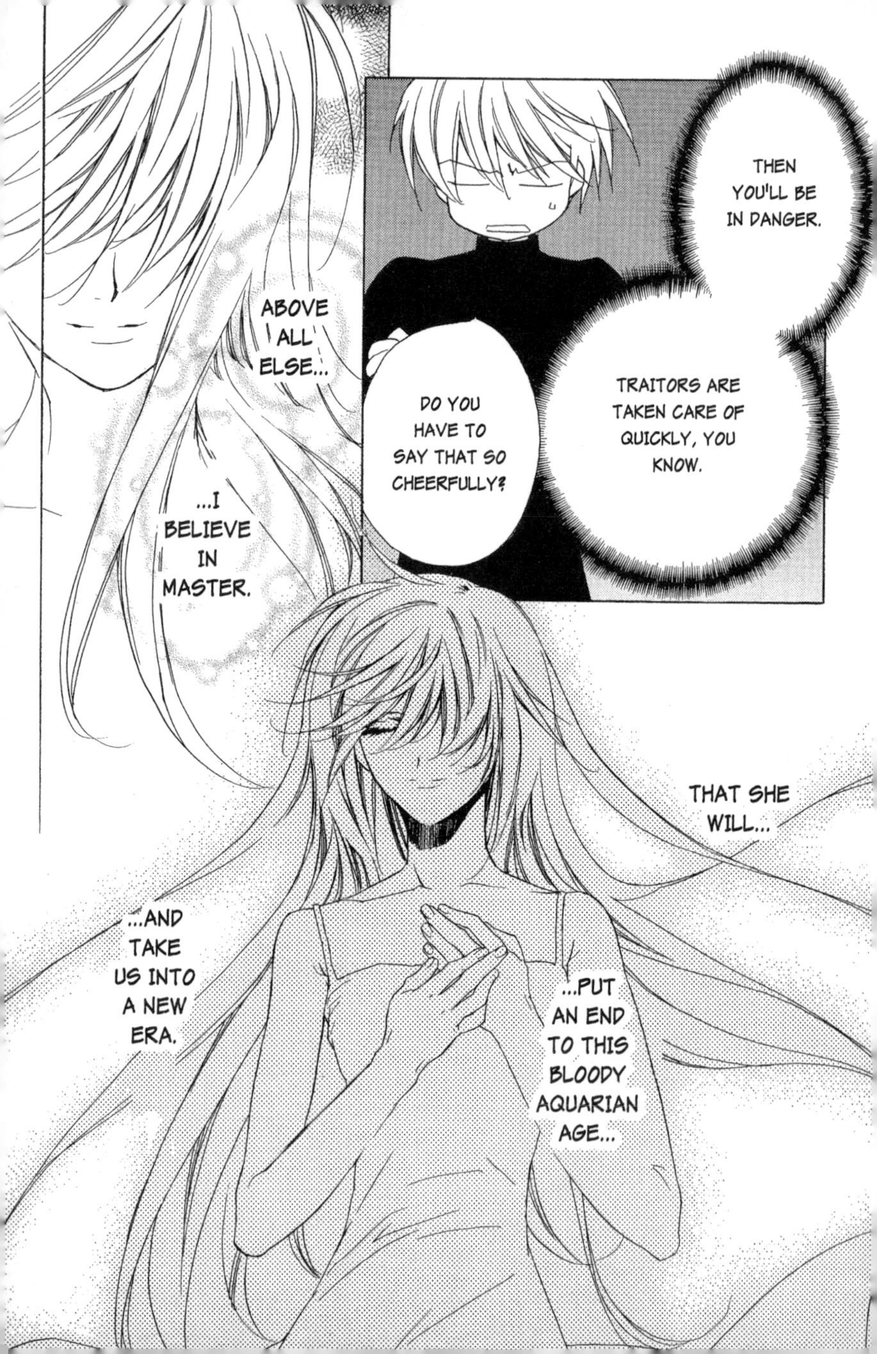
THEN YOU'LL BE IN DANGER.
TRAITORS ARE TAKEN CARE OF QUICKLY, YOU KNOW.
DO YOU HAVE TO SAY THAT SO CHEERFULLY?
ABOVE ALL ELSE...
...I BELIEVE IN MASTER.
THAT SHE WILL...
...PUT AN END TO THIS BLOODY AQUARIAN AGE...
...AND TAKE US INTO A NEW ERA.

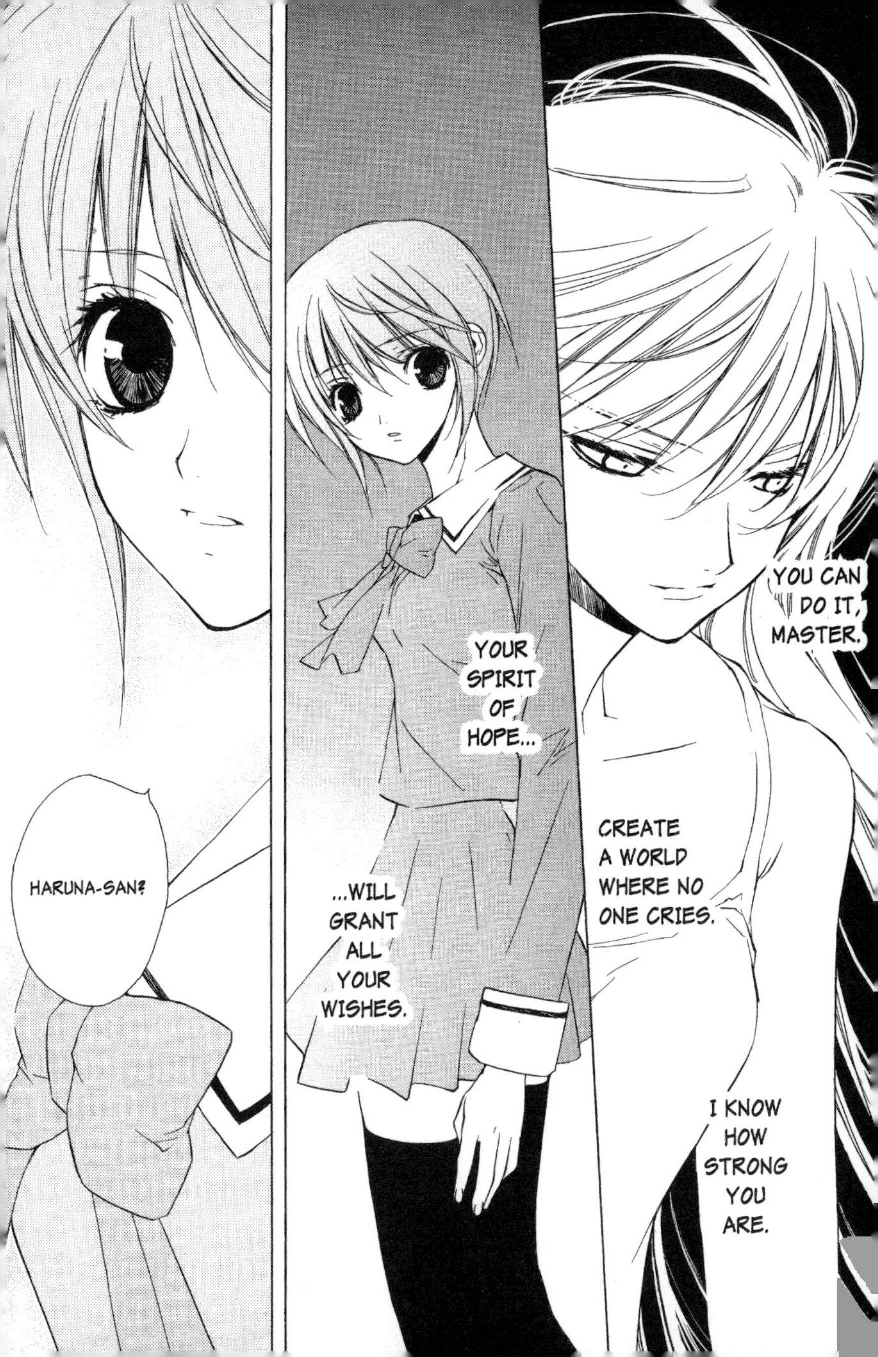
YOU CAN DO IT, MASTER.
CREATE A WORLD WHERE NO ONE CRIES.
I KNOW HOW STRONG YOU ARE.
YOUR SPIRIT OF HOPE...
...WILL GRANT ALL YOUR WISHES.
HARUNA-SAN?

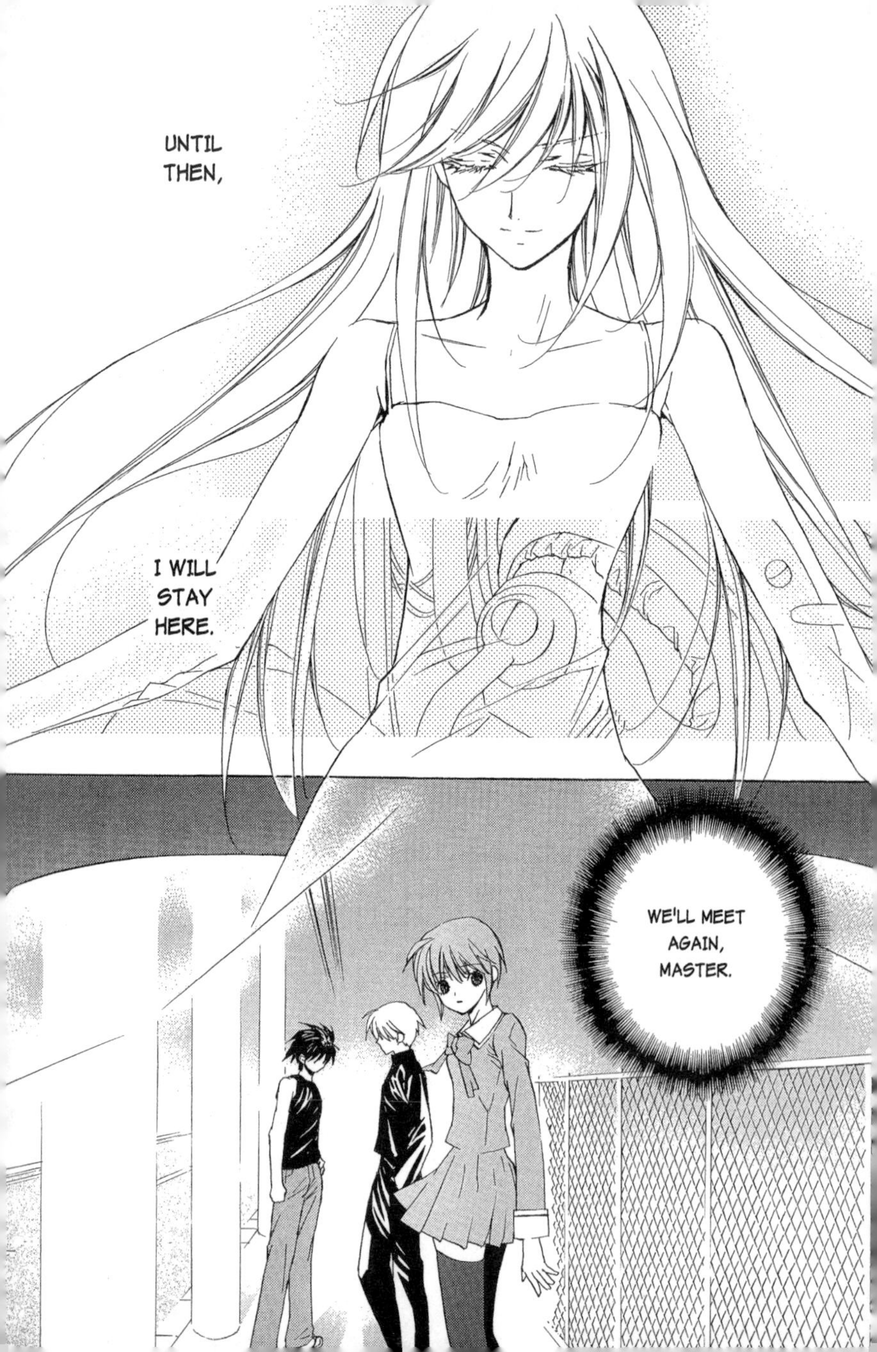
UNTIL THEN,
I WILL STAY HERE.
WE'LL MEET AGAIN, MASTER.

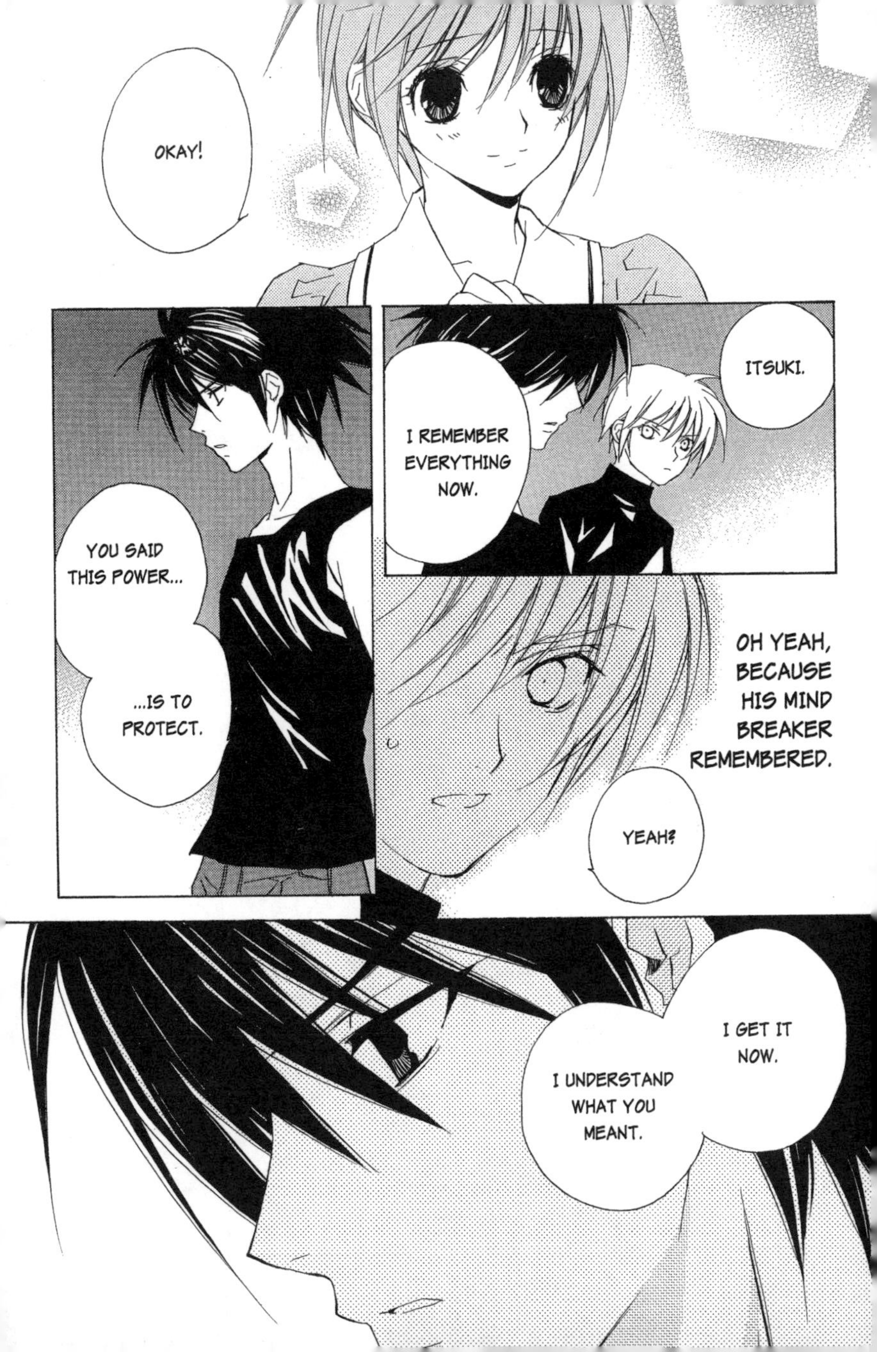
OKAY!
ITSUKI.
I REMEMBER EVERYTHING NOW.
OH YEAH, BECAUSE HIS MIND BREAKER REMEMBERED.
YEAH?
YOU SAID THIS POWER...
...IS TO PROTECT.
I GET IT NOW.
I UNDERSTAND WHAT YOU MEANT.

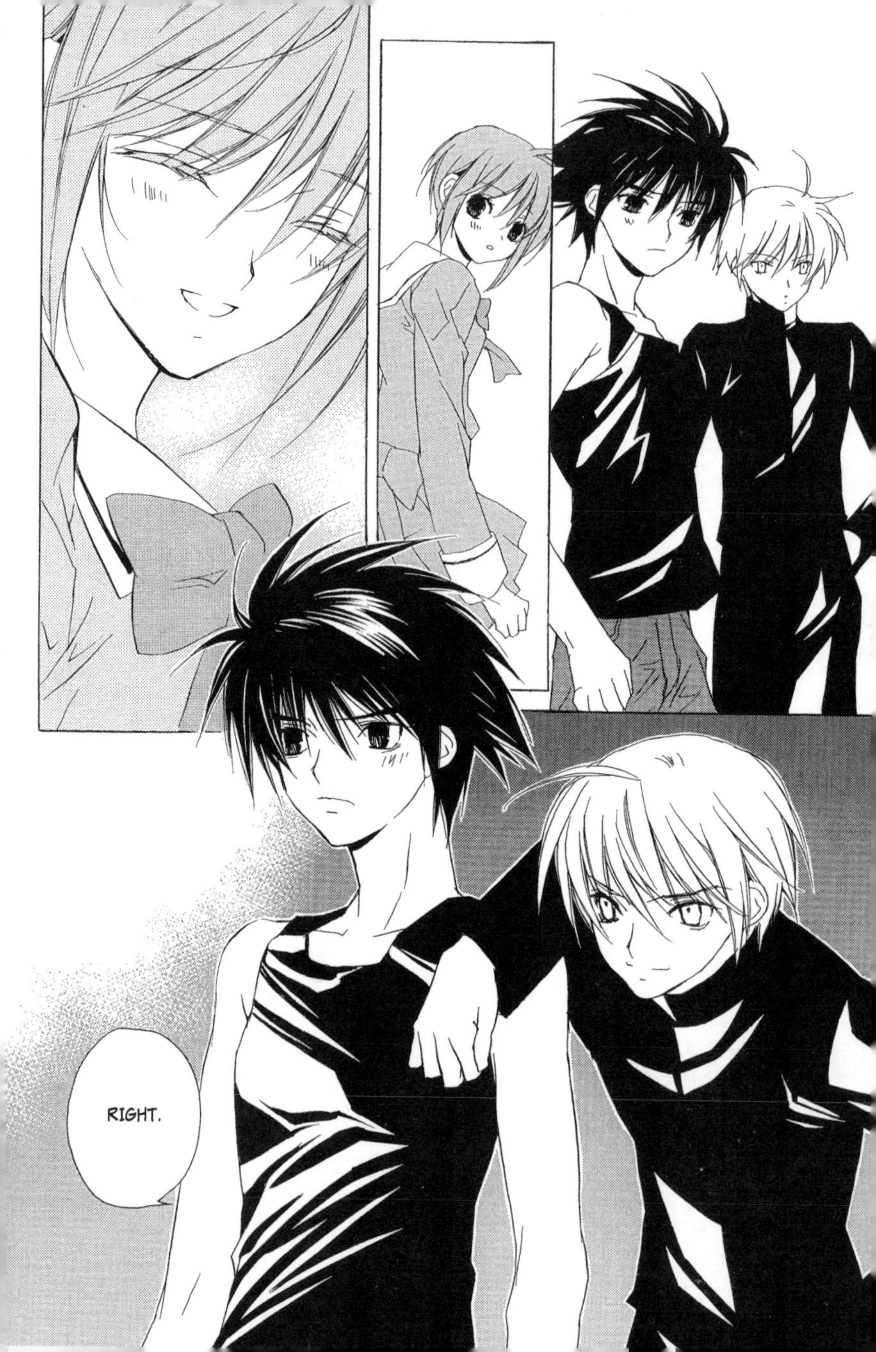
RIGHT.

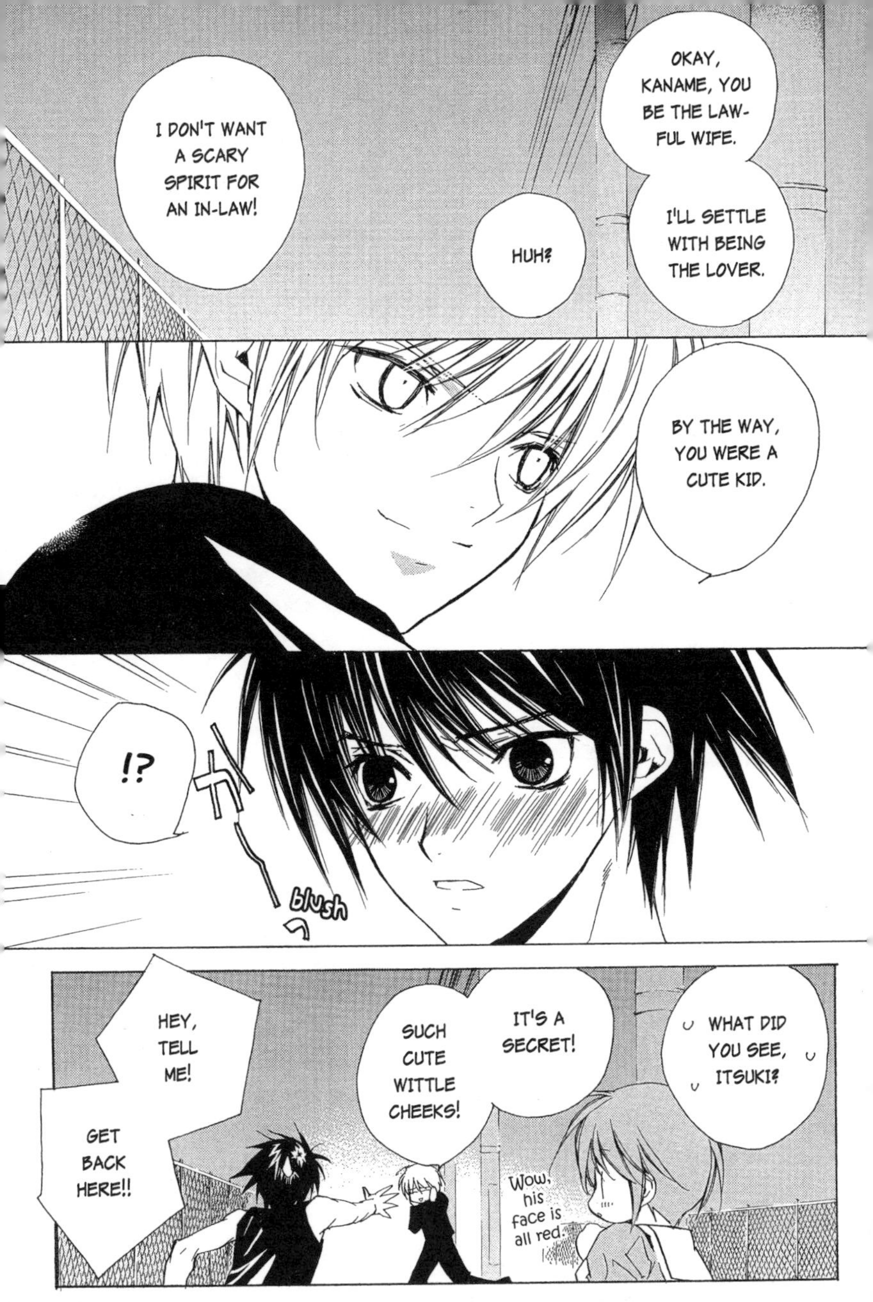
OKAY, KANAME, YOU BE THE LAW-FUL WIFE.
I'LL SETTLE WITH BEING THE LOVER.
HUH?
I DON'T WANT A SCARY SPIRIT FOR AN IN-LAW!
BY THE WAY, YOU WERE A CUTE KID.
!?
blush
WHAT DID YOU SEE, ITSUKI?
IT'S A SECRET!
SUCH CUTE WITTLE CHEEKS!
Wow, his face is all red.
HEY, TELL ME!
GET BACK HERE!!

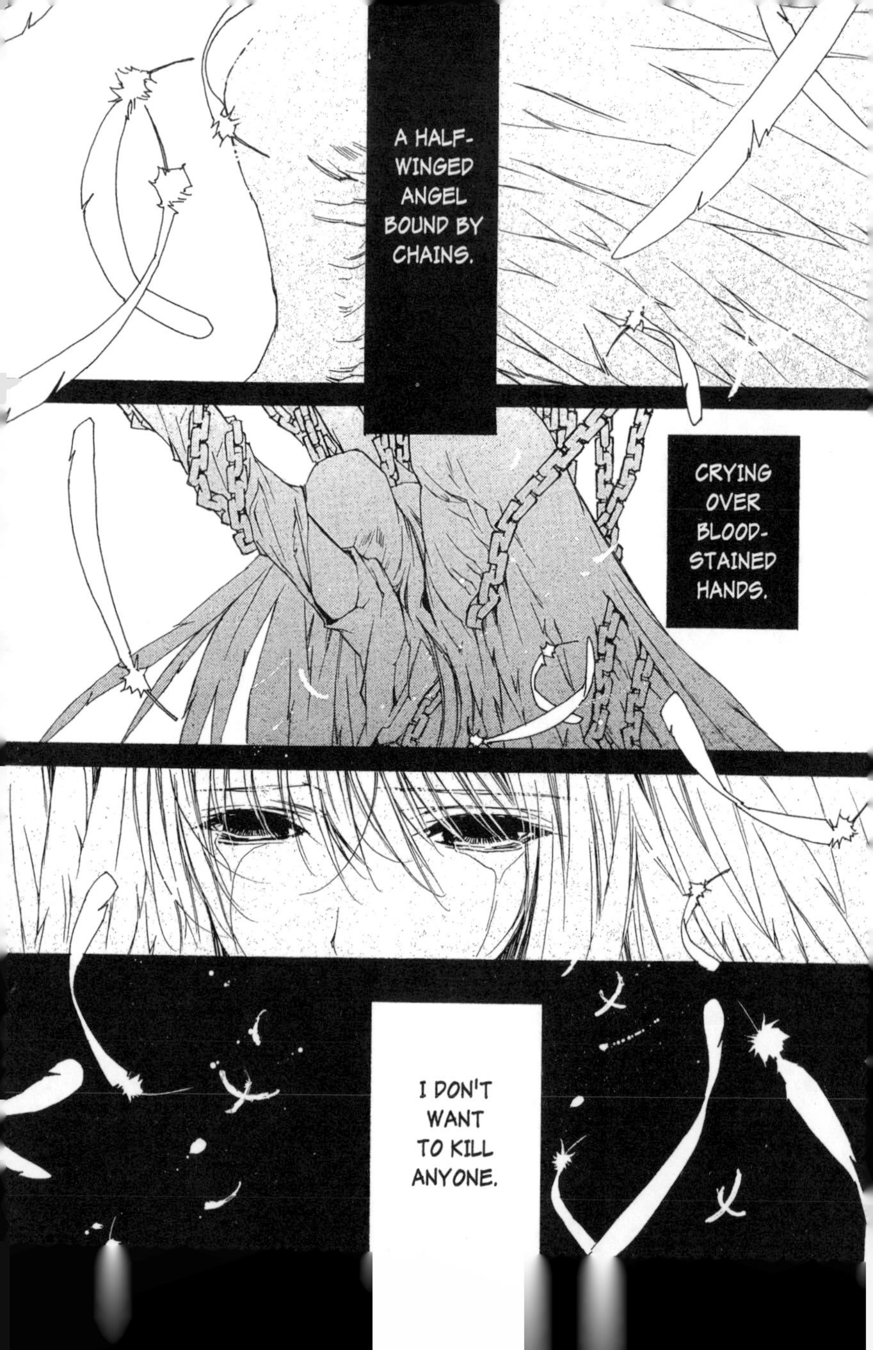
A HALF-WINGED ANGEL BOUND BY CHAINS.
CRYING OVER BLOOD-STAINED HANDS.
I DON'T WANT TO KILL ANYONE.

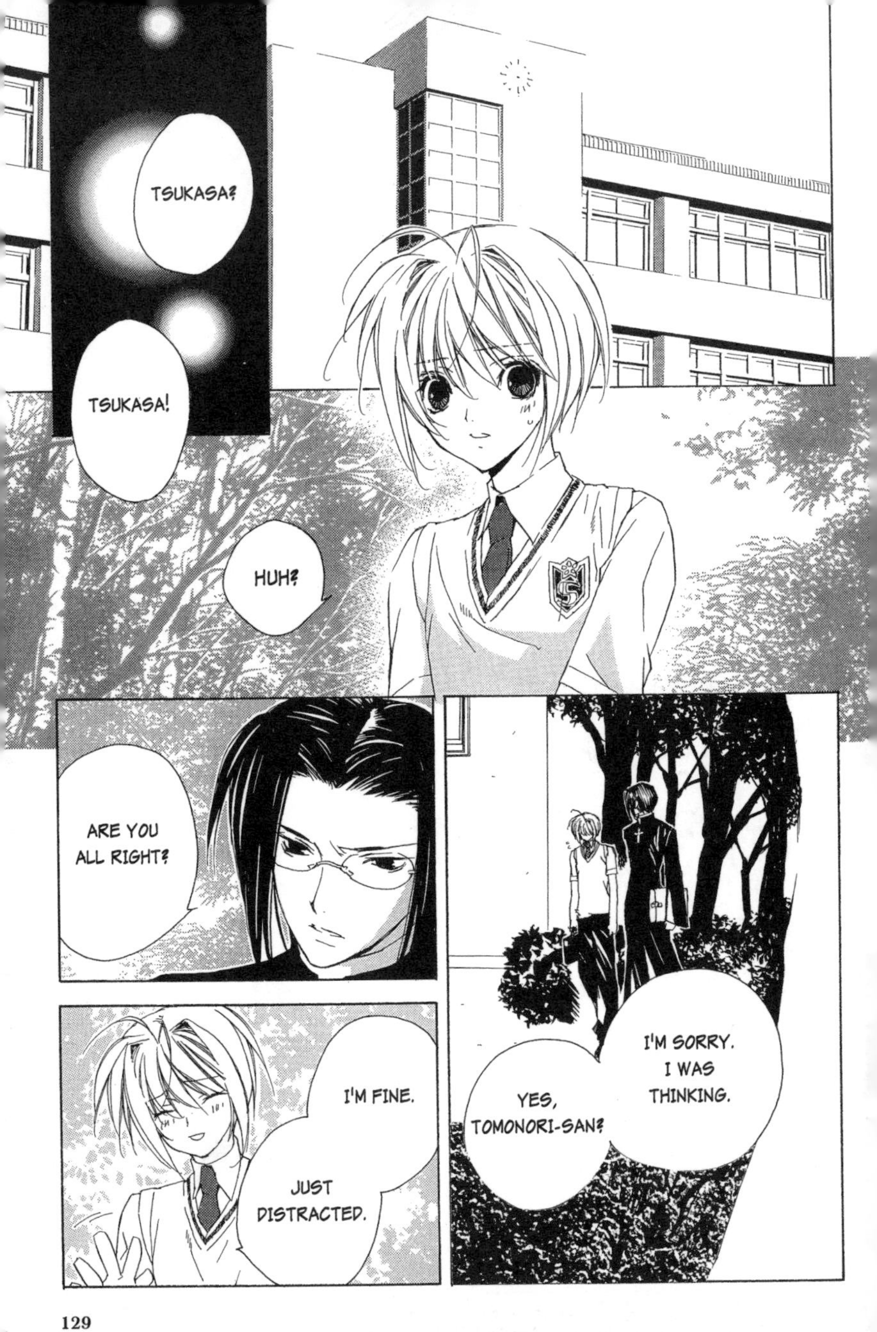
TSUKASA?
TSUKASA!
HUH?
I'M SORRY. I WAS THINKING.
YES, TOMONORI-SAN?
ARE YOU ALL RIGHT?
I'M FINE.
JUST DISTRACTED.

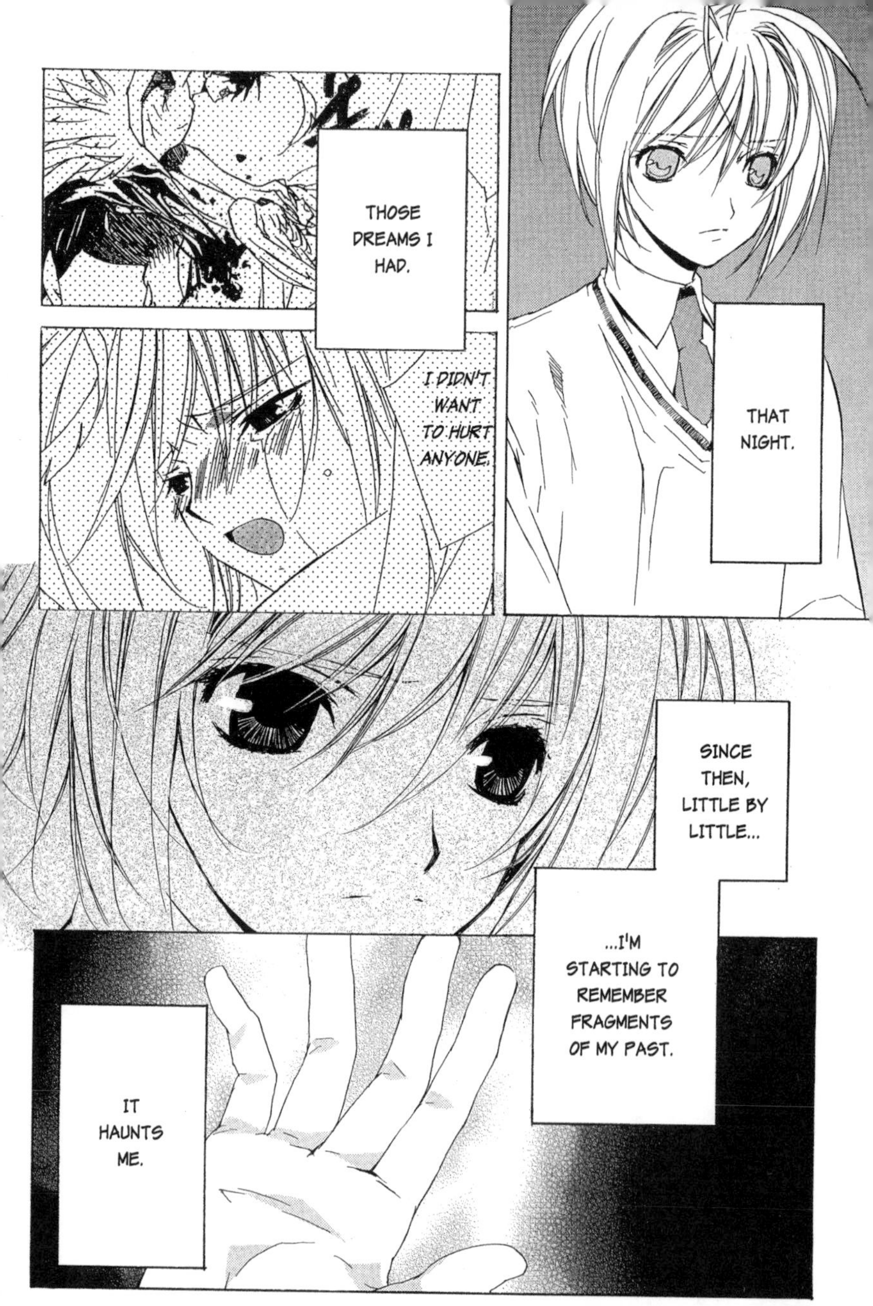
THAT NIGHT.
THOSE DREAMS I HAD.
I DIDN'T WANT TO HURT ANYONE.
SINCE THEN, LITTLE BY LITTLE...
...I'M STARTING TO REMEMBER FRAGMENTS OF MY PAST.
IT HAUNTS ME.

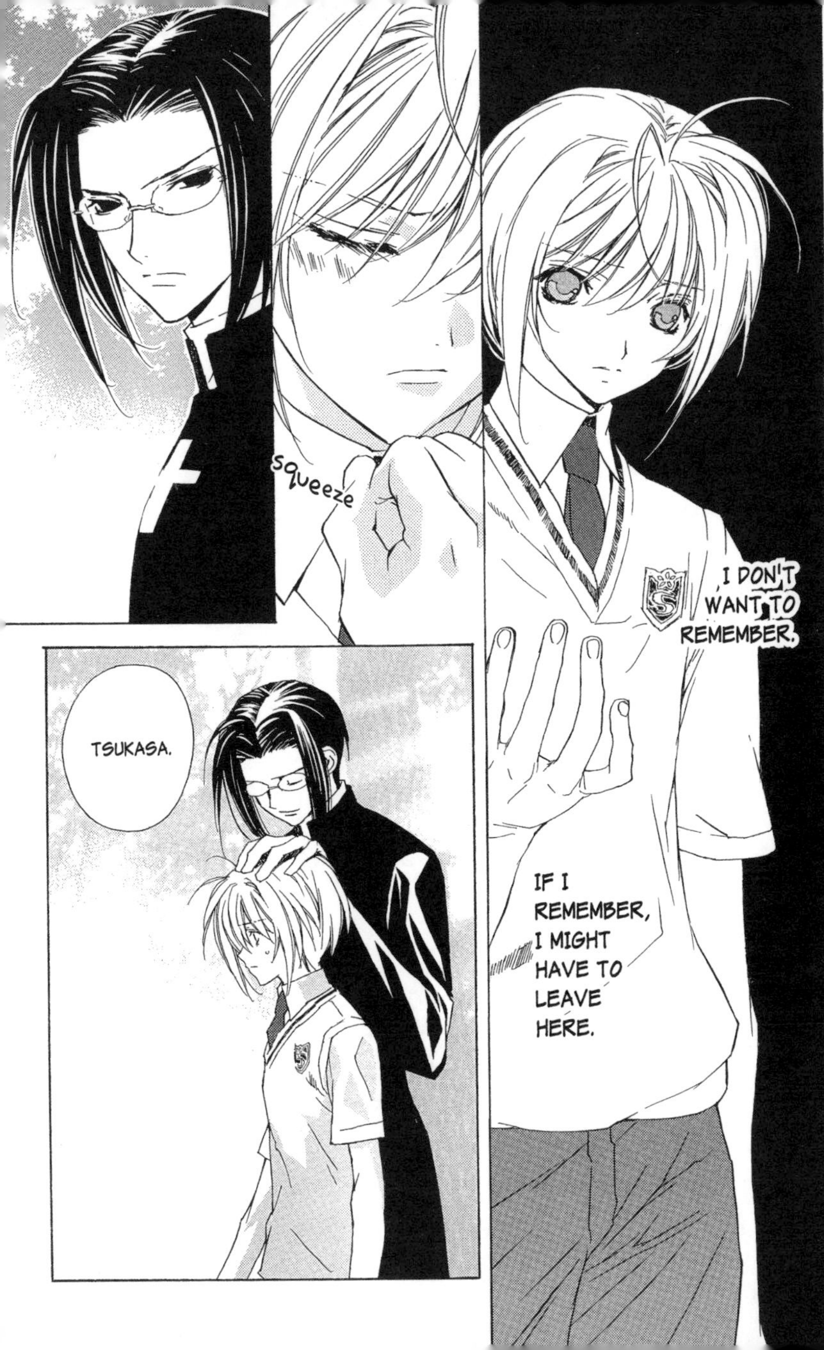
I DON'T WANT TO REMEMBER.
IF I REMEMBER, I MIGHT HAVE TO LEAVE HERE.
squeeze
TSUKASA.

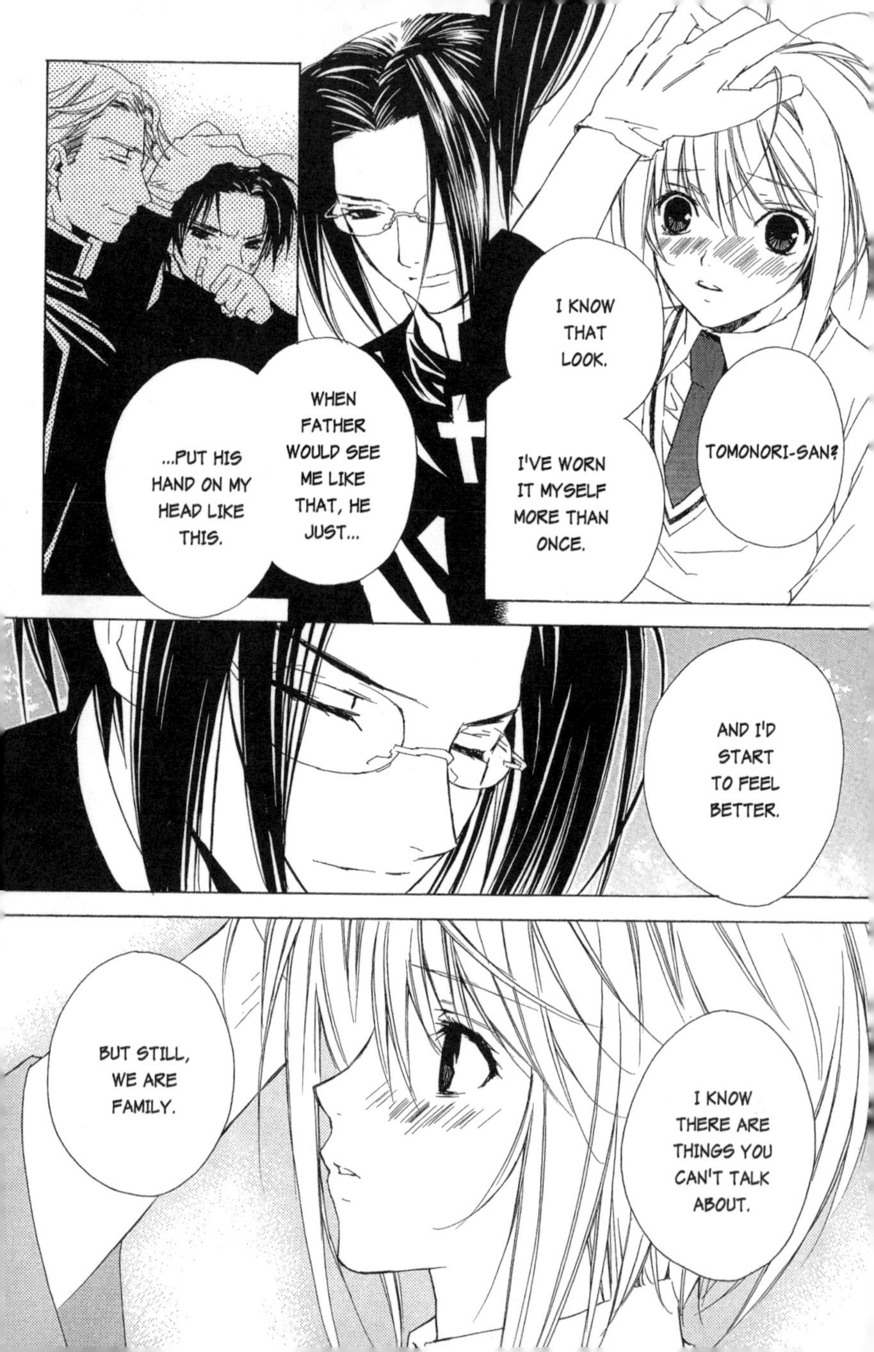
TOMONORI-SAN?
I KNOW THAT LOOK.
I'VE WORN IT MYSELF MORE THAN ONCE.
WHEN FATHER WOULD SEE ME LIKE THAT, HE JUST...
...PUT HIS HAND ON MY HEAD LIKE THIS.
AND I'D START TO FEEL BETTER.
I KNOW THERE ARE THINGS YOU CAN'T TALK ABOUT.
BUT STILL, WE ARE FAMILY.

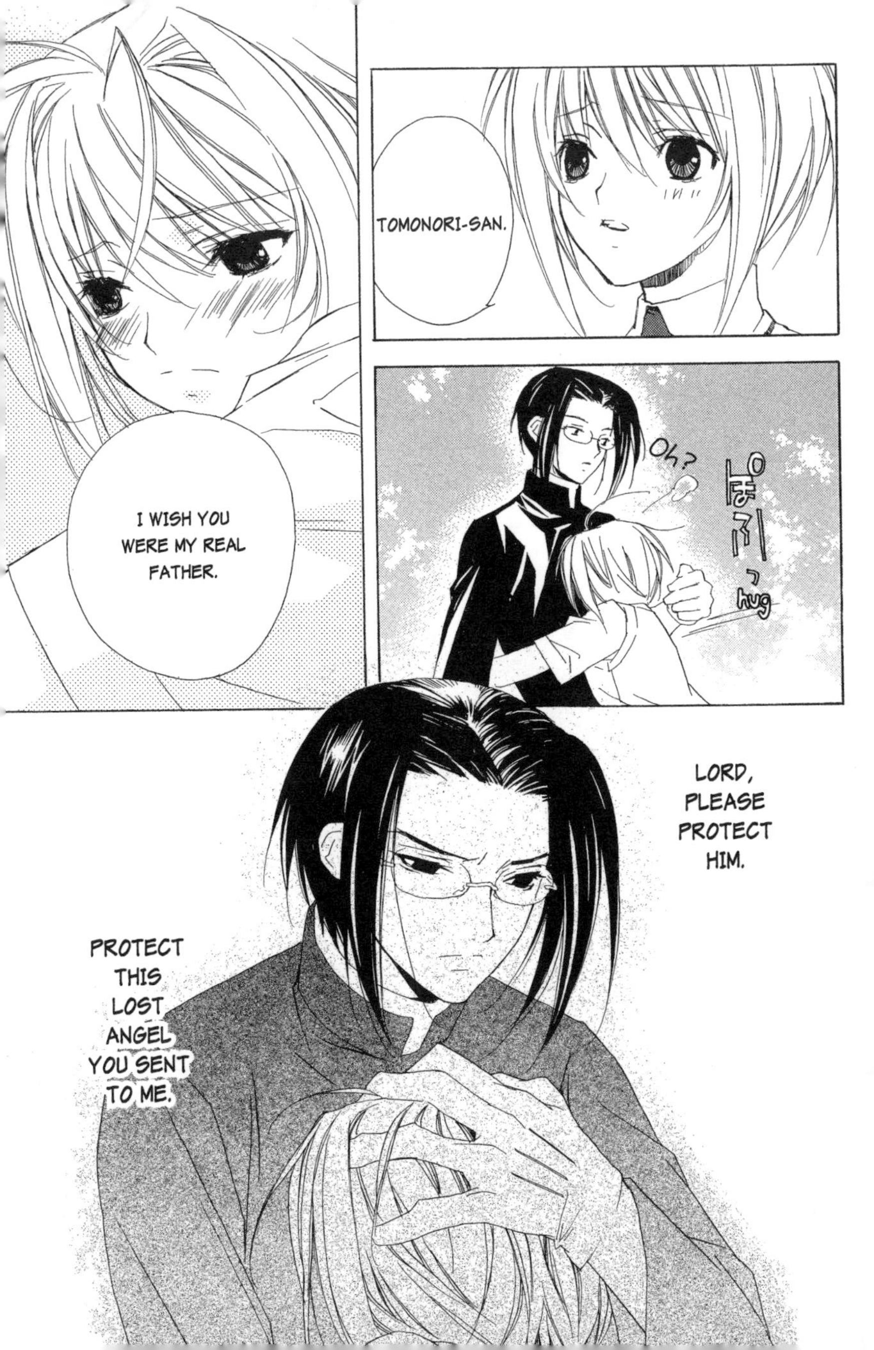
TOMONORI-SAN.
Oh?
hug
I WISH YOU WERE MY REAL FATHER.
LORD, PLEASE PROTECT HIM.
PROTECT THIS LOST ANGEL YOU SENT TO ME.

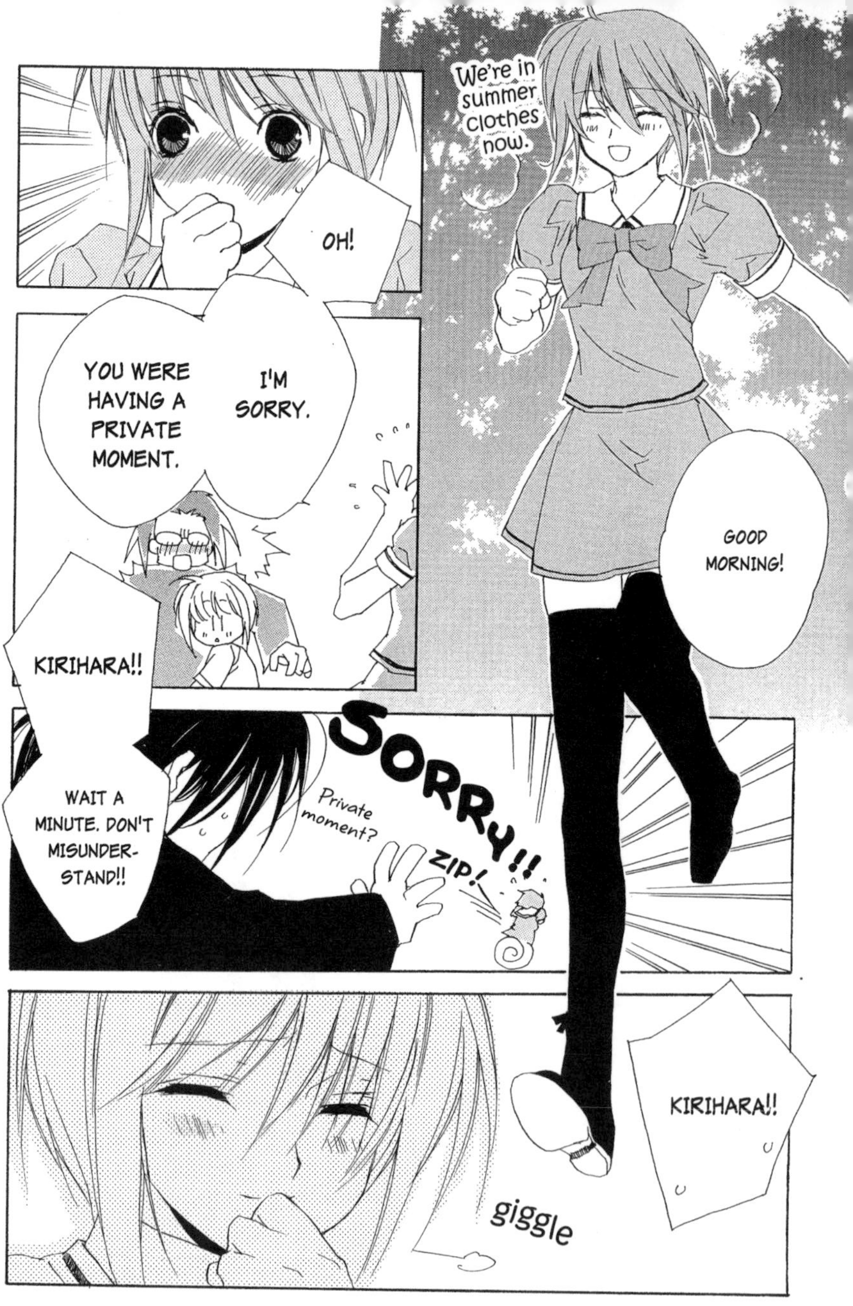
We're in summer clothes now.
GOOD MORNING!
OH!
I'M SORRY.
YOU WERE HAVING A PRIVATE MOMENT.
SORRY!!
ZIP!
Private moment?
KIRIHARA!!
WAIT A MINUTE. DON'T MISUNDER-STAND!!
KIRIHARA!!
giggle

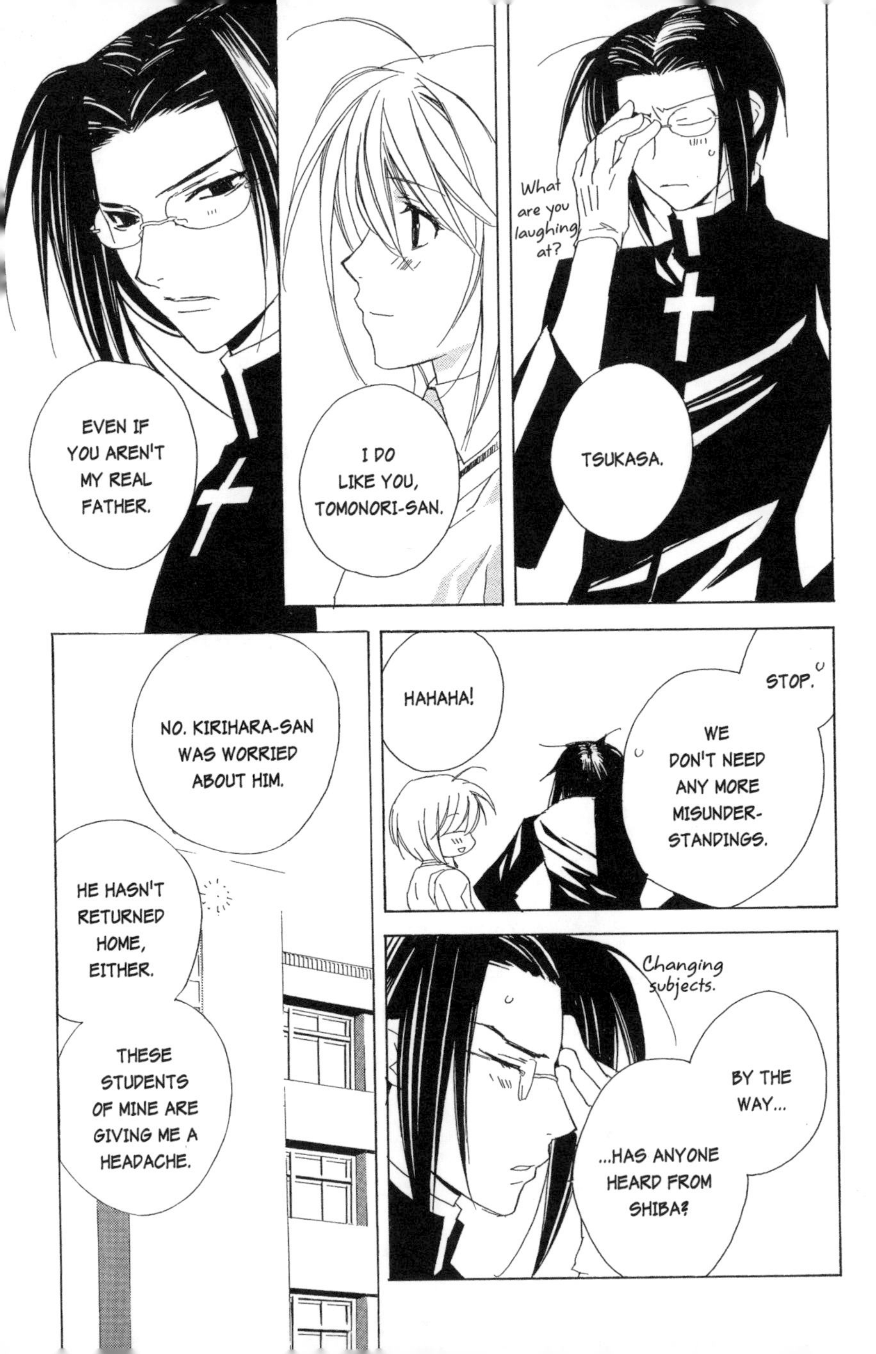
What are you laughing at?
TSUKASA.
I DO LIKE YOU, TOMONORI-SAN.
EVEN IF YOU AREN'T MY REAL FATHER.
STOP.
WE DON'T NEED ANY MORE MISUNDER-STANDINGS.
HAHAHA!
Changing subjects.
BY THE WAY...
...HAS ANYONE HEARD FROM SHIBA?
NO. KIRIHARA-SAN WAS WORRIED ABOUT HIM.
HE HASN'T RETURNED HOME, EITHER.
THESE STUDENTS OF MINE ARE GIVING ME A HEADACHE.

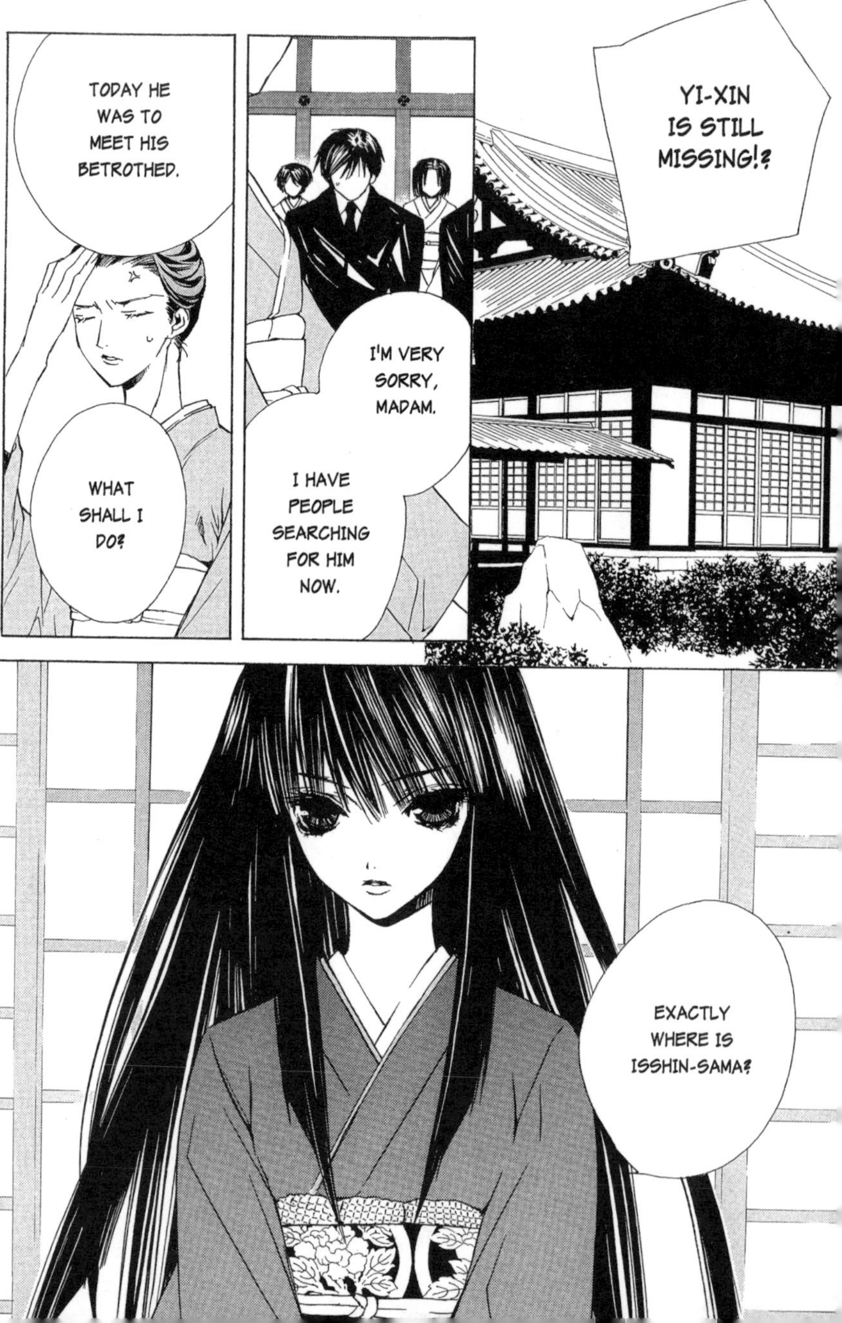
YI-XIN IS STILL MISSING!?
I'M VERY SORRY, MADAM.
I HAVE PEOPLE SEARCHING FOR HIM NOW.
TODAY HE WAS TO MEET HIS BETROTHED.
WHAT SHALL I DO?
EXACTLY WHERE IS ISSHIN-SAMA?

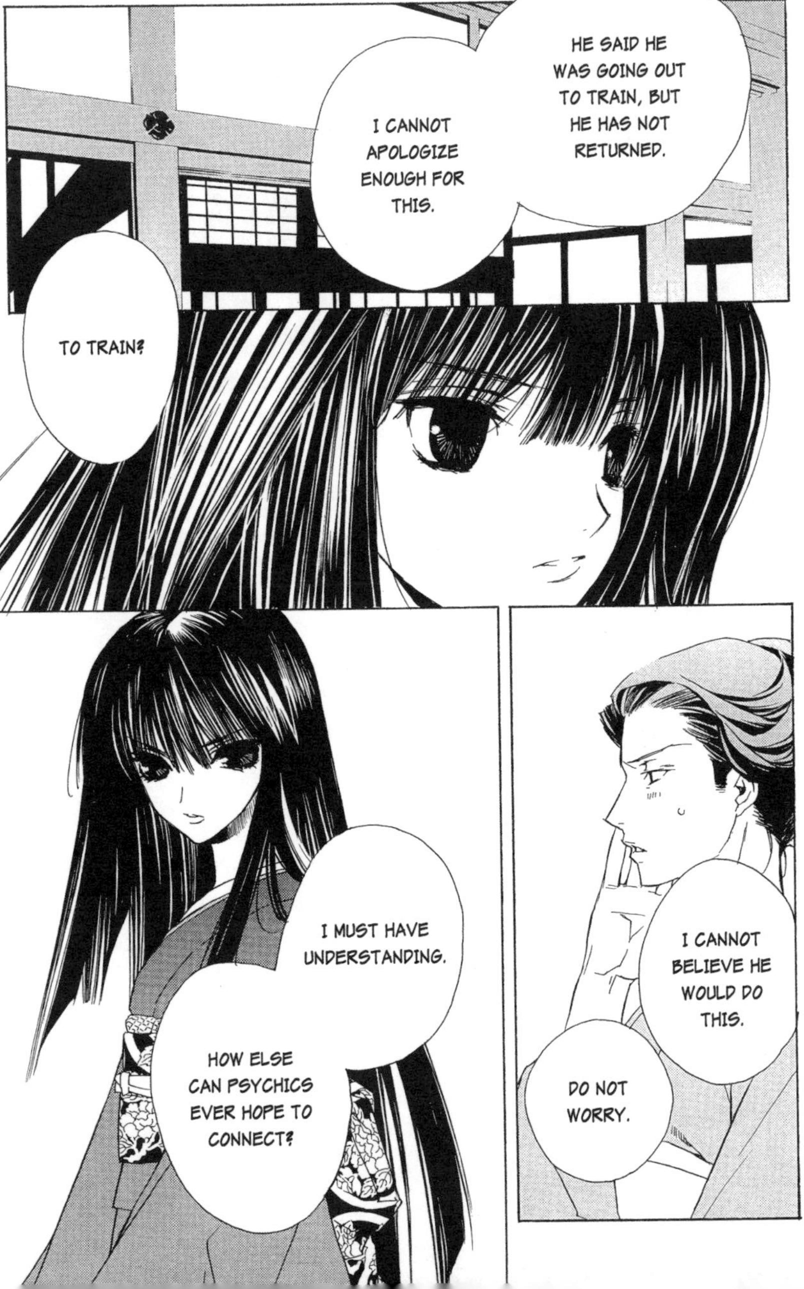
HE SAID HE WAS GOING OUT TO TRAIN, BUT HE HAS NOT RETURNED.
I CANNOT APOLOGIZE ENOUGH FOR THIS.
TO TRAIN?
I CANNOT BELIEVE HE WOULD DO THIS.
DO NOT WORRY.
I MUST HAVE UNDERSTANDING.
HOW ELSE CAN PSYCHICS EVER HOPE TO CONNECT?

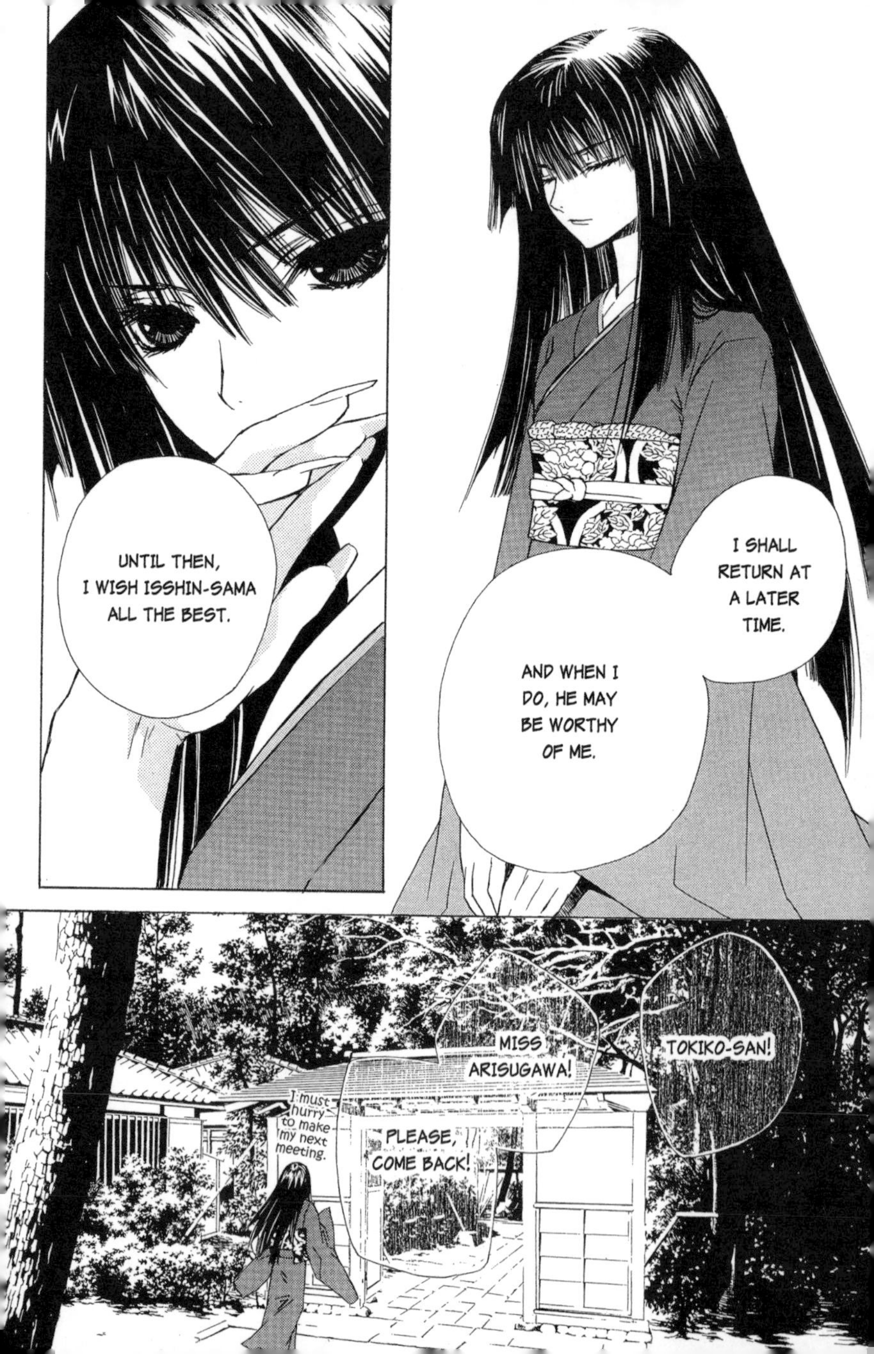
I SHALL RETURN AT A LATER TIME.
AND WHEN I DO, HE MAY BE WORTHY OF ME.
UNTIL THEN, I WISH ISSHIN-SAMA ALL THE BEST.
TOKIKO-SAN!
MISS ARISUGAWA!
PLEASE, COME BACK!
I must hurry to make my next meeting.

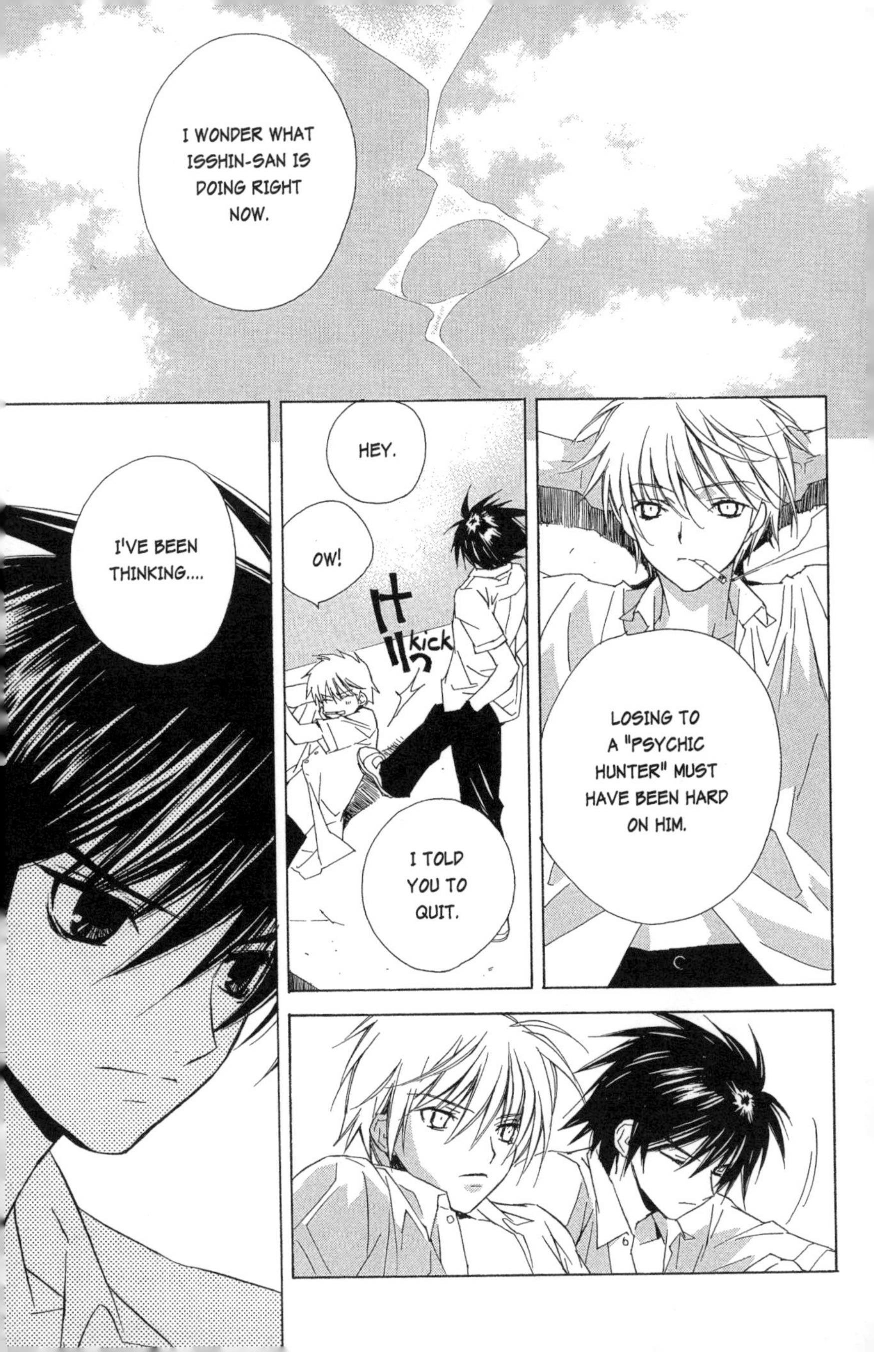
I WONDER WHAT ISSHIN-SAN IS DOING RIGHT NOW.
LOSING TO A "PSYCHIC HUNTER" MUST HAVE BEEN HARD ON HIM.
HEY.
OW!
kick
I TOLD YOU TO QUIT.
I'VE BEEN THINKING....

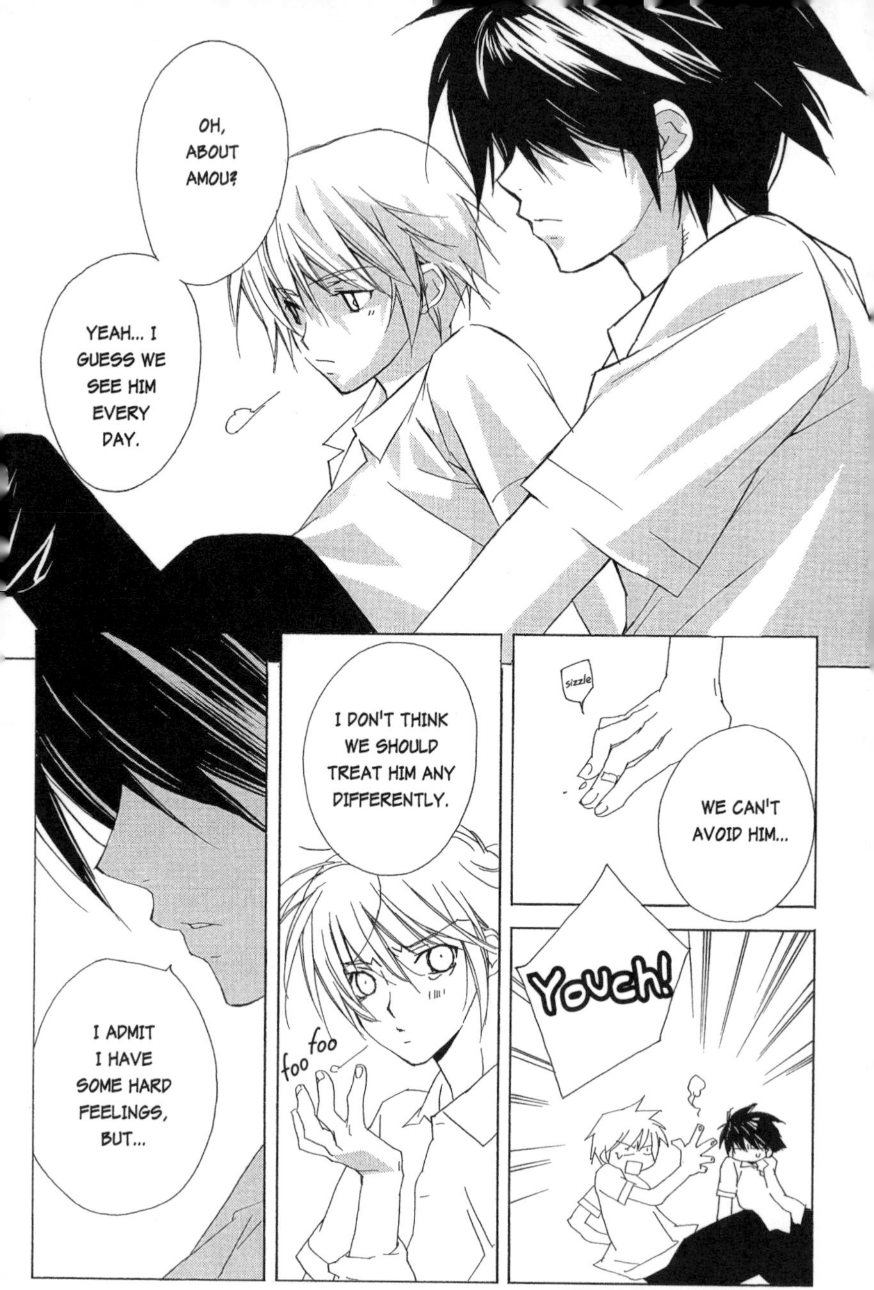
OH, ABOUT AMOU?
YEAH... I GUESS WE SEE HIM EVERY DAY.
sizzle
WE CAN'T AVOID HIM...
Youch!
I DON'T THINK WE SHOULD TREAT HIM ANY DIFFERENTLY.
foo foo
I ADMIT I HAVE SOME HARD FEELINGS, BUT...

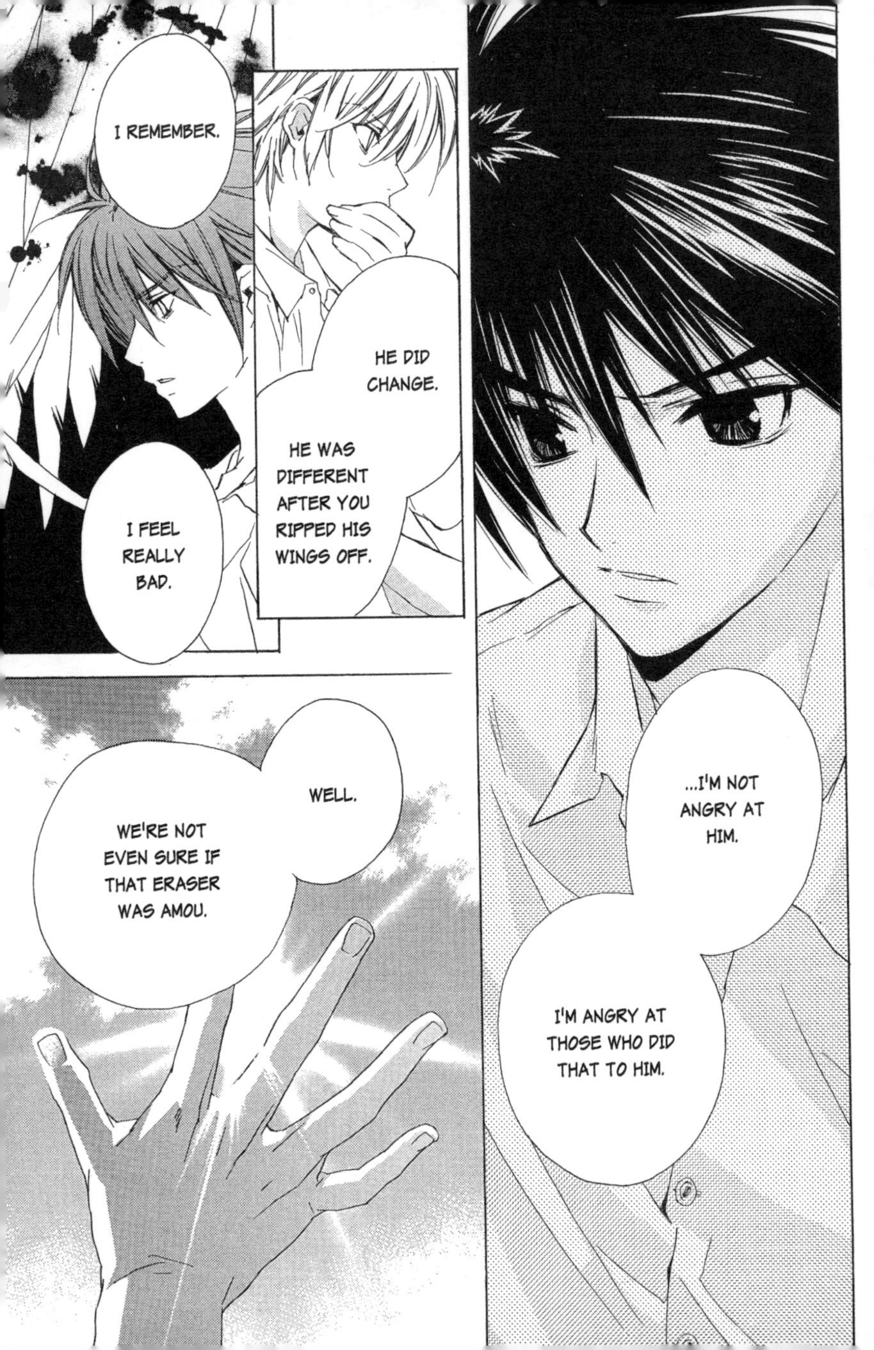
...I'M NOT ANGRY AT HIM.
I'M ANGRY AT THOSE WHO DID THAT TO HIM.
HE DID CHANGE.
HE WAS DIFFERENT AFTER YOU RIPPED HIS WINGS OFF.
I REMEMBER.
I FEEL REALLY BAD.
WELL.
WE'RE NOT EVEN SURE IF THAT ERASER WAS AMOU.

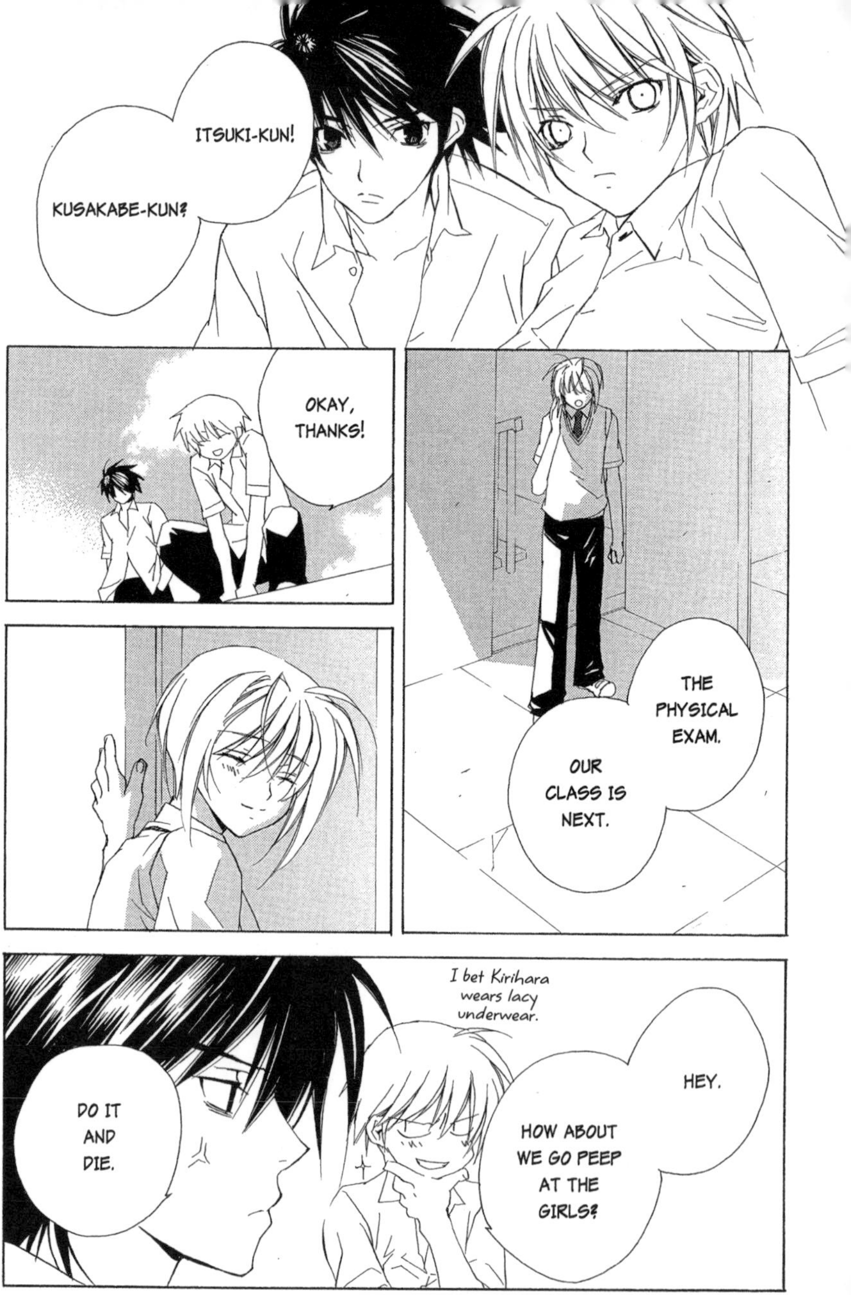
ITSUKI-KUN!
KUSAKABE-KUN?
THE PHYSICAL EXAM.
OUR CLASS IS NEXT.
OKAY, THANKS!
HEY.
HOW ABOUT WE GO PEEP AT THE GIRLS?
I bet Kirihara wears lacy underwear.
DO IT AND DIE.

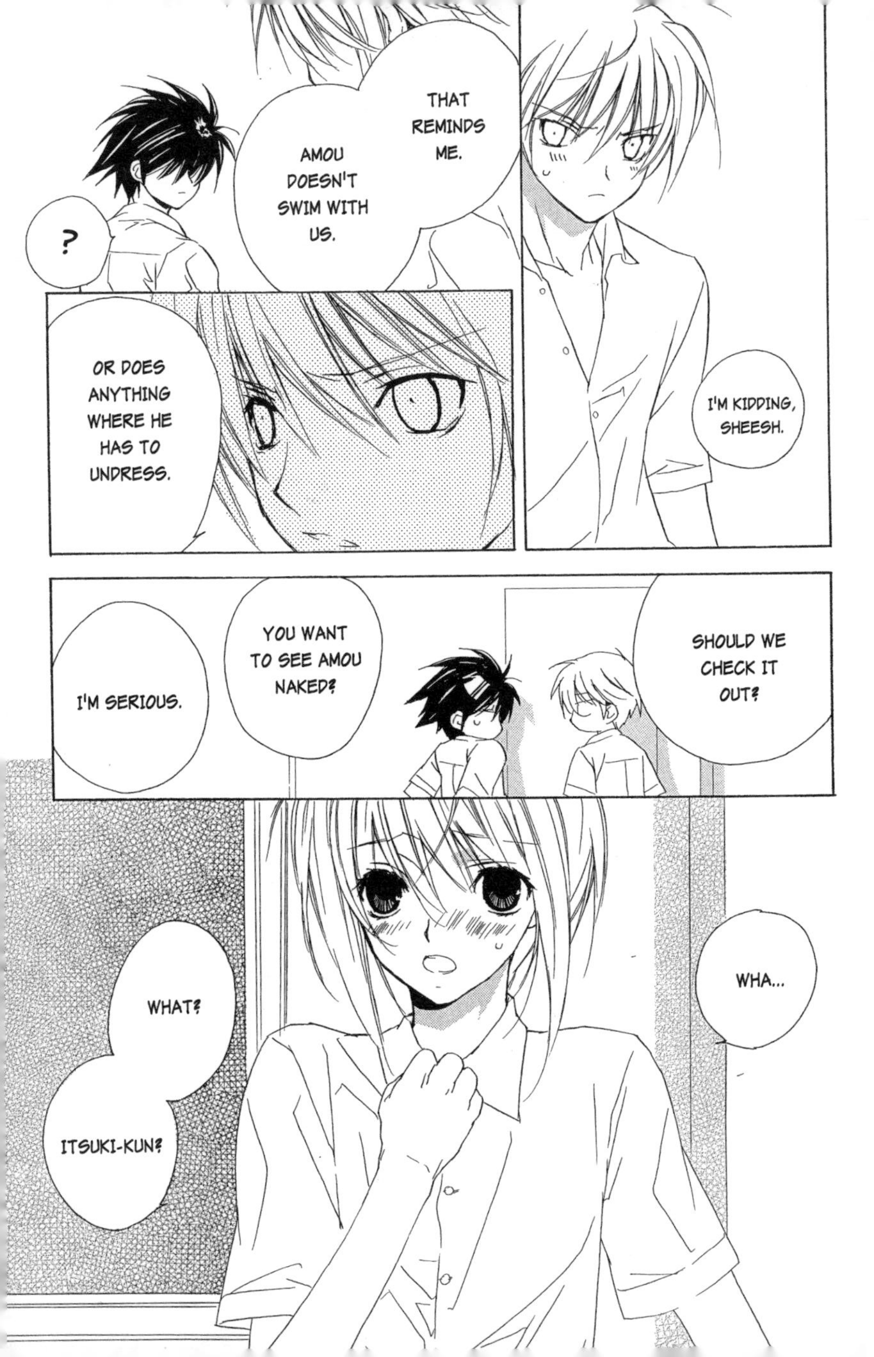
THAT REMINDS ME.
AMOU DOESN'T SWIM WITH US.
?
OR DOES ANYTHING WHERE HE HAS TO UNDRESS.
I'M KIDDING, SHEESH.
SHOULD WE CHECK IT OUT?
YOU WANT TO SEE AMOU NAKED?
I'M SERIOUS.
WHA...
WHAT?
ITSUKI-KUN?

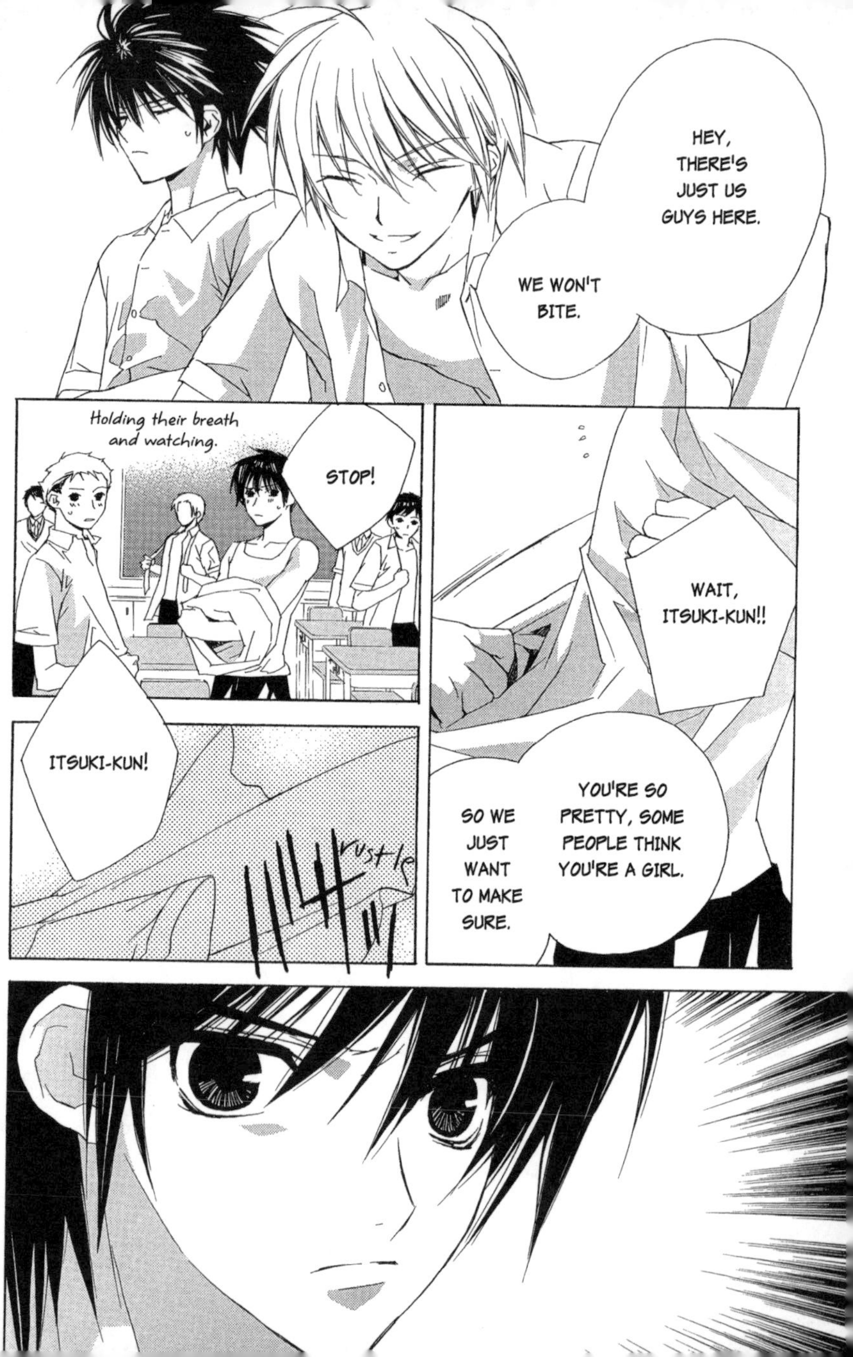
HEY, THERE'S JUST US GUYS HERE.
WE WON'T BITE.
WAIT, ITSUKI-KUN!!
YOU'RE SO PRETTY, SOME PEOPLE THINK YOU'RE A GIRL.
SO WE JUST WANT TO MAKE SURE.
Holding their breath and watching.
STOP!
ITSUKI-KUN!
rustle

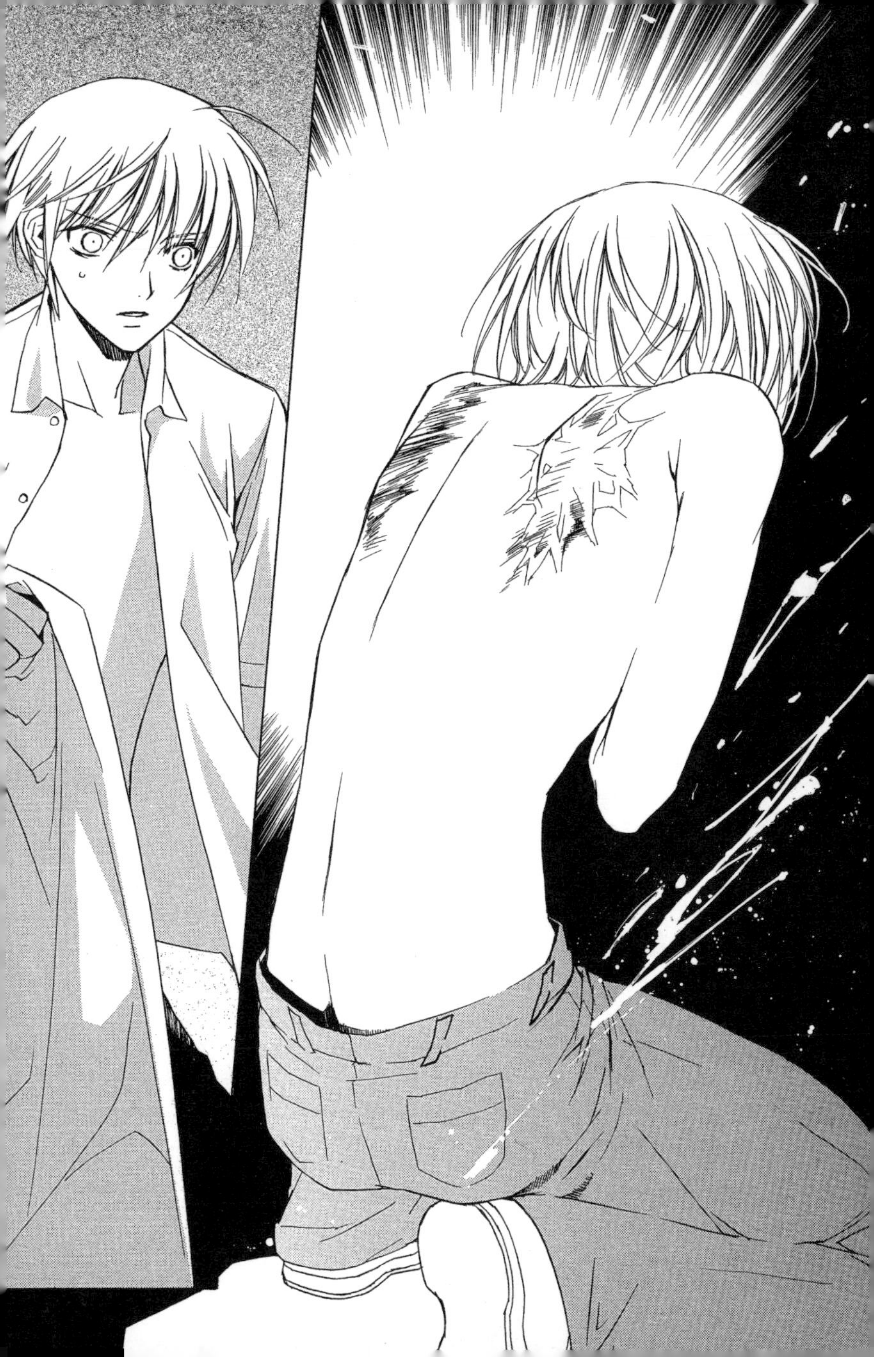

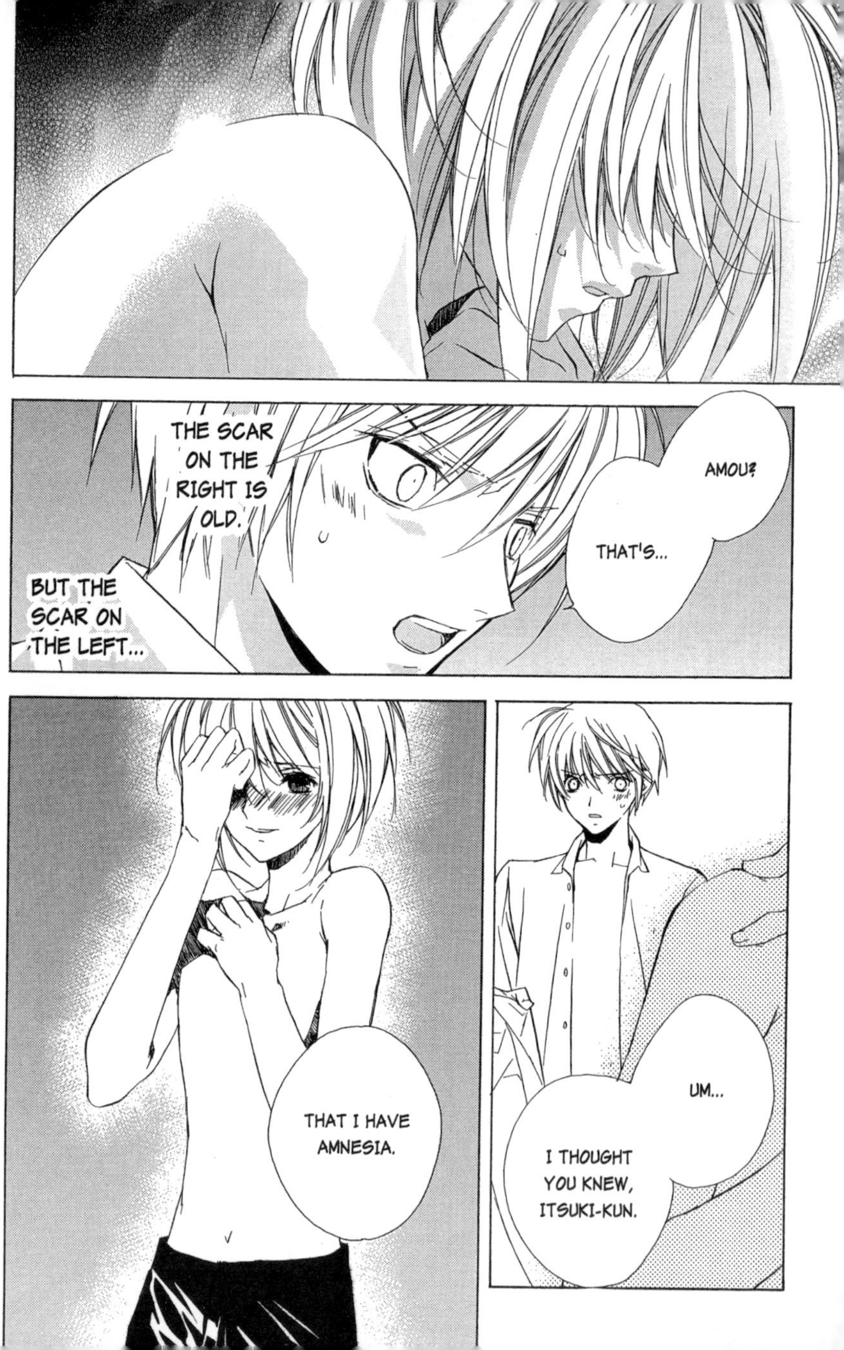
AMOU?
THAT'S...
THE SCAR ON THE RIGHT IS OLD.
BUT THE SCAR ON THE LEFT...
UM...
I THOUGHT YOU KNEW, ITSUKI-KUN.
THAT I HAVE AMNESIA.

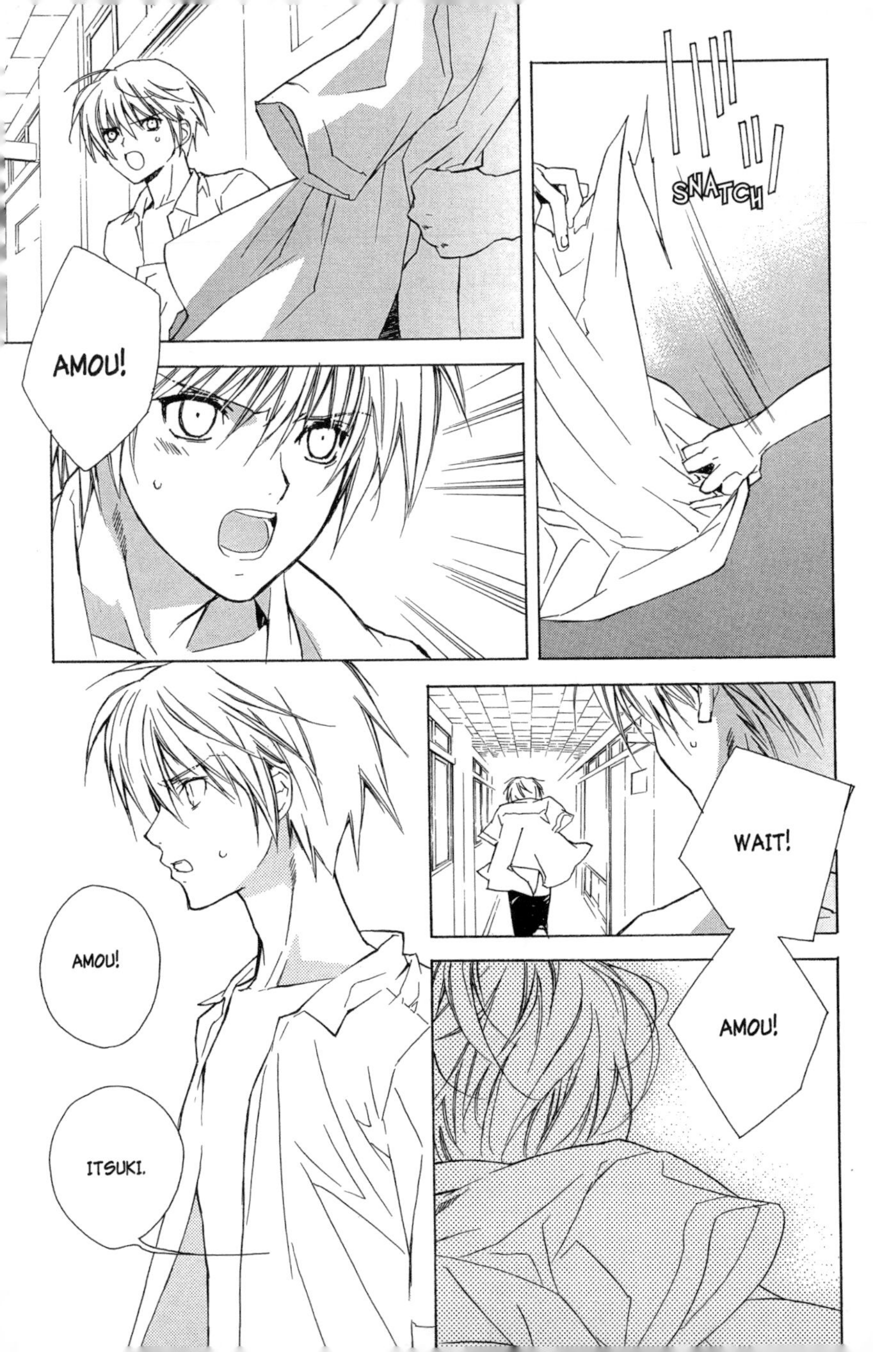
SNATCH
AMOU!
WAIT!
AMOU!
AMOU!
ITSUKI.

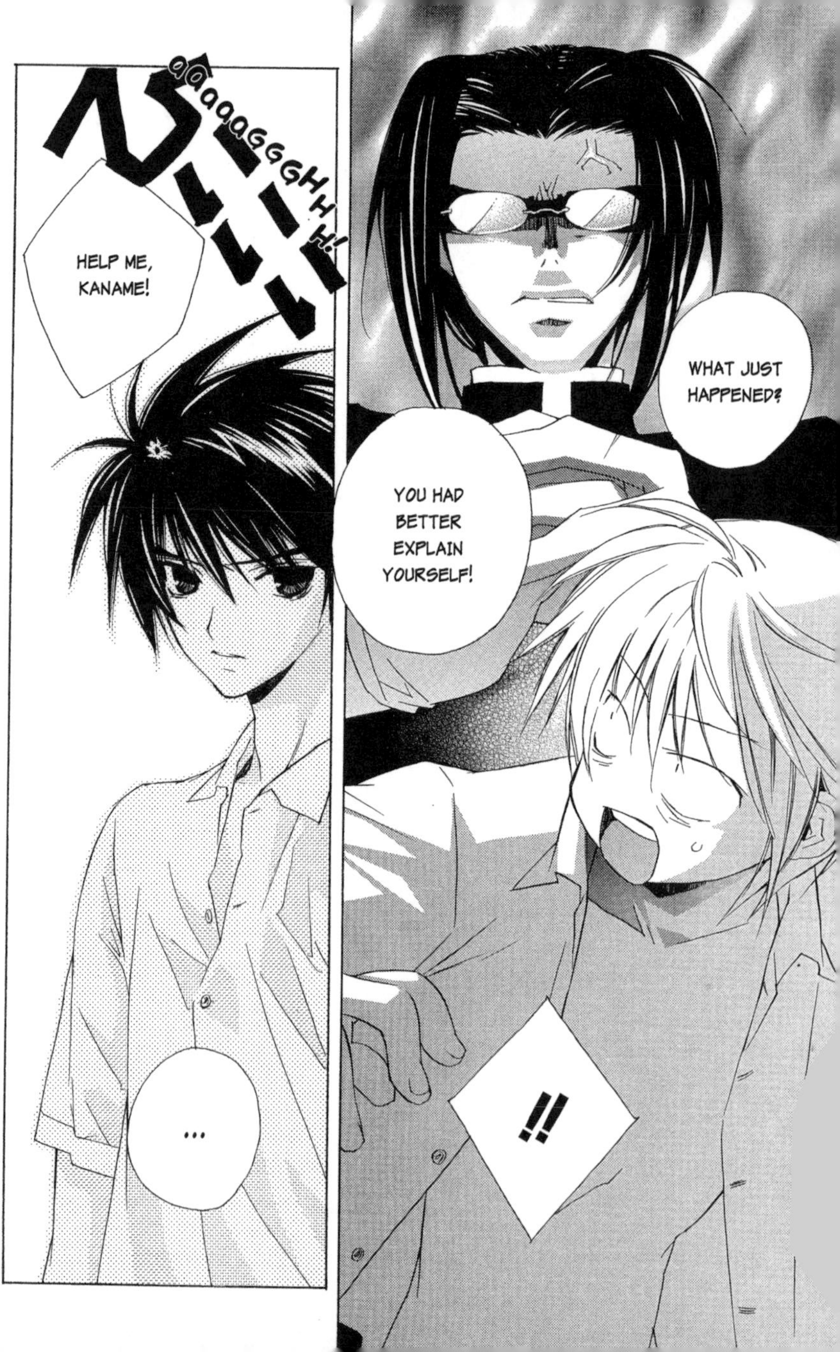

WHAT JUST HAPPENED?
YOU HAD BETTER EXPLAIN YOURSELF!
!!
aaaaaGGGHHH!
HELP ME, KANAME!
...

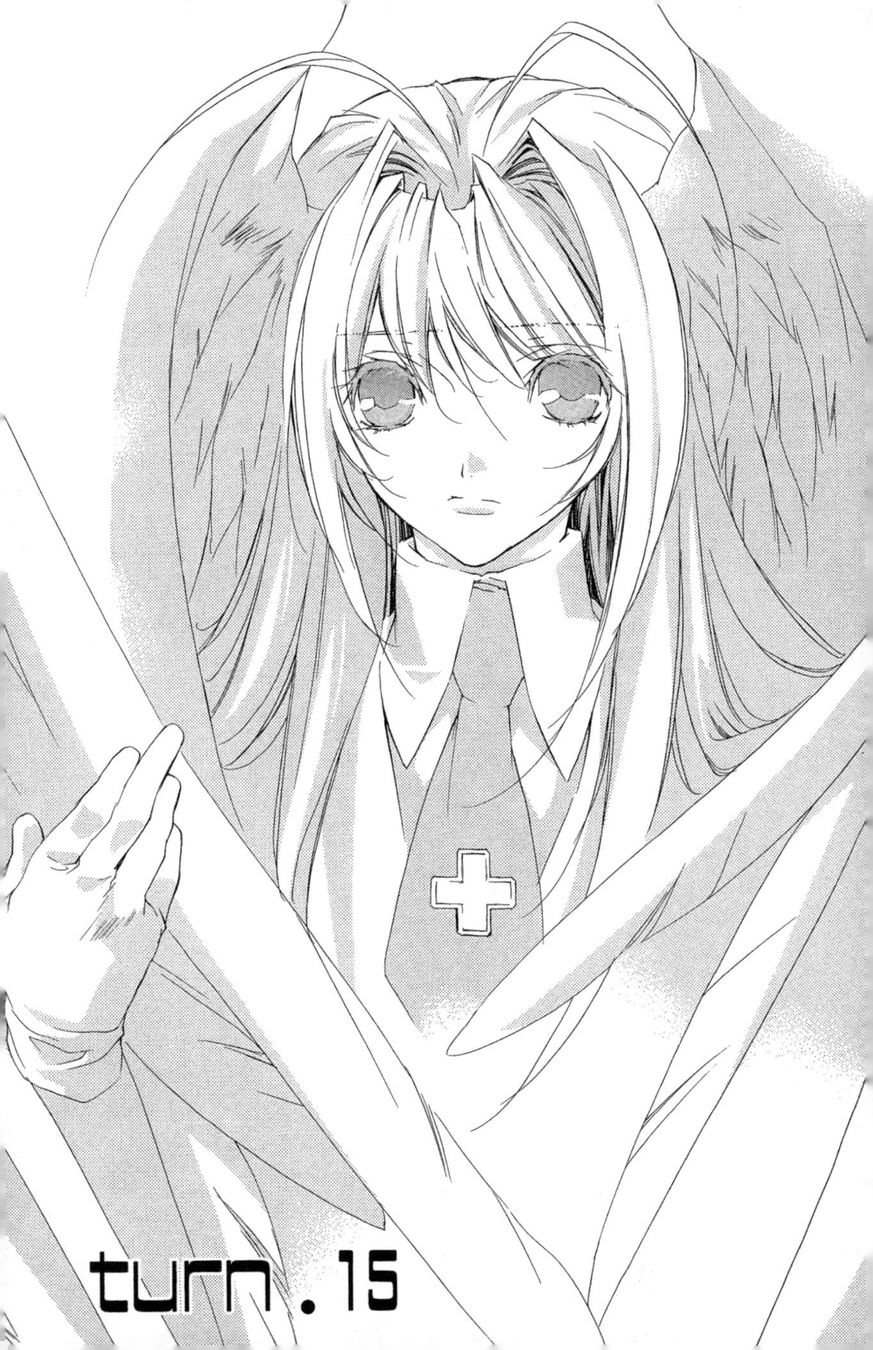
turn.15

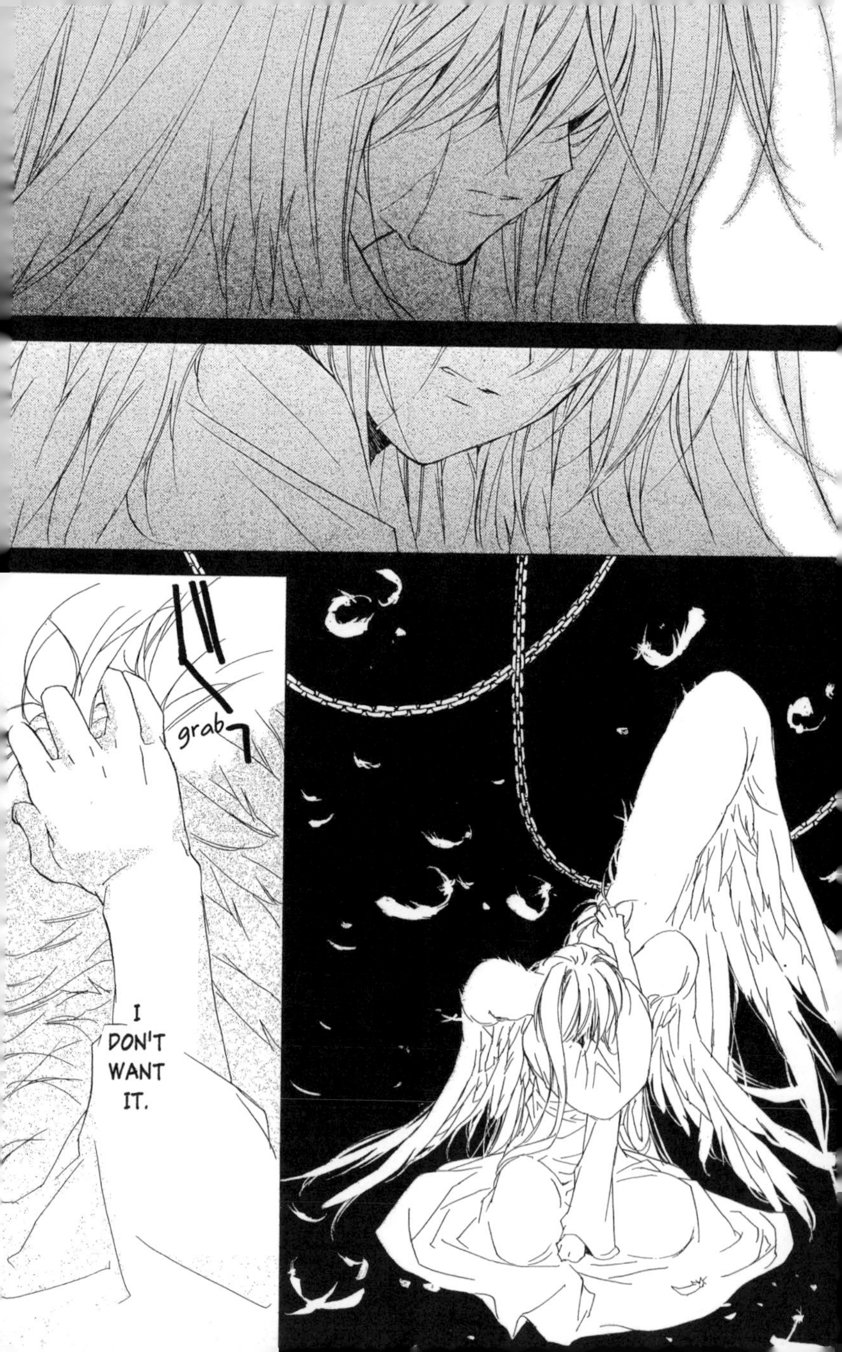
grab
I DON'T WANT IT.

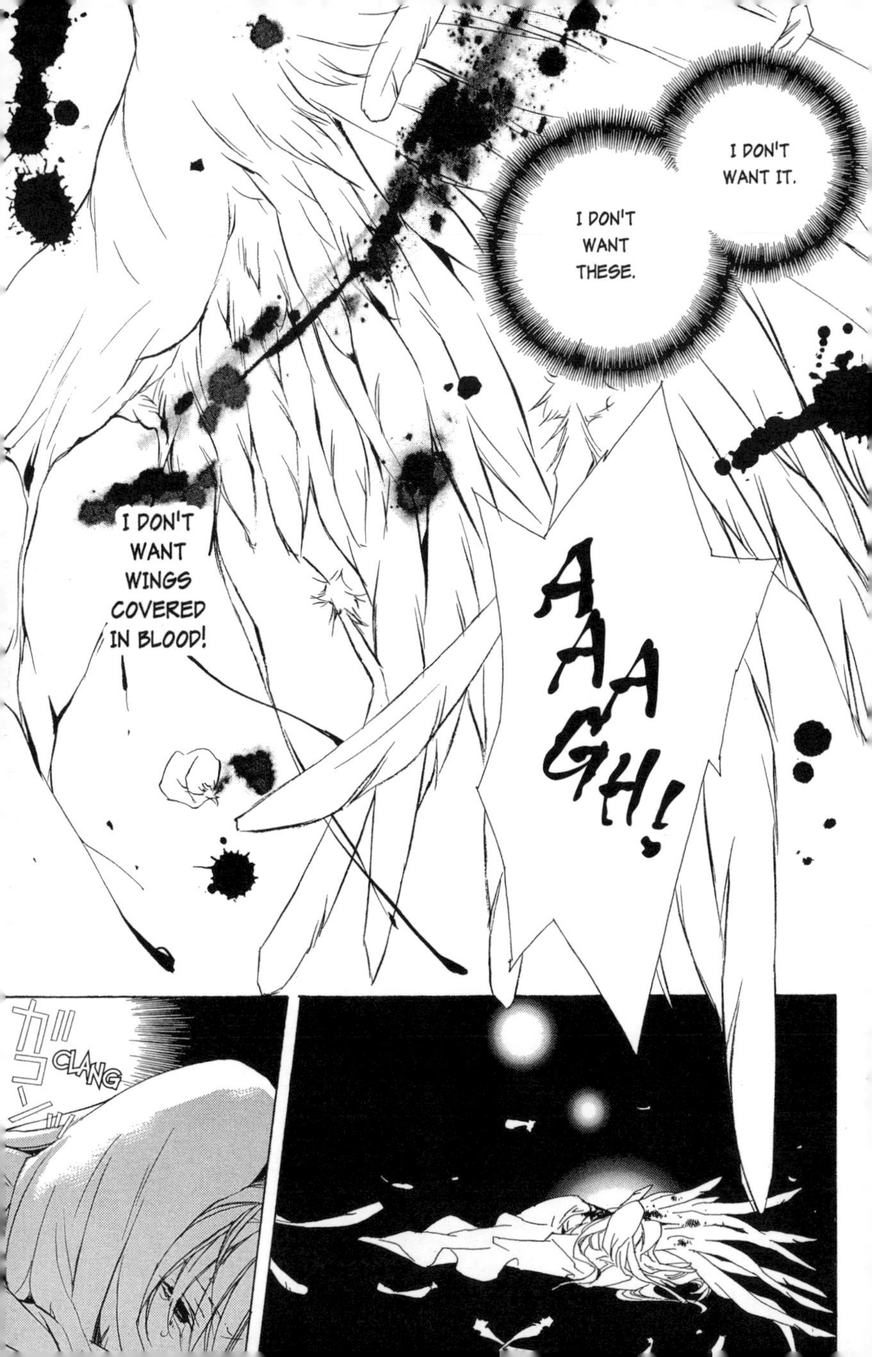
I DON'T WANT IT.
I DON'T WANT THESE.
I DON'T WANT WINGS COVERED IN BLOOD!
AAAGH!
CLANG

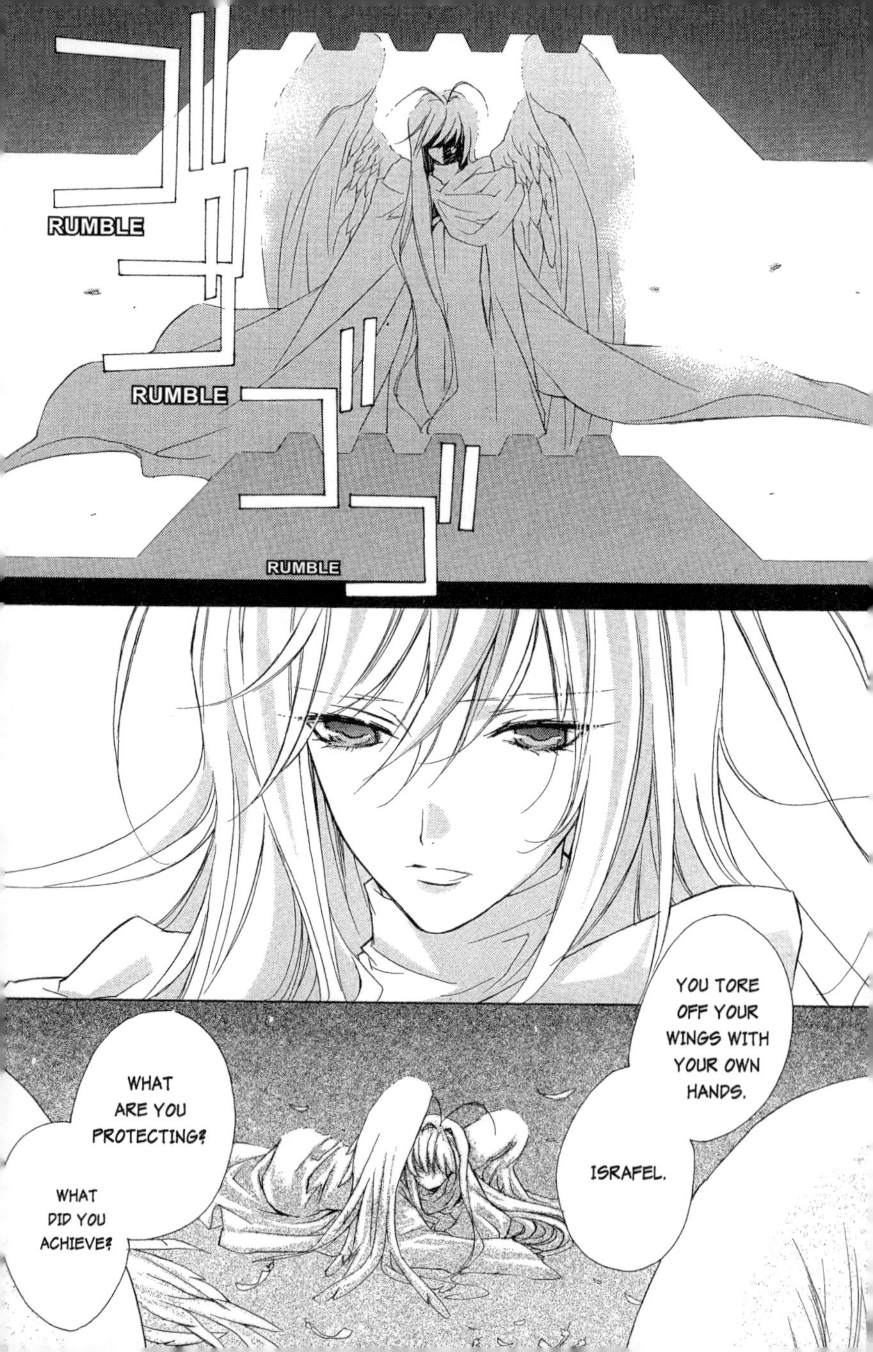
RUMBLE
RUMBLE
RUMBLE
YOU TORE OFF YOUR WINGS WITH YOUR OWN HANDS.
ISRAFEL.
WHAT ARE YOU PROTECTING?
WHAT DID YOU ACHIEVE?

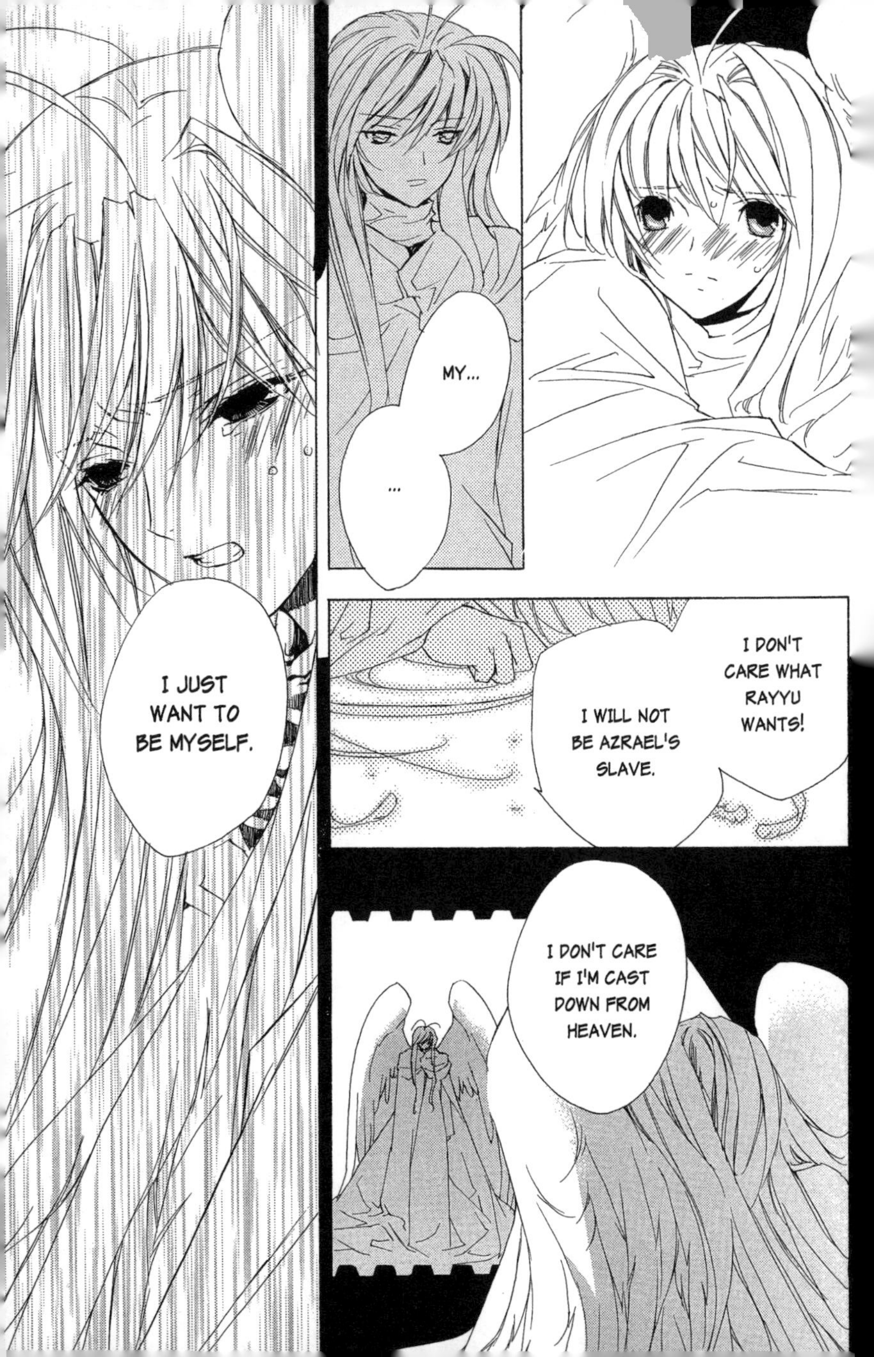
MY...
...
I DON'T CARE WHAT RAYYU WANTS!
I WILL NOT BE AZRAEL'S SLAVE.
I DON'T CARE IF I'M CAST DOWN FROM HEAVEN.
I JUST WANT TO BE MYSELF.

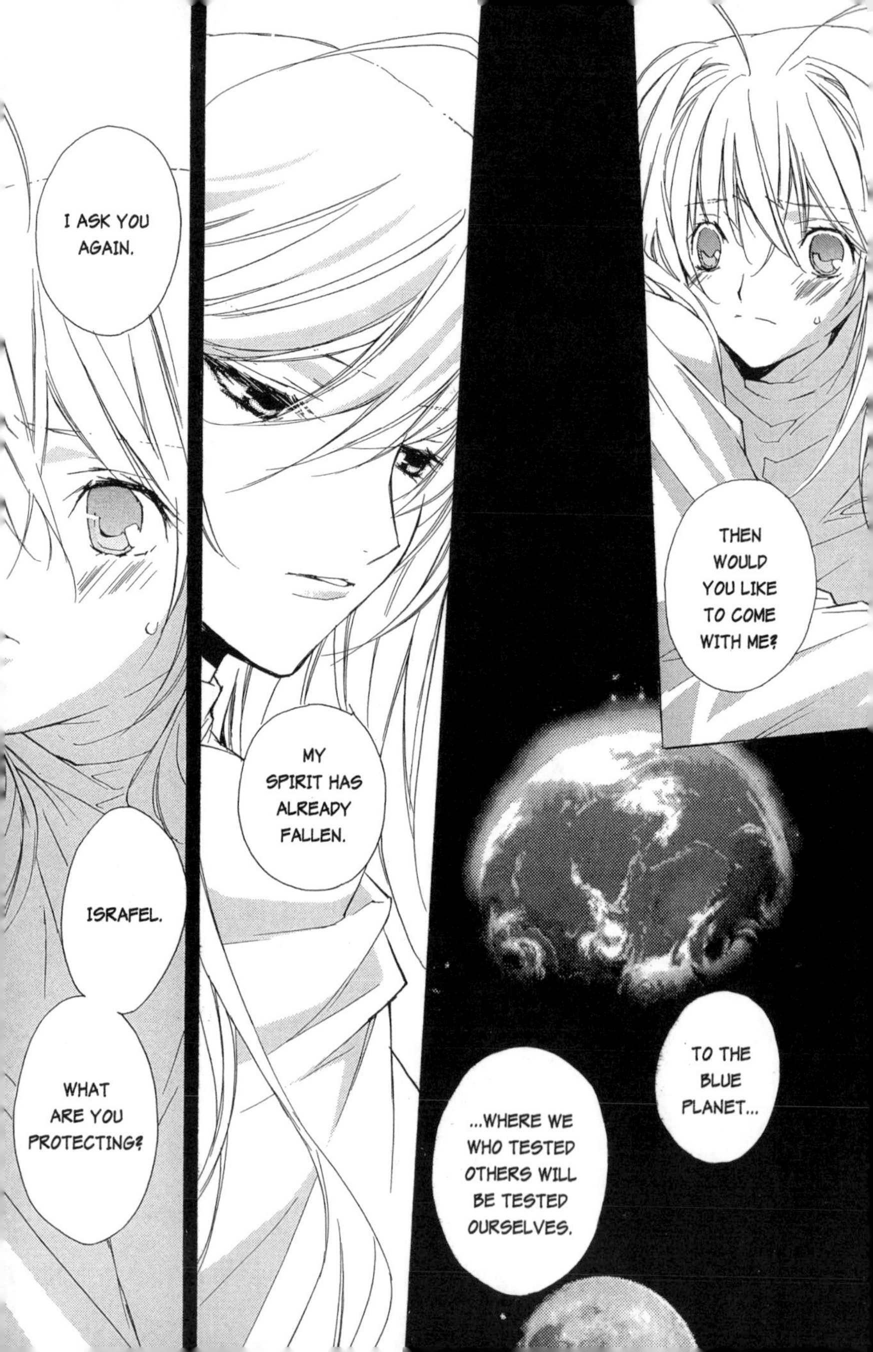
THEN WOULD YOU LIKE TO COME WITH ME?
TO THE BLUE PLANET...
...WHERE WE WHO TESTED OTHERS WILL BE TESTED OURSELVES.
MY SPIRIT HAS ALREADY FALLEN.
I ASK YOU AGAIN.
ISRAFEL.
WHAT ARE YOU PROTECTING?

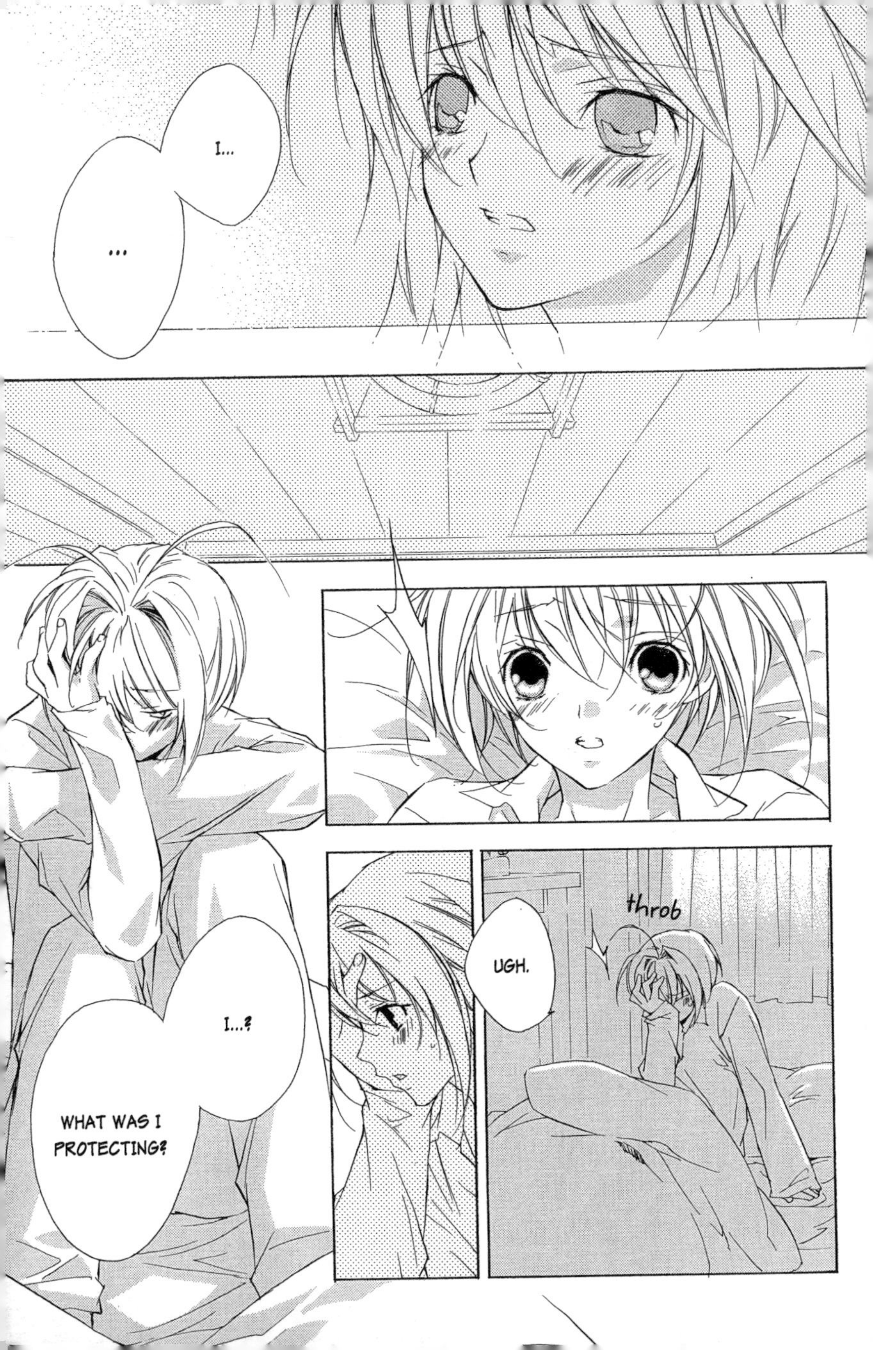
I...
...
UGH.
throb
I...?
WHAT WAS I PROTECTING?

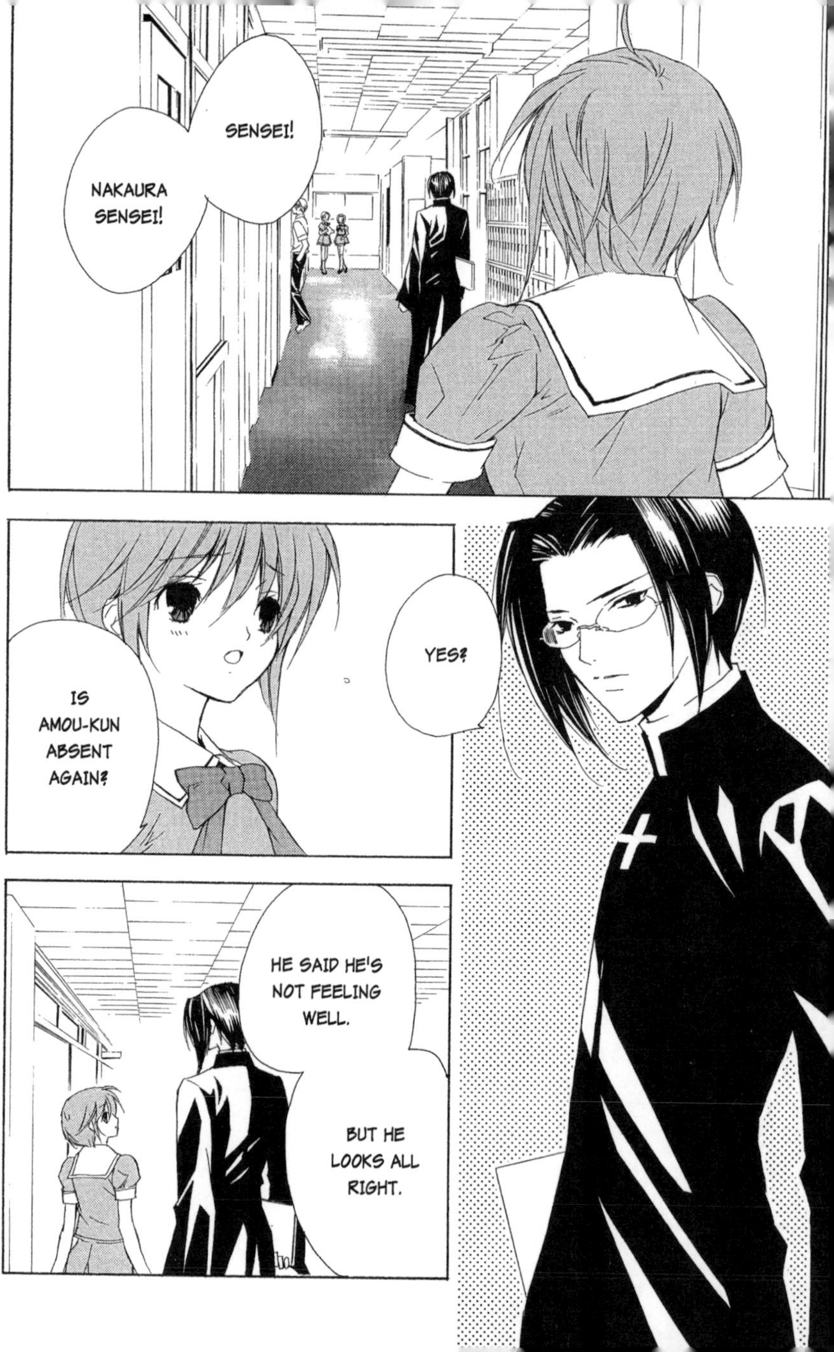
SENSEI!
NAKAURA SENSEI!
YES?
IS AMOU-KUN ABSENT AGAIN?
HE SAID HE'S NOT FEELING WELL.
BUT HE LOOKS ALL RIGHT.

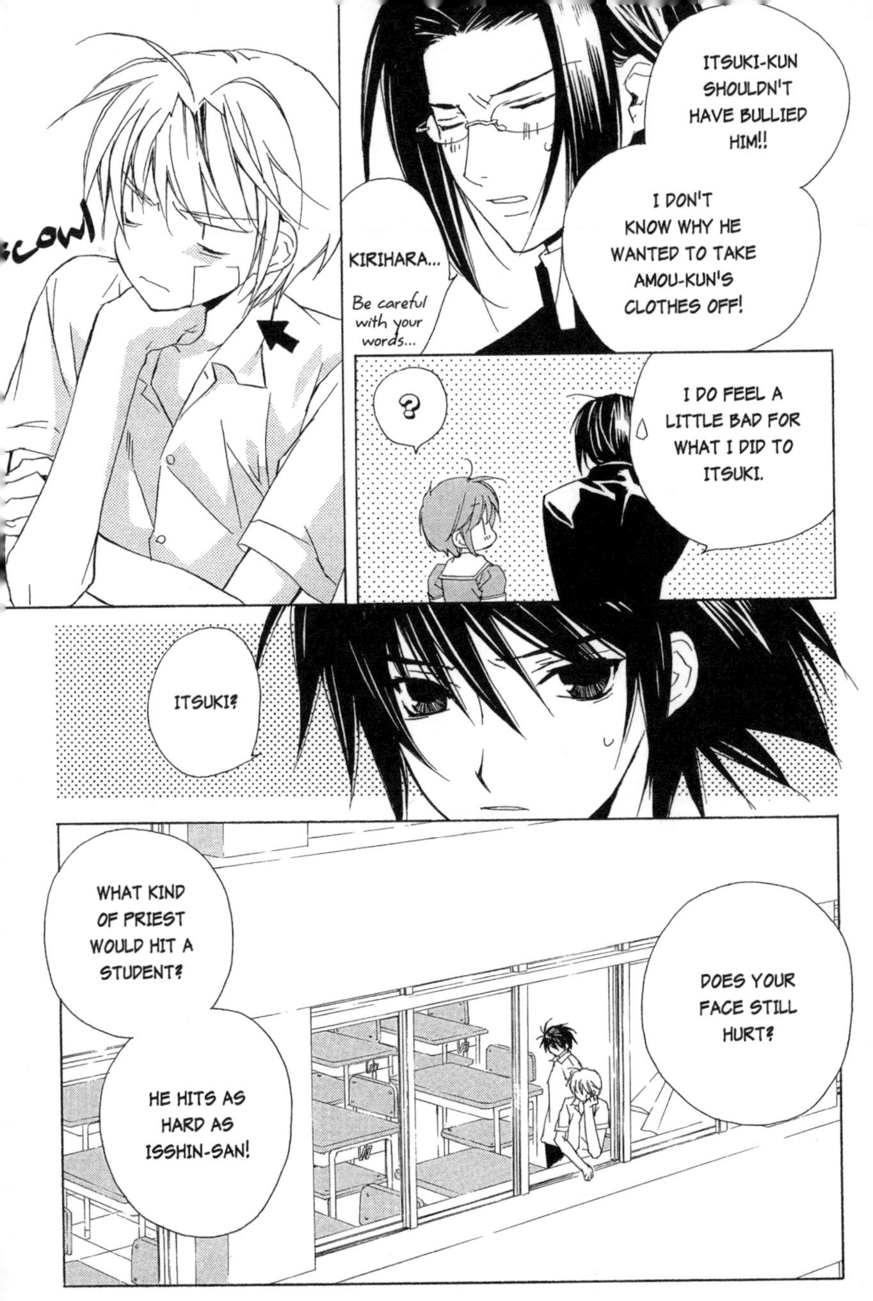
ITSUKI-KUN SHOULDN'T HAVE BULLIED HIM!!
I DON'T KNOW WHY HE WANTED TO TAKE AMOU-KUN'S CLOTHES OFF!
KIRIHARA...
Be careful with your words...
I DO FEEL A LITTLE BAD FOR WHAT I DID TO ITSUKI.
?
ITSUKI?
DOES YOUR FACE STILL HURT?
WHAT KIND OF PRIEST WOULD HIT A STUDENT?
HE HITS AS HARD AS ISSHIN-SAN!

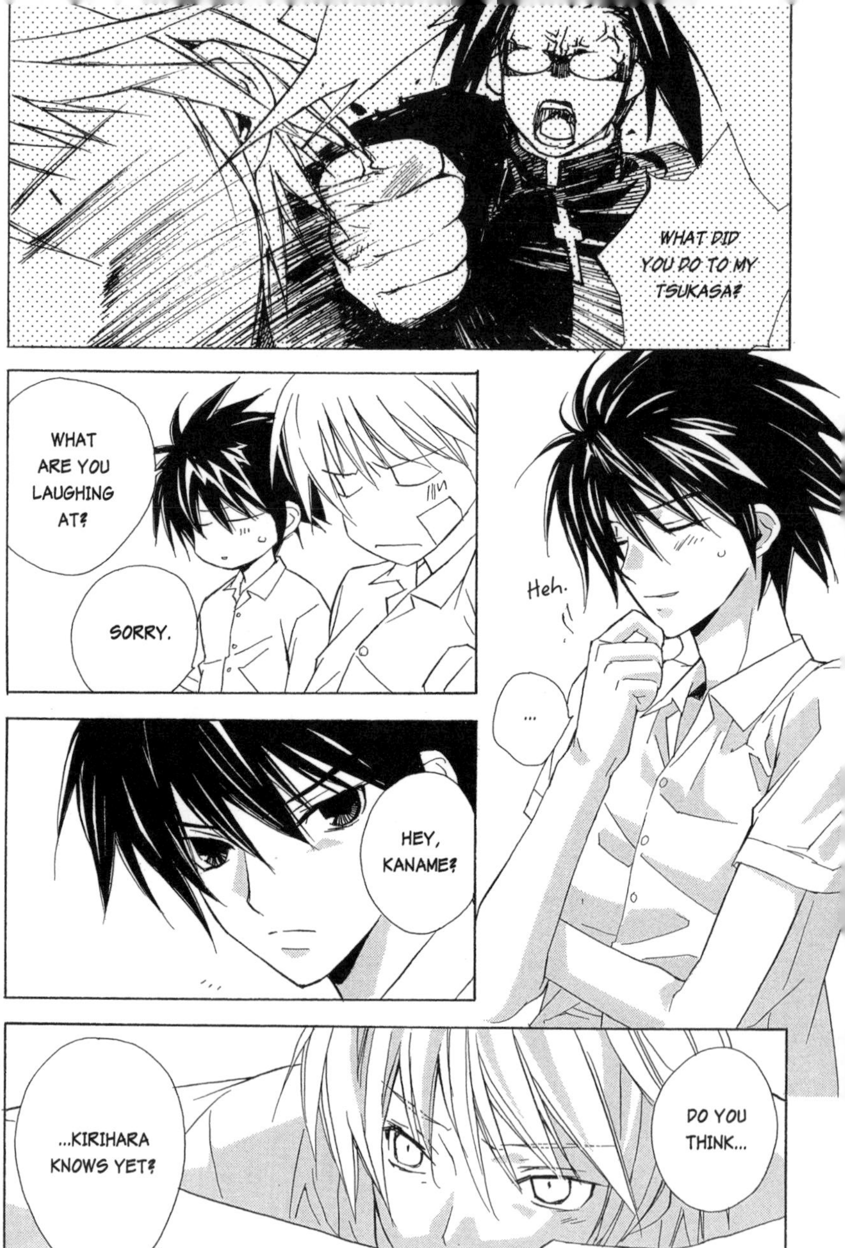
WHAT DID YOU DO TO MY TSUKASA?
Heh.
...
WHAT ARE YOU LAUGHING AT?
SORRY.
HEY, KANAME?
DO YOU THINK...
...KIRIHARA KNOWS YET?

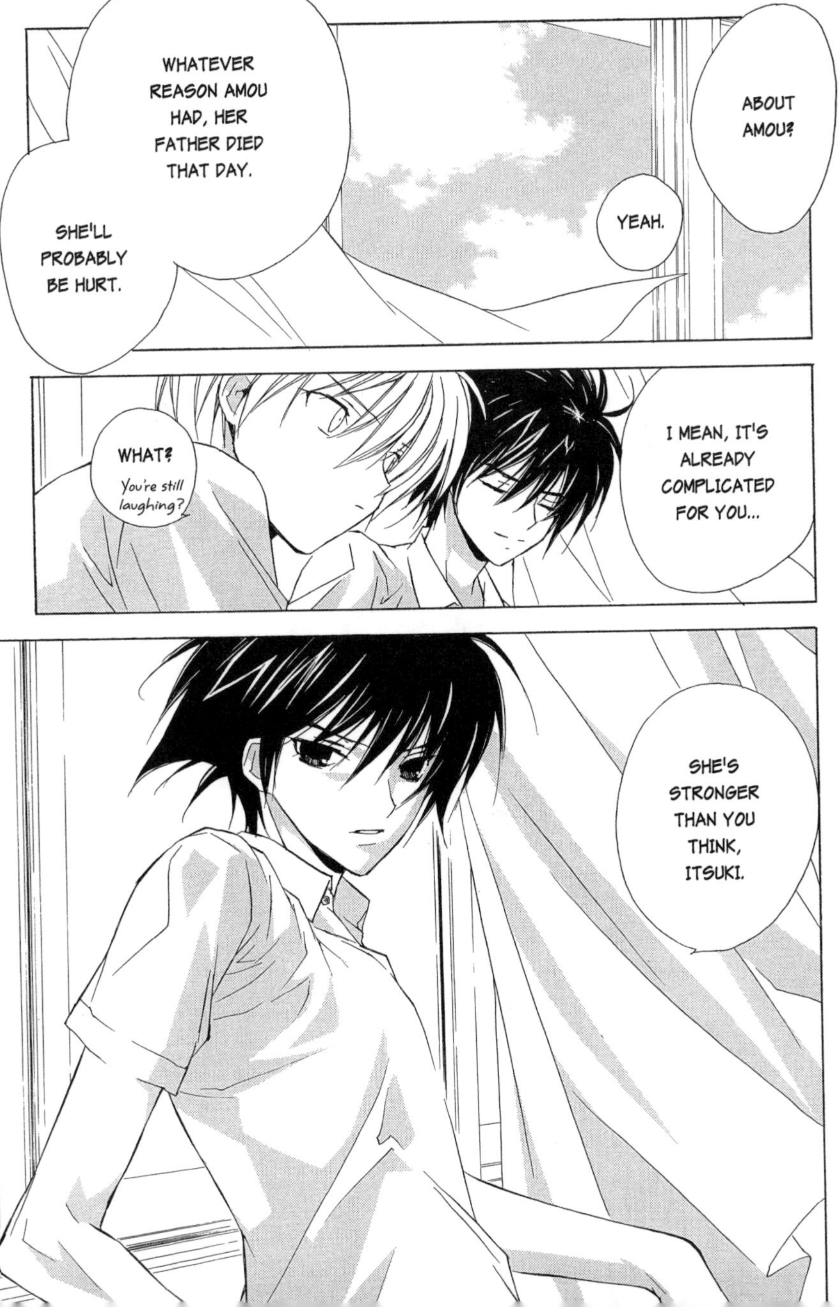
ABOUT AMOU?
YEAH.
WHATEVER REASON AMOU HAD, HER FATHER DIED THAT DAY.
SHE'LL PROBABLY BE HURT.
I MEAN, IT'S ALREADY COMPLICATED FOR YOU...
WHAT?
You're still laughing?
SHE'S STRONGER THAN YOU THINK, ITSUKI.

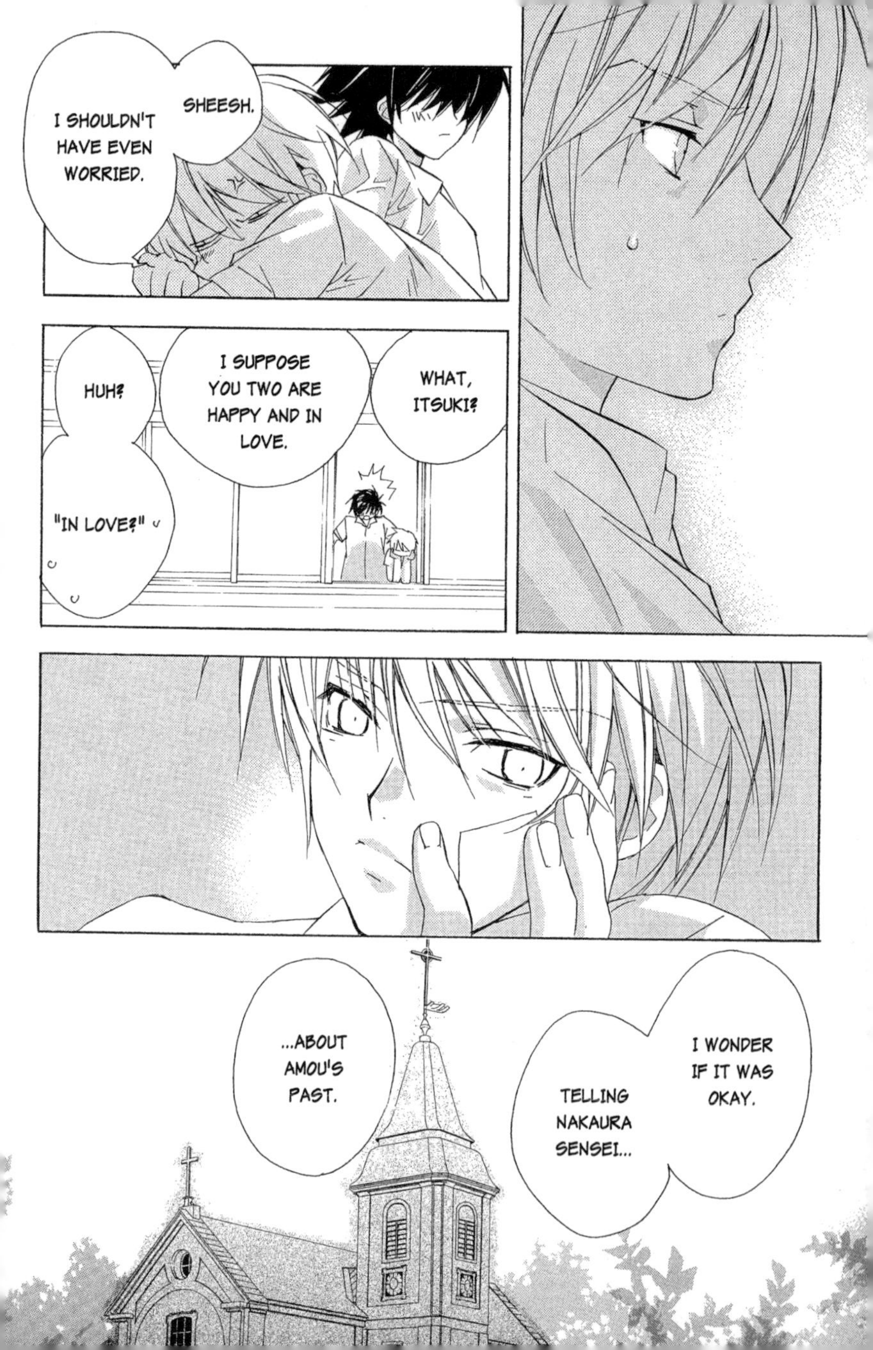
SHEESH.
I SHOULDN'T HAVE EVEN WORRIED.
WHAT, ITSUKI?
I SUPPOSE YOU TWO ARE HAPPY AND IN LOVE.
HUH?
"IN LOVE?"
I WONDER IF IT WAS OKAY.
TELLING NAKAURA SENSEI...
...ABOUT AMOU'S PAST.

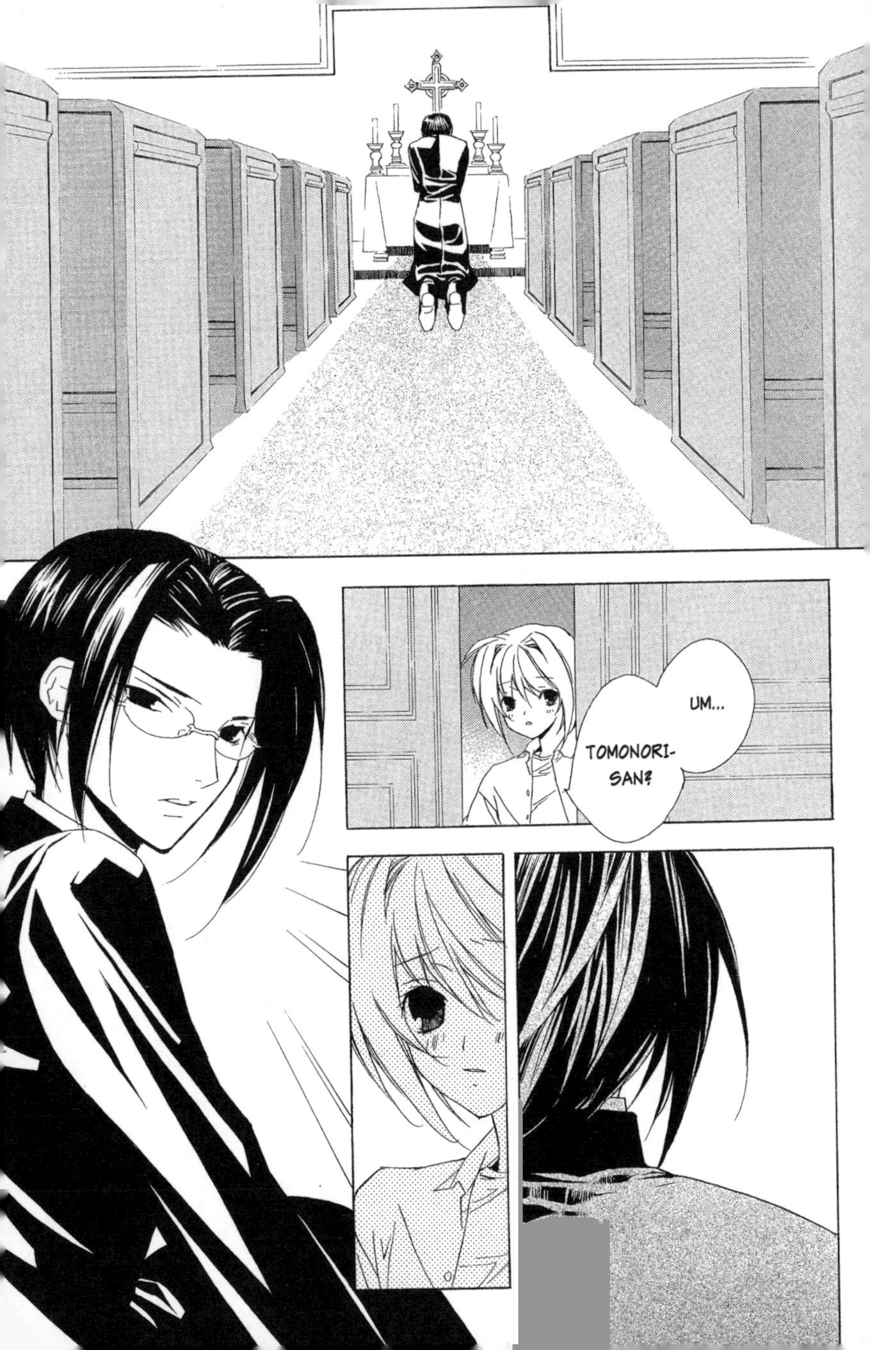
UM... TOMONORI-SAN?

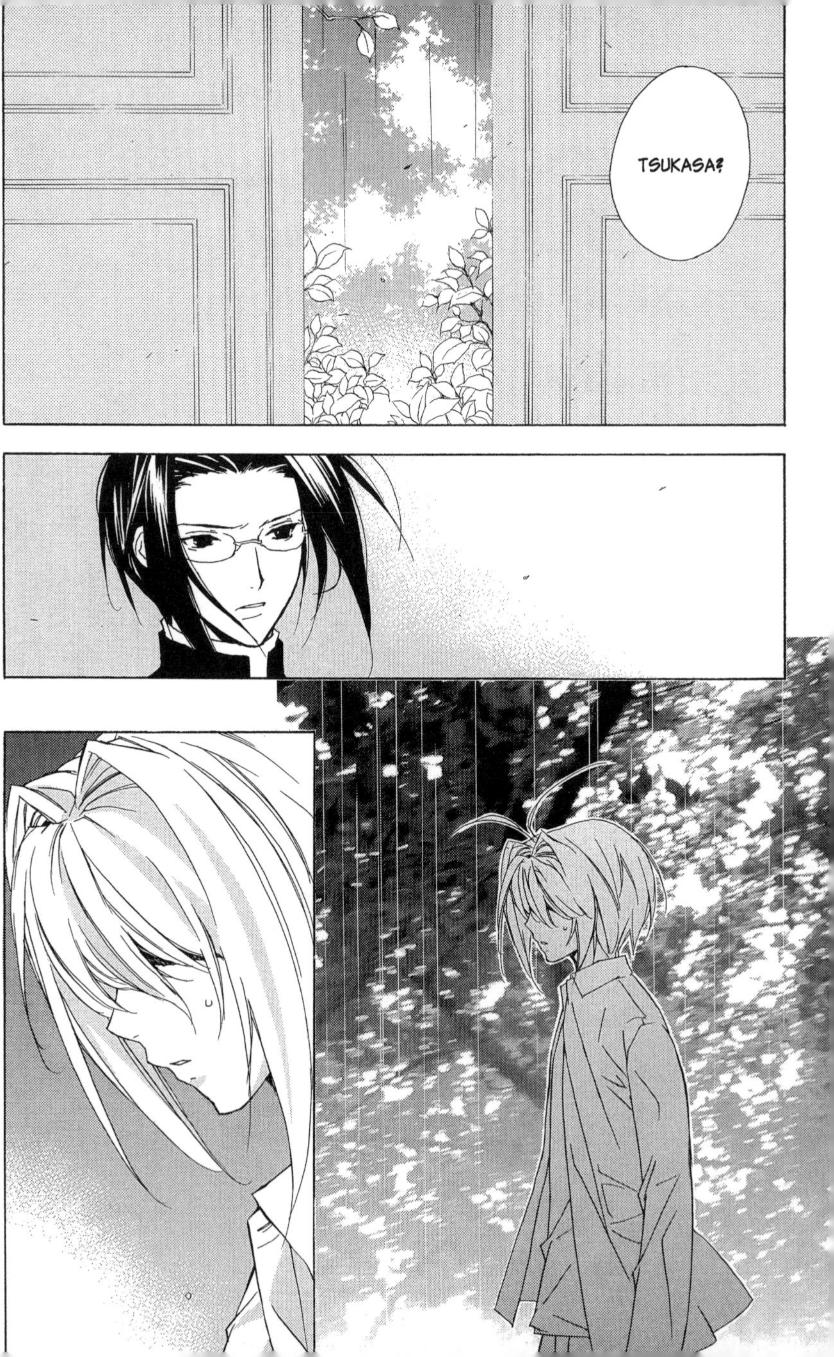
TSUKASA?

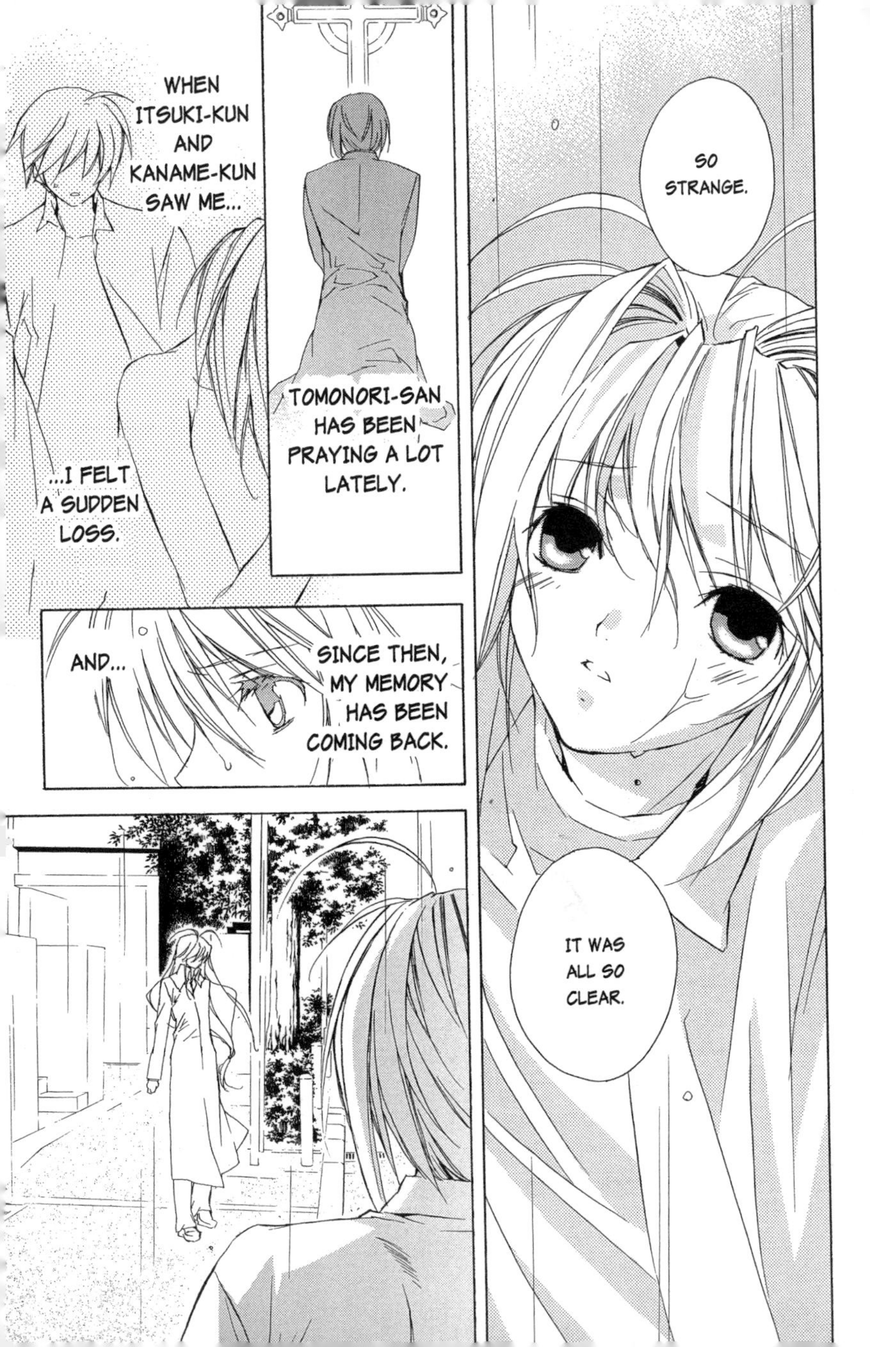
SO STRANGE.
IT WAS ALL SO CLEAR.
TOMONORI-SAN HAS BEEN PRAYING A LOT LATELY.
WHEN ITSUKI-KUN AND KANAME-KUN SAW ME...
...I FELT A SUDDEN LOSS.
AND...
SINCE THEN, MY MEMORY HAS BEEN COMING BACK.

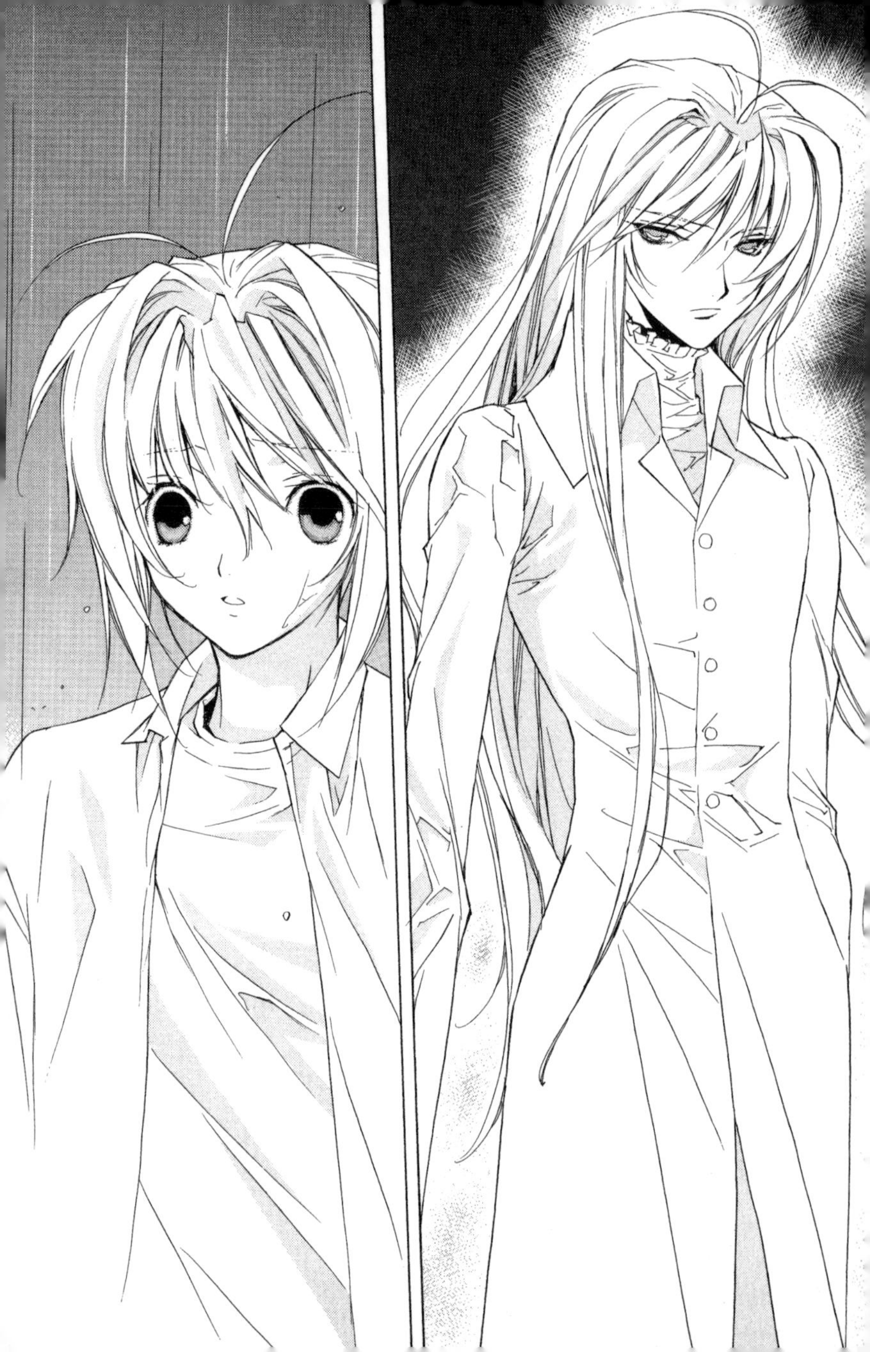

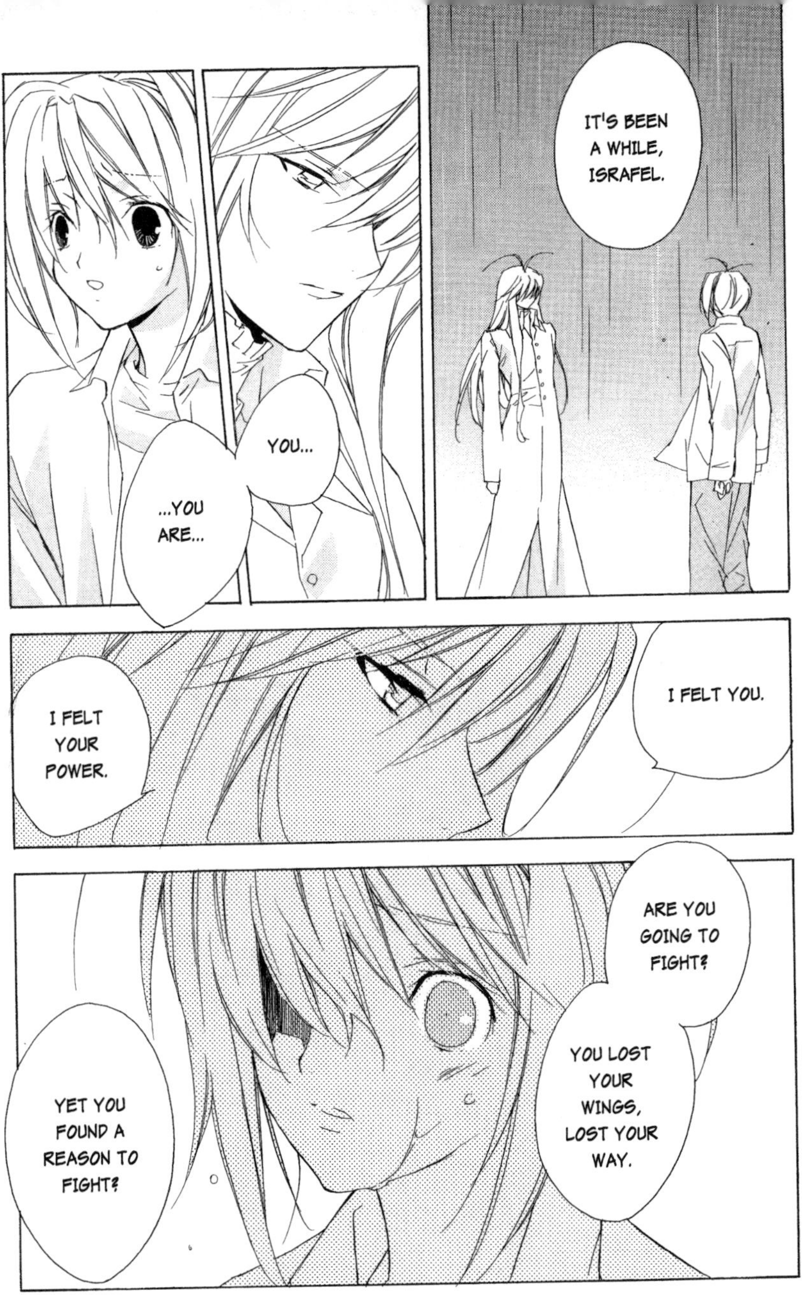
IT'S BEEN A WHILE, ISRAFEL.
YOU...
...YOU ARE...
I FELT YOU.
I FELT YOUR POWER.
ARE YOU GOING TO FIGHT?
YOU LOST YOUR WINGS, LOST YOUR WAY.
YET YOU FOUND A REASON TO FIGHT?

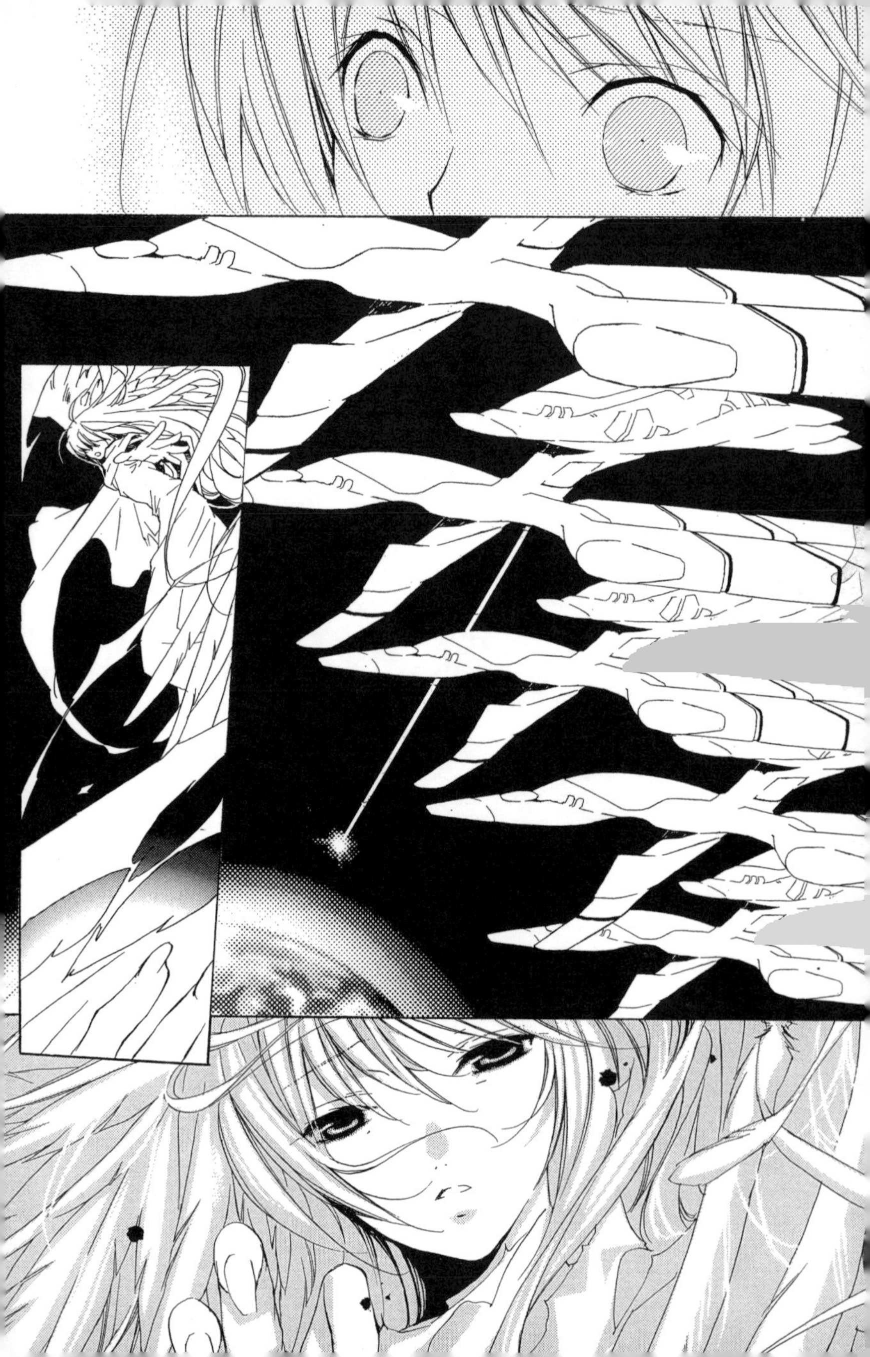

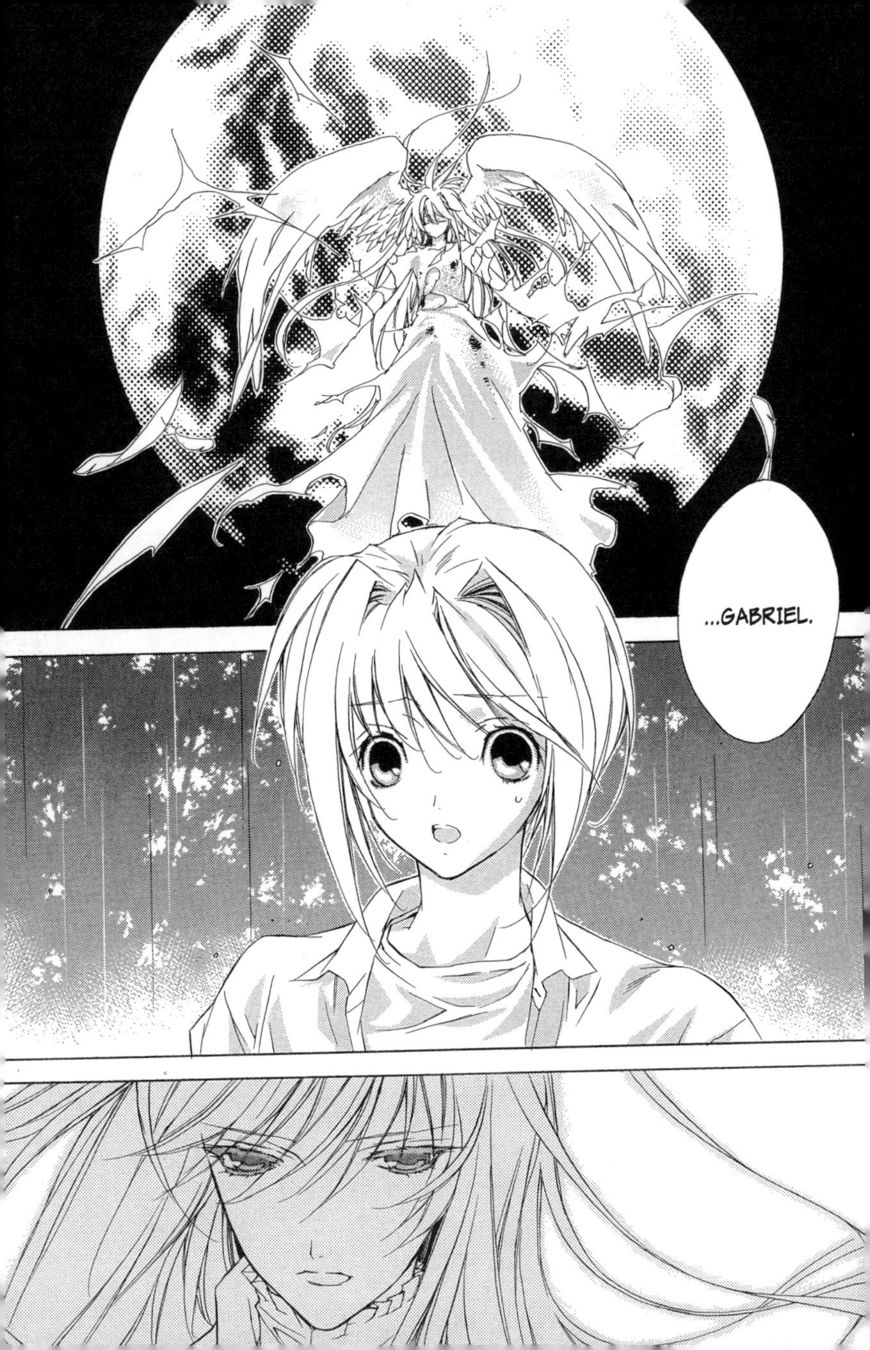
...GABRIEL.

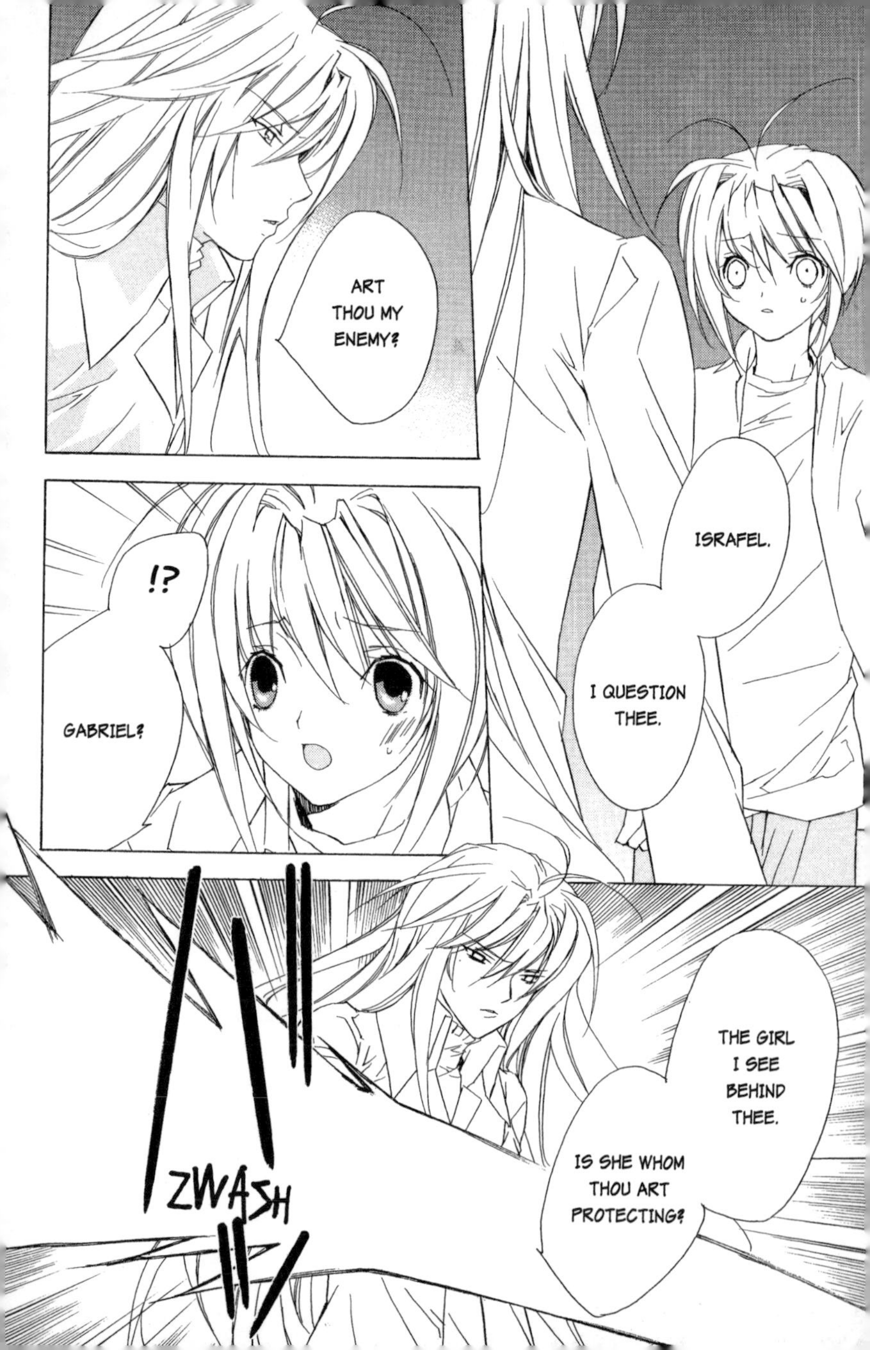
ISRAFEL.
I QUESTION THEE.
ART THOU MY ENEMY?
!?
GABRIEL?
THE GIRL I SEE BEHIND THEE.
IS SHE WHOM THOU ART PROTECTING?
ZWASH

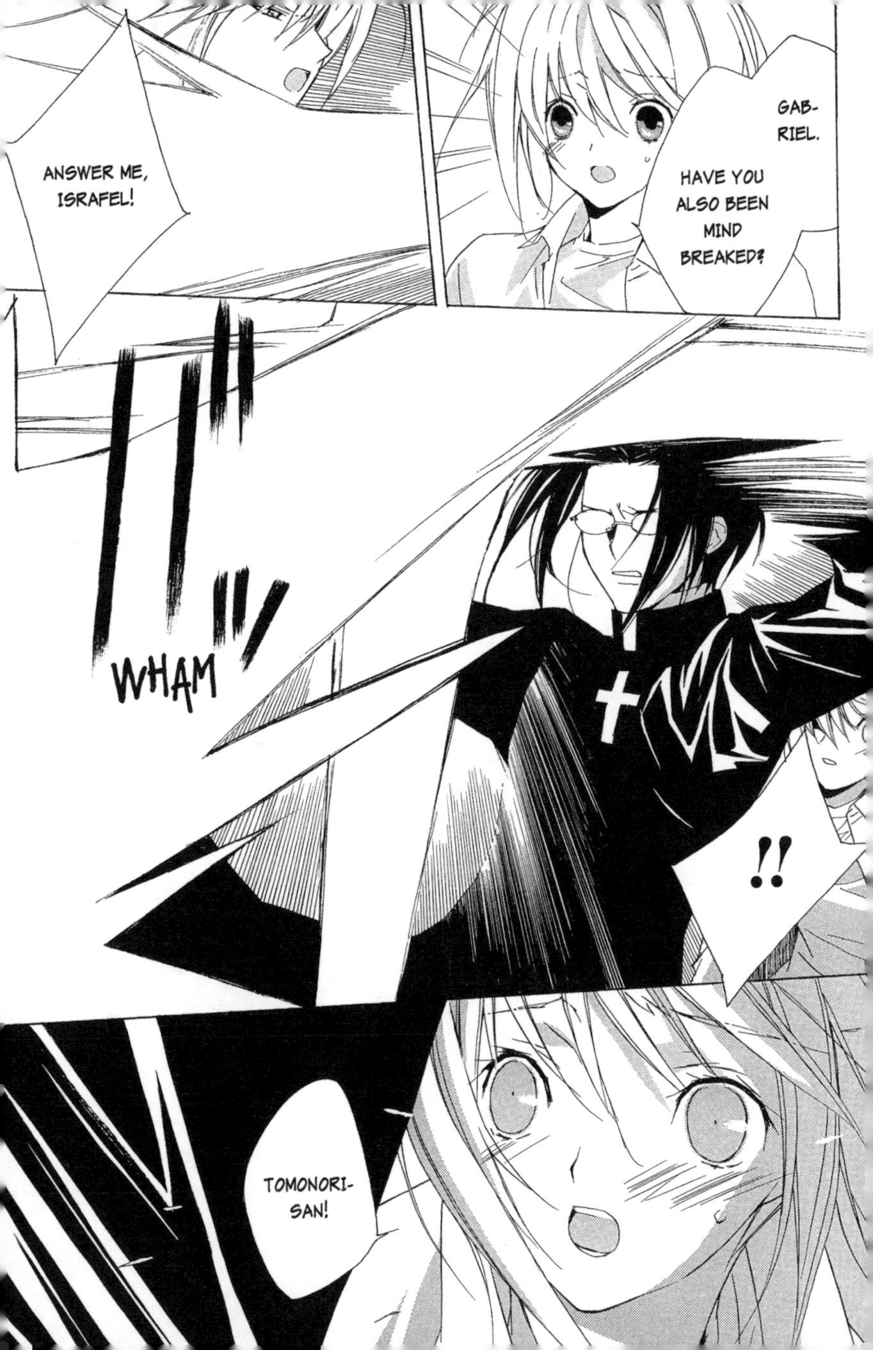
GAB-
RIEL.
HAVE YOU ALSO BEEN MIND BREAKED?
ANSWER ME, ISRAFEL!
WHAM
!!
TOMONORI-SAN!

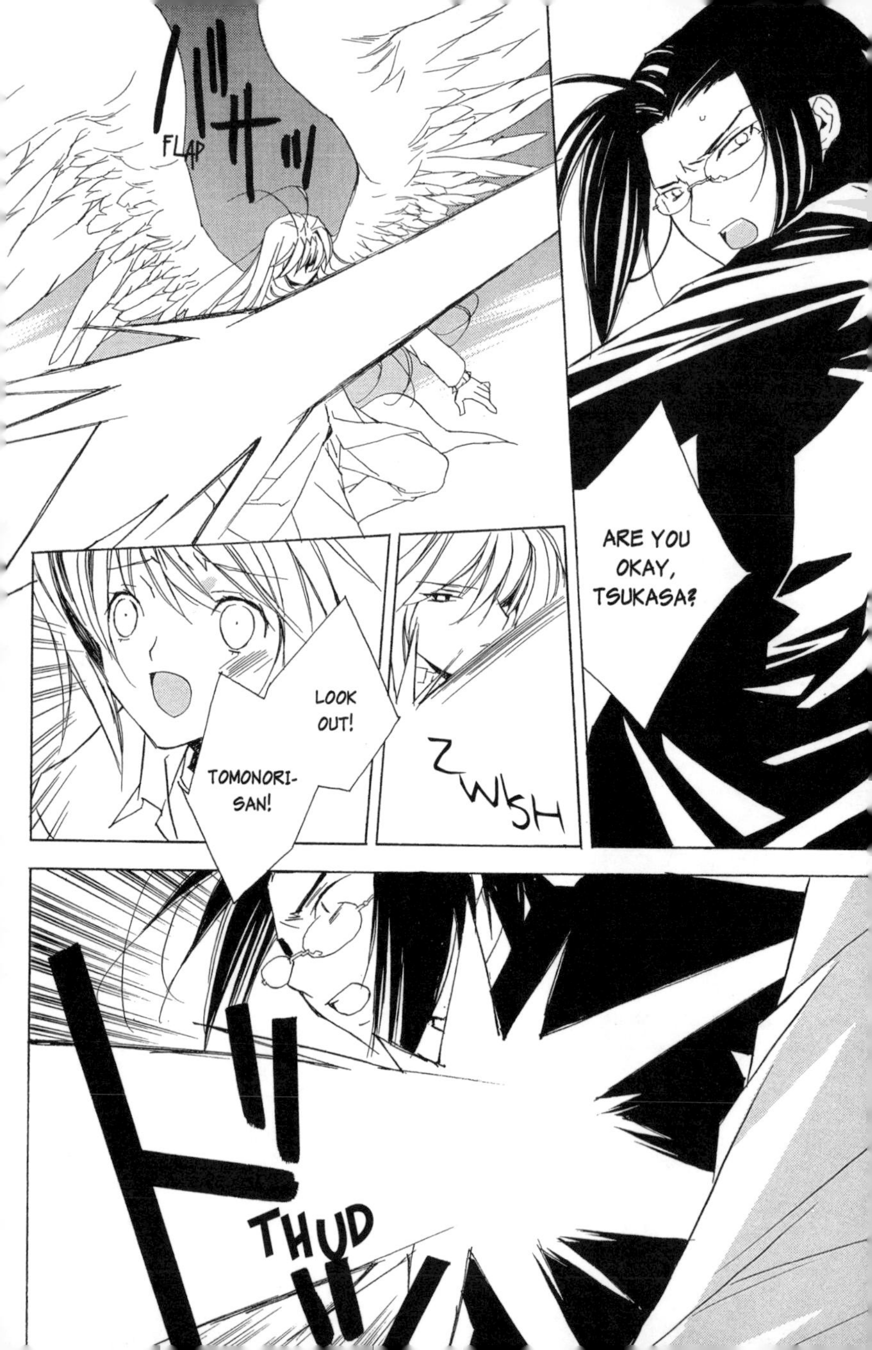
ARE YOU OKAY, TSUKASA?
FLAP
ZWISH
LOOK OUT!
TOMONORI-SAN!
THUD

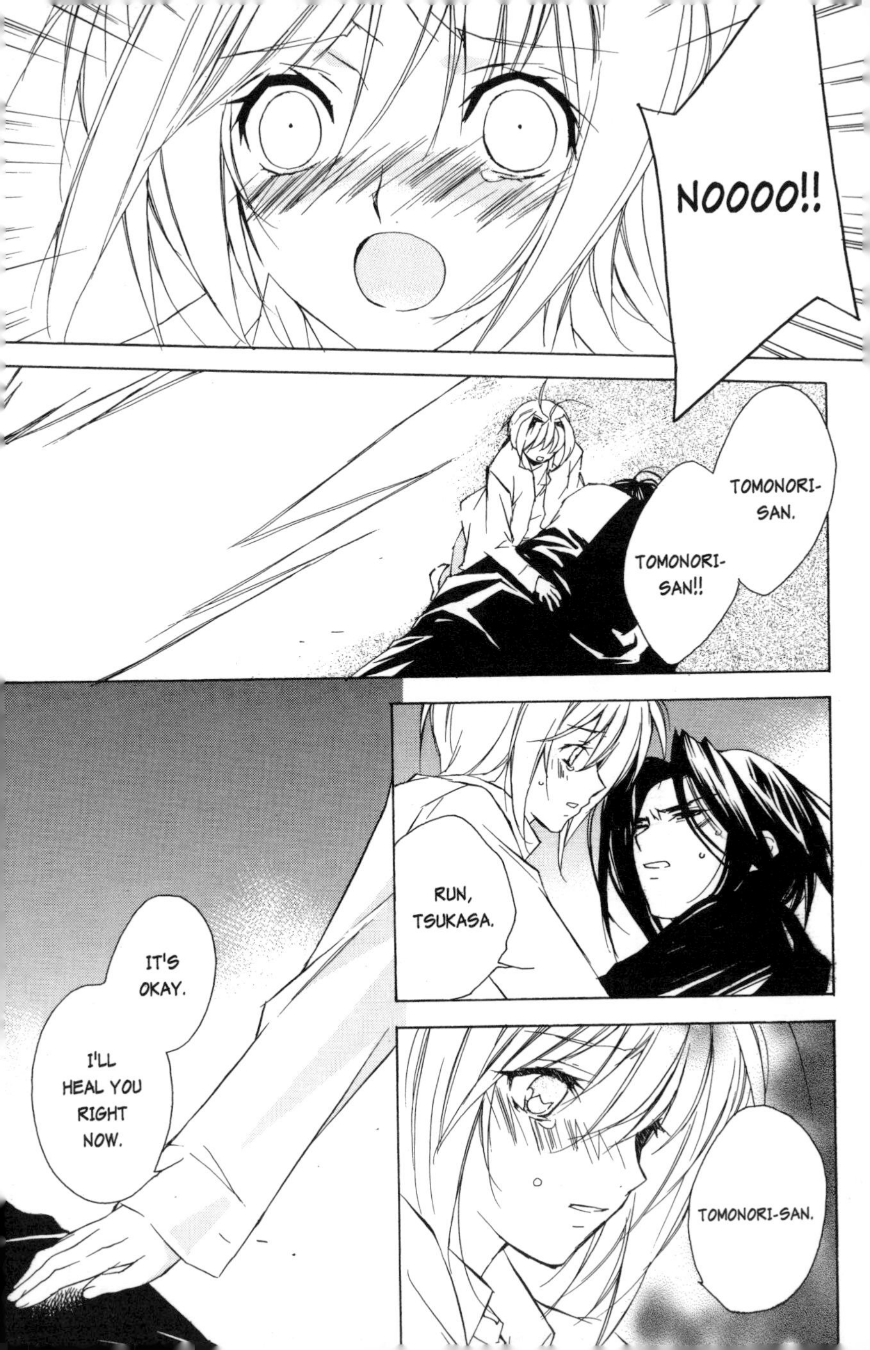
NOOOO!!
TOMONORI-SAN.
TOMONORI-SAN!!
RUN, TSUKASA.
IT'S OKAY.
I'LL HEAL YOU RIGHT NOW.
TOMONORI-SAN.

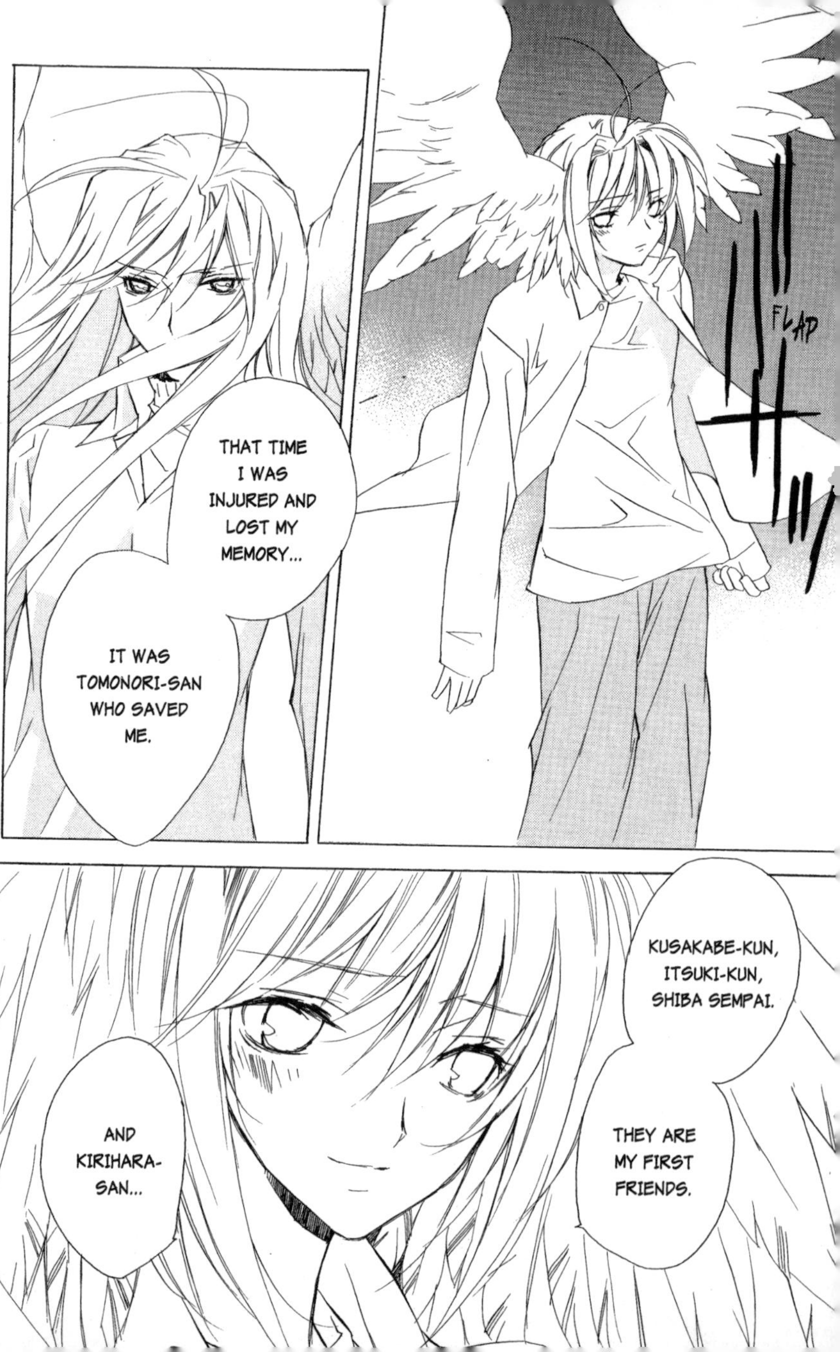
FLAP
THAT TIME I WAS INJURED AND LOST MY MEMORY...
IT WAS TOMONORI-SAN WHO SAVED ME.
KUSAKABE-KUN, ITSUKI-KUN, SHIBA SEMPAI.
THEY ARE MY FIRST FRIENDS.
AND KIRIHARA-SAN...

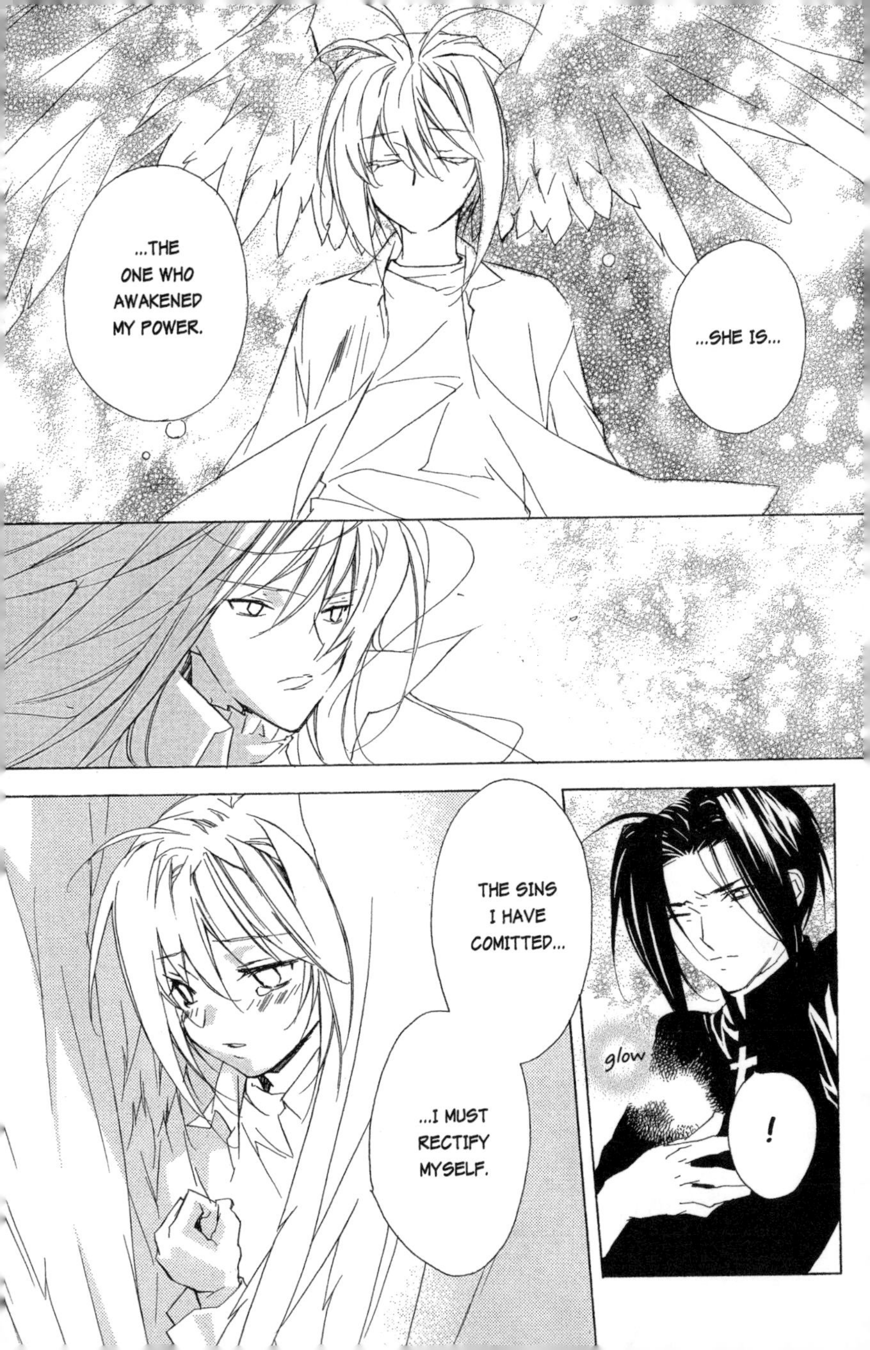
...SHE IS...
...THE ONE WHO AWAKENED MY POWER.
THE SINS I HAVE COMITTED...
...I MUST RECTIFY MYSELF.
glow
!

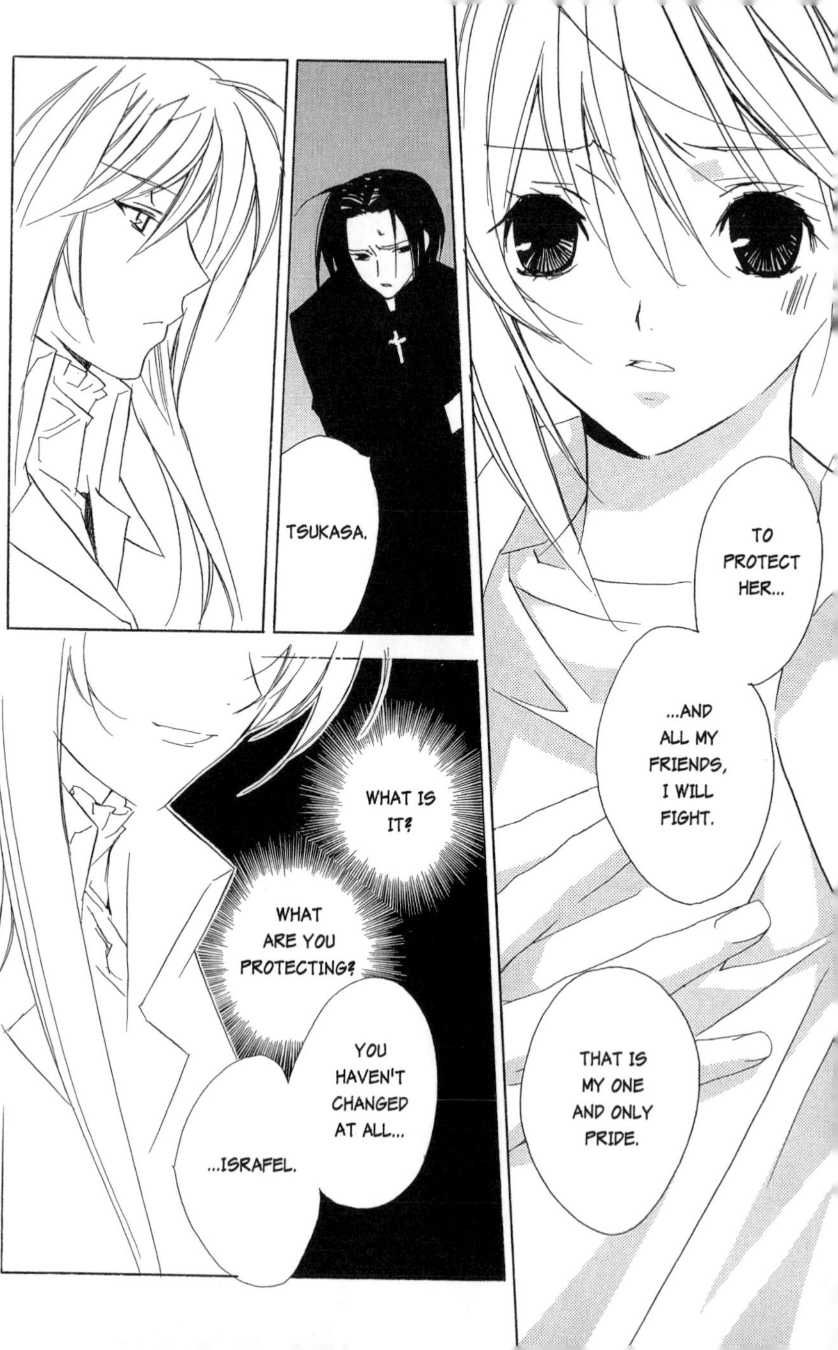
TO PROTECT HER...
...AND ALL MY FRIENDS, I WILL FIGHT.
THAT IS MY ONE AND ONLY PRIDE.
TSUKASA.
WHAT IS IT?
WHAT ARE YOU PROTECTING?
YOU HAVEN'T CHANGED AT ALL...
...ISRAFEL.

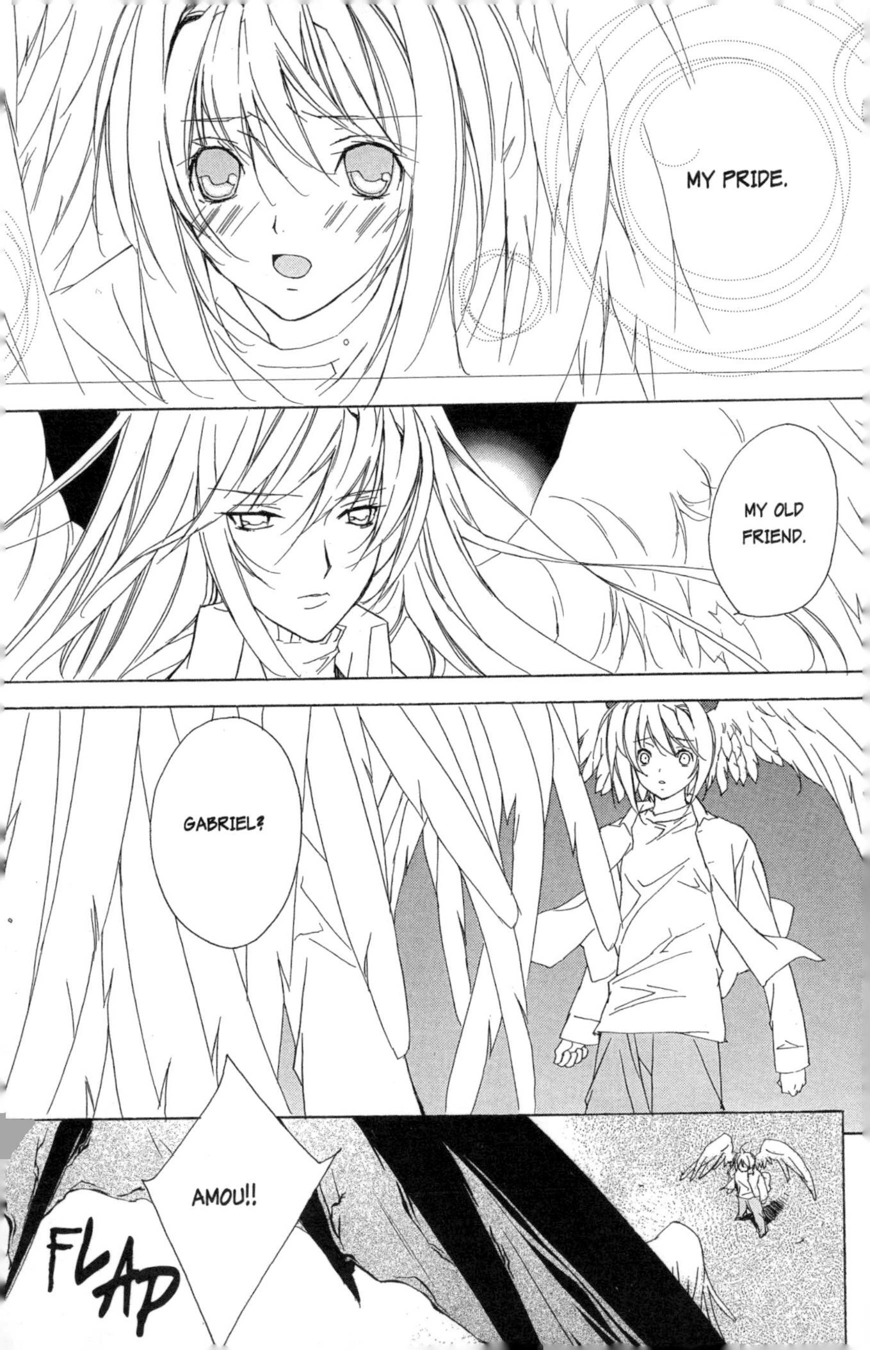
MY PRIDE.
MY OLD FRIEND.
GABRIEL?
AMOU!!
FLAP

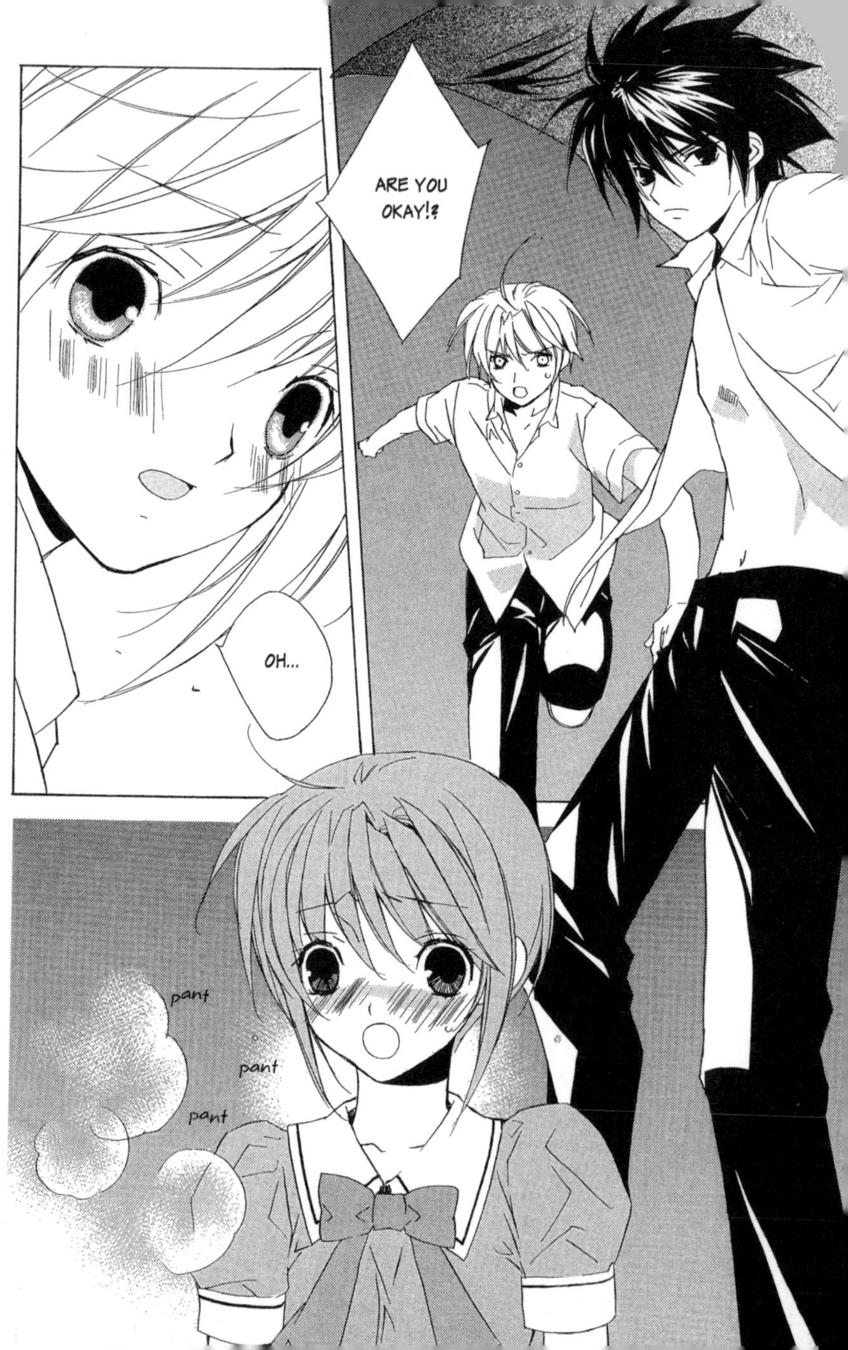
ARE YOU OKAY!?
OH...
pant
pant
pant

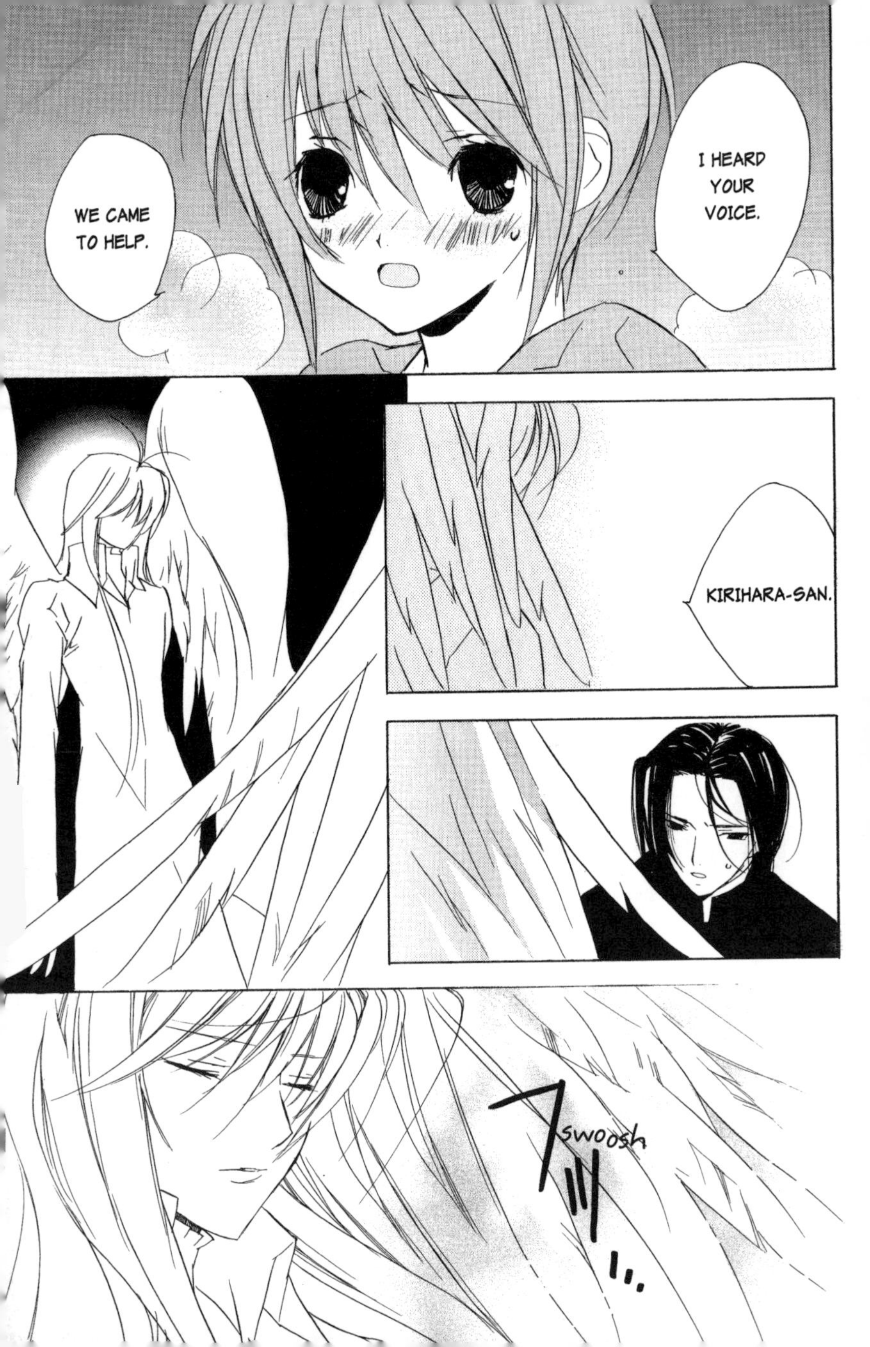
I HEARD YOUR VOICE.
WE CAME TO HELP.
KIRIHARA-SAN.
swoosh

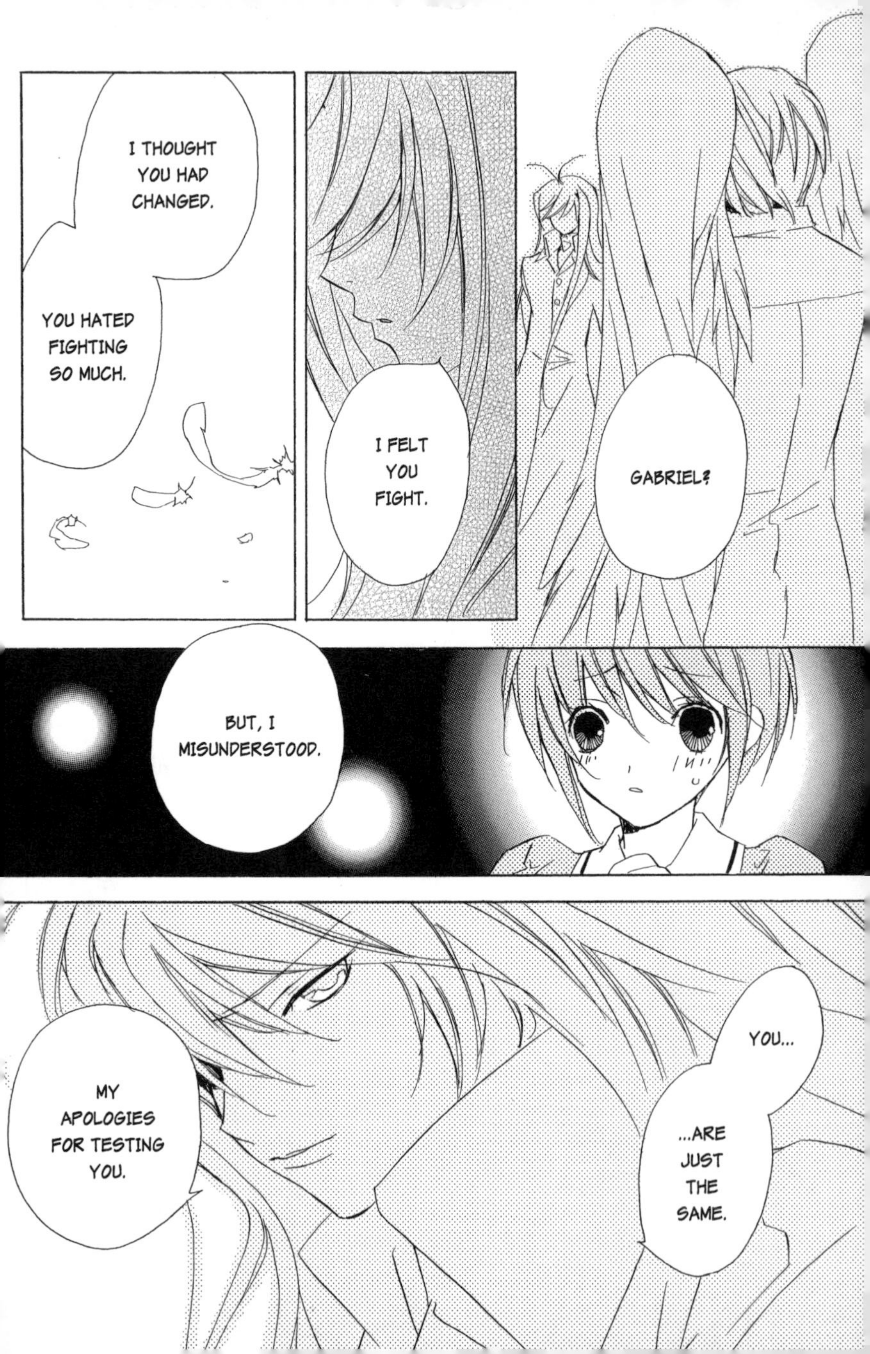
GABRIEL?
I FELT YOU FIGHT.
I THOUGHT YOU HAD CHANGED.
YOU HATED FIGHTING SO MUCH.
BUT, I MISUNDERSTOOD.
YOU...
...ARE JUST THE SAME.
MY APOLOGIES FOR TESTING YOU.

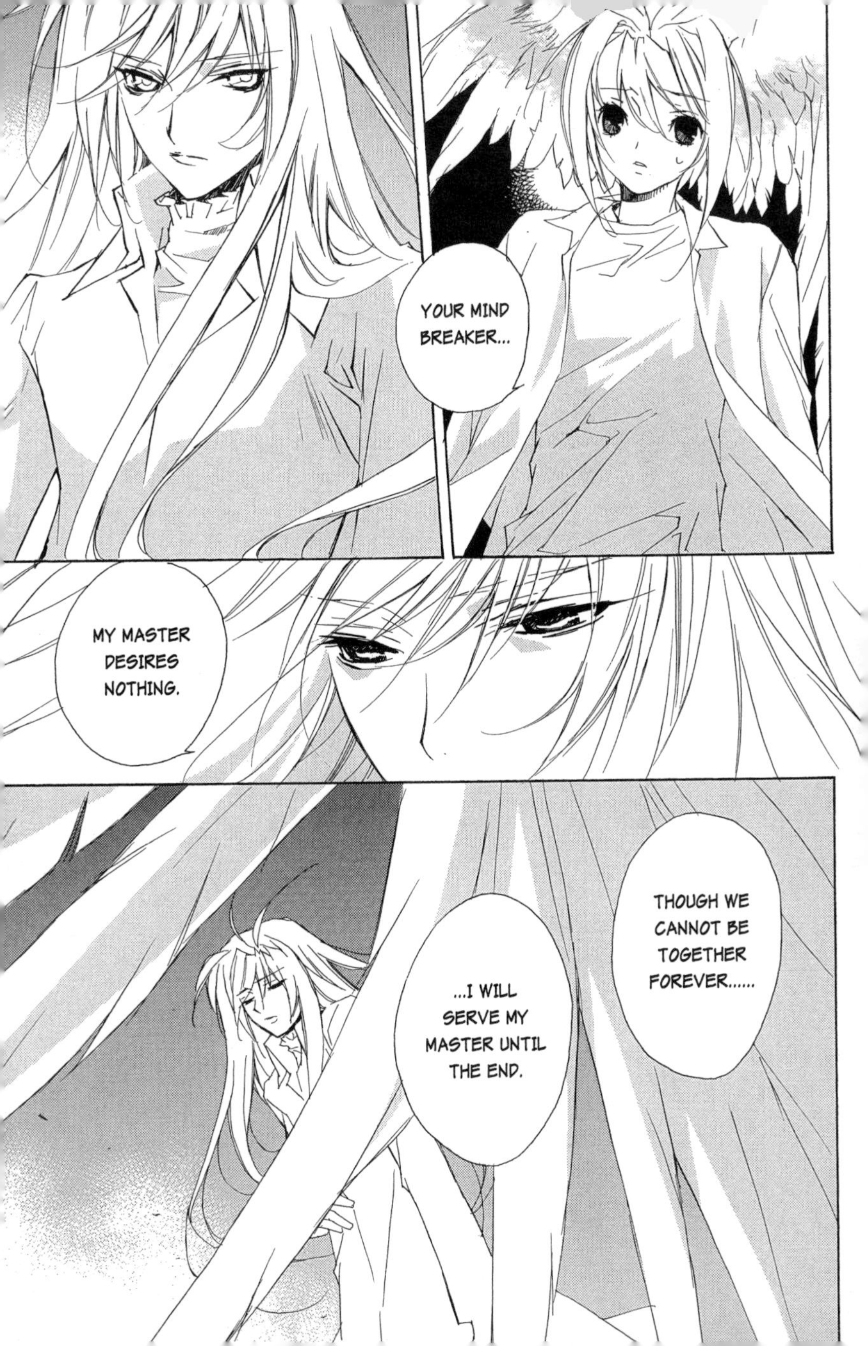
YOUR MIND BREAKER...
MY MASTER DESIRES NOTHING.
THOUGH WE CANNOT BE TOGETHER FOREVER......
...I WILL SERVE MY MASTER UNTIL THE END.

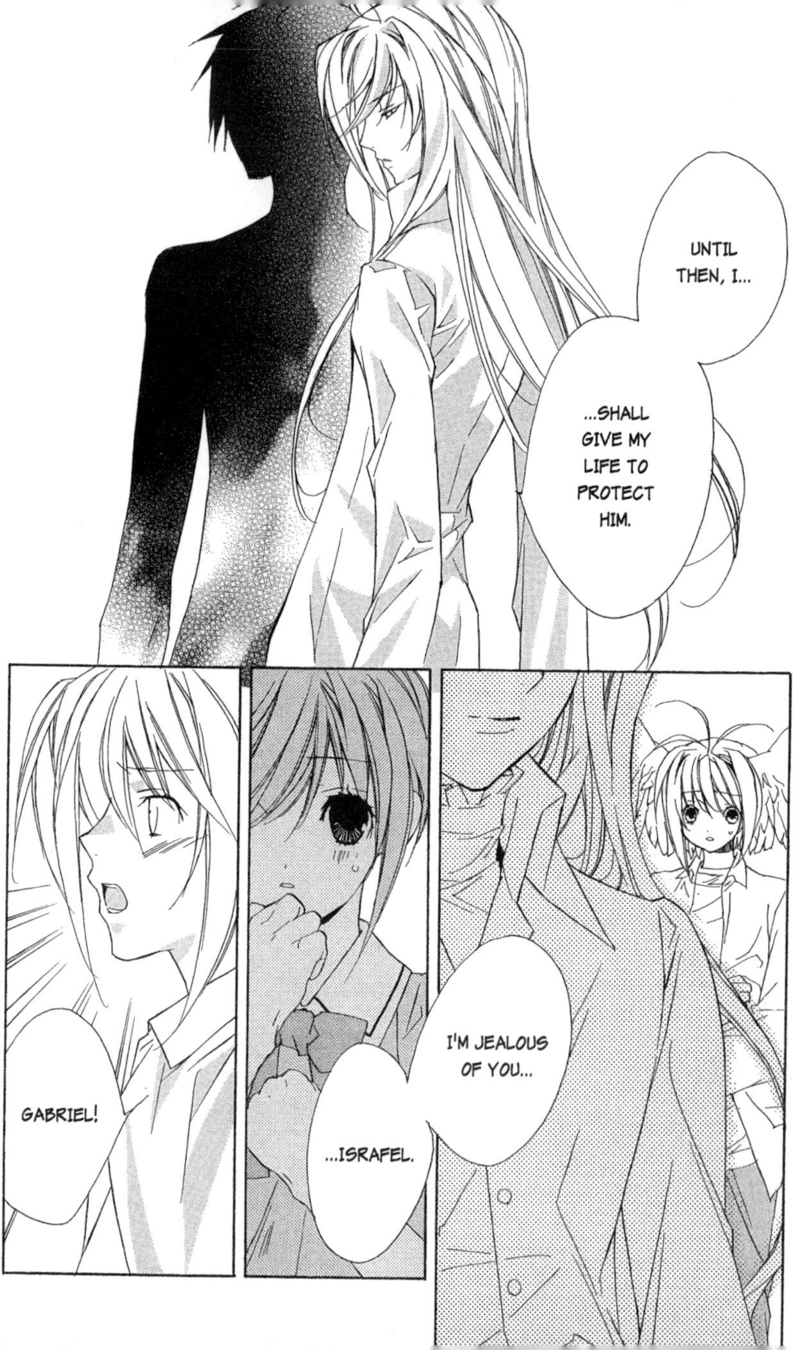
UNTIL THEN, I...
...SHALL GIVE MY LIFE TO PROTECT HIM.
I'M JEALOUS OF YOU...
...ISRAFEL.
GABRIEL!

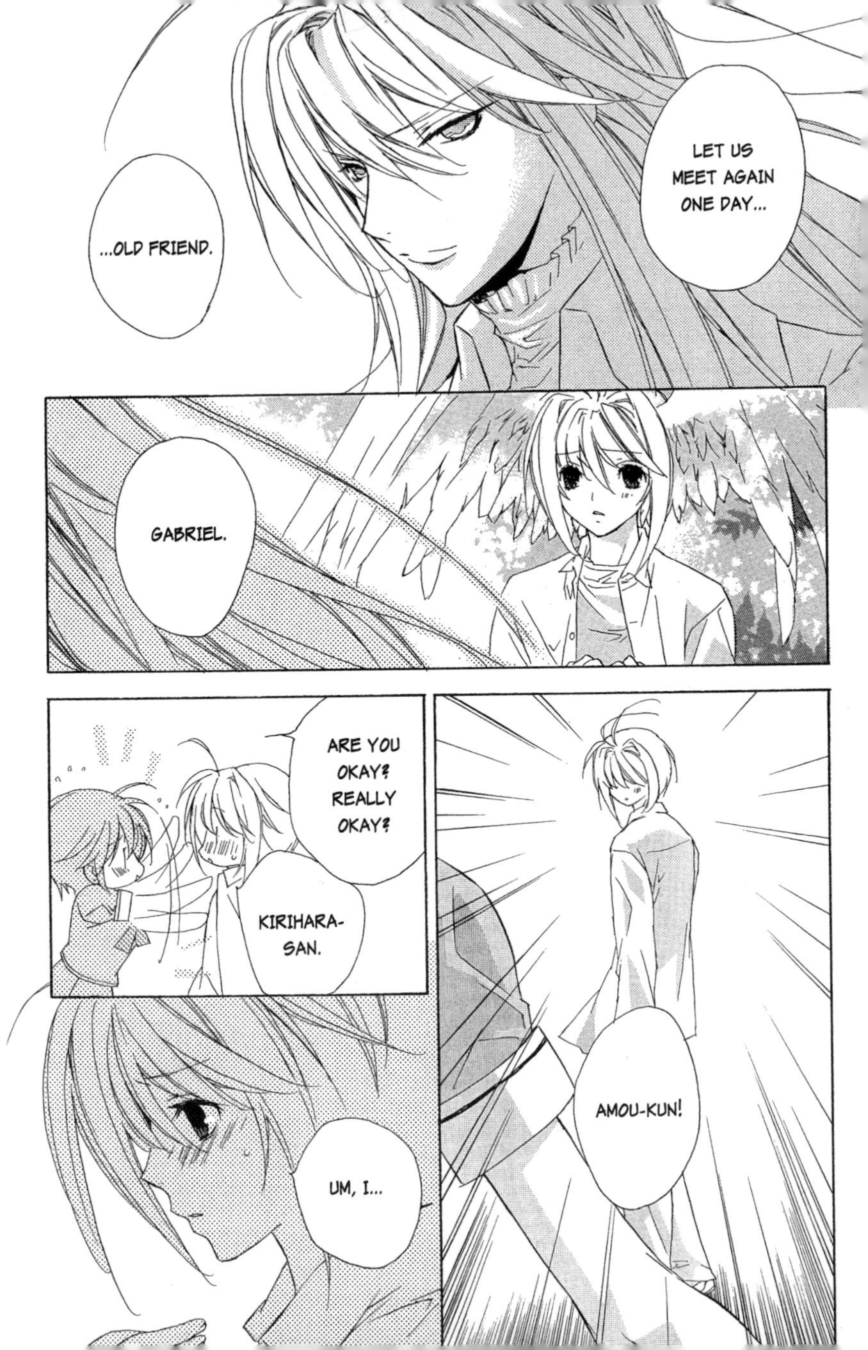
LET US MEET AGAIN ONE DAY...
...OLD FRIEND.
GABRIEL.
AMOU-KUN!
ARE YOU OKAY? REALLY OKAY?
KIRIHARA-SAN.
UM, I...

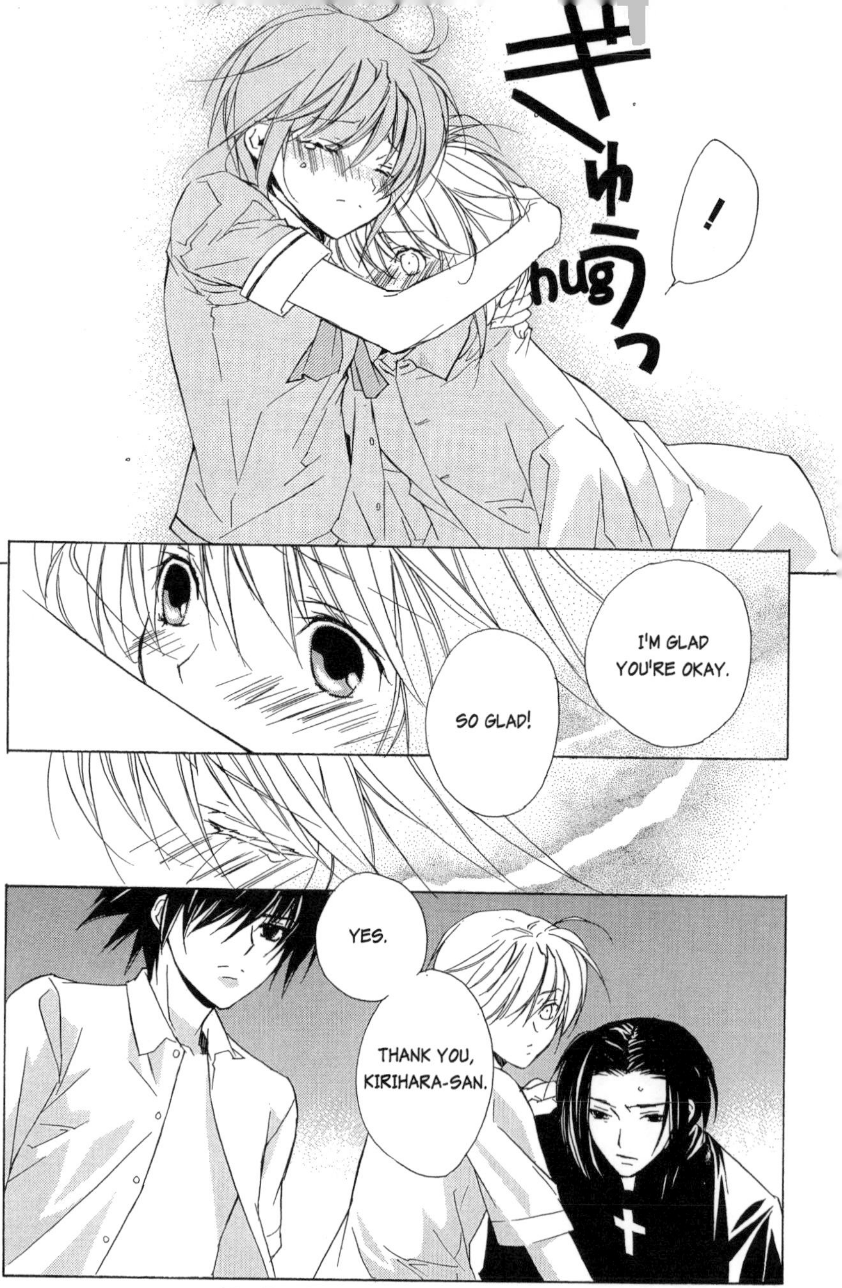
ギゅうっ
hug
!
I'M GLAD YOU'RE OKAY.
SO GLAD!
YES.
THANK YOU, KIRIHARA-SAN.

To Be Continued in Volume 4

The Adventures of White Rabbit

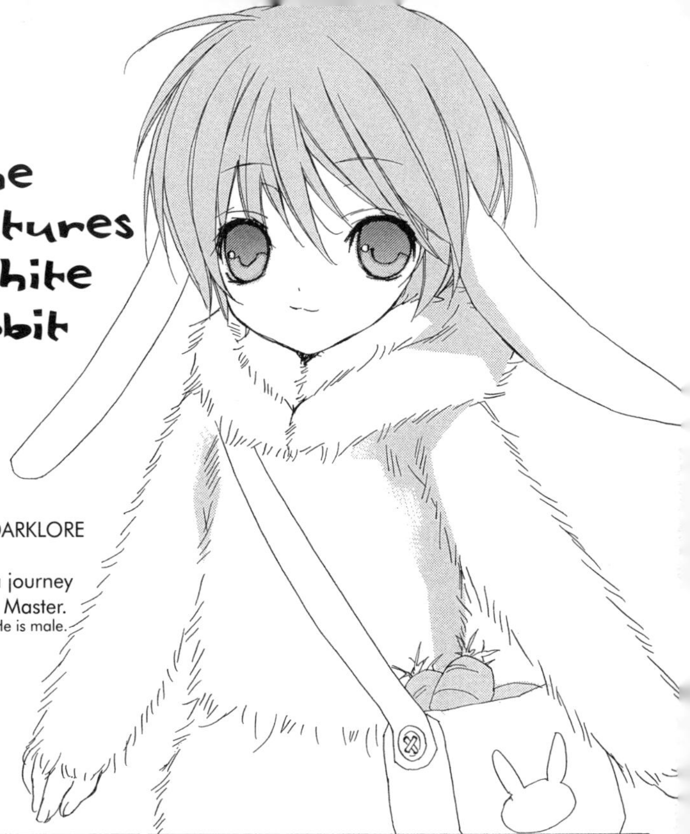

Faction: DARKLORE

He is on a journey to find his Master.

*He is male.

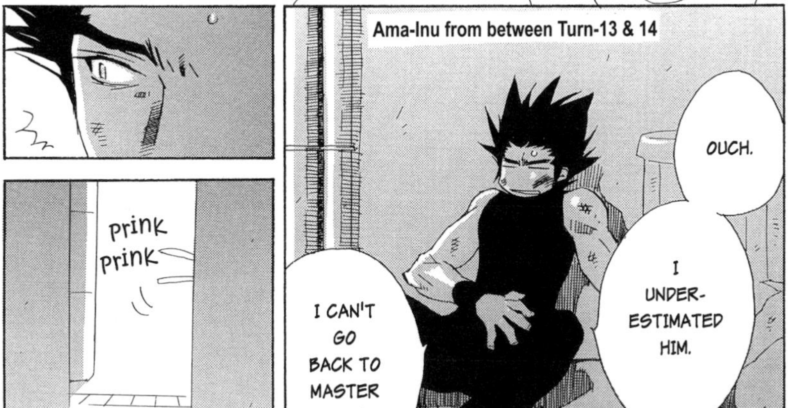

Ama-Inu from between Turn-13 & 14
OUCH.
I UNDER-ESTIMATED HIM.
I CAN'T GO BACK TO MASTER LIKE THIS.
prink prink

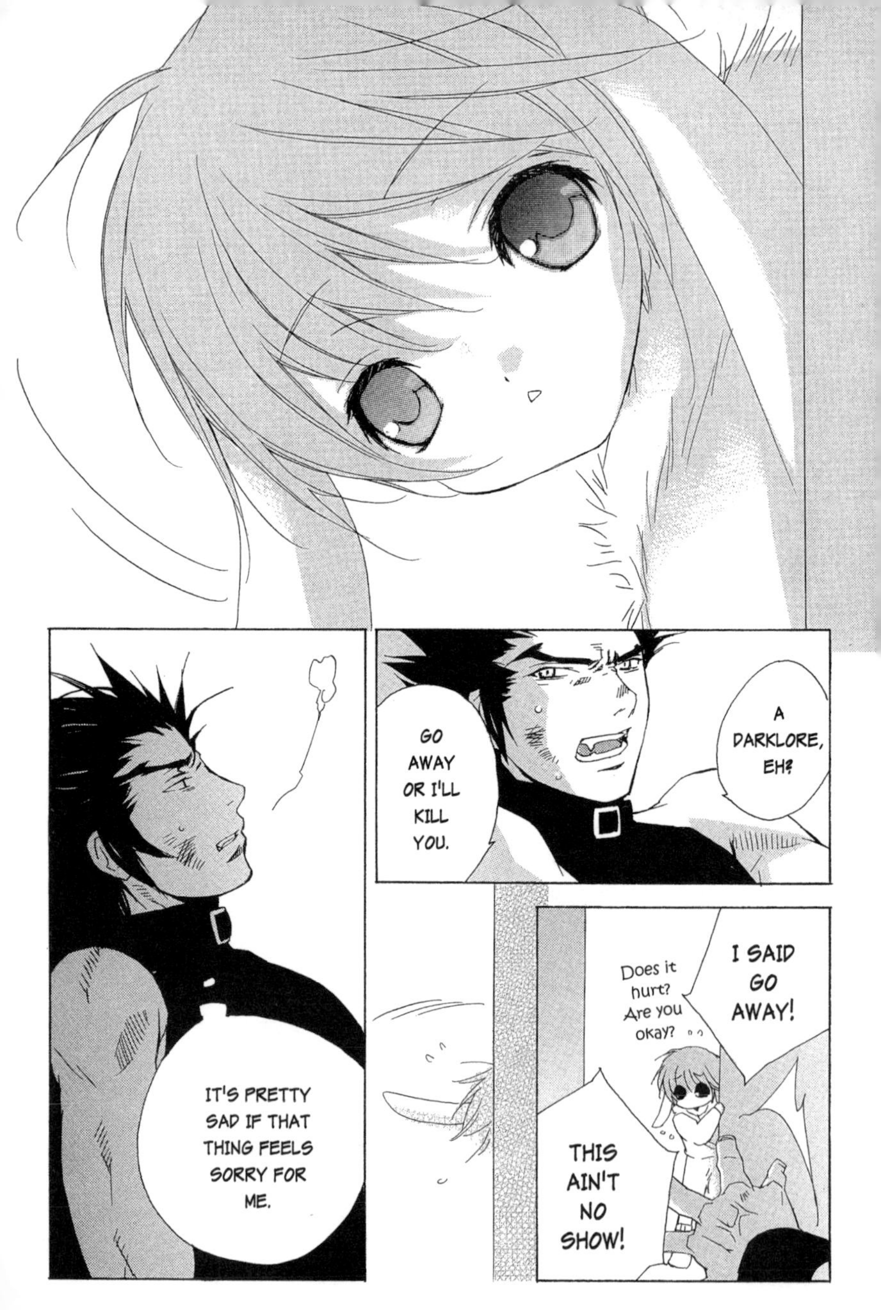

A DARKLORE, EH?
GO AWAY OR I'LL KILL YOU.
I SAID GO AWAY!
Does it hurt? Are you okay?
THIS AIN'T NO SHOW!
IT'S PRETTY SAD IF THAT THING FEELS SORRY FOR ME.

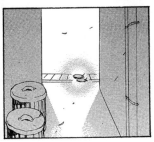

Carrots ♥

♪

The End

HMPH.

munch munch

JUVENILE ORION
TRANSLATION NOTES

A Note About First and Last Names
The characters in this story call each other by different names, sometimes using first names and sometimes using last names. Usually in Japan, classmates and teachers would call each other by their last names. Friends who are close call each other by their first names or nicknames.

pg. 15 San - A suffix; can be put after any name indicating respect.

pg. 17 Kun - A suffix; usually goes after a boy's name.

pg. 67 Sempai - The Japanese word for "senior." The direct translation is "you who came first." Kaname and Naoya call Isshin "sempai" because Isshin is older than them.

pg. 67 Sensei - Means "teacher" in Japan.

pg. 73 Onii-chan - Japanese word for "big brother."

pg. 85 Nee-san - Japanese word for "big sister."

pg. 134 Summer Clothes - The term used here was koromo gae, which means "change of clothes." This term is used when referring to the change of summer clothes to winter clothes and vice versa.

pg. 136 Tokiko Arisugawa - The only daughter and heir to the Arisugawa family, one of the wealthiest families in Japan. The Arisugawa family supports the ARAYASHIKI faction with their wealth and political power.

pg. 151 Rayyu - The commander-in-chief of the ERASER Earth Invasion Army.

pg. 151 Azrael - The Angel of Death. It is said that everytime he blinks, a person dies.

pg. 165 Gabriel - One of the central members of the ERASER faction. His hobby is to arrange and organize.

pg. 183 White Rabbit - A little DARKLORE who is wandering the Earth in search for a Master. His favorite food is carrots.

AQUARIAN AGE

JUVENILE ORION 4

オリオンの少年

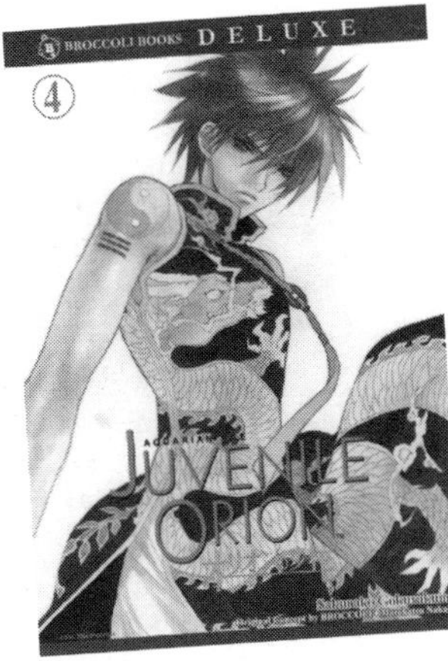
BROCCOLI BOOKS DELUXE
4
AQUARIAN AGE
JUVENILE ORION

Kaoru and her group continue their twisted game of hunting those with power, and Mana is their next target. Kaname, Naoya, Isshin, Tsukasa, and Tomonori rush to save her, but Kaoru's men stand before them.

Here's a sneak preview!

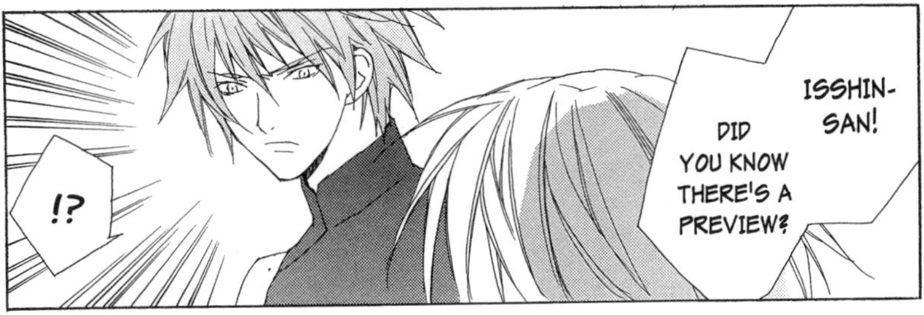
ISSHIN-SAN!
DID YOU KNOW THERE'S A PREVIEW?
!?

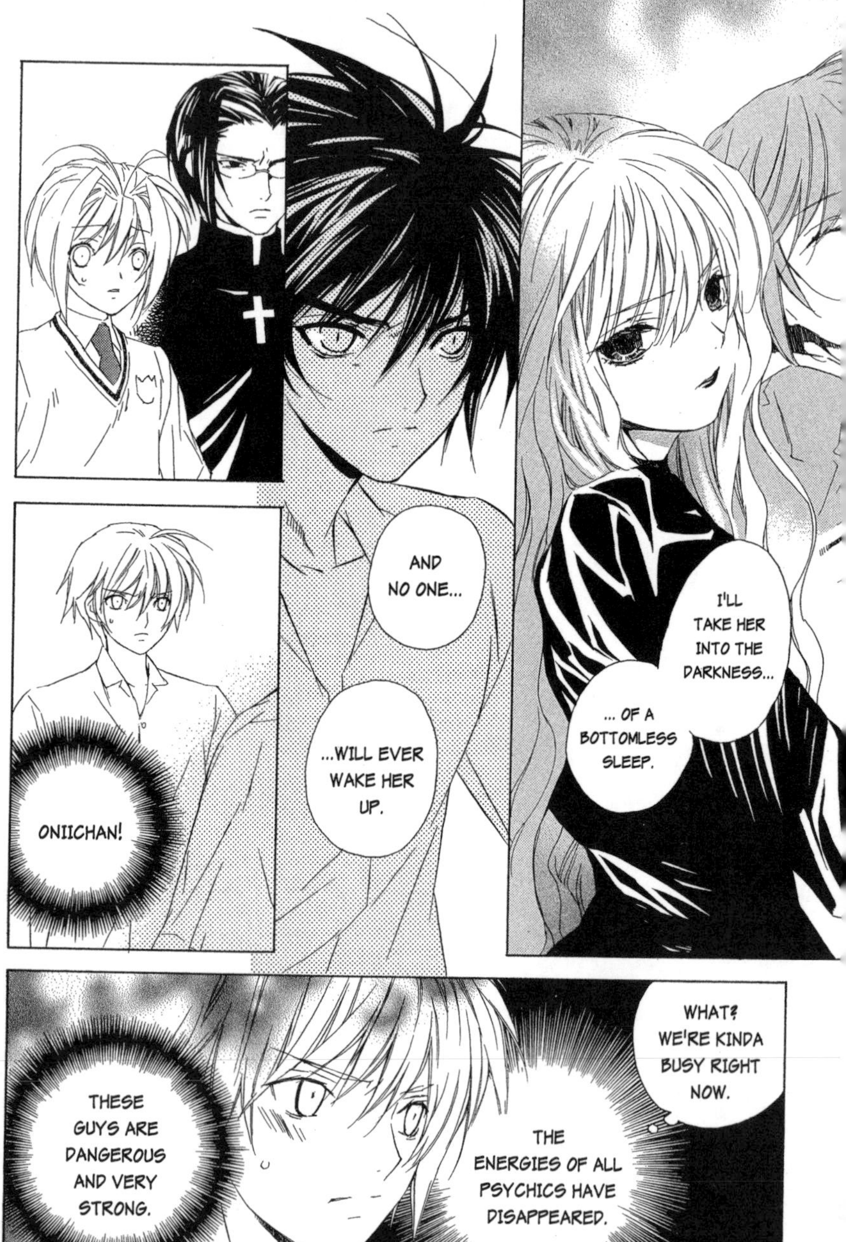
I'LL TAKE HER INTO THE DARKNESS...
... OF A BOTTOMLESS SLEEP.
AND NO ONE...
...WILL EVER WAKE HER UP.
ONIICHAN!
WHAT? WE'RE KINDA BUSY RIGHT NOW.
THE ENERGIES OF ALL PSYCHICS HAVE DISAPPEARED.
THESE GUYS ARE DANGEROUS AND VERY STRONG.

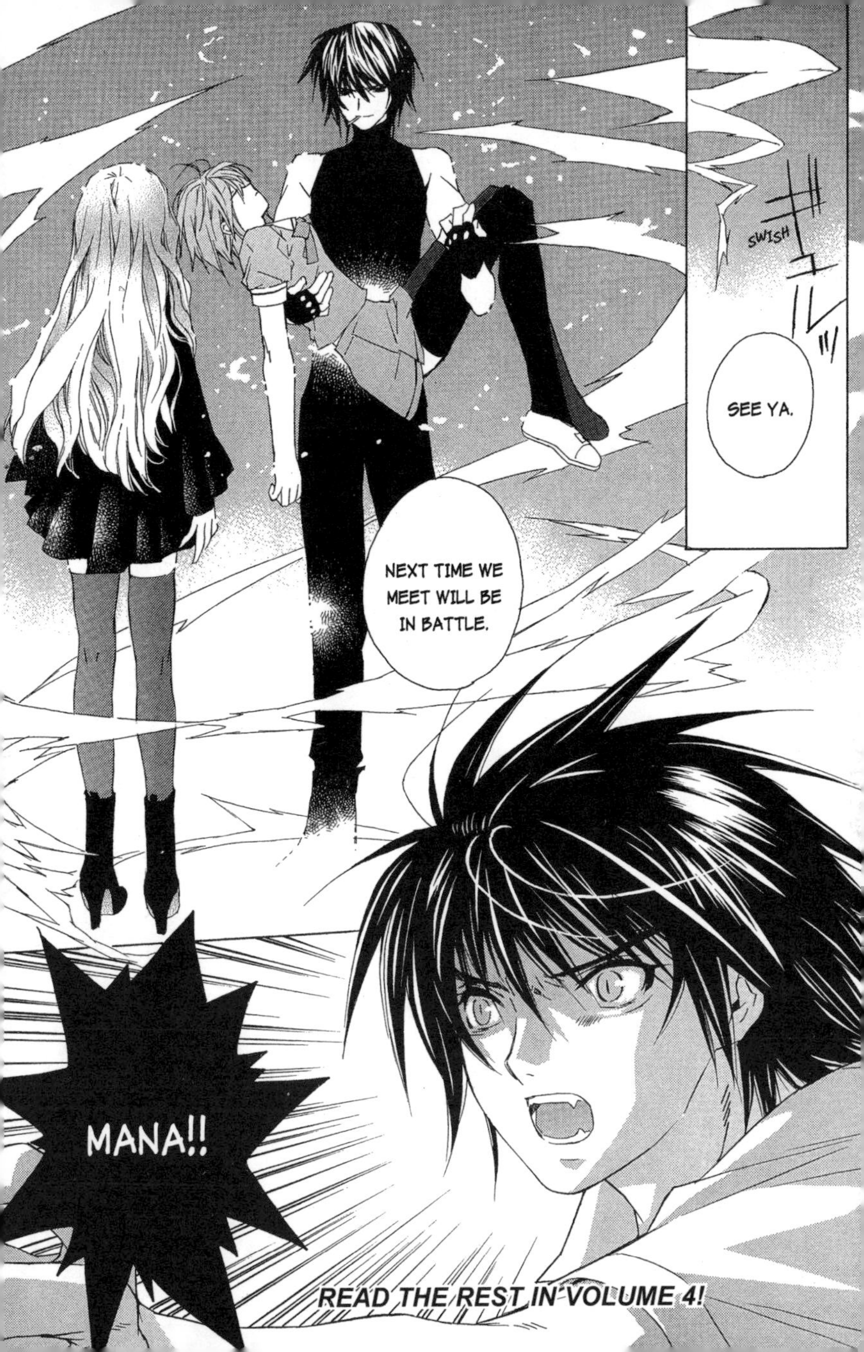
SWISH
SEE YA.
NEXT TIME WE MEET WILL BE IN BATTLE.
MANA!!
READ THE REST IN VOLUME 4!

JUVENILE ORION
THE CARD GAME

Aquarian Age is an original trading card game created by Broccoli that was first introduced in July of 1999. The unique game system and the illustrations featuring many talented artists in Japan have fascinated card game players of all kinds.

The Rules (continued from Volume 2)

Battle Example

Player 1 has Character A (Mental Strength 2/Attack Power 2/Defense Power 3) in the Control Area with 2 Power Cards.

Player 2 has Character B (Mental Strength 3/Attack Power 2/Defense Power 1) in the Control Area with 3 Power Cards.

PLAYER 2
CHARACTER B
3
2 1
2
CHARACTER A
2 3
PLAYER 1

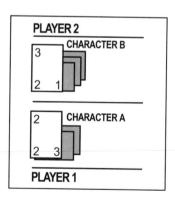

1) Player 1's Character A pays a Power Card and declares an attack.

2) Player 2's Character B pays a Power Card and declares a guard.

3
CHARACTER B
2 1
PAID POWERCARD
GUARD
ATTACK
2
CHARACTER A
2 3
PAID POWERCARD

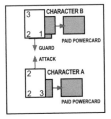

3) Character B's attack is 2, and Character A's defense is 3, so Character A will not be discarded. Character A's attack is 2, and Character B's defense is 1, so Character B will be discarded.

3
CHARACTER B
2 1
ATTACK
DEFENSE
2
CHARACTER A
2 3
ATTACK
DEFENSE

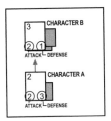

4) Player 1's Character A pays another Power Card, and attacks again.

5) Player 2 has no characters in the Control Area, and therefore cannot guard. So the player will take 2 points of damage.

PLAYER TWO'S DECK
2
2 3
CHARACTER A
PAID POWERCARD

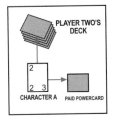

6) Player 2 will draw the top card from his Deck and place it faced up in the Damage Area.

7) The card was a Character Card, so the card will move to the Faction Area.

PLAYER TWO'S DECK
CHARACTER CARD GOES IN THE FACTION AREA

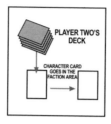

8) Damage was 2, so Player 2 draws another card and places it faced up in the Damage Area.

9) The card was a Break Card, so it will remain in the Damage Area.

PLAYER TWO'S DECK
BREAK CARD GOES IN THE DAMAGE AREA

Power Card Phase

During this phase, you can place Power Cards under characters in your Control Area or any of your active characters in the Faction Area. You can continue until you end your power phase or you run out of cards in your hand.

However, a character can only have Power Cards up to the number of their Mental Strength. When a character in the Faction Area has the number of Power Cards the same as their Mental Strength, the character will come down to the Control Area at the end of the Power Phase.

You can only control 1 character per faction in one turn. Characters with Mental Strength of 0 will come down automatically at the end of the Power Phase.

Faction Area
Control Area
2 CHARACTER A
1 CHARACTER B
2 CHARACTER C
2 CHARACTER D

2 CHARACTER A
2 CHARACTER B
0 CHARACTER C
Faction Area
Control Area

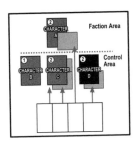

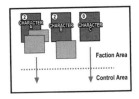

Discard Phase

During this phase, if you have more than 7 cards in your hand, you will need to discard cards until you have 7 cards.

Special Attacks

Mental Attacks

A Mental Attack is the ability to attack directly to the Power Card of the opponent's character instead of at the Defense Power. Characters with Mental Attack abilities have their Attack Power written in parenthesis such as (2).

For a character with Metal Attack ability, declaring an attack and declaring to guard is the same as usual. Paying the attack cost of one Power Card and guard cost of one Power Card is also the same.

The damage inflicted by a character with Metal Attack ability is called Mental Damage. When a character receives Mental Damage, it must discard the Power Cards placed on it. The number of Power Cards to discard is the same number as the Mental Damage.

Just as in a normal battle, characters inflict damage onto each other in battles that involve Mental Attack.

If a character does not have enough Power Cards to discard from the Mental Damage, the character is discarded. When the Power Card that is left is 0 or more, the character survives the attack.

When a character receives a Mental Damage and normal damage at the same time, the Damage Determination is done at the same time. If the character cannot endure either one of the damages, the character is discarded. When a player receives Mental Damage and a normal damage at the same time, the player must pay the total amount of damage from both attacks in the Damage Determination.

Please look in our other Aquarian Age releases for the complete rules for other styles!*

*Juvenile Orion uses a "Limited Style" set of rules and therefore, simpler than the other styles of the Aquarian Age trading card game.

CARDS WITH MENTAL ATTACKS

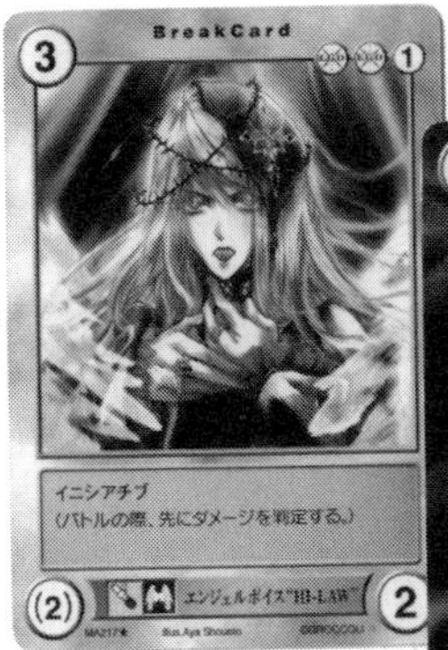
BreakCard
3
1
イニシアチブ
(バトルの際、先にダメージを判定する。)
(2)
エンジェルボイス"HI-LAW"
2

E.G.O.
Angel Voice "HI-LAW"

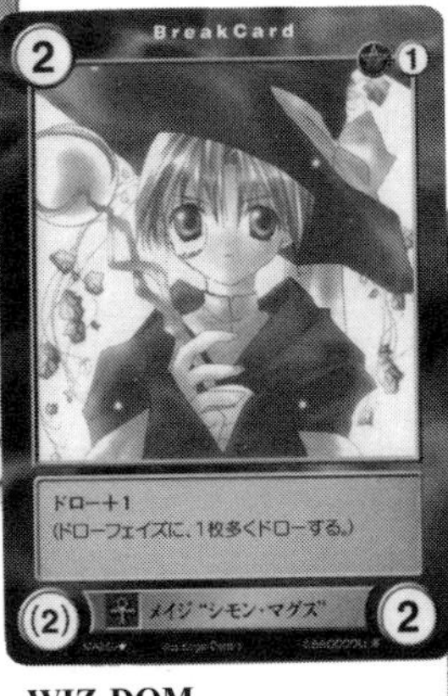
BreakCard
2
1
ドロー+1
(ドローフェイズに、1枚多くドローする。)
(2)
メイジ"シモン・マグス"
2

WIZ-DOM
Mage "Simon Magus"

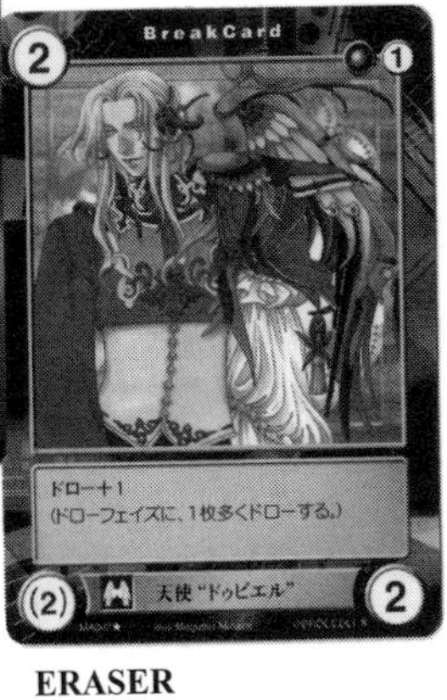
BreakCard
2
1
ドロー+1
(ドローフェイズに、1枚多くドローする。)
(2)
天使"ドゥビエル"
2

ERASER
Angel "Dubbiel"

Illustration by Aya Shouoto, Koge-Donbo, and Megumu Minami

JUVENILE ORION
SERIES 3 CARD LIST

No.	Faction	Rarity	Card Name	Artist
MA202	E.G.O.		Action Hero	Chifumi Ochi
MA203	E.G.O.		Baseball Player	Aya Shouoto
MA204	E.G.O.		Sergeant	Towa Ōzora
MA205	E.G.O.	★	Politician	Kaori Monchi
MA206	E.G.O.	★	Bodyguard Android	Soh Aoki
MA207	E.G.O.	★	Bartender	Yoshiko Agawa
MA208	E.G.O.	★★	Programmer	Chacha Tachibana
MA209	E.G.O.	★★	Junior High Student	Haruhiko Mikimoto
MA210	E.G.O.	★★	Delinquent High School Student	Kamon
MA211	E.G.O.		Body Builder	Kiriko Yumeji
MA212	E.G.O.		Mad Mechanic	Fun Fun
MA213	E.G.O.		Editor	Hiromi Torihito
MA214	E.G.O.		Spiritualist	Kazuki Shu
MA215	E.G.O.	★	Student Body President	Kamon
MA216	E.G.O.	★	Blaster	Yuuya
MA217	E.G.O.	★	Angel Voice "HI-LAW"	Aya Shouoto
MA218	E.G.O.	★	Deputy "Makoto Hikami"	Mieko Koide
MA219	E.G.O.	★★	Commander "Harold J. Thornton"	Shibuko Ebara
MA220	E.G.O.	★★	Rookie Police Detective "Makoto Hikami"	Mieko Koide
MA221	E.G.O.	★★	Telepath "Naoya Itsuki"	Sakurako Gokurakuin
MA222	E.G.O.	★★★	Rookie Police Detective "Makoto Hikami"	Mieko Koide
MA223	E.G.O.	★★★	Telepath "Naoya Itsuki"	Sakurako Gokurakuin
MA224	ARAYASHIKI		Immortal Hermit Apprentice	migi-
MA225	ARAYASHIKI		Three-eyed Monk	Koge-Donbo
MA226	ARAYASHIKI		Judoist	Tsubaki Enomoto
MA227	ARAYASHIKI	★	White Belt	Kaori Monchi
MA228	ARAYASHIKI	★	Discord Priest	Ryushi Takamura
MA229	ARAYASHIKI	★	Ancestor Spirit	Haruhiko Mikimoto
MA230	ARAYASHIKI	★★	Sumou Wrestler	Kamon
MA231	ARAYASHIKI	★★	Buddha Master	Kaori Monchi
MA232	ARAYASHIKI	★★	Purifier	Yuna Takanagi
MA233	ARAYASHIKI		Yamabushi	Reiko Shiratori
MA234	ARAYASHIKI		Tan-Kie	Ryushi Takamura
MA235	ARAYASHIKI		Vindhya Boy	Ringo Manda
MA236	ARAYASHIKI		Yojimbo	Yuna Takanagi

No.	Faction	Rarity	Card Name	Artist
MA237	ARAYASHIKI	★	Waiter	Aya Shouoto
MA238	ARAYASHIKI	★	Thunder God "Michizane Sugawara"	Yuuki Fujinari
MA239	ARAYASHIKI	★	Bass Player "Ying-Yang"	Banri Sendou
MA240	ARAYASHIKI	★	Shikigami "Cilang-Zhenyun"	J-ta Yamada
MA241	ARAYASHIKI	★★	Meikai "Yuge Kanata"	Kanan
MA242	ARAYASHIKI	★★	Tsuchimikado Head Family "Seimei Tsuchimikado"	Fubito Mikanagi
MA243	ARAYASHIKI	★★	Instructor "Isshin Shiba"	Sakurako Gokurakuin
MA244	ARAYASHIKI	★★★	Tsuchimikado Head Family "Seimei Tsuchimikado"	Fubito Mikanagi
MA245	ARAYASHIKI	★★★	Instructor "Isshin Shiba"	Sakurako Gokurakuin
MA246	WIZ-DOM		Homunculus Lilliput	Mako Takahashi
MA247	WIZ-DOM		Mafia	Yaya Sakuragi
MA248	WIZ-DOM		Opera Singer	Tsubaki Enomoto
MA249	WIZ-DOM	★	Pianist	Reiichi Hiiro
MA250	WIZ-DOM	★	Cowboy	Chata Tachibana
MA251	WIZ-DOM	★	Hustler	Fun Fun
MA252	WIZ-DOM	★★	Clay Golem	K2 Shoukai
MA253	WIZ-DOM	★★	Friar	NATU
MA254	WIZ-DOM	★★	Elementaler	Haruhiko Mikimoto
MA255	WIZ-DOM		Alchemist	Kazuki Shu
MA256	WIZ-DOM		Magic Grad Student	K2 Shoukai
MA257	WIZ-DOM		Guild Master	Chata Tachibana
MA258	WIZ-DOM	★	Troubadour	Chata Tachibana
MA259	WIZ-DOM	★	Guitar Player "Bardiel"	Kaname Itsuki
MA260	WIZ-DOM	★	Mage "Simon Magus"	Koge-Donbo
MA261	WIZ-DOM	★	Prince "Edward Albright"	Nori Kobari
MA262	WIZ-DOM	★★	Homunculus Azoth "13"	Kiro Hanehane
MA263	WIZ-DOM	★★	Crown Prince "Edward Albright"	Nori Kobari
MA264	WIZ-DOM	★★	Exorcist "Tomonori Nakaura"	Sakurako Gokurakuin
MA265	WIZ-DOM	★★★	Crown Prince "Edward Albright"	Nori Kobari
MA266	WIZ-DOM	★★★	Exorcist "Tomonori Nakaura"	Sakurako Gokurakuin
MA267	DARKLORE		White Rabbit	Sakurako Gokurakuin
MA268	DARKLORE		Troll	Towa Ōzora
MA269	DARKLORE		Mafia Devil	Kiriko Yumeji
MA270	DARKLORE	★	Wolf Boy	Kiro Hanehane

JUVENILE ORION
SERIES 3 CARD LIST

No.	Faction	Rarity	Card Name	Artist
MA271	DARKLORE	★	Demon Physician	Kiriko Yumeji
MA272	DARKLORE	★	Kentauros	Hideaki Hoba
MA273	DARKLORE	★★	Flirt	Reiichi Hiiro
MA274	DARKLORE	★★	Echo	Kaori Monchi
MA275	DARKLORE	★★	Shape Shifter	Ryushi Takamura
MA276	DARKLORE		Blue Demon	Soh Aoki
MA277	DARKLORE		Lizard Man	OKAMA
MA278	DARKLORE		Marandanti	Shibuko Ebara
MA279	DARKLORE	★	Vampire Noble	Keiichi Sumi
MA280	DARKLORE	★	Storm Tiger "COZY"	Fubito Mikanagi
MA281	DARKLORE	★	Aramitama "Susanoo"	Toru Azumi
MA282	DARKLORE	★★	Canine God "Yashaou"	Toru Azumi
MA283	DARKLORE	★★	Gedoumaru "Shuten Douji"	Makoto Sajima
MA284	DARKLORE	★★	Evil God "Kaname Kusakabe"	Sakurako Gokurakuin
MA285	DARKLORE	★★★	Canine God "Yashaou"	Toru Azumi
MA286	DARKLORE	★★★	Gedoumaru "Shuten Douji"	Makoto Sajima
MA287	DARKLORE	★★★	Evil God "Kaname Kusakabe"	Sakurako Gokurakuin
MA288	ERASER		Businessman Angel	Hiromi Torihito
MA289	ERASER		Missileborg	Lily Hoshino
MA290	ERASER		Snipeborg	OKAMA
MA291	ERASER	★	Cat Android	Reiko Shiratori
MA292	ERASER	★	Dead Copy	Kaori Monchi
MA293	ERASER	★	Disposed Android	Hideaki Hoba
MA294	ERASER	★★	Reconstructing Scientist	Fun Fun
MA295	ERASER	★★	Matrix Clone	Yuna Takanagi
MA296	ERASER	★★	Armorborg	Yoshisada Tsu2mi
MA297	ERASER		Messenger	CJ Michalski
MA298	ERASER		Thrones	CJ Michalski
MA299	ERASER		Part-time Borg	Fun Fun
MA300	ERASER		Dragon Warrior	Hikaru Mizusawa
MA301	ERASER	★	Fugitive Dragoon	Soh Aoki
MA302	ERASER	★	Angel "Dubbiel"	Minami Megumu
MA303	ERASER	★	Gunborg "Samuel"	Yuri Narushima
MA304	ERASER	★★	Angel "Shamshiel"	Haruhiko Mikimoto

No.	Faction	Rarity	Card Name	Artist
MA305	ERASER	★★	Canonborg "Samuel"	Yuri Narushima
MA306	ERASER	★★	Angel of Light "Tsukasa Amou"	Sakurako Gokurakuin
MA307	ERASER	★★★	General "Rik Heisenberg"	Koge-Donbo
MA308	ERASER	★★★	Lieutenant General "Ky Schweitzer"	Koge-Donbo
MA309	ERASER	★★★	Major "Coo Erhard"	Koge-Donbo
MA310	ERASER	★★★	Canonborg "Samuel"	Yuri Narushima
MA311	ERASER	★★★	Angel of Light "Tsukasa Amou"	Sakurako Gokurakuin

This is the list of Juvenile Orion trading cards that were produced for the Japan market, and not necessarily the United States. Moreover, even if the Juvenile Orion card game is made available to the US market, the cards listed and the translations used may not be the same.

Juvenile Orion Clear Poster

Great for walls or windows

Juvenile Orion T-Shirts

Two styles available

Juvenile Orion Drama CDs

vol. 1
Voice Actors are Tomokazu Seki, Hikaru Midorikawa, Tomo Saeki, Chihiro Suzuki, & Kousuke Toriumi

Juvenile Orion 2005 Calendar

Full color 12 x 12" calendar for 2005.

Get your Juvenile Orion merchandise at:
www.animegamers.com

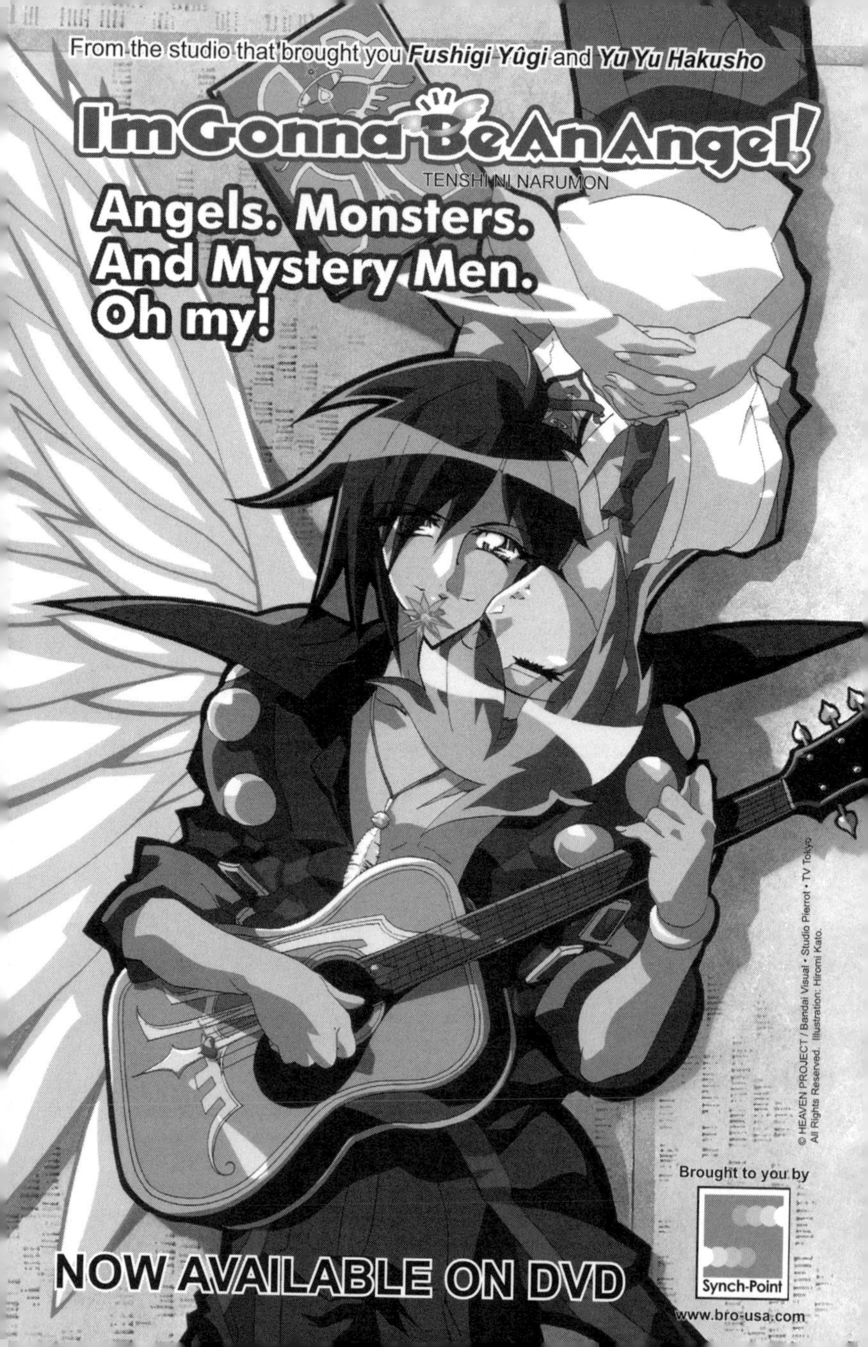
From the studio that brought you *Fushigi Yûgi* and *Yu Yu Hakusho*
I'm Gonna Be An Angel!
TENSHI NI NARUMON
Angels. Monsters. And Mystery Men. Oh my!
© HEAVEN PROJECT / Bandai Visual • Studio Pierrot • TV Tokyo
All Rights Reserved. Illustration: Hiromi Kato.
Brought to you by
Synch-Point
NOW AVAILABLE ON DVD
www.bro-usa.com

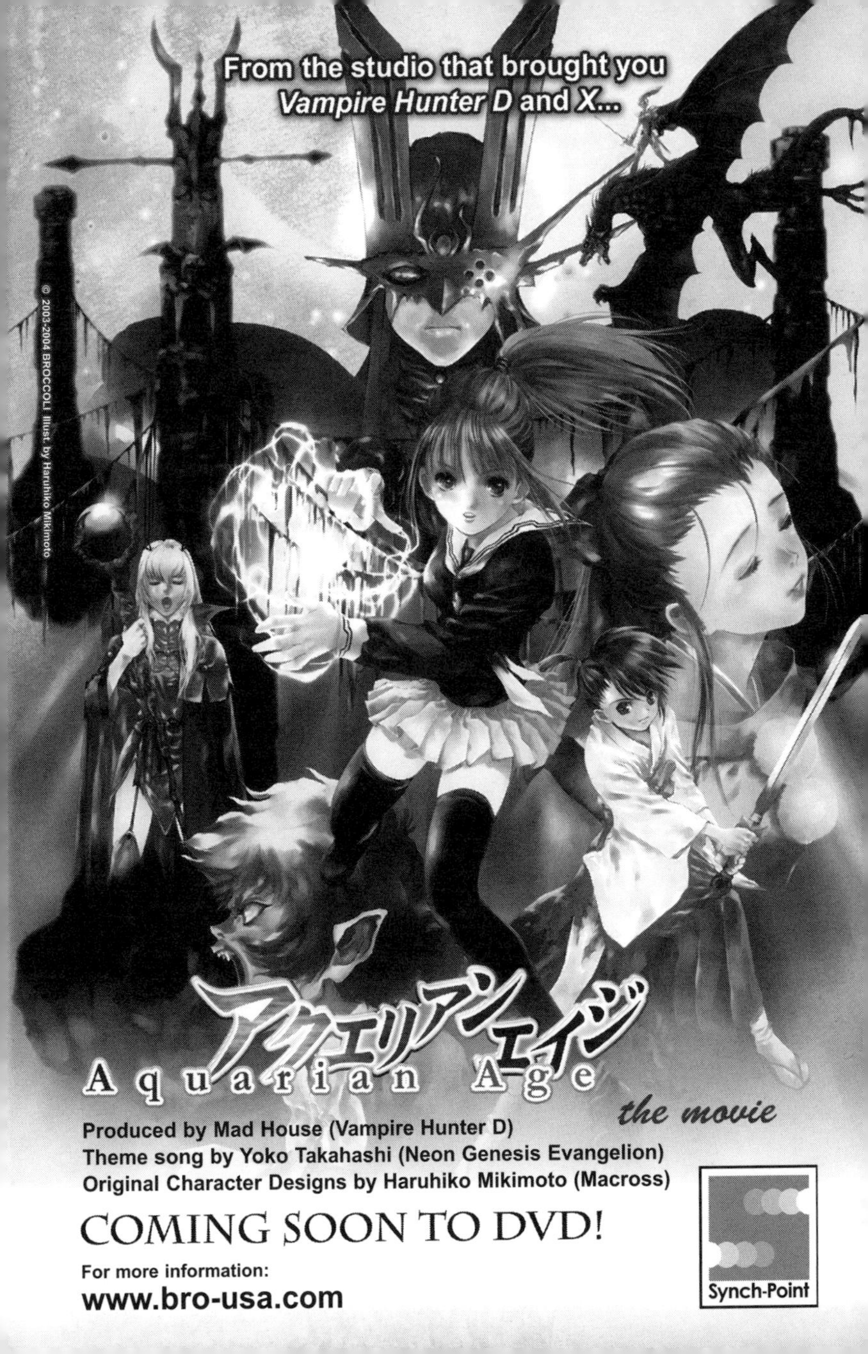
From the studio that brought you
Vampire Hunter D and X...
© 2003-2004 BROCCOLI Illust. by Haruhiko Mikimoto
アクエリアンエイジ
Aquarian Age
the movie
Produced by Mad House (Vampire Hunter D)
Theme song by Yoko Takahashi (Neon Genesis Evangelion)
Original Character Designs by Haruhiko Mikimoto (Macross)
COMING SOON TO DVD!
For more information:
www.bro-usa.com
Synch-Point

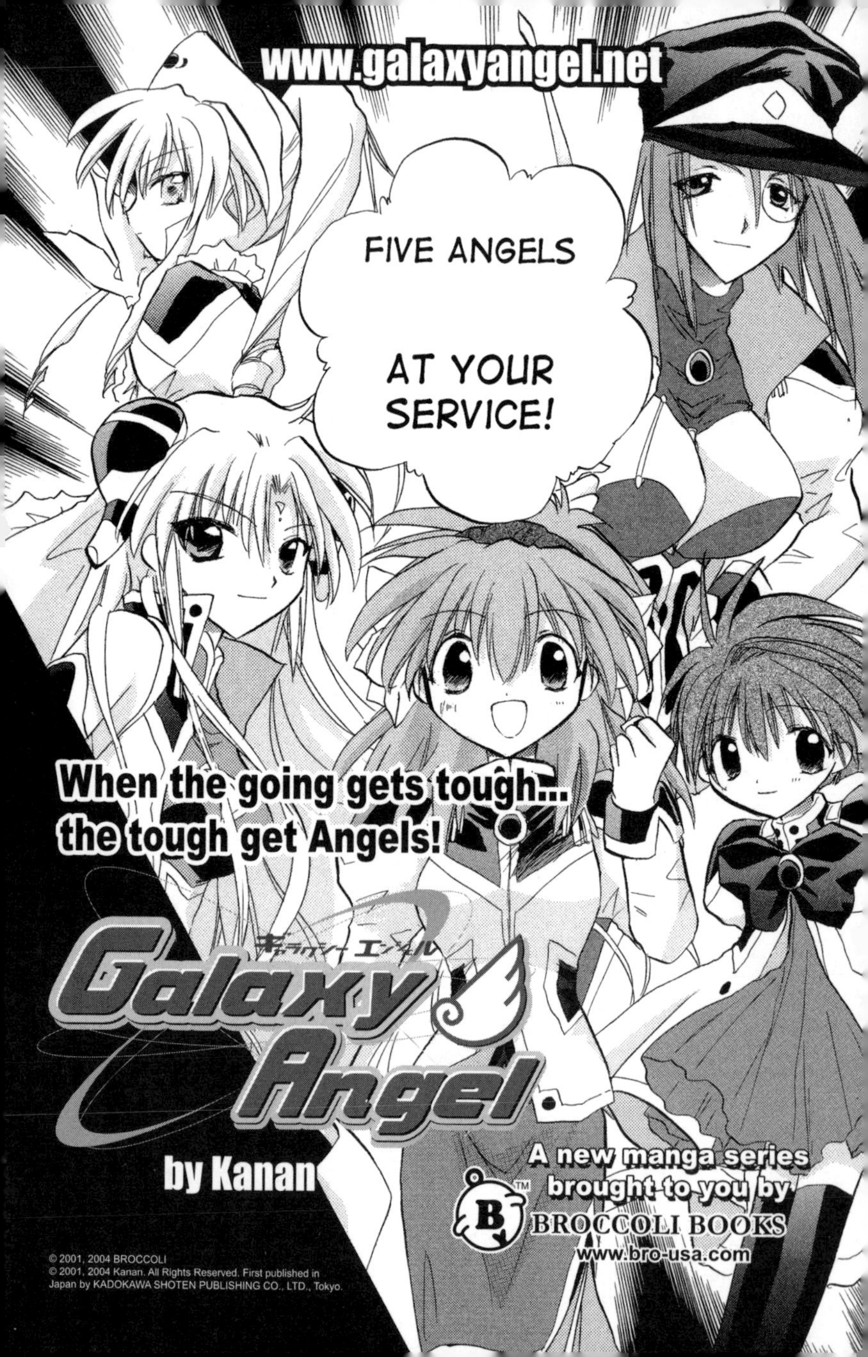
www.galaxyangel.net
FIVE ANGELS
AT YOUR SERVICE!
When the going gets tough...
the tough get Angels!
ギャラクシーエンジェル
Galaxy Angel
by Kanan
A new manga series
brought to you by
BROCCOLI BOOKS
www.bro-usa.com
© 2001, 2004 BROCCOLI
© 2001, 2004 Kanan. All Rights Reserved. First published in
Japan by KADOKAWA SHOTEN PUBLISHING CO., LTD., Tokyo.

STOP!
YOU'RE READING THE WRONG WAY!

This is the end of the book! In Japan, manga is generally read from right to left. All reading starts on the upper right corner, and ends on the lower left. American comics are generally read from left to right, starting on the upper left of each page. In order to preserve the true nature of the work, we printed this book in a right to left fashion. Those who are unfamiliar with manga may find this confusing at first, but once you start getting into the story, you will wonder how you ever read manga any other way!